Reconstructing Modernism

edited by Serge Guilbaut

Reconstructing Modernism:

Art in New York, Paris, and Montreal 1945–1964

The MIT Press
Cambridge, Massachusetts
London, England

Contents

vii   **Acknowledgments**

ix   **Introduction**
     Serge Guilbaut

1   ***Abstraction chaude* in Paris in the 1950s**
     John-Franklin Koenig

17   **Hot Painting: The Inevitable Fate of the Image**
     Jean Baudrillard

30   **Postwar Painting Games: The Rough and the Slick**
     Serge Guilbaut

85   **Cold War Constructivism**
     Benjamin H. D. Buchloh

113   **Marginality as a Political Stance: The Canadian Painter Jean McEwen**
     Constance Naubert-Riser

130   **New York as Seen from Montreal by Paul-Emile Borduas and the Automatists, 1943–1953**
     François-Marc Gagnon

144   **Greenberg's Matisse and the Problem of Avant-Garde Hedonism**
     John O'Brian

172   **Jackson Pollock's Abstraction**
     Timothy J. Clark

244   **The Monochrome and the Blank Canvas**
     Thierry de Duve

311   **Saturday Disasters: Trace and Reference in Early Warhol**
     Thomas Crow

332   **The Politics of Consumption: The Screen Actor's Guild, Ronald Reagan, and the Hollywood Red Scare**
     Lary May

369   **Cultural Cartography: American Designs at the 1964 Venice Biennale**
     Laurie J. Monahan

417   **Contributors**

The *Hot Paint for Cold War* symposium held at the University of British Columbia, Vancouver, Canada, in September 1986 could never have taken place without the generous help offered by numerous institutions, agencies, and individuals, to all of whom we would like to express our warmest gratitude. Within the university itself, the Faculty of Arts under the direction of Dean Robert M. Will and the Department of Fine Arts headed by Dr. James O. Caswell played an especially important supportive role. Funding was also provided by the Koerner Foundation, the UBC Alumni Association, and the Emily Carr College of Art. In addition, the conference enjoyed the fullest possible support of the Social Sciences and Humanities Research Council of Canada and of the Canada Council, whose subventions were further supplemented by the Cultural Affairs Division (Arts Promotion) of the Department of External Affairs Canada.

   To these various bodies, and to those numerous other individuals who worked toward ensuring the success of the symposium, we wish to extend our deep appreciation.

Serge Guilbaut

Introduction

Serge Guilbaut

I know, this will sound a little silly, but conservative America is
scared. The America which has been riding high since Ronald
Reagan's election is scared to see New York's world hegemony in
the arts going to the dogs, evaporating into thin air. I am not the
one who says this: it is the cultural spokesperson of the new
American right, Hilton Kramer, in the 1986 summer issue of his
magazine *The New Criterion*. Well, it is not panic yet, maybe just
a shiver, a certain nervosity, and quite a bit of irritation when
confronted with some of the realities of the New York high-
culture world. It seems New York is becoming too expensive for
young artists to live and work in. This turn of events is seen as
disturbing, because this news coincided with the mammoth popular extravaganza surrounding the anniversary of the Statue of
Liberty. Is it possible that American culture, like old Lady Liberty, needs to be freshened up? Jean Baudrillard in his latest
book *Amérique* seems to ask the real question: "Can Reagan be
considered an emblematic image of the present American society—a society, which, after having represented power, now
needs a facelift?"

Kramer is wondering—even if New York remains as strong as
ever—if some of its past vitality has not vanished. "This position
of dominance," Kramer remarks, "while rarely questioned as a
general proposition, no longer seems quite what it was even a few
years ago." This is a sad story indeed. But Mr. Kramer, who by
self-proclamation has become protector of all "good" interna-

tional American culture, a new type of Saint George battling and extirpating from under every American bed the ugly heads of the Marxist intellectual hordes, stands on guard. For the crusader, any questioning or criticism of New York's supremacy is as dangerous as a terrorist attack. That is why before this rumor has time to develop and amplify, before the rumor becomes a successful media event, the issue has to be controlled, even asphyxiated by the production of a poll in *The New Criterion*.

The questions posed are quite interesting:

1. In your field, does New York lead now, and will it continue to lead?
2. Is New York's perceived position of leadership real, or is it merely a matter of the concentration of media attention?
3. How has the cultural vitality of New York changed over the last two decades?
4. Can any decline of New York's central position in America's cultural life be seen as part of a general decline?
5. Were New York to lose its position of leadership, what would be the effect of this loss on American culture as a whole? etc.

Kramer received many cautious but on the whole positive answers from the various fields of the cultural establishment, but what was striking was the fact that the most negative answers came from art critics—in particular, from Clement Greenberg and Barbara Rose, two critics attached to another era of art production but still in touch with the different spheres of the art world. Their critique was devastating. Greenberg, despite acknowledging the continued dominance of New York as an attractive and validating center, thinks that what it validates now is hardly worthwhile. In Greenberg's mind, New York has become a sewer, a place from where diseases spread into the art world: "Now New York spreads bad taste, incubates it."

Barbara Rose's critique is even more aggressive, because she feels that New York has "sold its soul to save its face." There is of course a lot of nostalgia in Rose's text: nostalgia about the good old days when artists still believed in something, in values of the soul, in sincerity, in authenticity, etc.—all those values that the art world cannot take seriously any longer, now that the entire system has been analyzed, criticized, turned upside down but in the end accepted after auscultation. Now artists are anything but naive; they are instead practical, cool, effective, and a bit cynical.

Despite the nostalgia in Rose's account, a lot of what she says rings true, like the fact that "New York is a city for the consumers, not the producers, of culture." That's a sure sign of decline for the author, who tries to measure the achievements of New York with the old yardstick she has kept from the 1950s, when New York was still trying to mimic Europe. Today Europe is copying America, and New York is proud to be American, proud of its modern superficiality. As Baudrillard wrote, "America was a political power, she has now become a model." What Rose misses is the fact that New York has become the new sign of our modernity, a vertical desert where fashionable images enter into an endless process of permutation with no room for utopian desire. To paraphrase Baudrillard, what can you do after the end of utopia?

Barbara Rose now lives in Paris and Madrid. She is ecstatic about the earlier French socialist program for the arts, which has stimulated high culture—a last attempt to curtail the total victory of the entertainment industry. She is finding it difficult "to imagine America retaining hegemony in any but the lowest forms of the mass media." With the return of a right-wing government in Paris, there is much chance now to witness a renewed neck-and-neck race to win the crown for artificiality, banality, and hyperreality. In this democratic contest any modern city seems today to have a chance.

What is fascinating for our purposes is that the questions raised by Kramer, Greenberg, and Rose are the same ones posed by French intellectuals about the supremacy of Paris in the 1960s. And they were asked, of course, when Paris had been long gone from the forefront of artistic power. Moreover, it is at the moment when the traditional importance of absolute art centers is being replaced by a network of multinational galleries that proponents of a New York art (which is still equated with American art) are wondering if New York is still on top. The hegemony of centers has in fact vanished, since art is propagated at lightning speed simultaneously all over the Western world through gallery franchises like Castelli, Boone, Maeght, etc. and through magazines published in different languages, catering to different publics with different emphases. A series of short, inconsequential, dazzling flashes. One for Europe, one for America. Culture as *saucisson:* one mild slice here, one spicy slice there.

This was not the case, of course, in the early 1950s. Until 1948, in fact, Montreal, Washington, D.C., New York, and of course Paris thought it was possible for them to symbolize post-

war Western culture. It is to the story of this curious moment
that this conference was devoted.

The title of the conference, *Hot Paint for Cold War*, despite
its silly pun, addressed an important historical question: the relation between art and politics, between the production of Hot abstraction (this was the way, in Paris, that Abstract Expressionist
type of painting was differentiated from geometric abstraction,
called *Abstraction froide* in French) and the Cold War.

The questions debated at the conference, and in the essays
published here, were: What were the reasons for the simultane-
ous development in Paris, Montreal, and New York of a type of
painting based on spontaneity, abstraction, primitive traditions,
individualism, and freedom of expression? How much did the
success of this type of art have to do with the politics of the Cold
War? What kinds of relationship existed among the three cities
between 1945 and 1964? What were the reasons for the replacement of this art by neo-dada and neo-cold abstraction in the early
1960s? This topic is vast and we do not expect to answer all the
questions raised, but we hope to be able to spark some interest in
the study of international cultural relations in the post-1945
Western world.

What these essays bring, in their multifaceted approaches,
is a reevaluation of the serious attempts made by many painters
of the immediate postwar period to reconstruct the strength of
modernism after so many years of slow decay and violence
against it. To understand the intricate mechanism underlying the
reconstruction of a postwar modernist critical discourse seems
to be timely, as the reassessment of postmodernism and its excesses has become desirable and is already under way.

Why Montreal? Simply because it seems that, while well
known and by now very well established in Canada, thanks to the
important works produced by François Gagnon, the work of the
Automatists has rarely been put in relation to the Western aesthetic and the politics of the Cold War. It is time I think to stage
a confrontation.

The art of the Montreal Automatists like Paul-Emile Borduas, Marcel Barbeau, Pierre Gauvreau, Jean-Paul Riopelle, Fernand Leduc produced until 1950, as well as their discourse and
theories, relates quite closely to the best of what was offered
elsewhere. Particularly important was their sophisticated understanding of the theoretical side of Surrealism. They were so
much in tune with the avant-garde world and strategies that they

staged their very own rebellion against the artistic establishment two months before the famous "Irascibles" in New York. The young Automatists decided in March 1950 to boycott and criticize a juried show they considered too conservative, but the Canadian "Rebels," not having been transformed into a media scandal, as were the "Irascibles" by *Life* magazine, and also fighting against a weaker art scene than the one in New York, became only a footnote.

The relations between Montreal and Paris are well known; they were difficult and disappointing, fruitful only when Canadian artists were willing to become international by accepting the rule of Paris. They actually had to become "Parisians." That was their key to success. Riopelle took this road. Otherwise Paris was just a dream—as unattainable as was New York. Borduas was the perfect example of an artist closely in tune with the political and aesthetic issues of the day, profoundly aware of the ethical problems contained in the "new postwar abstraction," but unable to enter into a dialogue with the other art centers. He became a sad vagabond of modernism—traveling late in his career from New York to Paris, on his way to Japan, which he never reached—never able to impose his vision in international circles, always out of sync.

Since the "triumph" of American painting was decreed in the 1960s, it has been difficult to discuss anything in the art culture of the 1950s but Abstract Expressionism. In traditional writings, the New York art scene is generally simplified to the point of appearing monolithic. The art produced in Paris and Montreal is considered inadequate and is constantly minimized or dismissed. This was the picture until recently. It was a kind of embarrassment for artists and critics, who felt a sense of shameful inadequacy when hearing that their production did not correspond to the standards elaborated by the New York avant-garde. It was certainly the case of Paris, able only in 1981, in a wobbly way, to organize a show called *Paris/Paris*, in which it was finally possible to reflect on that crucial period in terms of a French art.

It is of course not the purpose of this book to dismantle the New York avant-garde, but rather to confront it with the other productions of the period and in particular to compare the New York "winners" to the European and Canadian "losers." It seems that critical revisionism, not the one that wishes to tumble heroes in order to replace them by new ones, is historically important. This approach has become possible only in the last few years. Why? Because it seems that the recent European artistic offensive, coupled with the success with which it has been greeted in North America, signals a redirection in the contemporary art world, a loosening up of the hegemony of the New York art scene, as Mr. Kramer has noticed. This, along with a critique of the postwar formalist dogmatism, would seem to make opportune a historical discussion and comparison of what is sometimes forgotten were very different, complex, antagonistic, but nevertheless very active art scenes during the period of the Cold War.

This proposed dialogue among historians, critics, painters, and art historians should extricate the discourse on the period from the "provincial chauvinism" that characterizes the majority of published works on the topic. Until now, these studies have been compartmentalized according to countries and blinded by national interests. No real comparative study exists because "the other" has been dismissed, and the history of this art has been a battle among narcissists. Each capital, discovering and defending its local heroes, produced local histories without any connections—outside of formal ones (and even then . . .)—to the other Western centers. And this despite the fact that exchanges among painters, intellectuals, and politicians between the centers were very frequent and important. For this reason some essays included here are not directly related to painting per se, but are designed to illuminate other facets of the cultural scenes.

The fact that only painters of Abstract Expressionism have reached the artistic pantheon does not mean that excellent painters, confronting the same types of issues as painters in New York, did not exist elsewhere. After the Second World War, few—including French painters—still believed in the formerly all-powerful Parisian Muse. She had been disrobed. She was still cute, but she had lost her mystery, her fineries. She did not seduce anymore. That was the way art critics and journalists talked about Paris in those days.

A cultural hegemony is symbolic; it works like a reliquary. Its strength consists especially in its presentation, in its surroundings—the gold, the gems, and so on. The war had destroyed the reliquary that enshrined the School of Paris. Once this was gone, all that was left were the old bones. How was it possible to make the world believe that these old bones were, in fact, the same as before, capable of doing the same old tricks? But of course they were not; the reliquary is very important, and until artists could set about to build a new one, they would gain no respect or veneration.

At the core of some of the following essays is the study of a very complex set of ambiguous cultural relations between Paris, Montreal, and New York and by the same token the slow transferral of artistic power from Paris to New York. The transfer taking place at the height of the Cold War was not made without some rancour and misunderstandings. But if in the 1950s the marriage between the United States and France was one of convenience (or of necessity), today the mood has changed. Paris loves New York, the Americanophobia has been replaced by a galloping Americanophilia. There is not a week without a long love article in the French press about the American dream, about the performance of the American economy. Only the leftist press sometimes wonders about this love affair. The *Nouvel Observateur* wonders if the famous American mouse, after so many calls for the installation of his kingdom in the Ile de France, is not dangerous after all, if a Disneyland in France would not totally destroy a way of life. American popular culture, as in the 1950s, can still be considered dangerous in its leveling power. The French people's fascination with American popular culture is always accompanied by a certain uneasiness. Indeed they still remember what happened to some of their stars, such as the co-optation by Hollywood of the diabolical, unkempt, and despairing existentialist nymphette Juliet Greco and her transformation into an elegant, soulless, happy star.

In the 1950s, though, for many French America was naïveté, still imitating Paris in many ways, with artists trying to be bohemians and Greenwich Village mimicking Montmartre—all those things that Parisian intellectuals liked to paternalize about. But America also meant determination and arrogance—as in the 1953 descriptions of the youth of the world by *Holiday* magazine. The French male was characterized as P'ti Louis, a relaxed farmer, a little dumb and a dreamer; the French girl was of course a high-fashion model interested in romance. The German man was the hard-working miner, serious and wilful. His partner was sporty and dangerous. The American woman was a doctor ready to save humanity from diseases and epidemics, while the American boy, religious and military, was ready to save freedom from the communist epidemic. It is not surprising that the Belgian Surrealists juxtaposed in 1956, in an ironic collage for a cover of their magazine *Levres Nues*, the Statue of Liberty and the flushing mechanism of a toilet.

This was the battle of images that was raging between the two countries; it has all disappeared lately. The new French liberalism, sometimes wilder than the American, is popular today in Paris. Now, it is fascination replacing aversion. There is actually a tumultuous race in order to beat New York at her own game. The fascination of the old European city with the hyper-reality of American culture is total and surpasses in certain domains the teacher, who is now more and more ready to recoil into a religious neoprudism.

It is in Paris now, it seems to me, that some experiences of modernity are pushed to the limits. It is Paris that organized a huge exhibition of advertisements on billboards in the Champs Elysées, transformed for the occasion into a Museum of Publicity, as if, as Jack Lang once said, advertisement was the real art of the 1980s. It is French television after all that is producing a very popular show where blindfolded young yuppies try, by caressing the half-naked bodies of several women, to recognize their wives. If they do, they are sent to beautiful Greece as a reward. There is no animality here; everything is controlled, slick, and proper. Of course, France never did lose its fame in matters of elegant/kinky sex, but now the cliché has been plastified.

It is in Paris again that one can find in one of the most popular left magazines a series of ads promoting sex by telephone. With "allo Pussy" it seems certain that France has definitively been reconnected to the most advanced terminal of Western culture. With this stimulating simulation Paris has become a serious contender for the postmodern spectacular culture. Maybe Hilton Kramer was right, after all, to wonder.

But what about Montreal in all this? Well, it's haltingly getting there; but Montreal still seems too real, too bland, still too modern! Nobody in big cities talks about Montreal. If somebody does, it is by accident, as in the latest book about America by Jean Baudrillard, in which Montreal is mentioned in order to symbolize everything New York is not. Montreal is the dark side of the moon, mysterious, unknown but real.

But there is hope for those who desperately desire Montreal to become as plastic as everywhere else. There is hope for Montreal to become really postmodern. With the drop in the Canadian dollar, the American film industry has invaded Montreal. The city, in fact, has become the double of New York, her simulacrum; and spectators don't seem to notice it, nor to mind. It is then not surprising (adequate, I would say) that it is Montreal and not New York that the publishers of Baudrillard's book *Amérique* chose to put on the cover. Or was it another error?

But since film has become our new reality, maybe through its imposture Montreal has finally arrived—like everybody else, onto the spectacularized world stage. For some, it's about time; for others it is sad that, as Baudrillard noted in *Cool Memories*, few places in the world are still able to be real in their violence, naïveté, or mystery. Where shall we go, he asks: Berlin, Vancouver, Samarkand?

*John-Franklin Koenig
in his studio, rue de
Lille, Paris, 1957*

John-Franklin Koenig

I made my way to Paris in September of 1948 as a graduate of the
University of Washington's Romance Languages Department,
with a minor during the last two years of my studies in a very
general art and architecture program. I had been in Europe
already during World War II, serving in the 11th Armored Division, and hating it.

My return to Europe was made for certain positive reasons:
it was also a flight from the United States for certain negative
reasons.

The positive reasons came from my experiences in Europe
after the Armistice. That summer of 1945 I was first in Austria,
not too far from Salzburg, and then in southwestern France, at
Biarritz. For the first time in my life I felt at ease, not out of
place. I had never been an "all-American boy," preferring reading to baseball, preferring to be an artistic young man rather than
a product of the _Reader's Digest_. I found in Europe for the first
time in my life a society that considered the intellectual as a person to be envied and admired, rather than someone who should
be scorned and shunned. In Europe the artist was high on the
social scale of society, rather than a somewhat dubious individual
on the fringes of it. "Monsieur l'artiste" had a role in the world,
even if he was not making money and was not necessarily successful. His role, his function could be prestigious, even glamorous, even if the artist lived in poverty in a garret. One was
concerned with the spiritual rather than the material status. Any-

one could be a shopkeeper, some could be bankers, but to be an artist, an intellectual, was a rare quality—a quality that was shunned by most people in the United States at the time. In the States, mediocrity was considered a virtue. William Faulkner talked of a mythical family, the Snopeses, whose mediocrity was one of their means of power and in which honor and the traditional values were something that could be bypassed and trodden upon. We must not forget that Rousevelt was our last truly intellectual president. One thing that was forgotten was that money and power could not lift anyone out of mediocrity even if one should so wish.

During the last few months of my Army life I had the good luck of being one of the chosen few who were able to go to one of the "GI" universities and schools that had been set up all around Europe after the Armistice. I was able to attend the GI university at Biarritz and to choose three courses. One of those which I chose was a general art course. Here we were taught about gouache works on paper à la Dufy, and had some elementary oil painting studies in the Impressionist style. This was my first, and last, painting instruction.

This period of my life in Europe, roughly from the autumn of 1944 to the late winter of 1946, was an extremely formative period for me. On reading Henry James in later years, and then reading his biography, I could closely identify with him and his characters, those passionate pilgrims in search of art and beauty.

Let us think back a minute to the autumn of 1948. Pollock was just really emerging as the Pollock we know. Mark Tobey, who was over fifty at the time, had just had his first successful New York show. Calder was fairly well known, but within a small circle: he was certainly not "established," nor living an opulent life.

It might be useful to consider for a moment the artistic situation of the New York School at the time. It seems to me strange and dubious that the role of the European refugees and emigres has been minimized and passed over by some of the leading critics of the time. A great part of the artistic milieu of New York and of the United States had been fashioned and influenced by the presence of such personalities as Max Ernst, Moholy-Nagy, Gropius, Bartók, André Masson, Hans Hoffman, Peggy Guggenheim, Mondrian, and many others. Today, one would have us believe that the Abstract Expressionists came as a sort of spontaneous combustion, that New York had nothing to learn from the rest of the world nor, for that matter, from the rest of the United States!

In the New York that I remember of 1947–48, the artistic milieu was fairly limited; there were not many galleries and these were patronized by only a small number of people. The Museum of Modern Art was a prestigious institution, but it was certainly not thronged by visitors.

When I arrived in Paris in 1948, the Musée National d'Art Moderne was a rather shabby affair. There were many great things, but it was a dreary, lifeless space. Jean Cassou, its director, had been appointed not so much for his artistic renown (he was a minor poet), but to reward him for his actions during the war. He was a bit like the president of that period, René Coty, dear and kind, but not a leader. Cassou was, hence, a *haut fonctionnaire*, but, unhappily, he was not even a very good administrator and certainly had no knowledge of contemporary art, the art which in France was evolving out of the period of the 1930s: Post-Impressionism, Surrealism, and in the background some nonfigurative art. Outdated figurative artists such as Dunoyer de Segonzac were very much admired. Cassou's collaborators had little more knowledge than he, at least as far as contemporary art was concerned.

Certainly, one of the most unfortunate aspects of the *fonctionnaires* of the art in France just after the war, and even on into the 1960s, was this lack of interest in what was going on not only in Paris, and France, but also in Europe. François Mathey of the Musée des Arts Décoratifs was one of the few exceptions, along with the director of the Musée de Saint-Etienne, Maurice Allemand.

Paris in late 1948 was still in the throes of the reconstruction. There were restrictions on food, textiles, gas, telephones, housing, coffee—everything. Governmental budgets were strictly controlled. I do not remember hearing anything very positive, or even anything at all, about the Ministry of Culture until Charles de Gaulle came back into power in 1958, when his vision of the *grandeur de la france* had him name one of the most prestigious authors, André Malraux, as the head of the ministry.

In 1948 André Marchand was hailed as the most important successor to Picasso, Braque, and Chagall; Bernard Buffet was the rising star of the younger artists. He came out of the "Miserabiliste" school, of which the lugubrious Gruber was the master. Buffet became the first figure in the art world of postwar

France to be marketed as a commodity. His friend, the publicist Berger, was later to "create" Yves Saint-Laurent.

Here I feel that I should speak of a very important factor in American life of the postwar period: the GI Bill, created by Senator Fulbright. Without this bill millions of young Americans coming out of the Armed Forces would have had a tremendously difficult time resuming their education. Some of these young men were to become America's most prominent artists. Servicemen were entitled to as many months as they had served, plus twelve months. For example, the thirty-three months I served in the Army entitled me to forty-five months of schooling; the equivalent of approximately five academic years. Once you had received a diploma from a school in your home state, you could do postgraduate time almost anywhere in the States, or in the world, provided you remained in your major field. This was the ways and means that provided a considerable number of GIs the chance to go to Paris. This situation continued until about the end of 1952, when almost everyone's allotted time had expired.

Politically, most of the students were liberal to left-leaning. One of the reasons for this was the disenchantment with political activity in the United States. For instance, there was a witch-hunting Canwell Committee on the University of Washington campus as early as 1946, which predated the era of McCarthy. We wondered why we had fought and died for freedom. The Greek royalty was helped back onto the throne with the Nazi-loving Queen Mother in the background. Foster Dulles became the Secretary of State; his family was considerably involved with the United Fruit Company, which in turn was involved with the continuation of the repression in Central America and Cuba. We all know where this led—and still leads. I could speak of many other acts and policies of the US government which resulted in our disillusionment at this time. Of course, in the 1950s the real scandal was Joseph McCarthy and his committee. Even in Paris we felt watched over and surveyed. There was good reason to believe that there were informers in our ranks, and we had to be careful, because if anyone acted up, his visa would be revoked.

In the days of late Stalinism, which culminated in 1956 with the terror of Budapest, there was not much enthusiasm for the other side and the narrow, dogmatic French Communist Party was certainly not admired. From 1948 until the early 1950s, Picasso, who had several beautiful shows of his paintings and the first showing of his ceramic plates, was the hero of the Communist Party. Later, when the Party adopted Stalinist Social Realism and proclaimed it as the only possible means of artistic expression, Fougeron was lauded as the great painter, the supreme model. The Communist cultural weekly *Les Lettres Françaises* became even more dull, dogmatic, and unconvincing. When Fougeron was abandoned, Fernard Léger became the artistic hero of the PFC: by this time his art had become so stereotyped that it was very easy to fit it into the dogmas of Social Realism. The fact that he was married to a Russian woman helped him achieve the status of artistic hero in the Party.

So here I was in the city of light in 1948, arriving to continue my studies at the Sorbonne, L'Alliance Française, and the Institut de Phonétique. The French education system is much more compartmentalized than the American system; there was no way for me to continue an art minor. Nor could an art student take advanced studies in literature. However, I think that my basic studies in the arts—beginning drawing and composition, beginning architectural drawing, interior design and ceramics—were very beneficial. My bible at that time was *Vision in Motion* by Moholy-Nagy, who had founded the new Bauhaus in Chicago in the early 1940s. This book was based on the policies and methods of training at the Weimar Bauhaus, where students were trained in a number of different artistic fields: theirs was a general training for the visual and creative mind. This was, of course, very far from the policies of the French Ecoles des Beaux-Arts. Arts and architecture were based on the arts of the past, including Greek and Roman antiquity. Le Corbusier was considered *fada*, demented. Picasso was very much decried; Miro was, along with the other Surrealist painters, highly suspect. Of course, any art that was close to nonfigurative was entirely out of the question. I know of a professor at the Conservatoire de Musique who, even in the late 1970s, refused to mention Hector Berlioz, whom he considered a dilettante upstart. The professors in the painting and sculpture sections of the different art schools and academies were, for the most part, traditionalists. Fernand Léger was one of the most "modernist" and well-known artists that operated an academy of painting; but all of his students were forced to paint à la Léger (*si l'on peut dire!*).

The only inventive and truly modern artist teaching at the time was Ossip Zadkine. He was not appreciated in France, although Sandberg of the Stedelijk Museum was a great supporter of his.

Hence it was perhaps just as well that I was not involved in any of the art schools then; I learned, like the art students, from friends and also from intense exposure to shows and museum collections. In 1948–49, I was still doing figurative work, except for some collage work. I looked to Picasso and Braque as my masters and also admired Klee, Miro, Calder, Moholy-Nagy, and Arp (particularly Arp's collages). During trips to Amsterdam and Basel, in 1949 and 1950, I saw works by Vortemberg-Gildewart, Sophie Taeuber-Arp, Van Tongerloo, Theo van Doesburg, Klee, and many others. By 1950 I was already on friendly terms with César Domela.

Of my close acquaintances, none were familiar with any contemporary artists except Picasso and Braque. One of these acquaintances was Jean-Robert Arnaud, a *pied-noir* from Algiers, who had a tiny bookshop on an obscure street, la rue du Regard. It seemed that the only passersby were widows and *religieuses*. They all carefully ignored the shop, for its windows were full of nonorthodox books, from Gide to Sartre, as well as Camus, Genet, the Surrealists, and others. Arnaud wanted very desperately to flee this small corner and move to Saint-Germain-des-Près, which was at that time the intellectual center of Paris, of France, and perhaps, of the world. The rue de Seine, which still harbors one of the greatest concentrations of galleries in the world, was nearby.

I became Arnaud's best customer when I was a student of French contemporary literature. I was delighted one day when I found about twenty hand-painted "Christmas cards" that I had left in Arnaud's shop overnight (done in ink and gouache, inspired by the likes of Klee) pinned up in his bookshop in front of the books. One of Arnaud's dreams was to have a small gallery joined to his activities. In the years that followed, I became associated with him and when my GI Bill ran out, I stayed in Paris and worked with him. We were able to move to Saint-Germain in early 1950, into a former bougnat/bistro that had a small space opening onto the rue du Four and a fairly large cellar underneath that had been used for storing coal, wood, and wine. We were euphoric about this move; however, in June 1950 our euphoria turned into despair. That was when war broke out in Korea. We were ready to flee to Argentina; neither of us wanted to serve time in any army. All my friends, especially my ex-GI friends, were panicky during this bitter time.

In that same year Richard Seaver, a fellow contemporary literature student, became a client and a good friend. Seaver was a good friend of Jack Youngerman and Ellsworth Kelly.

There was a great need for a gallery that would show young

*Party for Michel
Ragon, Paris, 1957,
collage/montage. Left to
right: Sugai, Michel
Ragon, James Guitet,
Huguette-Arthur Ber-
trand, Martin Barré,
John-Franklin Koenig.*

painters, and the idea Arnaud and I had for a gallery excited everybody. So, in the early winter of 1951 we decided to go ahead and rehabilitate the shop's basement. It was a big job to clean out what had accumulated over the years—coal dust, faggot fragments, broken bottles. We had to cover the grimy walls with the hundreds of gallons of paint donated by a developer friend. The first to show at our gallery was Jack Youngerman; it was his first show. He sold one painting to Edgar Kaufmann of the Museum of Modern Art in New York. The second to show at the gallery was Ellsworth Kelly. It was also his first show, but because he tabled his prices on those of established artists of the Galerie Denise René nothing was sold. With the mailing list given to us by César Domela we were on our way. Jack and Ellsworth both left for New York that summer to make their fortunes. Having been encouraged by Jack, Ellsworth, and Sandberg, I decided to search my own artistic fortunes in Paris, and stayed on. In 1952 and 1953 I had my first small shows of collages.

The gallery scene, in the early 1950s, was virtually closed to nonfigurative art and especially to younger artists doing this type of art. Lydia Conti opened a gallery in the 1940s with Hans Hartung, Gerard Schneider, and Pierre Soulages but was unable to continue. The painters were absorbed by Louis Carré for a while, but their works disappeared into his reserves; his best-known contemporary artist was Jacques Villon. The Galerie Maeght showed Kandinsky, Miro, Calder, and Steinberg and in 1949 showed Hans Hoffman. There were annual shows of young painters during those years, but they were discontinued. Denise René was certainly the most important nonfigurative gallery. As early as 1946 she had a show entitled *La Jeune Peinture Abstraite* with Hartung, Schneider, Deyrolle, Dewasne, Jacobsen, and Marie Raymond (mother of Yves Klein). In 1948 she showed Max Bill, Gorin, Magnelli, Schneider, Dewasne, Jacobsen, Herbin, Mondrian, Kandinsky, Mortensen, and Marcelle Cahn. Victor Vasarely was her chief advisor. André Bloc, the editor of *Architecture d'aujourd'hui* and *Art d'aujourd'hui*, was a powerful ally of Denise René. *Art d'aujourd'hui* was the best contemporary art magazine of its time.

Jeanne Bucher had a stable of semi-abstract artists, including Bissière. Out in the sixteenth arrondissement, Colette Allendy had a small gallery in her house; she showed more lyrical works alongside a mixture of figurative, Surrealist, and nonfigurative works. One of these artists was a Frenchman named Jacques Doucet, who belonged to the Cobra group.

The Galerie Huit, near Notre-Dame, showed a variety of young artists. The Galerie Facchetti opened in the early 1950s; some of its early shows were suggested by Michel Tapié, who proposed an "Art Autre" which included some American painters. The most important show of this early period was the 1952 Jackson Pollock show, which included works exhibiting a certain kind of return to figuration. Facchetti also showed in later years Paul Jenkins and Adja Yunkers. Tapié was later to become the chief counselor to the Galerie Stadler, which showed, among others, Claire Falkenstein and Norman Bluhm. Antoni Tapies had his first show there, before going over to the Galerie Maeght. Julien Alvard counseled Facchetti from the late 1950s until his death. The critic Léon Degand ruled, along with Vasarely, at Denise René. Charles Estienne advised Suzanne de Koninck, as well as the Galerie Kleber. Later, Jean Fournier of this gallery, in a new location and under his name, showed mainly American artists, among which were Sam Francis, Joan Mitchell, Donald Judd, and Shirley Jaffe.

As this partial list indicates, there was plenty of activity during the "heroic" years of the early 1950s. One reason why it was essential for the younger and lesser-known artists to have a place to show was that the two major salons were, each in its way, restrictive. The Salon de Mai was a mainly figurative and Surrealist salon which had Picasso as one of its figureheads. It was very difficult for young artists to show there unless they belonged to the stable of certain established galleries. The Salon des Réalités Nouvelles was under the direction of the artists clustered around Denise René, Léon Degand, Michel Seuphor, and *Art d'aujourd'hui*. It became the private domain of the hard-edge and "constructivist" groups. Anything outside this dogmatic expression was anathema.

There were few publications that talked about contemporary art. In addition to *Art d'aujourd'hui*, Charles Estienne had a column in *Combat*, Georges Boudaille was allowed to write small articles in *Les Lettres Françaises*, Robert Vrinat was a chronicler for some provincial papers and professional publications. Herta Wescher, besides writing for *Art d'aujourd'hui*, wrote for several German and Swiss publications.

Feeling the need for an organ through which his artists could become known, Jean-Robert Arnaud founded *Cimaise* (which means the wall on which paintings are hung). I was the General Secretary, meaning that I did all of the menial and administrative tasks, as well as distribution (on foot and bicycle across Paris),

Ode à Georges Carrey,
*1955, 39 x 39 in.
Collection of
Olivier Le Corneur.*

Mannheim Revisited,
*1955–56, 39 x 31½ in.
Collection of Jacques
and Renée Cate, Lyon.*

publicity, and translations from French into English and vice versa. The first four numbers were small brochures, illustrated with original linocuts by artists of the gallery. In that first season of 1951–52 he became friendly with several critics who offered small texts. Some of these critics were associated with *Art d'au-jourd'hui*—Roger van Ginderstael, Herta Wescher, and Julien Alvard—but they felt cramped and restricted by the narrow aesthetic policy the magazine followed under the quasi-dictatorship of Léon Degand and abetted by another doctrinarian, Michel Seuphor. Arnaud suggested that *Cimaise* be enlarged: instead of a small house organ, it could become a magazine dealing with the whole gamut of contemporary nonfigurative art. Ginderstael's tastes were mainly for painters whose *acte de peindre*, the painterly act, was visible and expressive, such as one could find in the early nonfigurative works of de Stael. Alvard was interested in a more atmospheric type of painting: his preferences were for the works of René Laubies and Frédéric Benrath.

Herta Wescher was, to my mind, the most knowledgeable critic on the Paris art scene. She began her career as an art historian in Berlin during the 1920s and had known most of the personalities of the Bauhaus and, subsequently, all of the international group clustered in Paris during the 1930s. Her tastes were eclectic and generous. She was also a specialist in collages; her book on collages through the 1940s is a definitive work. She was near to finishing the second volume from the 1940s through the 1960s when she died. She was a great model and mentor to me; her stories of the Dada era, of Kurt Schwitters and Hans Richter, gave me insights that flashed in later years when hype around Pop, Minimalism, *e tutti quanti* clouded the air. She was to be of immense help to me in the beginning, during my first two shows (1952 and 1953).

Another critic who soon joined the ranks of *Cimaise* was the young populist post-cum-critic Michel Ragon. His first painter friends were those of the Cobra group, Atlan being one of the best known. This group had its roots in Surrealism, *art brut*, and Expressionism. Appel and Corneille from Holland, Asger Jorn from Denmark, Svanberg from Sweden, and Atlan and Doucet from France were among its founders. Ragon was to become the most active young critic of the period. His older friends included Atlan, Soulages, and Hartung; he was also close to two young painters from Nantes, which was his home city: James Guitet and Martin Barré. These painters proposed a sort of abstract-landscape type of painting. A bit later Georges Boudaille would join the magazine, and Pierre Restany was asked to join at my suggestion in 1958. He stayed until the early 1960s, when he became the Pope of *Nouveau Réalisme*, and more or less found anathema almost all the other critics—and their artists—associated with *Cimaise*.

This scene was extremely rich, with all of its different tendencies coming from all sorts of different traditions and art movements. There were all kinds of rivalries, jealousies, and intricacies, along with all sorts of gossip and small scandals which everyone knew immediately. There were many galleries, each with its stable of artists and its friendly critic or critics. With the European system of contracts between galleries and artists, the gallery owners showed their devotion, their involvement, and their concern. Their commitment was doubly deep as it was both aesthetic and monetary. They were in a way forced to create activity and interest around their artists: their renown and, as the French say, also their "Biftek" depended upon it. With this rich milieu of strong personalities and committed persons, a whole "scene" could not be taken over by one personality or tendency. There could not be a total dictatorship of one movement, such as would be formed during the papacy of Clement Greenberg and the Abstract Expressionist school or during the time of Pop Art. On a promotional level, the diversity and rivalry was a weakness. But on an aesthetic and creative level, it led to a vital cultural permanence.

One of the serious weaknesses of the Parisian and French cultural scene was the lack of moral and material support from the French public and from the government. To my mind, an echo of this was the fact that a majority of the true creators, except in literature, were very often not French, and especially not Parisians. Even during the time of Malraux, after 1958, there was little improvement in support for the contemporary arts. Painting, sculpture, architecture, and dance were poor relatives until after 1968. The schools were poor and had insufficient programs; the museums did not buy, and did not even seem interested in looking, especially when the art was contemporary. We fell into the old French pattern, in which no one bought the Impressionists, the Post-Impressionists, the Fauves, the Cubists, the Surrealists, and the different forms of nonfigurative art until after the artists were well respected or dead. I remember that during the "heroic" period of the 1950s only the director of the Musée de Saint-Etienne, Maurice Allemand, visited the contemporary galleries, both large and small, regularly.

Several events that took place in the late 1950s were to help
the onward march of the contemporary arts. First, there was
the publication of the *Dictionnaire de l'art abstrait* of Michel
Seuphor. Then in 1958 Michel Ragon published his book *L'Aven-
ture de l'art abstrait*, in which, for the first time, the younger
generation played an important role. Then there was the first of
the Biennales de Paris, devoted to artists under the age of thirty-
six (in the first year, 1958, Carol Summers and I were among the
Americans who won prizes).

Of course the corporations, the banks, and the big companies were not involved. The American system of de-taxation
for companies and individuals that helps the arts and education
has never existed in France (even to this day, despite the valiant
attempts of the Mitterand government). The cultural scene
opened up after 1968, but prior to that, times were tough. Galleries and artists made their living through foreign collectors and
dealers or by organizing shows outside France. I think, too, that
the whole education system in American universities, with their
thriving and active art faculties, churning out thousands of potential artists, or at least people committed to the arts, was an extremely vital phenomenon.

Whereas the art and artists of the so-called "School of
Paris" began a steady decline from about 1958, the "School of
New York" took steady steps forward. The new art of the United
States started to be known in Paris as early as 1949: Charles
Estienne spoke at the time about a certain poetic aspect which
was typically American evident in the works of Hans Hoffmann,
during the show at the Galerie Maeght. Michel Tapié was the first
to bring Pollock to Paris, at Facchetti's, in the early 1950s. Arnaud showed MacDonald Wright, Moholy-Nagy, and other lesser-
known artists from New York; he also had two Americans, Joe
Downing and myself, in his small stable.

A very important exhibition of American art that included
Arthur Dove, Man Ray, and Alexander Calder as well as Ab-
stract Expressionists such as Pollock, Clifford, Still, Arshile
Gorky, Franz Kline, and Philip Guston took place at the Musée
d'Art Moderne in 1956. It caused a tremendous sensation in the
Parisian art world, and was vehemently attacked, of course, by
Beaux-Arts and *Les Lettres Françaises*.

I believe that it was in 1956 or 1957 that the Centre Americain of the rue du Dragon brought a show of four painters from
the Northwest (Tobey, Graves, Callahan, and Anderson) and four
sculptors from the East. It was possibly at this time that Tobey

made a contact with the Galerie Jeanne Bucher (where he was to show later), which would lead to his decision to settle permanently in Europe. It was probably at this time that he made the contacts that led to his striking show at the Musée des Arts Décoratifs in 1965.

Sam Francis arrived in Paris in the early 1950s and quickly made a name for himself in France and Switzerland (he was one of the many GIs taking classes at La Grande Chaumière). He was to be the center of a group of Americans who were installed, for the most part, in Montparnasse or as permanent fixtures at the Café des Deux Magots, which, as the centerpiece of the Saint-Germain, was like a center of the art world. It has been said that at the time, especially when the Biennale de Venezia was a great cultural event, you could sit in the Deux Magots and see the entire working art world come to greet you. Francis's decision to stay in Europe led to his being considered a renegade by the New York papacy. Norman Bluhm, Paul Jenkins, and I (among others) were to undergo this ostracism and chauvinism by the militants of the New York School for many a year. The low point was when an important show of Hans Hartung was organized by the Metropolitan Museum: it was boycotted and viciously attacked by the New York art community. It was considered normal for a New York artist to show in Europe, but not the contrary.

Concerning the artists of Quebec, Riopelle arrived at a fairly early stage and stayed on and prospered. His mentor and master, Paul-Emile Borduas, became known in Paris but not until a much later date and was never appreciated to the same degree.

One very important factor in the life of the triangle of Montreal/New York/Paris of the 1950s was that of Dr. Paul Lariviere of Montreal. He was a neuropsychiatrist and probably the only collector of contemporary art in Canada at the time (at least the only one who bought in all three centers). Part of his collection on loan to the Musée d'Art Contemporain, in Montreal, was the foundation of their permanent collection. His passionate and curious spirit was an example for the arts in Canada. Several younger collectors who tried to follow in his path later became gallery dealers, but they never had his original flair and dedication.

During the summer of 1958, I toured most of the United States in a Greyhound bus accompanied by my friend Michel Ragon. I had my first show back in the States at that time, after a ten-year absence—an absence due not to indifference or aggression, but purely to the fact that I did not have the money for a round-trip ticket to Seattle. Somewhat later I had two shows in Seattle and in 1963 had shows in Seattle, San Antonio, New York, and Montreal. It was during these years that I was able to see what was going on in the United States at this time. Among the people of the New York scene that Michel Ragon and I discovered in New York in 1958 was Leo Castelli, who was just getting started and was showing Rauschenberg and Jasper Johns. We also had a meeting with Franz Kline, who was pleased and rather surprised by his success. He was generally very mistrustful at the time and marveled at the system of long-range contracts with galleries that existed in Europe. In 1958 he said that he did not know from month to month if Janis was going to keep on buying his work, piece by piece. Another discovery was the great sculptor Louise Nevelson, who was relatively unknown at the time. We also visited Sam Kootz, whom we had previously met in Paris. He was one of the few dealers who continued to work with some European painters. Howard Wise had tried to do so in Cleveland and had succeeded to some degree; when he moved his gallery to New York, he could sell only New York painters. Martha Jackson had a few European painters, including Tapies, and her son tried, and failed, to make a go of it in Paris and New York. But there were very few who continued to work with any artist living in Europe from, let us say, 1962 on.

The triumph of Pop took place in 1964, with Rauschenberg obtaining the Grand Prize at Venice. I have never been able to convince anyone in New York that Pop was a new version of Dada, with Schwitters and some of the other artists of the Bauhaus or the "Berlin School" (such as Hanna Hoch) as masters. In about 1963 the level of chauvinism in the New York School had reached one of its highest levels of intensity. It was touted around that Paris as an art center was dead. No one even talked about other cities; they did not exist, they could really even be dead. In 1965 I had dinner at the house of Dore Ashton and Adja Yunkers. Dore had been the art critic for *Art News* and *The New York Times* in the mid-1950s. She went to live in Europe for a few years with her husband; when she returned she refused to join with the strict line of the hegemony of New York . . . and lost her job at *The New York Times*. At that same dinner was Mark Rothko. He stated that he felt as if he were dead; after having been brought to a pinnacle during the heyday of Abstract Expressionism, he was left in the heights where only museums and large corporations could acquire him. On the other hand he was no longer "hot"; no magazines even mentioned him, no young artists even tried to visit him. He was later to become severely alcoholic and to commit suicide. Another victim of this acceleration process was Philip Guston, whom I had met in 1962. In 1965 he was in a very difficult financial position and could not pay his dentistry bills. He had to go back to teaching. Years later he made a comeback, but for me it was a strange one. He had completely changed his style, had completely turned his back on his luminous work and was doing cartoon-like works, influenced by the Pop era and maybe *Zap Comics*. It amazes and frightens me to see the numbers of alcoholics and suicides in the New York art world, among people who are—or were—well known.

All these are incidents that I find very revealing. The exaggerated importance of hype, of marketing techniques, of speculation, have become an integral part of the negative side of New York. Paris is certainly not perfect, but the attitude of most of its galleries (especially in the time of which I am speaking) was supportive, and this on a long-range basis. And in recent years, the policies and actions of the Ministry of Culture have helped the creators, and brought a new element of imagination and vigor and even excitement into Parisian (and French) cultural life.

So who won the war of "Modern Art"?

I believe that peaceful coexistence and the free and adventuresome exchange of ideas and persons are far more enriching phenomena than the wars of dogma, where the enemy has to be destroyed so that he does not threaten your existence. I think that one of the great lessons to New York might come from the very make-up, the very idea of the United States. At the present time, New York's attempt at hegemony has antagonized the other great centers of the United States, who are coming to realize their intrinsic worth and the richness of the cultural activity of their own cultural center again, perhaps partly from getting slapped and even mauled by its trans-Atlantic friend. It has learned quite a few lessons (not all of them good). It just may well be that New York could learn a few itself in the future.

Jean Baudrillard

Someone should establish an anthropology of hot and cool, touching first of all, of course, on such well-known paradigms as cool societies, hot societies, hot war, cold war, cool media, hot media. It is tempting to try to work out direct links between them, but for our purposes all we need accept is that the period during which war grew "cold" is the same period during which cool media began to emerge—the dawn of mass television, the twilight of war and of history.

What I am hypothesizing is that by our acceptance of the Cold War we somehow exiled ourselves from history, because it was impossible for us to risk waging such a war; in so doing, we returned to being societies without history, cold societies in Levi-Strauss's sense. The orbital suspense of the war creates a kind of symbolic world balance, a balance of terror, yes, but one that is enough to keep history out, to eradicate its place. In the early years of the century and up until the post-World War II era, there was too much history, too much liberation, too much killing. With Auschwitz and Hiroshima, history reached its acme, it became saturated, the resultant explosion led to a freezing up that, in turn, led to implosion. Since it was impossible to advance, to go further, war froze, in the same sense that in film we speak of a picture's being "frozen," of a freeze-frame. War, and history with it, is somehow suspended, satellized, hyperrealized.

It is a unique situation: of course, violence still exists, events still "occur," but history no longer has meaning or finality. One event follows another, but they are basically inconsequential because they do not upset the symbolic order of terror, the world order of dissuasion (just as no decisive event can occur to shake the symbolic order of ritual in primitive societies). What is the meaning of abstraction in painting, if not this: a table is still a table, objects are always what they are, but there is no longer any sense, any significance, in representing them as such.

I take Canetti's proposition as epigraph: "A painful notion: that beyond a certain precise point in time history ceased to be real. As if, without being aware of it, the whole human species had suddenly taken off from reality. Everything that happened since has been untrue, but without our knowing it. Now our task and our duty must be to single out that moment and, until we have done so, we are forced to persevere in the present destruction" (*Provinz des Menschen*).

There are various plausible hypotheses about this disappearance of history. Canetti's phrase, "as if the whole human species had taken off from reality," irresistibly evokes for our contemporary astrophysical image repertoire the "thrust velocity" a body requires to escape the gravitational field of a star or a planet. Inherent in the image is the acceleration of modernity, of technology, events, the media, the acceleration of all kinds of exchanges and trade (economic, political, sexual)—in short, everything we mean when we use the word "liberation"—which has brought us freedom at such a speed that one day (and in this case we can, with Canetti, speak of a "precise" moment, just as in physics the "escape" point can be exactly calculated) we escaped the referential sphere of the real and of history. We are truly "free," in every sense of the word, so free that we have been thrust, accelerated (the speeded-up metabolization of our societies), out of a certain space-time, beyond a certain horizon where the real is possible, where the event is possible because gravitation is still strong enough for things to be reflected, to fall back upon themselves, and thus to have a certain duration and certain effects. A certain slowness (in other words, speed, but not too much), a certain distance (but not too much), a certain "liberation" (energy of rupture and change, but not too much)— all are necessary in order to produce this kind of condensation, this significant crystallization of events that we call history, this kind of coherent deployment of causes and effects we call "the real."

Beyond the gravitational effect that maintains bodies on a signifying orbit, the atoms of meaning spin out into space, once they have gained sufficient speed to break "free." Each atom follows its own meaningful trajectory into infinity and becomes lost in space—which is precisely what we are experiencing in our societies today, societies that are bent on speeding up the emission of bodies, messages, and processes in all directions and that have, in particular, with the help of modern media, created a simulated trajectory toward the infinite. Every fact, every feature—political, historical, cultural—is endowed by virtue of its power of media diffusion with a kinetic energy that thrusts it permanently out of the space proper to it and propels it into a hyperspace where, since it will never return, it loses all its meaning. There is no need to create science fiction: it exists, here and now, in our societies, with the media, the computer data, the circuits, the networks—particle accelerators that have destroyed the referential orbit of objects once and for all.

The consequences for history cannot be disregarded. "Narrative," the "recital of events," has become impossible, since it is, by definition (re-citing), the possible recurrence of a sequence of meaning. Today, through the impetus of diffusion, the circulative, total communication injunction, every fact, every event, is freed for itself alone: each fact becomes atomic, nuclear, and traces its trajectory in a vacuum. In order to be indefinitely broadcast, it must be broken down like an atomic particle, thereby attaining a counter-gravity thrust that can spin it out of return orbit, permanently separate it from history. Events no longer have consequences because they occur too rapidly; they are broadcast too quickly over distances that are too vast, caught up in the circuits; they will never return to testify to themselves or to their meaning (meaning is always an attestation). On the other hand, every cultural or event grouping must be fragmented, disarticulated, in order to fit into the circuits, every language must be reduced to 0/1, to binary numbers, in order to circulate—no longer in our human memories, but in the electronic, glowing memories of computers. No human language can withstand the speed of light. No historic event can withstand planetary diffusion. No meaning can withstand acceleration. No history can withstand the centrifuging of facts *per se*, the illimitation of space-time (and even: no sexuality can withstand its liberation, no culture its promotion, no truth its verification, etc.).

I have called this simulation. However, I would stipulate that simulation cuts two ways and that what I am putting forward here is, in turn, no more than an exercise in simulation. I am no longer capable of "reflecting" anything, I myself can only push hypotheses to their limits, remove them from their critical zones of reference, take them beyond the point of no return, thrust the theory into the hyperspace of simulation—whereby it loses all objective validity, but perhaps gains in coherence, that is, in real affinity with the system around us.

The second hypothesis regarding the disappearance of history is in a way the inverse of the first; it deals not with the acceleration of the process but with its slowing down. Again, it is directly derived from physics.

Matter slows the passage of time. To be more exact, time on the surface of a very dense body seems to pass more slowly. The phenomenon is accentuated as density increases. The effect of this slowdown is to stretch out the length of the light waves emitted by the body as received or perceived by the outside observer. Beyond a certain limit, time stops, the length of the light wave becomes infinite. The wave ceases to exist. The light goes out.

Here too, the analogical transfer is fairly simple. We need only think "mass" instead of "matter," and "history" instead of "time." We then see that when history falls under the influence of the gravitational pull of the astral body we call the "silent majority," it slows down. Our societies are dominated by this mass process, "mass" not so much in the demographic or sociological meaning of the word as in the sense (here too) of going beyond a certain critical point, a point of no return—not of acceleration (as in the first hypothesis) but of inertia. This is the most considerable event in our modern societies, the most subtle and profound trick of their history: the creation, throughout the course of their socialization, their mobilization, their productive and revolutionary intensification (for all societies are revolutionary in the eyes of the past), of a force of inertia, of an immense indifference and of the silent power of that indifference. Of what we call the mass. And this mass, the inert social mass, is not created by a lack of exchanges, of information or of communication; quite the contrary, it is the result of the increase in and saturation of exchanges, of information, etc. It is the product of the hyperdensity of cities, goods, messages, circuits. It is the cold star of the social, and history congeals around its mass, it slows down, events occur and subside with no effect. Neutralized, mithridatized by data, the masses in turn neutralize history, filter it out. They have no history, no meaning, no conscience, no desires. They are the potential residue of all history, all meaning, all conscience, all desire, all those fine things that, when brought into our modern world, have fomented a mysterious counterpart, ignorance of which (ignorance of this inertial force, this power of inertia, this inverse energy) is today wrecking every political, social, and historical strategy.

Here, we have the opposite: progress, history, reason, desire can no longer attain their "escape speed." They are no longer able to tear themselves away from the overly dense body that implacably slows their trajectory, that slows time to the point that we are now unable to perceive or imagine the future. All social, historical, temporal transcendence is sucked in by the silent immanence of this mass. We have already reached the point where political and social events can no longer exert enough autonomous energy to move us and seem instead to occur like a silent film in which we are—not individually, collectively—irresponsible. History ends here, and we see how: not for lack of players, nor lack of violence (there will always be plenty of violence, but violence must not be mistaken for history), nor lack of events (there will always be more events, thanks to the media and data processing!); it ends because it slows down, because of indifference and stupefaction. History cannot rise above itself, it cannot manage to envisage its own end, to dream its own death; and it shrouds itself in its own immediate effect, it exhausts itself in its own special effects, it falls in upon itself and implodes into "news." In the final analysis we cannot even speak of the death of history, since it will not have time to experience it. Its impressions will speed up, but its meaning will slow, ineluctably. It will finally grind to a halt and be extinguished, like light and time caught in the gravitational pull of an infinitely dense mass.

Whether the universe is indefinitely expanding or whether it is imploding toward an infinitely dense, infinitely small original nucleus depends upon its critical mass (about which there has been infinite speculation as new particles are "invented"). Analogously, our human history may be either evolutionary or involutionary, depending upon the critical mass of mankind. Has the history, the fate, of the species attained the speed necessary for it to break away and triumph over mass inertia? Are we, like the galaxies, caught up in an inescapable movement that is distancing us from each other at dizzying speed, or is this infinite dispersal going to end and the human molecules begin to move closer together in inverse gravitation? Can the daily growing mass of humanity get control over that kind of pulsation?

The human species has also experienced a "big bang": a certain critical density, a certain critical concentration of men and relationships controls the explosion we call history—the dispersal over space-time of formerly dense, hieratical and quasi-timeless nuclei. Today, we are faced with the inverse effect: the crossing of the critical-mass threshold (populations, events, data) leads to the inverse process of historical and political inertia.

On the cosmic scale we do not now know (and probably never will) if we have attained the breakaway speed and entered into a state of definitive expansion. On the human scale, with its more limited perspectives, it may be that the very energy used in the liberation of the species (the accelerations in the pace of demography, technology, and trade over the centuries) is creating a surplus of mass and resistance that is moving faster than the initial energy impulse and that it will inevitably impel us into pitiless contraction and inertia.

(I forgot to mention that the mass-effect is also simulative. Today, the masses are our model of social simulation, in which society can realize unhoped-for development but in which it can also find frustrations and drown in its own enlarged image. The masses are the purest product of society, and, at the same time, the most perverse).

This ending of history through historical excess, by surpassing history, has its counterpart in the field of the image. We must bear in mind the effect on the collective imagination during and after the last war of the many violent and ghastly pictures that conflict produced. Events and, of equal importance, their representation—above all visual—gave rise to deep trauma throughout the world. The war increased the image's potential for violence, it led to a hitherto unknown outburst not only of events but also of the way those events looked. At the same time, the very excess of the images killed the imagination. It became in a way impossible to imagine and to represent such horrors, such excesses. The human mind had nothing equivalent to them, reaction to them was impossible. So at the time, because of the impossibility of such things being conceivable, there was a brutal cooling off of the imagination, of feeling, with a parallel cooling off of history. And abstraction—in painting too—emerged from that impossibility of conceiving, of representing, such an outrageous and monstrous history. However, this abstraction, the abstraction of the 1950s, was not the subtle, analytical, experimental, classical—I would almost say felicitous—abstractionism of the prewar period. It was a desperate, nervous, pathetic, and explosive abstraction. It was the very abstract image of the Cold War itself, for the Cold War is abstract, it is something suspended, it does not break out, it is simultaneously conflict and deterrence, just as pictorial abstraction is simultaneously forms and forms deferred, a play of signs and a violent dissuasion of the signs of reality. In a word, if the Cold War represents a balance of terror, abstraction too brings a kind of terror to bear upon reality and its representation; it suspends events and denies appearance. It is a terrorist gesture, hot and explosive (here we are referring to "expressionist" abstraction), but it is also a part of an overall deterrence. Of course this is true of Pollock, not of Klee or of Kandinsky. The "hot" abstractionism of the 1950s is far more gestural and savage than it is geometrical and calculated. It is no longer an analytical deconstruction of the world, a nonfigurative mathematics of forms. It is a vehement manifestation, a challenge, a shout—expressionist in the sense of expressing, expulsing, in the sense of the exorcism, the conjuration, of the rejection and the violent bodily extraversion of the world by the image. "Classical" abstractionism is far more intellectual and critical. The later version is not critical, it is not really a denunciation, it is a holocaust of painterly signs, a holocaust of the world by the image, somehow reminiscent of the bodily holocaust of the extermination camps and of the imminent nuclear holocaust (from holocaust to hologram).

After the First World War Paul Valéry said, "Henceforth, civilizations knew that they were mortal." After the Second World War, after Auschwitz and Hiroshima, we knew that henceforth they were dead. From then on they were post-catastrophe civilizations, representations in light of catastrophe. A fatal strategy.

This fatal strategy bears examination, for art is never merely the mechanical reflection of positive or negative world conditions but, rather, an exacerbated illusion of them. It satiates itself with them, if we may use that term, it accentuates those negative conditions, it is their hyperbolic reflection. Abstract Expressionism, the "hot" painting of this period, is not just the equivalent, the reflection, of an imminent nuclear catastrophe, of some suspended threat; it goes further, it carries out that threat, it creates that catastrophe. It depicts annihilation by anticipating it, through symbolism. It does not attempt to avoid the threat or the catastrophe through any idealistic depiction; on the contrary, it goes beyond that and, faced with the threat of ultimate disappearance, it annihilates itself and gives every sign of its own disappearance as art. That is how it depicts the event, and not by giving it a critical meaning or by inventing some dialectical solution to it. Art is always a challenge, and if it engages in a contest with the world, if it resolves it, it is always by overstepping obstacles, by rising above them. The Germans have a word for it. *Steigerung*. It confronts a full, saturated system with the inverse and homologous systematics of a pure and empty gesture. Replying to the Cold War's blackmail threat of annihilation, it celebrates its own disappearance by an aggravated symbolic gesture. That is what "expressionism" means: the rage to create meaning even when there is no longer any sense—or criticism—to be made, when, faced with a world threatened with annihilation, the only effect it can produce is that of its own disappearance. It is the same felt need, the same fatal strategy that led members of the earliest Christian sects to commit suicide in order to hasten the end of the world and create the Kingdom of God. Ecstatic deaths designed to force the world into a corner, to compel reality and rise above appearances. Art has always done the same: it acts out, dazzlingly, its own appearance, its own disappearance; it incites reality to disappearance and thereby sets up, against the world current, the conditions for the Last Judgment. Indeed, modern art embarked upon this path long ago. Unlike classical art, it no longer employs that symbolic mastery of the presence and appearance of the world (which is possible only in a world in which things have a right to their own image, a world of meaning and resemblance), but employs only the symbolic mastery of disappearance. And, unlike classical art, its charm resides not in the seductiveness of forms but in the magic of its own disappearance. Since Hegel, perhaps, who was already writing about it, and throughout modern times—during which, we are forced to recognize, the conditions of a perpetual Cold War have always prevailed—but of course especially since the crucial period with which we are concerned, the magic exercised by art has been nothing but the magic of its own disappearance.

And the Cold War continues. It did not stop in the 1960s. Above and beyond the confrontation and tension between the two blocs, the mechanisms of dissuasion, the principle of deterrence, the neutralizing of meaning and reality and history, Hiroshima, Auschwitz, the nuclear world and extermination, radiation and chain reactions—it is all still going on, but readjusted to reflect itself, this Cold War, the war that never breaks out, not as a hot event but as a cold process, slow, endemic, administered in homeopathic doses, so to speak. No longer explosive, but implosive. We are atomically frozen, subjected to perpetual deterrence. And if the Cold War does not break out, if it does not explode, if, indeed, it is not really intended to explode, it is because its true function is to keep us deterred, chilled. In all this vast mechanism the cold media play a capital role. Television is creating a telefission of reality and the real world. It radiates and innervates the entire world via a network of cold images, images chilled by electronic distance. It creates in our systems for perception, imagination, and action a kind of catastrophe in the formal and topological sense that René Thom employs the word: a radical qualitative change in the entire system, just as nuclear science inaugurated catastrophe in the field of energy. It is simply that television is a catastrophe in slow motion, a cold catastrophe exuded over time, within minds. But it happens through the same kind of chain reaction, now an implosive one: it chills and neutralizes all the meaning and energy of events. Beyond the "hot" and negentropic concepts of energy and data, TV and nuclear power have the same dissuasive force of all cold systems. Beyond the presumed threat of explosion, of a hot catastrophe, nuclear power poses the threat of a drawn-out cold catastrophe, the universalization of a system of dissuasion and deterrence, the consequences of which are perhaps even worse.

There is indeed a chain reaction, but it is not the nuclear chain reaction but that of the simulacra and the simulation in which all the energy of the real is effectively engulfed, not in a spectacular nuclear explosion, but in a secret and continuous implosion, which is perhaps taking a more deadly turn than all the explosions that presently threaten us.

I'm not as far from hot painting as one might think, for it is that painting that is benefiting from this suspended explosion. There is nothing worse than this impending catastrophe, this invisible nuclear panic. Better a spectacular explosion and the spectacle of unleashed energy and destruction than slow, ineluctable deterrence. Better the parousia of catastrophe than some slow, viral cyrogenization. That is what, today, expressionism and hot painting are expressing: an explosive dream, a dream of energy liberated in its spectacular and pathetic form, a longing for intensity, for a deflagration of appearances, against the cold energy of simulacra and their distillation into homeopathic dosages within cold data systems. A last glimmer, a final attempt to transform into hot energy, into intense color and form—even if it should kill off painting itself—this is the implacable process of deterrence through freezing.

Expressionist painting is expressing the eruption of this chain reaction into the world of forms (including abstract forms), the eruption of gesture, matter, color, in a kind of fusion that shatters representation and form—like the nuclear chain reaction that vaporizes bodies and substances, that brings history to an end and ushers in new cold societies. Yet, at the same time, expressionist painting is protesting this involution of war into Cold War, this involution of the world into a frozen world, this involution of the imagination itself into the chilly images of television and the other cold media (to which painting itself has now largely acclimatized itself, in its pop, hyperrealist, conceptual, etc., guises). It is the last moment of illuminated painting in the context of historical darkness.

Translated by Richard Miller

Discussion

Benjamin Buchloh

I have a very limited question concerning a statement that you made in your talk and that also appears in your book *In the Shadow of the Silent Majority*. When I read it I was struck by it, and listening to you today made it even more striking. The soothing quality of the apocalyptic siren conveys an absolutely seductive image. The particular statement that I am referring to is your assertion that in the condition of total de-realization—the condition of total amnesia in the loss of history—we must not confound events with history. Do you think that any event, regardless of its magnitude, is simply another event in this ongoing staging of media events which we should not confound with history? There are many examples that we can quote; for instance, do you think that the attempt to resist the destruction of Nicaragua by the American government and the Contras is just another event that is staged by the media as an event in the ongoing chain of violence that replaces history?

Jean Baudrillard

I do not deny the painfulness of such events. They have been taken away from their space-time relationship and now they don't have a life of their own. This is contrary, for instance, to the war in Spain in 1936. Today's images are automatically projected onto us by the "cool" media and forgotten immediately. It is this process that I oppose to the historical process.

That is not to say that I deny that "hot" history, as it were, still exists. Of course, we bathe in it as human beings, but we are already immersed in a "cold," freezing sort of atmosphere which is propagated by the "cool" media. And, certainly, there is a fight—a constant struggle—between those two forms of life. Political commitment must be taken into account; it must be looked at within this context of the struggle between the "hot" and the "cold."

Thierry de Duve
Mr. Baudrillard has presented us with two models of history: one that says that it is accelerating, and another that says that it is freezing. Those models say that we are beyond the real. However, scientific use of models needs to be confronted with a reality, but since the hypothesis (that is, the model) says that there is no reality, we can no longer confront the model with a new reality. Thus the theory is tautological. Nevertheless, I think that Mr. Baudrillard has in mind to raise some questions about the political or practical views of his model—not the theoretical views— and that is what my question is.

Jean Baudrillard
I do not really mind being called a pessimist. I also do not mind the reference to models. Yes, I am referring to models. However, confronting models with reality is a classical tradition and today I find that basis impossible because models, to my mind, have absorbed reality. Consequently, there is no possible confrontation today because of this hegemony of models. There is no longer a determinant reality.

The political application of my point of view is not clear to me; I do not know what I can do with this standpoint from a political point of view. Yet I know that something has happened, and I can't go on believing that theory is still possible, as indeed it used to be. Theory can be reintroduced into the system; however, we have to assume that theory subverts the models. But again, the political applications of these steps are presently unclear to me.

T. J. Clark

I noticed an interesting shift in your point of view between what happens in your talk and what happens when you are confronted with a question about some particular political or historical instance or effect. It seems that that shift is built into your discourse in a way I find puzzling. On the one hand, your talk spoke of a protest, completed in reality, having disappeared: representation disappears. However, when you were confronted with questions from the audience, your answer seemed much more reasonable; you then began to describe a process of representation taking place: freezing, dissemination, et cetera.

In general, what seems most worrying here—and what gives your original discourse its comforting, and indeed apocalyptic, flavor—is that it has room inside itself in its first form for uneven development. It wants to see history as having ended and doesn't, for instance, build into itself the fact that history is still taking place. Even America is still face to face with and involved in some kind of crude, old-fashioned history in Managua or in Lebanon. It wants to see liberation, at the second level say, having taken place. Well, how do we deal with the resistances to that liberation in the last ten to fifteen years? It wants to see abstraction as having already happened. What do we do then with the sort of vehement and self-confident revivals of figuration in which we're surrounded? I think that there is, as I say, a sort of "shifting" in your argument.

One way of putting it would be to say this: in your discourse, it's almost as if you make yourself the spokesman—the representative—of a real which says that reality has finished. However, when you are confronted with more specific instances of what is happening, you retreat to what seems to be a much more plausible point of view. This view seems to accept that there is a struggle going on within the realm of representation and that all of the things that you are talking about—the inertia, the mass, the freezing, the end of history—are actually efforts at representation, control, and organization: efforts which indeed belong to institutions, to classes, and which are embedded in a certain kind of class struggle in the realm of representation still in history. Just how that goes side by side with the picture of these being a real—which is that there are only models, that the process of ending the real has happened—is, I think, what lies at the basis of all of what worries some of us.

I think that in the sphere of representation an object is always an object. This object is always the same and will be the same in the future. However, within a determinate moment, there is a phase in a system of values, or in a system of representation, where the object ceases to be an object—ceases to be determined by its utility and by the entire system of objects—and representation in painting is not possible as such. And you ask what happened? Well, what happened is something like a catastrophe. What happened—and I say this not at all in a pessimistic sense—is that something is over, and any object as such is beyond this vanishing point, beyond this point of no return with regard to self-representation.

Analogously, I can say that historical events are always events, but perhaps the same events are nowadays beyond this vanishing point. Perhaps between the two points—between interpretation and noninterpretation, similitude and dissimilitude, sense and nonsense—some catastrophe has happened. It is this that we must keep in mind and that must be reflected in our theoretical and political strategies. Just because historical events are from the beginning—and perhaps even before their beginning—recaptured by the media in a chain reaction of signs which are devoid of representation, does not make them any more representative. Representation by the "cold" media, especially, is a chain reaction: it is an exclusive form of representation. Of course, a chain reaction of "hot" representation is not possible. Nowadays we have to deal with chain reactions in history, psychology, and many things. This creates another universe of meaning: it is no longer the universe of representation. We do not yet have the code to deal with this new hyperreality, with this new universe. We can touch on it a bit with theory, but not very much. We can only apprehend it by anticipation.

Postwar Painting Games: The Rough and the Slick

Serge Guilbaut

C'est l'Président Truman
qui dit au vieux Shuman:
Faut signer mon pacte
car d'Hitler il porte la marque.
Il est pour faire la guerre à l'Union Soviétique
Aux pays populaires et au profit de l'Amérique.

Mais le peuple a dit non; il n'y a rien à faire
A l'Union Soviétique, on n'fera pas la guerre.
Nous n'serons pas les biffins des gros milliardaires.
Finalement ces requins mordront la poussière.

("Chant de la Paix," French Communist Youth Group song, 1951)

There will soon be an end to this (Korean) wicked war
When these hard-headed communists get what they're looking for
Only one thing will stop them and their atrocious bunch
It's if General MacArthur drops an atomic bomb . . .
They'll be fired up the middle and blinded all around
and radioactivity will burn them to the ground . . .
If there is any commies left, they'll be on the run
If General MacArthur drops the atomic bomb.

(Country and Western song "When They Drop the Atomic Bomb,"

by Jackie Doll and his Pickled Peppers, 1951)

The one-sided and mechanistic viewpoints of these two songs en-
capsulate the atmosphere of violence and mistrust that permeated Franco-American relations during the 1950s. They make
clear the rift that occurred in the late 1940s between France and
the United States over the Communist issue. This rupture was not
only felt in the political arena, but also, and perhaps even more
acutely, in the artistic and cultural realm. There, the mistrust
and misunderstandings were total and profound. The inability to
understand the very specific conditions of the creation of each
other's art as well as the difficulty in assessing the art on its own
terms, in relation to its own history, have continued and have
often kept art historians from clearly perceiving the issues that
were then so crucially at stake between France and the United
States.

When dealing with this postwar period and the artistic relationship between Paris and New York, one immediately sees a
bizarre kind of misunderstanding of the other, as if it were constantly operating in a blind spot. Moreover, as we will see later,
when the other did come into view, its image was invariably distorted by a reading based on false, incomplete, or skewed data.
But what one soon realizes is that there was, paradoxically, a real
desire to know about the other and, as soon as the image came
into focus, an irresistible urge to fit the other into a nonthreaten-
ing stereotype that had been constructed over many years:
America was violent, brutal, and free, while France was overcul-
tured, suave to the point of decadence, and riddled with inner
contradictions. One was rough, the other was slick. Interestingly
enough, both sides agreed on the validity of these clichés for dif-
ferentiating their two cultures. The catch was that each country
saw its characteristics as positive compared to the negative
qualities of the other. The real debate carried on throughout this
period was over which set of qualities should be seen to represent
the West's new postwar culture as a whole. Would it be French,
as tradition would have it, or American, as the new balance of
power seemed to imply?

What I would like to discuss in this essay are the cultural
implications of the Cold War of songs, of the popular "Rambo-
ism" (before the word) that the two songs cited above signify.
Things were of course not that simple; this polar division was
then, like now, much too crude. The Cold War rhetoric tended to
present two adversary empires striking at each other with every
bit of media available. The political reality, even in the 1950s, was

more complex, contradictory, and confused at times. It will then not be surprising to learn that the ideological positions and postures stricken by intellectuals were always intricate and often ironic. In fact, if one wants to understand the Parisian art scene from 1947 to 1951, one has to take into account this comment made by the poet Christian Dotremont of the "surréaliste revolutionnaire" group then allied with the Communist Party: When asked by a reporter from the newspaper *Carrefour* in 1948 what he would do if Russian troops invaded France, Dotremont in his best dialectical moment proposed this delicate answer: "No problem, I would take the first plane departing for the United States."[1]

This was not a mere quip, however, because this was very often the name of the game in France. It seemed important, imperative even for some of the most sophisticated artists, to play one side against the other so as not to belong to either. To be quartered was still, for some, the less painful position in these dangerous times. To acknowledge the game did not mean duplicity, but simply signaled political awareness and an astute stand in a very troubling situation, in which neutrality itself was heavily politicized during the Cold War.[2] Right from the start then, while the West was rebuilding its cultural image, one thing was clear: the traditionally friendly cultural relations between France and America were becoming extremely problematic.

My interest here does not lie in any uncritical revisionist revival of the art of the 1950s, nor in any nationalistic defense of Parisian art. Rather, what I am interested in doing, in light of the important and successful push by the Museum of Modern Art between 1948 and 1950 to impose Abstract Expressionism as the most advanced and significant modern art in America, is to try to show the fundamentally different sets of conditions under which French and American postwar art were operating. I will also try to show that despite some formal similarities, and some comparable reactions to the war and postwar culture, the pictorial discourses of modern art in the two countries were essentially different.

The years I am focusing on in this essay were in many ways the most important for the post-World War II period, because they happened to define the political and cultural shape of the Western world for the rest of the century. America knew that she had become the leader of the Western world and the main line of defense against Communist ideology. It quickly became clear that to secure a strong place in the postwar world, the United States had to acquire cultural supremacy, or at least wide cultural recognition, which would help convince the rest of the Western world that its military and economic hegemony was not dangerous, but could be trusted and followed. It had to be seen that America was in fact defending the same complex and cherished civilization as the Europeans. The problem for the American avant-gardists (and here I do not mean only the artists, but also their critics and museum supporters) was first to convince a portion of the home public that their work was as sophisticated as that of any European modern master. But the other step, of course, was to convince the Europeans of the American qualities. That would prove to be more difficult.

Very early on the American liberal elite realized the importance of high culture as an anti-Communist line of defense, but it did not yet know how to use it or how to manipulate it effectively.[3] France, on the other hand, had great experience in cultural imperialism. The problem was that Paris wanted to continue as if the war experience was just a glitch in an otherwise seamless historical continuum in which France's destiny, as always, was to shower the world with the aesthetics of her old artistic glories. The assumption was that the entire world, thirsty for high culture after all the barbarian madness, was going to turn once more toward the universal fountain of art: Paris. But art became rapidly entangled in the cultural politics of the Cold War, to the point that the old schema could no longer apply. It was nevertheless along these old lines that the French establishment as well as the avant-garde to some degree were misreading the new script. Their hopes, desires, and chauvinism crashed against the walls of cultural Cold War politics, and against economic and political realities of the new postwar world.

As if that were not enough of a problem, it soon became clear that in the French art world the unity and the very identity of the School of Paris were gone. In their place was developing a large mosaic of movements, of styles, of tendencies, all fairly clearly defined along political lines. In the United States, however, cultural and political scenes tended to be homogenized, erasing many asperities, and extremes were shrinking in size and in importance and were being absorbed by a greedy and fascinating center. Politically, liberals had virtually wiped out all Communist or Socialist alternatives and had won a key place in the American political spectrum.[4] In the art world, Abstract Expressionism was the leading force.

In France none of this had been possible. The French Communist Party was in fact extremely popular thanks to the prestige it had acquired from the important role—real and symbolic—it played during the resistance. The party was seen as a heroic and martyred nationalist entity. It also presented itself as the party around which the great majority of French intellectuals could rally, at least until 1947. After that date, without losing its impact, the Communist Party changed its previously more open postwar policy and, wanting to influence the restructuring of French culture, started promoting Social Realism against what in the 1930s they called bourgeois abstraction. This signaled the disintegration of the Parisian art scene and its reorganization along aesthetic lines, which were very often carved along political demarcations. What was nevertheless quite clear to everyone was that Paris, which had lost her political and economic strength, could not afford to lose her cultural prestige as well. All factions were in agreement on that. Both countries, then, were engaged between 1945 and 1953 in a kind of dialogue of the deaf, each talking to itself about the other, without assessing correctly the partner's cultural realities.

In the United States, under pressure from the right after the Boston Institute of Contemporary Art's antimodern manifesto of 1948,[5] the Museum of Modern Art and the Whitney Museum of American Art moved to save the most advanced form of modern art then becoming visible, what would be called Abstract Expressionism. Between 1948 and 1951, thanks to writings of Clement Greenberg and the activist involvement of major institutions, modern art was protected, repackaged, and presented as the most important movement for the new emerging postwar America. This was of course a very new phenomenon for the United States. As the events surrounding the ICA episode show, it is clear that Clement Greenberg, Robert Motherwell, Alfred Barr, and Nelson Rockefeller, to mention only a few with a certain ideological bent (which we can call a new liberal modernism separated from the watered-down academic modernism then very much in demand) were aware of the need to promote an art based on individualism, on freedom of expression, and in opposition to ideologically bound socialist productions.[6] This defense of the so-called "extremist" artists was of course possible because it could be easily demonstrated that modern art was safe for America, that it was not un-American, as many on the right attempted to argue, because the Russians, imitating the Nazis, were violently against it.

Modern art, and the most daring section of it at that, stood insolently between the two blocs traditionally opposed to it: the right and the old left. In America advanced modern art came to represent the new antitotalitarianism of the U.S., with all its ambiguities, just as the new art symbolized by the group of artists in the picture of "The Irascibles" published in *Life* magazine in 1951 was not coherent in its plan of action, only in its refusals and rejections.

This central, crucial position was in fact the argument Alfred Barr used in 1949 to convince Henry Luce, the director of *Life* magazine, to change his editorial policy toward the new Abstract Expressionist art. Barr again insisted that one should not fear modern art and showed that it was not designed to destroy American values. On the contrary, in a personal letter dated March 24, 1949, Barr told Luce that his fears were totally unfounded and that the new art should be defended by every American. Barr was concerned over the general wave of reactionary hostility toward advanced experiment in the arts and in particular toward Abstract Expressionism. This new type of art should be especially protected, not criticized as in the USSR, because this, after all, was "artistic free enterprise."[7] To win Luce to Barr's and MoMA's interests, the argument, even if specious, was in its strategic aspect clever, and it was expanded in several articles by Barr, Thomas Hess, and others in the following years.[8]

By March 1950, when MoMA, the ICA, and the Whitney Museum of American Art finally published a joint statement announcing their unflinching support of modern art, Abstract Expressionism was definitively saved and safe. This was a timely decision, as McCarthy had just delivered his famous anticommunist address on February 9. The pressure against liberalism was rapidly mounting, giving a new urgency to the defense of modern art. It seems then paradoxical that Robert Motherwell and Ad Reinhardt, in the introduction to a book published in 1951 (but written in 1950) and called, not without a tinge of defiance, *Modern Artists in America*, projected a tone of jubilation and hope. Modern art, they felt, had finally won an important place in American culture and had even succeeded in some ways in dominating the artistic scene:

Today the extent and degree of Modern art in America is unprecedented. From East to West, numerous galleries and museums, colleges and art schools, private and regional demonstrations display their mounting interest in original plastic efforts. One can say that by 1950, Modern Art in the United States has reached a point of sustained achievement worthy of a detached and democratic treatment.[9]

The tone here was certainly different from the one used by Motherwell and Rosenberg in December 1947 when in the introductory text of their new magazine *Possibilities* they wondered if the pressures of everyday life and the ascendency of politics in the social realm were not curtailing the possibility of the efflorescence of an American modern art.

Why this turnabout between 1948 and 1950? Were we witnessing at that time a loosening of the impact of politics? No, quite the contrary, since this was perhaps the worst period of the Cold War. If Motherwell and Reinhardt could applaud in 1950 the success of modern art and of abstraction, it was because they knew that after the Boston affair, and the united front constructed by major museums around the Museum of Modern Art, the new art had not only won definitively an important place in American culture, but had also found a symbolic role in international cultural politics.[10]

The rejection of a modernism of *juste milieu*, the modern humanistic and somewhat populist modern art defended by the Boston ICA in 1948, and its replacement by what was then called "extremist art"—Abstract Expressionism—signaled the importance attached by a section of American culture to an internationalist position. In the process though, modern art, in order to be acceptable in the U.S. and for strategic reasons, had to lose its negative, traditionally oppositional edge and be somewhat toned down, so as to be able to enter into the international arena as a positive alternative in Europe to Communist culture. It was the price modern art had to pay at that particular moment. Its symbolic victory was crucial, all the more so because a series of political events accelerated the Cold War paranoia. As the Korean War started on June 25, 1950, many were questioning the neutralist trend developing in Europe, and particularly in France. Many Americans, and new liberals especially, saw this neutrality as a gesture toward the Soviet Union. It seemed to them that Europe was being culturally destabilized, while Communist troops were on the military offensive in Asia.

It is because of this tense situation that after 1950 those artists who Motherwell had claimed were trying to avoid direct political engagement were actually not capable of achieving it. Their position, their work, their disengagement were all reworked, reideologized into the service of a cause not always in accord with their aspirations. On the other hand, those painters who wanted to continue, despite all pressures against it, an engaged painting, a realist work (like Ben Shahn or Philip Evergood), were forced through subtle pressures to drop their political stance of opposition in order to fit into a more central and less belligerent position. They became depoliticized, or rather humanized, and treated in their pictures the plight of humanity rather than the plight of the working class. This criss-crossing and slight permutation of emphasis allowed a type of cohabitation that enhanced the liberal image of America, thanks to the erasure of any controversial issues, thanks to a flattening out of the artistic landscape and a blurring of clear-cut ideological differences.

In this Cold War period, where the war was often more symbolic than real, except when it broke out at the periphery of the two major blocs as in Korea, the ideology of individualism was the weapon par excellence in the United States and dominated every sphere of social and artistic life. Individualism ran contrary to Soviet regimentation and also ran contrary to the artistic traditions of the 1930s, which had been one of group solidarity and unions. In 1948 Harold Rosenberg saw in the alienation of American abstract artists their move away from group involvement in order to become individual players. This was an early sign of the recreation of what had once made Paris glorious and special before the war, the independence and vitality of its artists, who were now crushed by the German victory. It was essential that this vitality now nurtured in America not be destroyed by Communism. But one has to be cautious here. It is not because this notion of individualism was elevated to such height that an avant-garde was not possible. Despite the fact that there was no group that could talk with one unified voice as most avant-gardes in the past, New York's new generation was recognizable as an avant-garde because of its oppositional discourse, thanks to its rejection of artistic options that seemed to them out of touch with the new postwar realities.

Certainly, these artists were rejecting the active corporatism of the 1930s and its united political action, but it was difficult in any case to do otherwise. Not only new private market pressures, but also the anti-Communist social trends were such that the culture was producing many interdictions and widespread cultural and political amnesia. Some words even became taboo so that unwanted connotations could be avoided. This is clear from the archives of Philip Evergood, a realist artist associated with the

Communist Party. A specific incident will illustrate the pressure under which one had to work in the U.S. at that time. In September 1950 Evergood sent the director of the Third Woodstock Conference the text of his address to the colloquium of art and museums. It was a plea for artists to unite in order to protect their profession. Sidney Laufman, the director of the program, in a comic attempt to be diplomatic, asked Evergood to censure himself:

> I should like to say one thing, and please consider this confidential and off the record. One thing that worries some of the conference committee very much is the bringing in of any political angle into our conference discussions, and your point 5 the whole containing observations on general world conditions and "the need" for great *Unity* among all interested and connected with the arts has seemed to carry that kind of an implication and has caused some anxiety. . . . You are well aware of how quick people are today in finding political bias in our most innocent expressions.[11]

Evergood obligingly complied, but not without humor: "I guess I was brash in using the word *Unity*." In this atmosphere, it was not surprising that the individualism of the avant-garde had replaced the unified cooperative structure related to the prewar revolutionary utopias. This was one of the major differences between Paris and New York art scenes, as we shall see. Another was the fact that America was intact and immensely rich, while France was ruined and destroyed, physically as well as morally.

While in August 1945 Truman could announce, "We can say that we end up this war as the most powerful nation in the world, and maybe as the most powerful nation in history," Sartre could only observe that "the peace which is vaguely announcing itself beyond the last few thunderstorms is an enormous world peace in which France holds only a tiny place." This tiny place was nevertheless rapidly becoming a crucial player in the Cold War theater. In fact, because of or despite her decline, France was now seen, in the words of the American ambassador in Paris, Jefferson Caffery, as the "keystone of the European reconstruction."[12] It was not surprising then that it was in France, in Paris, that the Cold War of propaganda had to be won. It was in Paris that the modern cultural image of America had to be secured, as a sign of calm strength of a country certain of its role as leader of the free world. The image of America in France was then becoming extremely critical in the struggle for the control of a portion of the divided French intelligentsia.

That is why in April 1948, when the Boston ICA was fighting a losing battle against MoMA's internationalism, the American Congress passed the Marshall Plan, a major aid program to Europe that would definitively shatter the last hopes of the isolationists for keeping America away from European turbulences. This ratification was of course crucial for France because her economy had been on the brink of collapse for several years. However, since May 5, 1947, since the withdrawal of the Communists from the government, there was even a risk of civil war or, even worse for some, the possibility that the Communist Party could win the elections. This became a constant preoccupation of Ambassador Caffery. Unlike England or Germany, two countries closely allied with America, France and Italy, because of their strong Communist parties, constituted weak links in the anti-Communist front. This occasioned interminable moments of fear and a constant reevaluation of the American image in France. American newspapers and magazines of this period present an Uncle Sam transformed into the fairy tale character who ritually spends time in front of a mirror to learn if he is still the most handsome and most loved person around.

The political situation was volatile in France and, as Caffery was constantly warning the State Department, was literally ready to explode. What the Americans were trying to protect in France, by at times even meddling into French internal affairs,[13] was a kind of centrist position not too different from the one at home, poised between two different but equally dangerous evils: the Communists and the "difficult to deal with" Gaullists.[14] To avoid any surprises, in late 1947 Congress allotted 150 million dollars in interim aid to France, despite or because of the fall of Ramadier's government and the ensuing political turmoil.

The year 1948 proved to be pivotal for post-World War II Franco-American relations. In the spring the European Recovery Plan passed in Congress, and France became a part of the Brussels Pact (European defense against the Soviet Union). It was clear by that time that France had opted for the Western camp in the Cold War. But the instability continued all through the year and in particular during the summer of 1948, when de Gaulle seemed to have been in a position of strength. An internal State Department policy paper on France produced in mid-September 1948 clearly identified the major difficulties confronting the U.S. and France: economic and political stabilization. The document again pointed up the key role France had to play in America's strategy to contain the spread of Communism in western Europe. In fact, during the fall of 1948, the French were given clear notice that American assistance was contingent upon the maintenance of a non-Communist government. That is why as early as 1947 Americans tried to evaluate not only the effect of American economic help, but also its ideological impact. For this purpose, Congress sent several delegations to France to observe results. The French people were still pretty suspicious of American capitalism, but how could it have been different when one sees how these commissions were actually working?

A picture from *Life* magazine published in October 1947 tells the story quite vividly. It shows several pudgy, superbly dressed, cigar-smoking congressmen inquiring at a poorly stocked vegetable market about the quality of the tomatoes and incidentally about the state of mind of the French working masses. Facing them stands a small, poor, scoffing peasant with beret. The document comes out as a real-life caricature of the capitalist. It was of course this type of arrogance and this type of dependency that made relations between the two cultures difficult. It is not surprising, then, that one could read in André Visson's 1948 book *As Others See Us* a lucid but pessimistic account of the Franco-American relations:

> The French suffer in their pride when they think that Americans to whom they owe their freedom, and to whom they must look for military protection as well as for economic recovery, are intellectually their "inferiors." . . . [The] French claim to represent the civilization of Man against the American civilization of the machine. . . . America, they say, is a great military and economic power, but a great moral and intellectual impotence. [15]

Though the Marshall Plan certainly eased the economic situation, it could not smooth over the tense symbolic frictions. In fact, it consolidated the different factions in French politics. As the left-leaning French Catholic magazine *Esprit* explained in a lucid article in April 1948, every section of the political French establishment was using the plan to entrench itself even more in its previous position:

LIFE

Vol. 23, No. 16

October 20, 1947

IN A PARIS STREET MARKET CONGRESSMEN WOLVERTON OF NEW JERSEY (CENTER) AND KEOGH OF NEW YORK EXAMINE SCRUBBY TOMATOES AT ABOUT 9¢ A POUND

U.S. CITIZENS LOOK AT EUROPE

Official and unofficial tourists find out for themselves why recovery lags

One newsworthy thing about Europe this fall is the number of Americans who are there. By year's end about 300,000 U.S. citizens—more than traveled abroad any year of the '30s—will have visited Europe. They include businessmen, farmers (pp. 34–35), just plain tourists. Whatever their status, they are getting a firsthand impression of Europe's food shortage, war damage and economic stagnation. The opinions they bring home to their friends and neighbors are bound to play a large part in shaping America's attitude toward aid to Europe.

Among the tourists were about a hundred congressmen who will have a chance to vote their convictions. One group is a special House committee headed by Chris-

tian A. Herter of Massachusetts (right), who decided five years ago to become a government expert and ran for office. Today he is one of the most respected men in Congress. In Europe his committeemen poked into market stands (above), talked to cabinet ministers and ordinary citizens, assembled 17 trunkfuls of data. When they returned last week on the Queen Mary, they announced that they were impressed by Europe's need but also by its complacency—they had found too many Europeans who were sitting back waiting for the U.S. to play Santa Claus. This combination of hardheaded realism and awareness of Europe's plight was exactly the kind of talk likeliest to get the Marshall Plan passed by Congress.

CONGRESSMAN HERTER views New York harbor after his six weeks in Europe.

31

Les Lettres Françaises,
June 10, 1948

The attacks of the French Communist Party against the Marshall Plan have always had a character of both passioned violence and at the same time a particularly striking technical imprecision. . . . On the other hand, Socialists, Popular Republicans (*republicains populaires*) and the Radical Party (*radicaux*), have always preferred to see the most favorable aspects of the Marshall Plan. In the plan's grand design, they saw only evangelical disinterest, generous concern for the future of civilization and the world economic equilibrium, total lack of any ulterior motive of political domination. . . . In the face of the overly black Epinal images of the Communists, another was devised, painted with the most vivid and seductive colors but no less distanced from reality.[16]

The extreme division of the Parisian art scene made acceptance of a type of consensus impossible. The violence of a very impressive media campaign in the popular and powerful Communist press did not allow it to coalesce after 1947 when the party rejected the validity of abstract art. As mentioned in *Esprit*, the Communist Party also had an active anti-American propaganda campaign developing. The "Peace Offensive" begun after 1947 was most impressive in its relentless attacks on American culture and life-style as well as in its portrayal of a warmongering America. During this offensive, the Party, knowing the importance of the French cultural image, had gained the support of a great number of very well-known intellectuals, such as Tristan Tzara, Roger Vailland, Louis Aragon, Paul Eluard, Pablo Picasso, Fernand Léger, Jean Lurçat, Edouard Pignon, André Fougeron etc. In this battle for the soul of France, art became one of the most precious elements of the equation, but it was unable to offer a rallying point. No viable center could be carved out of the political or artistic scenes. The Parisian art scene looked like a shattered mirror. Each faction's dream was to reassemble the fractured pieces so as to be able again to reflect the grandeur of France, but in its own image.

As if by enchantment, as soon as the Communist ministers were expelled from the government, the Communist Party realized that only one artistic style could effectively represent the working class. Social Realism was revamped and became the communist aesthetic yardstick. This type of art was direct, easily understood by the masses, and had its roots in French history (David, Courbet). The poet Aragon became the theoretician,

André Fougeron the lead painter.[17] Thanks to its powerful press,[18] the party was able to promote this style forcefully and through controversy monopolized the discourse on art until 1953.[19]

In the 1948 Salon d'Automne, for example, André Fougeron ignited a battle that became known as "La Bataille réalisme-Abstraction." At the center of the controversy was his painting *Parisiennes at the Market.* It was a fairly large painting depicting stern housewives trying to find something to buy in a poorly stocked market. While mimicking the Renaissance tradition, which he had just studied in Rome for a year, and divesting traditional forms of their usual use, Fougeron also subverted them by transforming happy, transparent light on the faces of angels and virgins into dark shadows over the profiles of baffled, suffering working-class women. Fish depicted in a realistic manner seemed as sad as the housewives in this thoroughly pessimistic canvas. The outrage from the bourgeois press was directed at the unsophisticated techniques displayed by the painter as well as at the subject matter: the presentation of drastic shortages of food for the working class. This type of painting, which was able to hurt the bourgeoisie, was exactly what the Party was looking for—an antidote to the meaninglessness of what was seen then as imported American abstraction. That is why in a panegyric on Fougeron in 1947 Aragon could say:

> The same cancer eats away language, disintegrates any language under our very eyes. It seems that suddenly man's honor is placed into silence, into non-said. The artist forbids himself to signify like the poet to sing. Epidemic suicide, voluntary resignation? The painter this time is an accomplice. In fact, he thinks that he acts on his own will. But look who the crime is profiting. Who controls it?[20]

Obviously the hand of the CIA was seen inside the hollowness of abstraction, manipulating French creativity, draining it of any thought and power. That is why an art like Fougeron's was important in its political ramifications. Realism was a strategy and the brush a weapon in the service of the working class. Painting could unveil the atrocities perpetrated by the ruling class against the workers. America, with her support of capitalist institutions in France, was of course one of the main targets of Aragon. That is why the poet could say that this type of realism

André Fougeron, Les
Parisiennes au Marché,
*1947–48, oil on canvas,
76 x 50¾ in. Collection of
the artist.*

had wide and crucial ramifications. Realism became simultaneously a dam against the flood of abstractions and a fierce offensive weapon against capitalist decadence: "André Fougeron," Aragon explained, "in each of your drawings the fate of figurative art is at stake, and you shouldn't smile if I tell you that the fate of the world is at stake as well."[21]

The equation between abstraction, silence, non-said, and American art should not surprise us, because during 1948 and 1949 many American abstract artists were exhibiting at the Salon des Réalités Nouvelles: Bauer, Llya Bolotowsky, Robert Motherwell, Zceron, William Baziotes, Pearl Fine, Hilla Rebay, etc. It was easy then for the Communist Party to equate abstract art with American decadence and reaction.

Communists were not by any means the only ones to equate abstraction with America. The right as well, and for different reasons, was lamenting this trend. Jean Cocteau, for example, returning from a visit to the United States in 1949 (a necessary trip for every serious French intellectual since De Tocqueville), had to say something about his experience after encountering the beast.[22] Like a true inspired angelic poet, he wrote his letter to the Americans in the sky, while flying between New York and Paris. His impressions were not, despite the heavenly environment, very ecumenical, in particular when it came to cultural matters. Capitalism, he said, parodying Churchill's famous phrase, had created a "gold curtain" separating Europe from America. But he felt that Europe could still help America to become real by teaching her what she lacked the most: luxury. All she had, poor soul, was comfort. Art was of course what Cocteau had in mind when he mentioned luxury. Americans, he said, considered art a distraction, when it should be considered a ministry. Understanding the fact that America was in the process of dominating the Western world, Cocteau warned that money was not all, that America would be able to rule only if it encouraged culture:

> You will not be saved by weaponry, nor by money, but by a thinking minority, because the world is expiring, as it does not think (*pense*) anymore, but merely spends (*depense*). America does not understand France, because from the outside our culture seems in ebullition, seems on the brink of bubbling over, but it is a boiling water which produces wonderful iridescent bubbles, unmatched anywhere else.[23]

The other difference was of course that France was really cultured, according to Cocteau, attached to a long past, far from the dryness of technological culture. That is why the aristocratic Cocteau hated what he saw when visiting the Museum of Modern Art in New York. What he saw with amazement reminded him of Taylorism, of assembly-line art:

I saw an unforgettable scene at the Museum of Modern Art. In a very clean day care center, 50 little girls painting on tables covered with brushes, inks, tubes, gouaches. They were painting looking away, putting their tongues out in the fashion of those trained animals who learned to ring a bell. Nurses were looking over these young creators of abstract art, and gave them a slap on the wrist if, by accident, what they were painting was representing something, was leaning too closely toward realism.[24]

America was definitely too abstract, too dry, too square for the poet.[25] But no doubt the realism concocted by the Communist Party in Paris was too strong as well for Cocteau to approve. What about the alternative realism just being produced in Paris? It was being cooked up by the middle-of-the-road establishment, which always wanted to see in the arts the expression of humanity, feelings, and drama. Bernard Buffet became their symbol. In July 1948, while a major exhibition of Louis David was on display at the Orangerie, an exhibition was put up in opposition to the Social Realist trend. It was called *Manifeste de l'homme temoin.* The catalogue debunked abstraction as well as social messages. It insisted also on the importance of man, not the Marxist social man, but rather the natural one, "an eater of red meat, of French fries, of fruit and fromage, and a girl chaser." Realism was back, with a popular existentialist twist. A depressive style, complete with subdued colors, wheezing drawing, and hieratic composition. Everyday life as crucifixion. Bernard Buffet, André Minaux, and Bernard Lorjou—three existential realists—won the critics' prizes the same year, and became instant celebrities.

If for many artists in Paris it was difficult to equate abstraction with the CIA, with America, as the Communist Party and the bourgeois art press was doing, it was hard nevertheless to find anybody in the French artistic world before 1953 who could talk positively about American art. The United States was generally seen as a culturally dry, unsophisticated, crude, antihumanistic, and cold land. The country was young, violent, and technological, good for movies but not fit to participate in the old traditional discourse of painting. It took at least five hundred years of practice to arrive at the perfection of the School of Paris. New York, it was felt, was a little bit short. And when an American artist like Hans Hofmann was discussed seriously, emphasis was put on his ability to represent the strident, primitive American environment. His exhibition in 1949 at the Galerie Maeght was one of the rare exhibitions of an American painter to be held in Paris, and it was dismissed quite rapidly. The unsigned critique in *Arts* unfavourably compared the "terrifying inhumanity" reflected in the paintings with the French Latin sensibility charged with the "sentimental poetry of man." Charles Estienne, in both his promotional text for the Galerie Maeght's own art magazine *Derrière le Miroir* and in a shorter version in *Combat*,[26] used the same old clichés to describe the American's work. He could not avoid talking about the rash, violent, and electric American light, compared to the refined and sensitive Parisian one. Using a kind of eighteenth-century theory of climates, he explained the violent characteristics of color in Hofmann through the qualities of the American continent. To reach the French public, Estienne recycled clichés to explain the artist's apparent harshness and rawness: Hofmann was in touch with the new continent, and his work advertised an apparent chaos, charged with explosive force, vitality, and virginity. It was a kind of Western rawness that populated some French dream of America: unrestrained spaces and wild behavior. He wrote:

> Hofmann's palette seems to me to be always an octave too high; it appears out of sync, or better, overcharged, like the high tension light and like the human and physical reality of which it is a frank and even brutal expression. But this imperfection through excess (and not because of lack) provides something to make us reflect. And we can prefer it to a thin precision through lack, and often through emptiness, or to frail and archaic accords of the minuet, we can prefer these splashes and these vitamins, this abundance, even this dishevelment, this so natural disrespect for taste, this generosity, in the end, which is the sign of adventure and risk, like the great American nature, skyscrapers and movies, forests and savannas intermixed, which is its place of origin.[27]

Estienne was attracted to nature because it was antagonistic to culture, the sign of the School of Paris, which the critic was in the process of subverting. His description, though certainly sympathetic to the work of Hofmann, was playing a domestic role as well. Estienne knew well that his cartoon-like description of American culture was not specific to the art of the United States, but also applied to a new trend in postwar French art. This trend had been visible and discussed since 1946, when Edouard Jaguer, allied with Surrealism, published an important article called "Les chemins de l'abstraction" in the leftist newspaper *Juin*. The piece was a call for a new contemporary direction in art, in gear with modern concerns. To make his point clear and immediately visible, he chose to place an Abstract Expressionist drawing by Hans Hartung between reproductions of Piet Mondrian and Wassily Kandinsky (1909 period). Hartung's abstraction was then presented as the perfect contemporary expression between Mondrian's refined abstract utopias and Kandinsky's mystic poetic emotion. For Jaguer, the enemy was the decorative effect of the academization of geometric abstraction, because it did not correspond to the orgiastic and apocalyptic present, and subsequently could not be called modern: "Confronted with these cheerful or austere mosaics, we stay indifferent (apart from the pleasure to the eye). In no way do these decorative elements relate to our apocalyptic age. We cannot recognize ourselves in them."[28]

This lucid analysis was followed by an active promotion of a type of abstraction fed by, but disconnected from, Surrealism. With Michel Tapié, Jaguer organized in July 1948 a particularly important exhibition called *Black and White*. This exhibition of works by Jean Arp, Camille Bryen, Jean Fautrier, Hans Hartung, Georges Mathieu, Francis Picabia, Michel Tapié, Raoul Ubac, and Wols was a kind of manifesto. Jaguer's text, printed on the invitation, was combative, Surrealist in its formulation, but also an attempt to carve a contemporary mood out of the historic situation. For Jaguer the new postwar man wanted to express a new emotive reality that the old aesthetic molds could not contain. He said:

> One cannot live with an open heart in old houses. And the monotonous slices of elected form and of the banal rectangles do not have anything to do in a world turned upside down by pure expressivity. For all these artists reunited here, what matters is the conquest of a subconscious but real place and not merely the derisory satisfaction of the accomplishment of plastic duty.[29]

Michel Tapié, on the opposite page, was even closer to formulating a theory of postwar art, of a new reality, opposed to the Communist one.

> There never was a system that was not liable to break down as soon as it came to be shown alongside REALITY, the latter having been divested of all those many varied kinds of realism which are ever soliciting the mind to use them as ways of not seeing it as it really is.[30]

Composition, rules, mathematics are all there in order to put the poetical (read liberating automatism) potential of art into straitjackets:

> Let all the classes, and clinics, be flung open, and the fun of the air and microbe-menageries, all the denizens of the realms of the incoherent and the inchoate, be let loose, that they may at once invade the pictorial rectangles of painters and burst thereon like bombs.[31]

Important here, besides the recurrent themes of Surrealism, was the concept of the "incoherent," the "inchoate," which became for Tapié the symbol of the new art and which derived from what Georges Bataille had named the "formless" in the 1920s. (*Informe* in French). The job of the Inform, as Rosalind Krauss has explained,[32] was to undo formal categories, to deny that each thing has its proper form. Things are shapeless, unfinished, or crushed, inside out like a spider crushed underfoot. For Bataille the Inform was like the "crachat," the spittle: a category encasing everything the bourgeoisie could not swallow, a kind of "part maudite," as Bataille named it later on—the part of culture that was pushed aside, the incongruous, the evil, the damned, the sick. Tapié, who was part of the underground Surrealist group La Main à Plume[33] with Jaguer during the war, knew well Bataille and his para-Surrealism. What he put in relief was the bankruptcy of a certain type of abstraction (the cold/geometrical), which many artists in the late 1930s recognized as a utopian fraud when violence, destruction, corruption, and war were engulfing the world.

Already by 1938–39 for many artists on the left, the continuation of an art production, especially geometric abstraction, whose theories had often been developed during the 1920s, seemed, at best, out of touch with the realities of the new age, which was then being defined as the end of utopia. In addition, confronted with Fascist crowds and the uniformity of masses behind Stalinism, concrete art, with its refusal of individualism, was considered dubious. More and more, the masses seemed to be at the heart of the authoritarian danger, and individualism seemed its antidote. That is what Bataille was emphasizing then. Opposed to the passivity of crowds, even questioning the validity of democracy and humanism, Bataille was searching for a heroic and Nietzchean individualism. The art of Mondrian and followers did not seem to be able to take into account the ever-growing violence and destruction then sweeping Europe. "Purity" was giving way to the "Formless," as Bataille said. The spittle was replacing the square. Wols was replacing Mondrian. The "Society's suicides," to take a phrase from Antonin Artaud, were replacing the optimistic dancer of the Charleston: Mondrian. This is what Michel Tapié meant when he wrote in the magazine *Reverberes* in 1938 that he was finally discovering that the famous armchair used by Matisse in describing his paintings was, in fact, nothing more than a toilet seat.

This awareness of the inadequacy of realist and concrete abstract language for the contemporary experience had been growing in the late 1930s in Paris, but under tremendous pressure. Artistic discourse and production gravitated around a void, a kind of historical black hole that tended to consume, prevent, or implode any kind of modern experimentation. The force of the historical moment, for a while at least, did not allow a new artistic discourse to be implemented or developed in Paris. Time actually ran out. Many progressive artists left Paris for Marseille in 1940 on their way to New York.[34] Nothing could really be implemented in Paris during the occupation; everything had to wait until the liberation. But theories about the impossibility of painting were kept alive in some Surrealist circles. Pessimism, darkness, suspicion of any positive position were respected. In fact, as the Surrealist poet Georges Henein said in 1941, despair was what counted; it was something one could relate to in these difficult years.

We are living in one of those historical moments sufficiently disagreeable to inspire in everybody a violent desire to get out of it. But we consider that what is most important is not to get out of it, but to avoid getting out by walking backward. And in order to get out of it humanely, a good general culture is maybe less important than acquiring a certain sense of despair. Because despair is not a stagnant milieu where bathe forever the imaginations of weak people. Despair does not wait. Despair is torrential. Despair forces doors. Despair blows cities apart. Despair is the thunderstorm under which unprecedented worlds of deliverance will ripen.[35]

In these conditions, for the "Informel" artists, Social Realist art and the Communist Party usually positive imagery were unacceptable, and geometric art, "cold abstraction" as it was known in Paris, seemed fossilized, historicized, dead by asphyxiation in its geometric matrix. If a form of art could at all represent or talk about contemporary reality as Jaguer was demanding, it was certainly not to be a pure art. It was going to be a dirty art, a decrepit art, Moribund and pessimistic, at the edge of deliquescence, a rotten art. An art like an open wound. It was going to be an art like Wols's, an art that Sartre could endorse, an art, as Sartre understood after a visit to the Museum of Modern Art in 1945, totally different from what Americans were supposed to like. In his book *La Mort dans l'Ame*, Sartre leveled a ferocious attack on American culture and on American intellectuals who loved and supported clean, safe, lifeless, and sterilized abstract art of the Mondrian kind. After his visit to MoMA with its large collection of geometric abstraction, Sartre decided that Mondrian's art, his boogie-woogie and mechanized utopian world, was indeed symbolic of American culture: a utopia turned into nightmare, an air-conditioned nightmare. He wrote: "The wing in which Gomez finds himself contains fifty canvases by Maudrian on the white walls of this clinic: sterilized painting in an air-conditioned room; nothing suspect, here one is protected from microbes and human passions."[36]

At the time these very lines were written, though, this partial descriptions of American taste was being contradicted by the passionate amoeba-like Surrealist-abstract production of the new generation of New York artists. While European painters exiled in New York brought to American artists a sense of urgency and professionalism, in Paris this urgency, this excitement had been replaced by a form of helplessness and active despair to the point that Wols, for example, liked to compare himself to a tunnel.[37]

It is clear that until 1953 Social Realism (a not particularly optimistic brand of it) had a very important visibility and, to some extent, even credibility in Paris. But the engagement of these artists with the working class, and by the same token with Stalinism, was challenged by painters highly suspicious of Stalinist propaganda. This refusal did not mean an alliance with bourgeois realism either. Using as a starting point, as the American painters had done, some Surrealist techniques and theoretical discourses, French painters were investigating the edges of bourgeois culture for a means of expressing this new Orwellian age. Convulsive abstraction seemed for many painters to be the only way to crack the cage. There was among artists, in France, as in the United States, a real fear of being "engaged," of being caught up in the political machine. There was certainly a kind of "disengagement" at work, but, and this is important, not a total distancing. What one can clearly see is a certain retreat from direct politics without losing sight of the art product's entanglement in the ideological struggle. Symbolically, the connection between the aesthetic object and the social milieu was never severed, especially since just to refuse certain codes of representation was, in Paris, enough to definitively locate one in the political debate. In these conditions, adding to the confusion, one did not even have to express a direct political opinion to be labeled.

The artists of the generation bursting onto the French art scene at war's end had found new intellectual heroes. They were dialoguing with Sartre's *Qu'est ce que la litterature?* and E. M. Cioran's *Précis de Decomposition*—moving between an engagement in art with an art of disengagement and the neutrality of unbelief.[38] Sartre was an important figure, because while being profoundly politicized, he accepted a certain autonomy of art, emphasizing the classical modernist motto that "the painter did not want to trace signs on canvas but wanted to create a thing." Having said this, though, he hastened to add that he would prefer a type of painting which could provide "Liberty through allusion." Propaganda in painting was for him anathema.

The philosopher Cioran presented a more radical, detached position, but one that in its pessimism and dispirited irony was central for some of the new artists working in Paris. Many could recognize themselves in this sharp text about the danger of believing. Cioran's position encapsulated quite well what the new abstract artists and their supporters were after:

He who loves unduly a god, forces others to love him, ready to exterminate them if they refuse. . . . If man loses his faculty of indifference, he becomes a virtual assassin . . . because faith exercises a certain form of terror . . . the major persecutors are found among martyrs whose heads have not been cut.[39]

It was this distancing, this caution, despite the artist's total emotional involvement, that was at work in some of the French abstract painters; it was an echoing of some of the concerns presented by some abstract American artists at the same time.

Pierre Soulages, to take one of the most famous examples of a postwar French painter well advertised in the United States, was keenly aware of the political situation, of some of the moral as well as politically impossible positions confronting the leftist avant-garde. He was part of a large group of artists (from Cobra and Jean Dubuffet to Raymond Hains and Jacques de la Villeglé) who were trying to develop a humble art, far away from and in opposition to the sophistication of French tradition. Soulages was not an expressionist or gestural painter, but an artist highly suspicious of the traditional language of art, of its usual ties with representations of nature. That is one of the reasons why, in his earlier production, he avoided the use of regular paint and used walnut stain. The choice was important. This was not industrial paint like that Pollock used, but artisan material, low key and fragile. This, allied with the use of common housepainter's brushes, signaled that painting, for too long over-glamorized, had to return to the roots of the trade without forgetting the specificity of the social conditions at the base of its production. This was also the signal (and a liberating one at that particular time) that one did not have to paint like Fernand Léger in order to be on the side of the underprivileged. It was an important message at a time when Social Realism was forcefully promoted and debated in Paris.

Soulages investigated carefully the properties of different tools, materials, and colors. What was needed, he thought, was something also discovered by some American avant-garde artists like Pollock: the exploration of simple gestures, the discovery of elementary rhythms, the salvation of the tools of painting from storytelling, from a condescending remapping of nature. For Soulages, painting had to relearn how to breathe, to walk, to talk. This apparent brutality, simplicity, was in fact the creation of a new alphabet. Under the destruction of the old bankrupt painted world, Soulages was rebuilding an independent vocabulary, aligning new tools.

We can see then how far Soulages was from the "Informel" type of painters or from gestural abstraction, despite the continuous attempt to link his work with Franz Kline along formalist lines. In fact, Soulages's pictures were close to being materialist. They were a discourse on the variations of application of paint to

Pierre Soulages, Pein-
ture, *1948, 25¼ x 19½ in.
Centre National d'Art
et de Culture, Georges
Pompidou, Paris.*

canvas, a dialogue with the imprint of a marked canvas, a relaxed organic relation between form and artist (an easy give and take, Pollock would say), a respiratory exercise, breathing life into old structures, in traditionally discarded materials and colors—a humane painting without the humanism. That is what Soulages explained in an interview about abstraction in June 1950:

> For a painter, the problems posed do not precede the solutions. They are born from the work [along] with it. I don't believe I find what I am looking for except in the process of painting: this does not exclude the fact that my painting could come out of a desire for certain forms rather than others, but it is only once painted that these forms tell me about this desire. It is at this precise moment that I bring in modifications, the precisions that I feel necessary as well as new forms which force me to question earlier ones. . . . Painting, as I envisage it above, is not a "pure" art opposed to a "realist" art. It is not a gratuitous art, certainly not a pure play of forms. It is a process which engages man at the same time, the world. Man, the spectator as well as the artist.[40]

Jean Fautrier, with a series of pictures painted during and after the war called *Les Otages* (*Hostages*), came to represent another pole of French painting. In a sense, he was very close to Soulages in his interest in producing an art grounded in basic textures and basic emotions, but very different in his exaltation of *métier* and his handling of abstract vocabulary. If Soulages expressed the biological mechanism of abstract vocabulary, Fautrier literally embalmed the last efforts and ultimate failure of representation. Fautrier was, it seemed to many, the typical painter of the Inform.

Fautrier took a very gruesome topic, one quite literally unrepresentable: the Holocaust. His task was ambitious but quite difficult if he cared not to exploit and sentimentalize such a painful topic. In this case, even allusion could be overplayed. Following the liberation, a large public could indeed relate to suffering and torture, to mutilation, killings, and decay. The Communist Party itself was supporting such imagery but transferred into heroism, into a form of *image d'épinale*. Fautrier, who painted extraordinarily powerful expressionistic dead rabbits à la "Soutine" before the war, found, with the horror of the camps still very present, a way to talk about the unspeakable by withdrawing

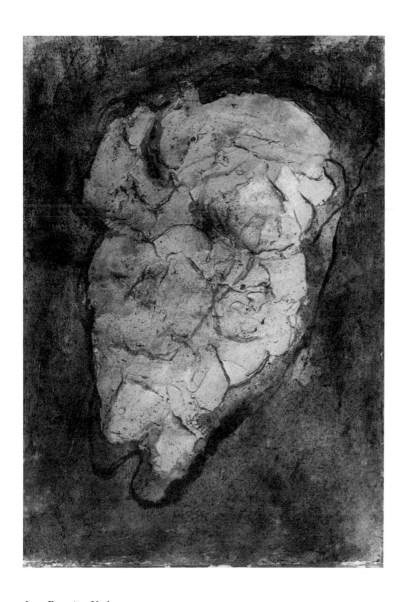

Jean Fautrier, Nude,
1943, oil on paper, 21½ x
15 in. The Museum of
Contemporary Art, Los
Angeles, The Panza
Collection.

Wols, Le Grand Or-
gasme, *1947, oil, 63¼ x*
50¾ in. Private collec-
tion, Paris.

from direct discourse and replacing it with allusions, connotations. The physical, painful, difficult construction of layers of transparent, thin papers on the canvas, the pulverization of white paint, the transformation of painting stuff into raw, decayed, palpitating material, became a metaphor for the suffering many still felt in France. These paintings were like raw wounds, open for investigation in their beautiful display, but accompanied by an abstract type of repulsion, a nausea ever present through association, through a procession of painful contemporary connotations. What is special in Fautrier is that he makes these connotations barely visible, transforms them, buries them under an avalanche of technical virtuosities.

We are here at the edge of the Inform, at the edge of figuration, when the drawing, the image, when the corpse, the stump, the flattened face, all in an advanced state of decomposition, tend to subside, to be transformed into soil, into *matière* (matter). But this one is of course an archaeological *matière*, with signs of history buried in it, in order to jolt the casual viewer into recalling elements themselves buried in one's memory. Proust's madeleines, with their nostalgic taste, were here transformed into putrefied limbs that recalled war's horror and insisted on the lingering postwar pessimistic taste of ashes.

Francis Ponge saw very well the connection with Bataille's concept of the Inform. He talked about these paintings as spreading like a pool of water or, rather, like a swamp,[41] as if the forms, the shapes, no longer had the strength to stand up but only instead the dubious pleasure of spreading themselves in an obscene display of beautiful abandonment.

This ugliness, this obscenity, this transformation of violated bodies into crusty mudpies, into impure excrements, was vitrified, embalmed, covered with varnish and colors as if the smell were too strong, as if the life of the studio could clean the death of the camps. If this was the Inform, if this was a spit, it was a dry one, too clean it seems for what Georges Bataille had in mind, despite the fact that Fautrier produced a series of illustrations for Bataille's book *L'alleluiah* in 1947.

Wols was perhaps closer, because in his work there is none of the respect displayed by other artists for the material of painting. What happens here is the collapse of mediations, the erasure of culture in order to find nature at all cost. And this nature is not the peaceful, ordered, genteel nature of Bissière; it is chaos. It is not even the balanced and controlled chaos of Jackson Pollock, but a direct explosion on the canvas. Here there is no complicated build-up of layers of paint or elaborate strategies, but the understanding that the studio language, the painter's work, was definitively unable to transcribe the effect that life had on the individual. What we have is painting as vomit, achieving two complementary tasks: a desperate release and at the same time a screaming denunciation. This was the end of the tunnel, the announcement of the final literate decrepitude of modern painting in a furor of colors and scratches, of the marks of knife cuts—a literal ritual killing. If Fautrier painfully covered over what he had done like a shameful cat, as Paulhan discovered, Wols was a sardonic and hurt exhibitionist. Here lies the scattered parts of the Renaissance project ciphered through Picasso and Matisse, under the atomic light, and full of vapors of rum. It's a coroner's report written in a Baroque manner, like a fireworks display.

For Sartre such a painting could not talk about wars, about the United States, about the Cold War; but the texture somehow could. The violence of the application of paint could indicate the violence outside. The battle among the masses of paint, the dazzling fling of colors covering each other, struggling for survival on the stage of the canvas, was a struggle alluding to ours in life. That's all painting could really do, but it was crucial for the new generation of French abstract artists.

In the Trenches of Critical Discourse

In this war of ideas and images, it was important for the United States to be regarded as a serious leader of the West and not only as a *nouveau riche*. With the beginning of the Korean War in 1950, the image of America became even more important because Picasso was leading the cultural side of the Communist "peace offensive" and a strong "neutralist" movement was developing in Paris, stubbornly refusing to take sides in the raging Cold War. To counteract these deadly trends, Senator Benton, former Assistant Secretary of State, proposed in March 1950 a vast Marshall plan in the field of ideas, and in April of the same year President Truman proposed a "Campaign of Truth." It was not enough to inform the public, he said, it was also necessary to actively combat Soviet influence. For that purpose, Congress voted 111 million dollars to be spent before June 30, 1951. Finally, in September 1951, what the president called a "psychological offensive" was launched, which prompted a transformation of the United States Information Agency in Paris. This was the sign of a more sophisticated but more aggressive offensive,

designed to enlist French people into the anti-Communist struggle without alienating them.[42]

The stategic battle for the minds of the public, a sort of gi-
gantic symbolic chess play, where the fate of the world was to be
decided, was going to be hot and long. On the artistic scene the
outcome would be definitively determined only in 1964 with the
victory of America's young Robert Rauschenberg at the Venice
Biennale.

In face of the well-organized American cultural machinery,
Paris was as divided as ever. But America, despite her will and
organization, was confronted with two difficult tasks: how to bypass, despite an all-out attack against the School of Paris itself
by Michel Tapié, the sumptuous remains of Matisse, Picasso,
Bonnard, Villon, Léger, and others, and how to erase from the
French consciousness that traditional cliché image of Americans
as merely materialistic and technical, as good moviemakers but
poor painters.

Though there were similar artistic trends in France and
the United States, born from a common postwar experience,
the similarities were not emphasized. Only differences were
stressed, and these were differently appraised. The war of images turned into a duel between two antagonistic set of logos:
American violence, roughness, and subjectivity against French
rationality, decoration, and gloss. Clement Greenberg was one of
the few critics who could see the importance of such an emphasis
on differentiation. Even if artists did not always understand what
he was after, Greenberg succeeded in characterizing American
abstract painting as rough and violent. Perhaps just as importantly, enumerating a one-sided if not totally fictitious set of
"French art characteristics," Greenberg was able to transform
the arrogant Gallic Cock into a classy purring pussycat.

The battle that began in the pages of *Nation* on September 9,
1950, between Greenberg and the English critic David Sylvester
illuminates the importance of this change. It demonstrates the
inability of some Europeans to grasp what was then at stake,
deeply buried in numerous layers of paint, but that Greenberg,
Alfred Barr, and others had been able to extract. The fact that
Sylvester was not French does not diminish the strength of my
argument. His defense of the "School of Paris qualities" shows
how difficult it was to disturb the traditional Western standards
of quality. This heated exchange was important because it flared
up while America was involved in an all-fronts counter-offensive
against Communist cultural efforts. September 13 was, in fact,

the beginning of the so-called psychological offensive, which emphasized the importance of cultural affairs in the propaganda war. While Sylvester's diatribe in the *Nation* and the State Department's offensive were obviously not directly connected, they were caught up in the same highly volatile political moment.

Sylvester's article, "The European View of American Art," reviewed the American section at the Venice Biennale. Not able to recognize what he knew of the traditional makeup of American art, Sylvester was disappointed. What he saw instead was what he called an over-German tendency in the American expressionist works:

> Overestimation of the importance of self-expression, and frenetic automatism which stems from the early Kandinsky. Both these tendencies represent the seamier side of America—sentimentalism, hysteria, and an undirected and undisciplined exuberance. There is no echo at the Biennale of the quality in which America's greatness lies—its use of technology to make the most of nature.[43]

For him, as for many Europeans, Alexander Calder represented the typical American artist: a friendly but naive brute, funny but reflecting "the essential genius of America—its capacity to make things."[44]

It was exactly this impression of one-dimensionality that the American liberal elite was trying to eradicate around 1950. In his response to Sylvester, Greenberg defined what could be called the new American line. He justly placed Sylvester's critique in the realm of politics. He said that Europe was accustomed "to think[ing] of Americans as cultural Barbarians," and that Europeans were uncomfortable with "their present military and economic dependence upon the US."[45] He impugned Sylvester's critical competence and attacked the traditional selection prepared by Alfred Frankfurter (which included Lee Gatch, Hyman Bloom, and the "Pompier" Rico Lebrun, as he was called by Greenberg) in order to publicize the freshness and the importance of the three artists selected by Alfred Barr (Willem de Kooning, Arshile Gorky, and Jackson Pollock).[46] He concluded by guessing why Sylvester had thrown so much animosity into the discussion: "At Venice, they must have looked too new—beyond freshness, and therefore violent." For Greenberg, who had not had the privilege of going to Venice like Sylvester, it was indeed important that those three artists looked "violent," too new, be-

yond freshness, "raw" in fact. Well, they had to at this precise
time, for the American artist was directly confronting Parisian
painters, operating now on the same modern intellectual level
(not just the technical one to which they had been reduced for
so long), on the same plane as the Europeans. What was clever
was the fact that on top of this Europeanization of painting were
added the clichés of American specificity: honesty, freshness,
roughness, excessiveness. So what one got was a revitalized
French painting that could only be made by Americans: stronger,
new and improved.

Sylvester did not understand that America was changing its
looks, moving from *Technicus Homo* to *Homo Picturis*. This, for
Sylvester, was the world upside down. The total confusion of
signs was becoming intolerable. Moreover, why was Greenberg
so arrogantly sure he was on the right track in supporting paintings which to Sylvester were contemptible because they represented a romanticism that "gets hot and bothered over nothing
and reminds [him of a Steig] drawing called 'I can't express
it.' "[47]

Robert Motherwell, like Greenberg, understood the necessity of the move. It was necessary to put American art into a new
mold but one that would function on the international scene. In
a catalogue for an exhibition at Frank Pearl's Gallery in Los
Angeles, he clearly underlined the differences between the Paris
School and the New York School. In New York "they are always
lyrical, often anguished, brutal, austere, and 'unfinished' in comparison with our young contemporaries of Paris."[48] At the same
time, the French critic Michel Seuphor, while acknowledging the
attraction of some of these quailities, preferred what he saw as
the velvet and silk of Paris to the cutting steel metal of New
York.[49]

What is complicated and fascinating in this duel is that, at
this exact same time, some French artists and critics in Paris
were also trying to define a new type of art in opposition to the
traditional School of Paris and were using some of the same arguments as the American critics. Artists from *Art Autre*, which
included some of the Informel artists, were attacking the traditional Parisian image with new values like authenticity, violence,
and individualism. But Michel Tapié, the creator of this concept,
in his desire to collect an international group, did not differentiate between nationalities. He showed Pollock, Mathieu,
Tobey, de Kooning, Hartung in a universal front. Tapié of course
thought that all these individuals would coalesce, find an easy

space in his structure, under the umbrella of a renewed Paris, as had been true in the past.

For American critics, especially Greenberg, this was not enough. New York had to play a larger, more dominant role, not just be integrated into Tapié's world. The concept of universalism was important, but it had to be designed according to American models of strength and violence and be seen to be emanating from America. That is one of the reasons why, despite all Tapié's enthusiasm, *Art Autre* eventually fizzled, even though there were some very successful individuals in the group.

Sartre understood very well the reason for this shifting cultural power. In an article published in the American magazine *Commentary* in 1950, he declared:

> Americans receive ideas from us that are half dead and have absolutely no power to excite them; and this is so not only because their continent has different problems, but mainly because Americans do not see these ideas as their future. On the contrary, they see them as something that belongs to the past in relation to themselves, as the false future of a country of which they consider themselves to be the true future.[50]

Along with the new international power of the United States, Sartre could see the progressive transformation of international cultural values: "Cultural ideas, quite independently of their internal value, have a potential for diffusion that depends upon the economic or military importance of the country supporting them. They acquire a certain universality."[51] He could see the danger for France. He could see cleary that French prestige and her power to universalize her aesthetic choices were passing, as was her political power. For him, at that time, only a France at equal distance from Russia and the United States could be saved from oblivion, from confinement. Sensing this change, Julien Alvard, in a pessimistic moment, even went so far as to wonder why some young Americans still bothered to flock to Paris:

> Isn't she now an old capital with the heavy makeup of a Western world already long past maturity and slowly rotting into a frivolous Byzantinism? What should be said about this so-called superiority in the arts, of this imperialism which is no longer but a shadow of a shadow? . . . The light is coming from somewhere else now . . . but still.[52]

Yet still . . . Paris could still attract good painters from all over the world: Jean-Paul Riopelle, Sam Francis, John Koenig, Ellsworth Kelly, Jack Yougerman, Joan Mitchell. . . . Yes, for many, Paris was still fascinating, but often for the wrong reasons. James Baldwin, the American writer, tells us in a very sharp analysis of the exodus of artists to Paris in the 1950s that what young artists were looking for was "the legend of Paris, not infrequently at its most vulgar and superficial level."[53] And what they found instead was a kind of incomprehension quite difficult to handle, an unwillingness by the French to acknowledge that Americans did not all represent what French intellectuals in their majority rejected from American culture. He wrote:

The American wishes to be liked as a person, an implied distinction which makes perfect sense to him, and none whatever to the European. What the American means is that he does not want to be confused with the Marshall Plan, Hollywood, the Yankee dollar, Television, Senator McCarthy. What the European, in a thoroughly exasperating innocence, assumes is that the American cannot, of course, be divorced from the diverse phenomena which make up his country, and that he is willing, and able, to clarify the American conundrum.[54]

The shifts in the assessment of French culture were often quick and profound:

With the air of a man who has but barely escaped tumbling headlong into the bottomless pit, he tells you that he can scarcely wait to leave this city, which has been revealed to the eye of his maturity as old, crumbling, and dead. The people who were, when he arrived at Le Havre, the heirs of the world's richest culture, the possessors of the world's largest esprit, are really decadent, pernicious, self-seeking, and false, with no trace of American spontaneity, and lacking in the least gratitude for American favors. Only America is alive, only Americans are doing anything worth mentioning in the arts, or in any other field of human activity: to America only the future belongs.[55]

Let us add that the contours of the Parisian past were still very much revered by Greenberg in the late 1940s and early 1950s. He praised the Apollonian art of Matisse, for example, but as a product reflecting a different age, another culture, which one could certainly regret, but which was gone forever. This type of art, as good as it might have been (and still was in certain cases), could not compete with the rashness of the modern post-atomic world. In this nostalgic but calculatingly myopic view, the postwar era was empty of a strong native and contemporary creative presence in Paris. The best of French art, according to Greenberg, was in the past; nothing could compare with the new American strength. He considered the most violent, tough painter of the School of Paris, Picasso, as a "minor league" draftsman and in a state of total decadence as a painter.[56]

Nevertheless, Picasso was still considered a great symbol of modern art. That is why in 1948 when modern art was under attack in America, liberal intellectuals turned to him for help. J. J. Sweeney, for example, sent him a telegram after the publication of the Boston Manifesto, asking for his help in proclaiming the importance and safety of modern art. What they did not anticipate was that Picasso still stubbornly believed in the subversive quality of modern art, in its essentially antibourgeois predestination. The process of pacification and appropriation in which liberal American intellectuals were involved seemed indecent to the Spanish artist. He exploded. The recognized modern master could not accept this embrace, this deadly promiscuity. To sign this document he felt was like losing his soul in a kind of Faustian gesture.

Sweeney's telegram read:

SERIOUS WAVE OF ANIMOSITY TOWARDS FREE EXPRESSION PAINTING SCULPTURE MOUNTING IN AMERICAN PRESS AND MUSEUMS STOP GRAVE RENEWED PRESSURE FAVORING MEDIOCRE AND UTILITARIAN STOP ARTISTS WRITERS REAFFIRMING RIGHTS HOLD MEETING MUSEUM MODERN ART MAY FIFTH STOP YOUR SUPPORT WOULD MEAN MUCH TO ISSUE

Picasso's reaction, according to Françoise Gilot, was:

The point is art is something subversive. It's something that should not be free. Art and liberty, like the fire of Prometheus, are things one must steal, to be used against the established order. . . . How can I support an idea like that? If art is ever given the keys to the city, it will be because it's been so watered down, rendered so impotent, that it's not

worth fighting for . . . . Only the Russians are naive enough
to think that an artist can fit into society.

And with that he threw the telegram into the wastepaper
basket.[57]

Picasso's position was, throughout this period, a strange and
at the same time a quite powerful one. Indeed, he could be seen
successively as a role model for the Communist Party, as a savior
of the beleaguered American modern art, as anti-American in his
many appearances on podiums with Communist Party dignitaries
in the Peace Offensive campaign, and also as the major France-
based artist being sold in the States by Samuel Kootz.

Since 1950, one knew, thanks to the strenuous efforts of
Alfred Barr, Nelson Rockefeller, and Thomas Hess, director of *Art
News*, that modern art was in no way a Communist plot to destroy
Western values. They had also done well in convincing most
Americans that it was, in fact, a sign of freedom. But it was
disturbing, to say the least, to see Picasso in the Salon de Mai
1951 showing a picture titled *Massacres de Corée* which accused
America of committing atrocities during the Korean War. The
work was, to be sure, an elaborate commentary on art history,
from Goya to Manet and Picasso himself, but it was a critical
contemporary message as well, a new *Guernica* in which America
had replaced Germany. It is true, the American public and intelligentsia had praised *Guernica* in time of war, but this use (and
direction) of modernism for propaganda purposes against the
United States deeply upset New York's modern art community,
especially because for many years Picasso had been portrayed
as a freedom lover, a depoliticized naive genius whose love for
peace had been exploited by the rapacious Communist Party.
This denunciating painting undermined all this. To put it mildly,
it was considered treason. Thomas Hess expressed his disbelief
in a letter to Barr:

Art News has been offered a picture story on some recent
Picasso paintings, including one of some soldiers shooting
some naked women and children. I have heard that this picture represents American soldiers committing an atrocity on
North Korean civilians. Do you know if this is true or is it
simply an atrocity of war picture reminiscent of Goya's 3 of
May? Alfred Frankfurter heard somewhere that it was
painted specifically as a piece of communist propaganda . . .

*Samuel Kootz in his
New York gallery with
Picasso's show in 1947.
Archives of American
Art, Samuel Kootz
papers.*

a rumor that had passed me by. We feel rather honour-
bound to publish it as a story, but are quite reluctant to get
into the various political problems unless we know exactly
what they are i.e. is the artist actually taking on an active
political role, or simply commenting as an artist on a world
situation?[58]

Barr's response was short but to the point: "Yes anti-American
propaganda, though Picasso might dismiss this as he dismissed
the fact that the painting Guernica was political."[59]

It was quite disturbing for American modernists that this
Picasso work was too close to everyday life, to real politics.
American modern critics were by that time convinced that the
greatness of modern art had been the progressive withdrawal
from any discursive statement. Art had won over politics, over
ideology. Why did Picasso—for many the major figure of this
trend—renounce this hard-won position for such a blunt "engagement" in the Korean conflict? Of course Picasso's participation in a Communist-sponsored peace congress was a continual
problem for American intellectuals. Picasso was not only be-
traying the confidence of modernists, but also taking pleasure in
it. With a kind of demonic perversity, did he not in 1952 transform a Romanesque chapel into a Temple for Peace with luminous frescoes? And this, to complicate matters a bit more, in the
same month when Matisse, who all knew to be a friend of the
Communist poet Aragon, was inaugurating his new frescoes for
the Dominican chapel at Vence. These French people were
definitely too perverse, too complicated. Americans could not
and did not want to understand these decadent intricacies. The
complexity of the French art scene and French political life, the
inability of American culture to take into account the cultural
and social importance of Communism after the war in Europe
(Picasso said once that he did not understand all this fuss and
fear about Communists as he lived everyday in harmony with
them; in fact his baker and his newspaper man were Communists
and were quite normal and decent people) gave rise to a flurry of
articles about the incomprehensible and obscure maze of French
politics.

The irony of all this was that after a struggle of many decades, the United States had finally accepted Picasso's work and
genius. Why did he have to confuse them now with his politics?
As Joseph A. Barry in the *New York Times* said with humor in a
long and famous article on the difficult master, "The red period

*Pablo Picasso and
Peace Dove: "It is now
almost as widely known
as the Soviet Hammer
and Sickle."* Life, *Jan-
uary 29, 1951.*

"Non-Communist Dove shown with designer Jean Paul David." "The Dove that Goes Boom," Life, *January 29, 1951.*

Pablo Picasso, A ta Santé Staline, *drawing for the seventieth birthday of Stalin.* Les Lettres Françaises, *March 9, 1950.*

The Two Picassos: Politician and Painter

His position as an artist stands unchallenged, but his political beliefs present a puzzle.

By JOSEPH A. BARRY

VALLAURIS.

ON a height in the town of Vallauris, a day's drive from Paris, Pablo Picasso, now almost 70, lives in a two-story, honey-colored villa called "La Galloise," and creates in a many-roomed studio near by that was once a perfume factory. With him is his family—Françoise Gillot, not quite 30, the mother of his two children, and the children, Claude, who is 3, and the year-old Paloma. While he pays little attention to newspapers or current events, Picasso is, nevertheless, rather political these days—a Communist, and one who will not be moved by any consideration of the contradiction between his political and his esthetic positions. But in Vallauris, Picasso has entered upon a new phase of creation, a new manifestation of the artist's restlessness that took him from Barcelona to Paris at the age of 19.

His curious passion about new forms led Picasso less than four years ago up the steep, two-mile road from Golfe Juan, where he was staying, to Vallauris for the annual pottery show. Again and again he returned, fascinated. Finally, he asked Mme. Suzanne Ramié, whose craftsmanship he most admired, if he might not try his hand on her potter's wheel.

To get closer to "Madoura," the Ramié workshop, Picasso bought—in the name of Françoise Gillot—his eight-room villa. Daily he went to "Madoura" to work—to draw, paint and incise new images on clay. With the same exhaustive intensity that produced the fecund "harlequin" paintings of 1904 to 1906, Picasso took the ancient art of pottery and in a similarly short span of time restored its primitive beauty and imprinted his own touch of genius.

But now the "ceramic" period is over. Picasso is about to pour his restless talents into yet another mold. A new label must be added to the twenty or thirty already pasted to his past periods and critics will inevitably announce that "Picasso has changed again!" But Picasso has not changed: "Really it is not that," Gertrude Stein once pointed out. "He empties himself and the moment he has completed emptying himself he must recommence emptying himself, he fills himself up again so quickly."

PICASSO, the ever-emptying crucible of art, is filling these days with ideas about a "temple of peace." The *Conseil Municipal* of Vallauris, which made him an honorary citizen last summer, has invited Picasso to decorate the old chapel next to the town hall. For some time it housed Picasso's bronze sculpture, "Man With a Sheep." But Picasso preferred his statue standing "in the middle of the market place with the vegetables piled all around it," and that is where it is today.

By no coincidence Picasso will start turning the vaulted Romanesque chapel into a "temple of peace" this spring or just about the same time that Henri Matisse will be inaugurating the Dominican chapel that he has been building and decorating at Vence, eighteen miles away. Such has been the nature of their long rivalry that Matisse had indicated his intention of creating a chapel about three years ago, or roughly when the Museum of Antibes was being dedicated to Picasso for the extraordinary work done there—the fauns and satyrs, fishscapes and pottery.

THUS twentieth century art tends to revolve on its Picasso-Matisse axis. And it would be non-human for either one to be indifferent to the other, however indifferent they both are to most of their fellow-painters.

Similarly with Matisse. After a chat in Vence several years ago in connection with the contemplated chapel, he gave his interviewer a message for Picasso. "Tell him," he said mischievously, "that you came down here all the way from Paris to photograph my chapel." (The chapel, at the moment, was made of cardboard, and sat on a table at the foot of Matisse's bed.)

Before dropping in on Picasso, Matisse's visitor returned to Vence to look at the almost finished chapel, accompanied by a lady who had known both masters since the Nineteen Hundreds. More in the way of provocation, then, than information, Picasso was given an unfavorable impression of Matisse's progress. "It's nothing but Beaux Arts studies," Picasso was told within five minutes after the meeting at Villa La Galloise. "Matisse has become dull, academic."

"He always was," said Picasso unwarily (and unusually). "After all, a man is the same through the years—he uses the same passport—and it's good that he is."

"He had a certain élan when he was young," said the lady. "His flowers, for instance."

"Oh, yes," said Picasso, "they had a perfume, the perfume of handkerchiefs."

"It didn't persist," said the lady.

"No," said Picasso, "it faded, like flowers," and abruptly changed the subject.

Picasso's thick Spanish accent, his brief, often oblique, figures of speech, make him hard to follow. But not when he speaks of his own chapel. "I've been thinking about it lately," he told his visitors. "Do you know it? It's a nice chapel, with good stones and good lines. As soon as it gets warm, I'll start working. I'll make it a sort of 'temple of peace' showing people enjoying themselves. I'll paint the people on one side and war on the other."

"And in the middle?" he was asked.

"The public," he laughed, "getting it from both sides!"

THERE was time for little but a quick look at the villa's sparsely furnished room with the studio couch at the far end and two paintings that looked like Picasso's from a distance—but turned out to be Mme. Gillot's—before Picasso put down Claude's chubby little sister, Paloma, pulled on the sheepskin jacket he had picked up in a Polish market place and took his party out through the newly weeded garden down the hill in the gray, chauffeur-driven Oldsmobile *(Continued on Page 33)*

JOSEPH A. BARRY, manager of The New York Times Sunday Department bureau in Paris, is both a patron and reporter of the arts.

Picasso: The Red Period.

Drawing by Al Hirschfeld

"Picasso's Red Period," The New York Times Magazine, May 6, 1951.

of Picasso was certainly more difficult to understand than his cubist one."[60]

But the shock went a little deeper than the annoyance produced by Picasso's gesture. Picasso's peace offensive was in the end really the proof that one could not trust Paris to effectively fight and counteract Communist cultural aggression. That had been, after all, the purpose of the active campaign in France orchestrated by the USIAS.

To clarify the situation and to pressure Picasso into becoming more reasonable, a letter was sent in December 1952 by the American Committee for Cultural Freedom, just founded by James Burnham, James T. Farrell, Arthur Schlesinger, Jr. (vice chairman), and Sidney Hook and affiliated with the Congress for Cultural Freedom (an organization that one can characterize, at least until 1953, as pursuing right-wing liberalism in its active fight against Russia and Communism in the field of ideas),[61] but to no avail. Many American artists signed this petition asking Picasso to withdraw his public support of a regime which they emphasized would suppress the type of art Picasso himself produced. In a letter to Alfred Barr dated December 2, 1952, Irving Kristol mentioned that he could count on the signatures of Greenberg, Sweeney, Alexander Calder, Motherwell, Pollock, and Baziotes, who were all members of the committee.[62]

In 1952 modernism seemed to be totally divided, split into a hard and a soft look, between Peace and Freedom, between form and content, between Paris and New York. But to protect the old illusion of modernist homogeneity, a last and most impressive attempt was made by the United States to create a universal cultural front orchestrated by Americans. In 1952 the French magazine *Preuves*, the mouthpiece of the American Congress for Cultural Freedom, helped organize, and publicized heavily, a large exhibition of modern art at the Musée d'Art Moderne in Paris. The exhibition, called *Oeuvres du Vingtième Siècle*, dealt with the major European modern movements from Impressionism to Picasso. This extravaganza was specifically produced, according to *Preuves*, to show that only free societies were able to create great art. This unprecedented involvement of American cultural interests in the Parisian scene was the most powerful statement yet of America's total commitment to the championship of the tradition of modern art and freedom.

The introduction to the catalogue written by Jean Cassou, the new curator of the opened Musée d'Art Moderne, is interesting in what it shows of his uneasiness with his new alliance with the American side after years of critical flirting with Communism. His text is a kind of apology for the lack of originality of the show, as if other considerations were the engine behind such an enterprise. He says:

> No one better than this prespicacious and warm mind (J. J. Sweeney) could have chosen a group of works with such determined and positive characteristics. But a difficulty presented itself, arising from the considerable number of exhibitions, which, for many years, had allowed every capital of the world—and especially Paris—to see again and again all the great masterpieces from museums and collections the world over: it was then necessary to try to show in the present exhibition little-known works or, even better, those never before seen in Paris.[63]

The exhibition was symbolically important because it signaled to Parisians themselves that the United States was determined to fight for modern culture on the international scene and was leading the fight against a Russian culture reminiscent of Fascism. The exhibition was able to show, thanks to a display of "universal" modern art blossoming in the West, how important it had become to protect the old modern tradition. Paris and what it had symbolized for so long had to be protected, restored, propped up, even if against her will. In this case, the exhibition was like a scaffolding, like a brace, keeping the modern tradition alive in the face of incessant assaults from outsiders and from within Paris itself. This strategy seemed necessary when one realized how weak the Parisian bohemian tradition appeared to be, particularly as demonstrated by Picasso's lapses. He had in fact painfully demonstrated that Paris could no longer be trusted in this crucial battle for the soul of the Western world. Now the scene was set for the American avant-garde, promoted as forceful, virile, violent, and "universal," to play its role on the international stage.

As Julien Alvard remarked, the light now was indeed coming from a different source. Or rather, thanks to American scholarship, money, and collections, a new kind of energy was burning inside the old exhausted Parisian vessel: an imported one.

Notes

1.
Christian Dotremont, cited by Edouard Jaguer in an interview with the author, Paris 1986.

2.
An important debate about this issue of French neutrality raged for several years and reached its peak around 1950–51. The debate was essentially centered around the famous editorialist of the newspaper Le Monde, called "Sirius," and around Professor Etienne Gilson. Many of the new liberal cold warriors equated this position with a form of treason. For them, neutrality was akin to a pro-Soviet position. See John T. Marcus, Neutralism and Nationalism in France: A Case Study (New York: Bookman Associates, 1958).

3.
In an effort to publicize the cultural achievement of the United States, the State Department organized a show in 1946 called Advancing American Art. The show, due to relentless attacks by the right, had to be recalled from Europe, and the works bought by the agency had to be sold.

4.
See Mary Sperling McAuliffe, Crisis on the Left: Cold War Politics and American Liberals, 1947–1954 (Amherst: The University of Massachusetts Press, 1978).

5.
In 1948 the Boston Institute of Modern Art decided to change its name to Institute of Contemporary Art, declaring that modern art was too obscure and too difficult to understand. It has often been misleading. It was also a bit passé. See Serge Guilbaut, Dissent: The Issue of Modern Art in Boston (Boston: Northeastern University Press, 1985).

6.
It was Nelson Rockefeller who was instrumental in insisting on the similarities between attacks by the right against modern art and those leveled by Nazi and Communist regimes. See Lloyd Goodrich's letter to Jim Plaut, February 13, 1950, ICA Archives.

7.
Alfred Barr to Henry Luce, March 24, 1949, Archives of American Art, MoMA, Alfred Barr Papers, Roll 2171. Surprisingly, this interesting letter has not caught the attention of Irving Sandler and

Amy Newman, who published the papers of Alfred Barr, Defining Modern Art: Selected Writings of Alfred Barr, Jr. (New York: Abrams, 1986).

8.
See A. Barr, "Is Modern Art Communistic?", New York Times Magazine (December 14, 1952); Thomas B. Hess, "Is Abstract Art Un-American?", Art News (February 1951).

9.
Statement by Robert Motherwell and Bernard Karpel, Modern Artists in America (New York: Wittenborn, 1951). This important book was in fact an attempt to document thoroughly the modern art scene in America. As this was the only volume, it seems that the modern explosion was too widespread to be recorded after 1950.

10.
See Serge Guilbaut, "The Frightening Freedom of the Brush" in Dissent: The Issue of Modern Art in Boston (Boston: Northeastern University Press, 1985).

11.
Letter of Sidney Laufman to Philip Evergood, August 17, 1950. Evergood responded in August 1950; Evergood Papers, Archives of American Art.

12.
Jefferson Caffery, as cited in Steven Paul Sapp, "The United States, France and the Cold War: Jefferson Caffery and American-French Relations 1944–49." Ph.D. dissertation, Kent State University, 1978, chapter five.

13.
Jefferson Caffery was constantly warning the State Department of the danger of destabilization in France. About the U.S. meddling into French internal affairs, see in particular, ibid., p. 276: In light of Marshall's candid admission that 'covert political warfare' was being conducted by U.S. agents inside France, it is evident the statements of the Secretary of State, Hickerson, Labouisse, Caffery and others to the effects that non-Communist French governments should receive American support 'by all reasonable means short of direct interference in the internal affairs of the country' were mere window dressing designed to shield the truth from the public. What they actually meant was that 'direct interference' was to remain hidden from the public eye."

14.
See ibid., p. 270.

15.
André Visson, As Others See Us (New York: Doubleday, 1948), p. 125.

16.
François Goguel, "Le Plan Marshall devant les partis Français," Esprit 144 (April 1948), p. 620. This was also Irwing Howe's analysis: "Like anticapitalism, anticommunism was a tricky politics. Both could be put to the service of reaction, both became prey to ideological racketeering, both carried with them moral and political perils that no one could have anticipated in earlier times. Just as ideologues of the far right insisted by some ineluctable logic opposition to capitalism had lead to Stalinism terror, so ideologues of the authoritarian left said that anti-Communism had to lead straight to the Cold War strategies of John Foster Dulles and Dean Rusk. These were arguments for the simple, slogans for dummies." A Margin of Hope: An Intellectual Autobiography (New York: Harcourt Brace Jovanovich, 1982), p. 207.

17.
André Fougeron was a Picasso follower in the 1930s. He changed his style after the war in or-

der to put his talent at the service of the party. The stylistic change occurred in 1947 while working on a painting called Femmes d'Italie after his return from Italy, where he went after receiving the prestigious Prix National de la Direction des Arts et des Lettres in 1946. See Fougeron: Piéces Détachées 1937–1987 (Paris: Galerie Jean Jacques Dutko, 1987).

18.
The Communist press was extremely diversified and powerful, especially from 1945 to 1950: Les Lettres Françaises, La Nouvelle Critique, L'Humanité, Europe, Les Cahiers du Communisme, etc.

19.
See Jeannine Verdés-Leroux, Au Service du Parti. Le Parti Comuniste, Les Intellectuels et la Culture [1944–1956] (Paris: Fayard/Minuit, 1983), in particular pp. 269–328.

20.
Aragon, Preface to a catalogue of drawings by Fougeron (Paris: Les Treize Epis, 1947).

21.
Ibid.

22.
This has in fact become a tradition, from Paul Morand in the 1930s, Claude Levi-Strauss in

the 1940s, to Jean-Paul Sartre, Simone de Beauvoir, Philippe Sollers, Marcellin Pleynet, and Jean Baudrillard.

23.
Jean Cocteau, Lettres aux Americains *(Paris: Grasset, 1949).*

24.
Ibid.

25.
The idea of American painting being too abstract runs all through the discussion that year in France. Brassai in his memoirs says that Picasso was annoyed that Samuel Kootz always wanted the most abstract works. Brassai tells us that Kootz looking at Picasso's paintings would say: "I don't like them very much, they are not abstract enough." Brassai, Conversation avec Picasso *(Paris: Gallimard, 1964), p. 315.*

26.
Combat *(January 17, 1949), p. 4.*

27.
Charles Estienne, Derrière le Miroir 16 *(January 17, 1949).*

28.
Edouard Jaguer, "Les Chemins de l'abstraction," Juin *(October 1, 1946).*

29.
Exhibition invitation card, Edouard Jaguer Archives.

30.
Ibid.

31.
Ibid.

32.
Rosalind Krauss, "Corpus Delicti," October *(Summer 1985), pp. 31–72.*

33.
For a fascinating history of the underground group La Main à Plume, see Michel Fauré, Histoire du Surrèalisme sous l'occupation *(Paris: Table Ronde, 1982).*

34.
For this episode see Varian Fry, Assignment Rescue *(New York: Scholastic Book Service, 1970).*

35.
Georges Henein, Preface to Kamel Telmisany's exhibition, February–March 1941, cited in Alexandrian, Georges Henein, Poêtes d'aujourd'hui *(Paris: Seghers, 1981), pp. 31–32.*

36.
Jean-Paul Sartre, La Mort dans l'Ame (Les Chemins de la Liberté), *volume 3 (Paris: Gallimard, 1949), p. 26. Cited in George Howard Bauer,* Sartre and the Artist *(Chicago: University of Chicago Press, 1969), pp. 70–71.*

37.
Archives (Wolfgang Schulze) Wols, Centre Georges Pompidou, Paris, C4 No. 3880.

38.
These two books were first published in 1948 and 1949, respectively.

39.
E. M. Cioran, Précis de Décomposition *(Paris: Gallimard, 1949), p. 13.*

40.
Pierre Soulages, "Réalisme et Réalité, Esprit *168 (June 1950), p. 922.*

41.
Francis Ponge, Notes sur les Otages *(January 1945) (Paris: Seghers 1949), p. 30.*

42.
In a confidential report about the "psychological offensive" dated Paris, October 16, 1950, emanating from the American embassy and signed by William R. Tyler, Public Affairs Officer in Paris, we learn that the Paris delegation was in the process of changing the outlook of the agency according to "psychological offensive" guidelines:

It may be worth reporting here the following basic policy considerations which have been borne in mind, particularly in determining how additional funds for information work in France should be spent:

1) To increase the USIE establishment in all its media, and merely along existing lines of activity would be unsatisfactory. Additional funds and greater discretion in their utilization should be exploited in such a way as to stimulate and facilitate activities by the French themselves in critical areas of French opinion. . . .

2) Rather than increase the amount of material distributed by the USIS, there should be extreme flexibility of programming according to the priorities listed above and by the employment of means which French groups and organizations will often themselves suggest and support.

3) Certain USIE activities are by their very nature relatively unresponsive to short-term special projects of the kind envisaged above. Among these activities are the library, the "projection of America" type of film in the documentary film program, the Fulbright Exchange of Persons Program, and in general the cultural relations activities and assistance to private U.S. artistic and educational work in France.

State Department Archives, Washington, D.C., File NND 852917 (511.51/8.1650 and 511.541/10–1650).

43.
David Sylvester, The Nation (September 9, 1950), p. 233; Clement Greenberg reply The Nation (November 25,

1950), pp. 490–492; Sylvester reaction, pp. 492–93.

44.
Sylvester, "The European View of American Art."

45.
Greenberg, The Nation (November 25, 1950), p. 490.

46.
In the archives of Alfred Barr there is a letter from Barr asking Nelson Rockefeller to lend him Gorky's Calendar for his section of the Venice Biennale. Barr apparently did not have enough time to prepare his section as he had been called in at the last minute by Alfred Frankfurter because of, as he put it, "an international emergency that had arisen in connection with the American Pavilion in the Venice Biennale." Archives of American Art, Roll 2198, letter 1363.

47.
Sylvester, "The European View of American Art," p. 233.

48.
Robert Motherwell in a famous short introduction, "The School of New York," written for the exhibition Seventeen Modern American Painters (Beverly Hills: Frank Pearls Gallery, 1951), p. 3.

49.
Michel Seuphor, Art d'Aujourd'hui (June 1951), p. 25.

50.
Jean-Paul Sartre, "A European Declaration of Independence," Commentary (January–June 1950), pp. 407–414.

51.
Ibid.

52.
Julien Alvard, Art d'Aujourd'hui (June 1951), p. 25.

53
James Baldwin, "Encounter on the Seine," in Notes of a Native Son (Boston: Beacon Press, 1955), p. 109. First published in The Reporter as "The Negro in Paris," June 6, 1950.

54.
Ibid.

55.
Ibid. See also the diatribe against the decision of Lawrence Calgagno to return to San Francisco and his anti-Parisian declaration in Time (October 17, 1955).

56.
It has to be said at this point that Greenberg, in his excitement over his discovery of Jackson Pollock, totally overlooked what was then being produced in Paris. He never even

bothered to write about exhibitions of "School of Paris" artists showing in New York during those years. Not a word of Wols, Soulages, Hartung, Bram Van Velde, etc. Contrary to what Hilton Kramer says in his strategic embrace of Greenberg's writings (see "Clement Greenberg in the Forties," The New Criterion [Summer 1987], pp. 1–6), the so-called serious attention given by Greenberg to French painters in the essays of the 1940s was directed to well-established French painters, as if nothing had been produced since the 1930s. This was certainly comforting, as it apparently still is for Kramer, but very far indeed from the historical truth. The essays published by John O'Brian make painfully clear that if Greenberg could recognize the important achievement of some American young artists, he totally missed the major European figures of the postwar period. And when Dubuffet was mentioned, it was in a grand paternalistic manner in order to aggrandize Pollock's stature.

57.
Françoise Gilot and Carlton Lake, Life With Picasso (New York: McGraw-Hill), p. 197.

58.
Thomas Hess, in Alfred Barr Papers, Archives of American Art, Roll 2178, letter 66.

59.
Alfred Barr reply, ibid.

60.
Joseph Barry, "The Two Picasso's: Politician and Painter," New York Times Magazine (May 6, 1951), IV:2, pp. 17, 38.

61.
On the history of the ACCF, see Christopher Lasch, "The Cultural Cold War: A Short History of the Congress for Cultural Freedom," in The Agony of the American Left (New York: Random House, 1966), pp. 61–114.

62.
Irving Kristol, letter to Alfred Barr, Alfred Barr Papers, Archives of American Art, Roll 2178, letter 169. Preuves ran in its first issue in March 1951 an article called "Un réquisitoire soviétique contre Picasso," p. 7.

63.
Jean Cassou, Introduction to the catalogue L'Oeuvre du XXe Siècle. Cassou was the respected chief curator of the Musée d'Art Moderne in Paris. He had a long fellow-traveler history. In 1949 after a visit to Yugoslavia, he became convinced that Stalinism had manipulated the famous Rajk trial for propaganda purposes. He published a long article upon his arrival in France in the magazine Esprit, defending Tito's position. This article was for many the beginning of the pulling away from the French Communist Party. While repositioning himself in the Cold War debate, he forcefully denied the assertion made by his old Communist comrades that he was rejoining the American camp. See "Il ne faut pas tromper le peuple: la révolution et la vérité," Esprit (December 1949), pp. 943–948.

Discussion

Audience

I'm a little confused about what might be called point of view.
Are you presenting the fact that Americans used their artists in a
cultural offensive as a surprising thing for them to do? Or a bad
thing for them to do? Or a shocking thing for them to do?

Serge Guilbaut

Who do you mean by them?

Audience

The American government . . . the cultural agencies.

Serge Guilbaut

Well no, it's a normal thing to do. What I mean is that this had
been quite a strong tradition in the past. The French, as you
know, did it admirably well in the nineteenth century. The problem in the post-1945 era was that the French (and here I mean
painters, critics, politicians, and dealers) did not want to understand that the era in which they were for so long calling the shots
had just past. French culture did try to reassert itself on the
world art scene, but could not in the end reinstate its former
glory. After 1945 the French could not reassert their formal
hegemony in the Western art world for many reasons, not only
because they had lost the economic and political power necessary
to produce a hegemonic culture, but also because the new diversified, and one could even say totally divided, art scene, split
along strong political lines, could not propose a united front, a
clear successor to the old successful, School of Paris aesthetics.
Indeed, Paris had lost the ability to universalize her aesthetic
choices. But this does not mean, of course, that Paris did not
have very interesting painters and intellectuals searching for a
new way to express the postwar world. What they lacked was
clout, and also some understanding of a new situation which they
often could not grasp for lack of humility.

To discuss this shift, to try to understand how this shift of
cultural power from one country to another (including behind-the-
scene political manipulations) is not, I want to add, fed by some
desire on my part to try to replace New York's achievement with
a hypothetically better French solution. For some, to be interested in explaining the complex reasons for the production and
success of a new art as well as giving some reason for the shift of

cultural power is immediately equated with lack of sensitivity for pictorial problems. In fact, this type of art history, I think, finally permits one to reevaluate works and theoretical texts in a different light, reinjecting into them the sort of urgency that they had when first produced. To criticize, analyze, put into question some assumptions of Abstract Expressionism (more particularly of those who have evaluated it in the past), is not, as some would like to believe, to reject it in favor of some Stalinist aesthetic solution. This is the simplifying language of the Cold War à la *The New Criterion*. It is stupid. I reject it totally.

There are always, of course, those who, blinded by their own prejudices and dreams, will not accept a rereading of history that chips away some of the glitter they helped to accumulate through years of positive stories. What is happening now is that this type of critical reevaluation is not really discussed or tackled, but instead attacked on chauvinistic or personal grounds—never on historical bases. It's a pity indeed. And let me add rapidly that the situation in France on that score is not any better. In fact, it might even be worse, despite some encouraging signs around the active group of former Jean Laude students.

So the answer is yes; it is a normal thing to do. So if it is normal, I do not know why this should not be integrated into the discussion of the effects of the art in question. It is not dirty; it is the way it has always been in international relations. But it has to be addressed, not assumed that it doesn't matter.

Audience
There seems to be a parallel between your talk and Jean Baudrillard's. You both tend to treat Abstract Expressionism as a free-floating signifier which the American State Department and the CIA grabbed, appropriated, and used for their own purposes. You both maintain that the French and the Soviets were in a similar struggle to grab their own free-floating signifier. It seems that the artists during this period don't exist in this discussion, except for Picasso, where you have an explicit intention clarified. However, what about de Kooning? You don't talk about him as an expressive agent, and you tend to treat him as an homogenous agency of American imperialism. That seems a little bit bizzare.

Serge Guilbaut
I have explained at length somewhere else how artistic discourses rooted in the Marxist tradition of the 1930s transform themselves during and after the war into an active liberalism.

Now the fact that artists say that they are not involved politically does not mean that their work, through association, does not carry political connotations. Yes, Picasso is direct about this; he supports the Communist Party (the French party, not Russia, but that's another story). But I would say that some of the Abstract Expressionist painters also made their allegiances very clear in the 1950s; they were not naive, or peons. They actually signed a letter against Picasso's position and against Communism, along with well-known Cold Warriors like Clement Greenberg and Irving Kristol, for the American Committee for Cultural Freedom in 1952. At that time, as one can learn from the wonderful archives of Alfred Barr, Calder, Motherwell, Pollock, Baziotes, all belonged to the committee. What I am saying is that by 1952 these artists, continuing the interest in social issues they inherited from the 1930s, did not see anything wrong with their political affiliations with Cold Warriors. But to say that de Kooning or Pollock were working for the CIA, the answer is of course no.

Audience

But the question that I am trying to raise is: What does de Kooning's expressive purpose amount to? I mean, you can't really argue that de Kooning paintings are representations of the Cold War. Clearly, they don't constitute an attempt to amplify American prestige.

Serge Guilbaut

Well, I never said such a thing. I do not know where you got that idea. The problem is not posed in those simplified terms. I am analyzing here the effect, the meaning of a new style, a new approach to painting, the ideological content, so to speak, of a specific form, at a precise historical moment. It is one thing to understand the rhetoric or agenda of a new style (intention), it is another, both being intertwined, to study its effects in culture. What I would say is that this type of expression came about through a major disillusionment with social and political life around the beginning of World War II and rapidly, under the pressure of the Cold War, became, not a representation of it, but a reaction to it, a way to deal with it, a way to try to keep away from the ideological walls which were closing on each individual at that time. In that sense, yes, I would say that Abstract Expressionist artists were Cold War artists, but so was Philip Evergood or Soulages, for that matter

Your project is a dismantling of this idea of deconstructing a certain American idea of liberal democracy. But there is one side element that I wish you would be a little bit more concrete about: the fact that people like Greenberg and others in the late 1940s and in the 1950s could be so positive about the individual artist.

It seems to me that the isomorphism, if you want to call it that, of people like de Kooning with Schlesinger is not simply caused by some kind of state of mind, but is the outcome of the solution that these people experienced in the late 1930s with the Popular Front. For example, to dismantle the idea of the individual artist obliges you to provide us with an alternative and to refer vaguely to the Communist Party of France in the 1940s. I don't think that it's adequate to say that the Communist Party of France and other Communist parties in that period were all identified in the minds of many artists and intellectuals with the Stalinist period in which the so-called artistic groups became part and parcel of a dictatorship; which is to say that the Soviet dictatorship had regressed to below the level of liberal democracy at that point. And if that's the case, and those are the alternatives, how could artists opt not for freedom? You seem to leave out this aspect of the regression of the Soviet state far below the level of ordinary civil rights in capitalist countries.

Serge Guilbaut

You are right to say that it was, for historical reasons, possible to reinscribe the notion of the individual in the schema of things in the 1950s in America. But you have to remember that this acceptance was slow in coming, and artists were at first very cautious about this rediscovery (this of course corresponds to the end of the WPA program and the opening up of a new free market for art) because for many—taught in the Popular Front tradition—it was important to remember, as Robert Motherwell himself said at the time, that "one needs to save the individual but without individualism." Your position is, I believe, similar to that of those disillusioned leftist American intellectuals who became supporters of America in the 1950s without properly assessing the consequences of their shift. To say, like Dwight MacDonald in 1952, "I choose the West," against Norman Mailer's "I do not fit in this dichotomy" is again to play the Cold War game which the Reagan presidency has accustomed us to lately: If you criticize us you must be for the other side. There is no room in that sketch for a critical alternative. And there *was* one in the 1950s, in France, in politics, as well as in the arts. But of course that alternative, that critical "neutralism," was branded by Washington as a "Communist plot." In the arts, some creators were not all accepting the frozen Cold War positions. One needed a lot of despair or a lot of irony to carve an alternative spot, but that was done. I am thinking of the Cobra group, for example. Artists who refused to be forced to choose between two imperialisms, between Social Realism and the mystical humanism of Rothko (note that I did not say Pollock; one day it will be nice if we can discuss the major differences of art practice among the group). From the "surréalisme révolutionnaire" to "Cobra" to Soulages and Guy Debord, an alternative caught at times in violent discussions was opening in certain small circles in Paris, rendering possible a critique of individualism, of American policies, without falling into the arms of Stalinism. I am, of course, fascinated by this complex cultural struggle and sympathetic to those who refused easy and Manichean solutions.

Benjamin H. D. Buchloh

America is the bearer of a new civilization, whose task is simultaneously to cultivate and industrialize a continent. It is the ideal ground on which to work out an educational principle which strives for the closest connection between art, science, and technology.

László Moholy-Nagy, *The New Vision,* 1938

Between the "Triumph of the Will" in 1936, and the "Triumph of American Painting" in 1958 (the year of the European tour of *The New American Painting*), art history also witnessed a number of relative failures. One such failure was that of geometric reductivist abstraction—in particular, Russian and Soviet Constructivism—to reenter Western European and American reception in the post-World War II period. In this essay, the exemplary subject is the artist Naum Gabo (a member of the *historic*[1] avant-garde) and his fate within the discursive, institutional, and economic spaces of the newly established, thriving postwar culture—the neo-avant-garde.

The problematic reception in 1948 of Contructivism and Gabo's transition from avant-garde to neo-avant-garde artist raises two questions: First, what personal, aesthetic adjustments and what historical, political adaptations were required of Gabo? Second, what determined the critical reception of Gabo's work, inside the history of postwar culture, for example, by one of the major critics of the American neo-avant-garde, Clement Greenberg? What maneuvres was Greenberg obliged to perform, initially to accommodate Gabo's work, then to exclude it from integration into the critical, institutional, and aesthetic framework of the 1950s?

Naum Gabo left Moscow in 1922 for Berlin. In the early 1930s, after a brief stay in Paris, he fled the German Nazis to settle in England, where he remained until his departure, in 1946, for the United States. Why he left England then remains unclear; after all, this was the country he later frequently called his "real home." He had a firmly established circle of friends there, many of whom occupied increasingly powerful positions. Further, Gabo's apparently nonproblematic continuation of the pre-war tradition of geometric abstraction had found at that time more credibility and critical support in the British Isles than anywhere else in Europe.

Gabo, the artist, emerged from the history of Soviet Constructivism just when this type of reductivist geometric practice was about to lose all credibility in the United States. Gabo, the citizen, arrived in New York just when any association with the Soviet Union had become increasingly suspect, and definitely a liability, given the American climate of vindictive anti-Stalinism and aggressive anti-Communism.

In fact, a typical strategy during this period was to decry the threat of Communism by pointing to the cultural aberration in Soviet art and architecture, exemplified by Socialist Realism. Thus in 1948, in "Irrelevance versus Irresponsibility," Clement Greenberg wrote, "The truly new horror of our times is not, perhaps, totalitarianism as such, but the vulgarity it is able to install in places of power—the official vulgarity, the certified vulgarity."[2] Similarly, in the first major American art magazine article on Gabo, Serge Chermayeff (then director of the New Bauhaus, Chicago, and later of the Institute for Design) presented Gabo by juxtaposing his work with several pages of Socialist Realist painting.[3]

By contrast, Gabo's own attitude had not at all been that of the fervent anti-Communist he would soon become after his arrival in the United States. Only four years earlier, in a rather obscure journal (*World Review*, published in London and dedicated to contemporary Soviet politics and culture), Gabo had written:

Many students of Russian art are inclined to wonder whether
that art, in its contemporary phase, does really represent the
genuine spirit of Russia, and whether it is not annihilated by
the imposition of the leading ideology of the government
party. . . . Their main argument can be summarized thus:
Russian art is no longer the free expression of a free artistic
mind; it is supervised by a very strict and dogmatic tendency; it is no longer interested in that free development of
all sorts of experiments which is so necessary to the progress
of a creative mind; any possible advance is held back by the
attempt to keep art on the level of the masses, whereas it
should be just the other way round. Such arguments, plausible as they may sound to the layman, are fundamentally
misplaced. . . . But there was and is another very important
side to the Russian attitude towards art: that to the Russian
mind, art represents a social phenomenon, first and fore-
most; it is the expression of a collective event, and the work
is valued mostly from the point of view of its social utility. It
is, and was, valued almost entirely in so far as it accom-
plishes an obvious social function for the use of all and not
merely a few privileged ones.

This stream of naturalistic art, with an emphatically social theme, is flowing now broad and deep in Russian art,
and it is entirely irrelevant whether that art is, at the present
stage, of high or low quality, from the point of view of refined
Western technique. . . . It is true that, at the moment, the
constructive movement is not encouraged in the Soviet
Union, but this may be an inevitable and, to a certain extent,
understandable phase of transition, which need not alarm
any artistic mind. One has to bear in mind that for more than
twenty years, the Soviet Union has been developing itself
under potential wartime conditions. The abstract movement
is still in the process of growth and has not yet found its full
application in the life of the masses. It has, nevertheless,
slowly penetrated, and is continuing to do so, in the shaping
of the edifice of the New Union. In due course and through
these demands, it will also find its way into the emotions and
aesthetic demands of the masses.[4]

These sentences are as surprising as they will remain rare. While
there is no shortage of ideological justifications for Socialist Realism in the Eastern/Western European debates of the 1930s and

1940s, one would not find such a position affirmed among Soviet emigrés. Most astonishingly, Gabo's position recognized the complicated dialectical relationship between progressive modernist geometrical abstraction and reactionary neoclassicist figurative Socialist Realism. Further, it dared to consider the historical reality of Socialist Realism as a necessary transition stage in a long process of cultural consciousness-raising and political education among the masses. Most provocatively, Gabo's attitude courageously argued that this phenomenon might be partially dependent on the precarious conditions inflicted on the new state by external military threats—at first from German Fascism and later from American Cold War anti-Communism.

For Socialist Realism to appear sufficiently horrifying after 1945, Western (American) intellectuals had to argue that after 1922 party politics made it impossible to work in any other mode, unless an artist were willing to face deportation, imprisonment, or death. After his arrival in the United States, Gabo became one of art history's eyewitnesses; along with his brother, Antoine Pevsner, he gave an account of that moment in Constructivist history that would be endlessly repeated, in almost literally identical terms, by scholars such as Herbert Read, George Heard Hamilton, Andrew Carnduff Ritchie, Eduard Trier, Robert Goldwater, and many others, from the early 1950s into the late 1970s. The "master statement," issued in 1949 by Gabo himself, read:

> At the end of the Civil War, they (i.e., the Party) took over cultural affairs and were given the job of drawing up our programmes. It only took them a few years to liquidate everything alive in art. They closed the School and brought in new teachers. . . . The party's hostility soon became very disturbing. We were attacked from all sides and no longer had the right to reply. To do so would have meant prison. Our only remaining choice was exile.[5]

It is now understood that this particular period of artistic transformation was occasioned by an internal artistic debate, which, among other consequences, led to Gabo's and Pevsner's departure from the Wchutemas (Gabo was never an officially appointed faculty member, although he shared a studio and periodically gave seminars). While apparently rabid and unrelenting, this debate certainly did not involve Party officials, but rather included artists like Malevich, who insisted on the departure of Kandinsky and Chagall, and like Rodchenko, who forced out into the open conflicts between the Productivist program and the increasingly aestheticized Constructivist practices of Gabo and Pevsner.[6]

It seems reasonable to assume that El Lissitsky was addressing, among others, the work of Gabo and Pevsner in his essay on "The New Russian Art." He wrote:

> And finally, the materials were imbued with a symbolic meaning: iron stood for the willpower of the proletariat, glass was as clear and pure as its consciousness. Thus, a new sculptural body had been constructed, but it was not at all a machine; it did not perform any work and did not serve any utilitarian function. But this art still had one merit, in that it ruptured the old conception of art. Thus, the process of transcending the institution of art altogether began. . . . The position of the artist in the world was changed: the materials of his profession became more vaired; new conditions of reception emerged. Nevertheless, the artists still moved on the same old orbit. The merit of Tatlin and his colleagues consisted of the fact of having acquainted artists with actual space and contemporary materials. . . .
>
> But this group ended up in a kind of *fetishism of materials* and forgot the necessity of a new plan.[7]

In contrast to the extremely well-informed scholars and general audiences of the pre-war period,[8] the European and American public of the immediate postwar years was completely ignorant of that aspect of Russian and Soviet avant-garde history and its critical debates, and they would remain so for at least another twenty years. The work of these artists (and the corresponding concepts of writers and theoreticians) would be censored from reception by those who actually witnessed the transformation from Constructivism to Productivism and who had emigrated to the West, like Gabo, Pevsner, and Kandinsky. From then on, that history would be simply disavowed by such witnesses and ignored by historians and critics determined to write the history of twentieth-century art according to the perspective provided by these witnesses.

In his classic 1967 study *Painting and Sculpture in Europe, 1880–1940*, George Heard Hamilton candidly described this perspective:

> As Malevich's influence declined, the task of opposing the materialistic direction of Tatlin's and Rodchenko's teaching

fell to two artists, Naum Gabo (1890–1977) and his elder
brother Anton Pevsner (1886–1962). . . . Long after they had
left Russia, where Socialist Realism had become the dominant Soviet aesthetic, Gabo and Pevsner, through their work
and activity in Western Europe and America, maintained the
tradition of Russian abstract design. It is only an historical
accident that their mode of expression . . . has since been
known as "Constructivist" and was eventually so accepted
by the artists themselves. The latter term properly should
be identified with a social and political point of view which
would grant the artist none of the automomy, and the work
of art none of the spiritual primacy, which they have
demanded.[9]

The strategies for such a reorganization of the history of
Constructivism now seem obvious: first of all, it was necessary to
disinherit the actual historical participants and to deny the development of the movement; then, to erase its commitment to mass
audiences and ignore its utilitarian dimensions; and finally, to
reorient it toward European and American concepts of artistic
autonomy and modernism.

To achieve the first task of successfully disregarding those
artists who, in fact, developed Constructivism, it was crucial to
establish oneself as the movement's originator and leader: Gabo
and Pevsner both dedicated themselves with considerable eager-
ness to the dissemination of this myth. In a 1947 article in the
Waterbury *Sunday Republican* of Gabo's new Connecticut
hometown, the artist was already describing himself as the
"founder and leader of the Constructivist school."[10] Or, as the
New Yorker critic Robert Coates phrased his version of the same
testimony, presumably freshly received from the witness, "In
fact, since the death, a while ago, of their great co-peer Moholy-
Nagy, they [Gabo and Pevsner] just about are the Constructivist
movement."[11] It should be remembered that at this time Tatlin,
Rodchenko, Stepanova, Melnikov, and two of the Vesnin
brothers were still alive and working in Moscow (El Lissitzky had
died in 1941).

The most astounding reconstruction of Constructivist history, however, was performed by Pevsner in an interview with
Rosamond Bernier for the French journal *L'Oeil*. She introduced
her article with the formula that by now had become standard:
"The founders of the Constructivist movement, Antoine Pevsner
and his brother Naum Gabo, were forced, by the political events,

to leave their country." She then proceeded to ask Pevsner about the other Constructivist artists in the group, and he replied:

> There were no others. I repeat it again and again: it was only Gabo and myself who invented Constructivism. Tatlin and Rodchenko picked up our ideas, but they falsified them by applying them to a functional art that was subjected to serve practical purposes. By contrast, we have always declared . . . that we were partisans of pure art, of *l'art pour l'art*.[12]

For Gabo and Pevsner, this was the very moment in which to secure for themselves the mythical role as originators and to block for postwar audiences that space for the reception of Russian and Soviet Constructivism. Western European and American audiences were as eager to reconstruct the institution of modernist high culture as they were anxious to depoliticize the heroic tradition of its opponents—the *historical* avant-garde of the 1915–25 period. However, the avant-garde tradition had to be reinstituted in such a way that it would supply the radical aesthetic goods without the political strings originally attached to the Dadaists' and the Constructivists' work, especially to that of their Productivist followers. This unlikely synthesis of contradictory postwar needs could be successfully performed only under the guise of a complete abstraction of the Constructivist avant-garde's artistic practices (here, artistic practices include their *aesthetic* commitment, as well as their *social* and *political* involvements). Gabo and Pevsner performed this abstraction by fusing these irreconcilable contradictions in their work, and they were adequately rewarded: soon they would be considered as the first, the *true*, and the *only* "Russian Constructivist" artists, and their work would actually dominate all art historical accounts and sculptural histories of the 1950s and 1960s.

In addition they provided the ideological argument to legitimize this blatant falsification of the Constructivist project. Gabo wrote:

> My art is generally recognized as the art of Constructivism. But the word "constructivism" was also claimed in the 1920s by a group of "constructive" artists that actually wanted to *liquidate* art. . . . They requested that the artist should devote his life to the construction of material goods. . . . My friends and I opposed this conception. . . . I believe, by contrast, that art is an elementary, real part of human life, the

most immediate and effective means of communication among the members of human society.[13]

The final task, then—the conventionalization of the avant-garde and its reorientation toward the autonomy concept of modernism—was accomplished through a renewed commitment to an antimaterialist, anti-utilitarian notion of art, evident here in the abstract universality of art as "a means of human communication."

Thus, the antimodernist assault on the presumably autonomous status of art (mounted, and, in many instances, successfully achieved by the Constructivist and Productivist aesthetic of the Soviet avant-garde) was refuted. This reconstruction necessarily erased those voices which, since the 1920s, had clearly criticized the inherent conceptual limitations of the modernist legacy and the type of Constructivist sculpture produced by artists like Gabo and Pevsner. It is to these voices that Gabo refers with a typical Cold War term, calling them the "liquidators" of art.

As early as 1926, the Productivist theoretician Boris Arvatov had attacked that very notion of a self-sufficient purity Gabo now attempted to resuscitate in 1948:

> While the totality of capitalist technology is based on the highest and latest achievements and represents a technique of mass production (industry, radio, transport, newspaper, scientific laboratory), bourgeois art, in principle, has remained on the level of individual crafts, and therefore has been isolated increasingly from the collective social practice of mankind, and has entered the realm of pure aesthetics. . . . The lonely master is the only type in capitalist society— the type of specialist of "pure art"—who can work outside of an immediately utilitarian practice, because his work is not based on machine technology. From here originates the total illusion of art's purposelessness and autonomy, from here art's bourgeois fetishistic nature.[14]

While there is no certainty that these statements by Arvatov and El Lissitzky were written with specific reference to Gabo and Pevsner, both identify the problem of the *fetishism* of so-called Constructivist materials, and this problem is pivotal in any reconsideration of their work. El Lissitzky had been among the first artists to understand that the concept of autonomy in modernism was particularly problematic: it stood in manifest contradiction to the assertion that the work would simultaneously provide an experience of formal, material, and structural radicality, and, thereby, anticipate and implement social and political "progress."

One of the key concerns of Constructivists and Productivists had been the disentanglement of their practice from this mythology. Further, they attempted to develop strategies and production procedures that would concretize their aesthetic and political commitments, according to the original implications of the modernist critique: they sought to activate and expand its audience, to abolish the work's cult and exhibition value, to deny its falsely auratic status, and, most importantly, to actually develop new strategies that would gradually anchor aesthetic practice to the social and political reality of the new mass-audiences.

El Lissitzky's statement reveals his foresight about Constructivism's eventual transgression of modernism's aesthetic limits: he foresaw that it would, at that point, inevitably cling to a mythology which claimed that new materials and production procedures had inherent progressive values. However, such materials and procedures originally had been developed as *functional* strategies, intended to dismantle governing aesthetic preconceptions rather than carry perceptual or actual value and meaning, *qua material* or *qua process.*

It must be remembered that the Constructivist commitment to industrial materials in sculpture originated both from an emphatic Futurist embracing of industrial mass-culture reality and from an anti-aesthetic impulse that insisted on the work's contingency and ephemerality. Opposed to traditional emphasis on sculpture's presumed universal validity and static perpetuity, this new sculpture underlined temporal, functional, and dynamic qualities (see, for example, El Lissitzky's 1920 design for a "Tribune for Lenin"). The work of Gabo and Pevsner (and most of Moholy-Nagy's) fulfilled the worst expectations about the fetishization of materials and process that El Lissitzky and Arvatov had anticipated. In fact, this "Perspex School of Constructivism" pretended that the contradictions within the modernist aesthetic could be resolved, at least superficially, through the use of new technological materials (celluloid, perspex, nylon, wire, chrome steel), in whose inherent qualities they believed. However, it is on the level of materials that their sculpture acquired its mythological qualities in the first place: to its postwar audience, these qualities signaled the perfect fusion of their apparent devotion to scientific and technological progress, on the one hand, and, on the other, "spiritual autonomy" and "exquisite abstract beauty," as the English critics put it.

During the reconstruction period, the dominant notion of industrial progress refused to address any of the social, economic, and political questions posited by the Constructivists. Further, such works had appeal because this fetishization process was so ideally suited to disembody Constructivist sculptural practice and to make this new sculpture appear truly progressive; it embraced technology and industrial production, providing new high-culture icons, for both the collective adaptation to industrial consumption and the incumbent industrialization of culture itself.

Paradoxically, we learn that as late as 1936—in apparent contradiction to their postwar commitment to pure, autonomous spirituality—Gabo and Pevsner were perceived as potential builders for monumental, utilitarian arthitecture. Here, for example, is Alfred Barr's (presumably) unintentionally comic statement:

> Pevsner is more powerful, more intellectual in his approach and more inclined to force his materials so that . . . his constructions take on superficially something of the character of sculpture, while Gabo's are more in the spirit of architecture. Some of Gabo's constructions have, in fact, been projects for semi-architectural monuments, but it is his pupil Lubetkin, and not himself, who has had the privilege of designing the Constructivist Penguin Pond for the London Zoo.[15]

And even after the war, some of these architectural visions materialized, albeit in somewhat different contexts and for unexpectedly different patrons. The promotional text for the publication of Gabo's A. W. Mellon lectures (delivered in 1959, published in 1962), stated: "Among his most famous works are *Construction Suspended in Space.* Baltimore Museum of Art: a constructed relief in the U. S. Rubber Co. Building, Rockefeller Center, New York; and a free-standing 85-foot construction in Rotterdam, Netherlands (for the department store de Bijenkorf)."[16]

To accomplish this complex ideological mission, on the level of formal and structural definition, all of the specific features of Constructivist sculpture had to be mythified. Transparency of construction and transparency of the sculptural body had been among the essential strategies in the works of Kobro, Medunetzy, Iogansoii, Rodchenko, and the Stenberg brothers. These strate-

gies had originally increased the perceptual awareness of the
constructed (temporary and transient) function-oriented qualities
of this new art. This emphasis on its constructed nature, and its
continuous transformation resulting from the collective social
production process (the *Machbarkeit,* as Bertolt Brecht would
call it) implied an equal emphasis on its participatory dimension
and contextual contiguity and on the abolition of the contemplative mode, in favor of the activating mode of the new tactility in
art, as Walter Benjamin would describe it.

By contrast, with Gabo and Pevsner, as well as Moholy-
Nagy, transparency had acquired a "purely visual" value. This is
evidenced in Moholy-Nagy's statement: "This composition demonstrates three types: transparent walls, circumscribed by the
thick edges of the plastic or wire. One is moderately transparent
(rhodoid), the second perfectly transparent (plexiglass), and the
third supertransparent (air.)"[17]

The second, equally important paradigmatic feature of Constructivist sculpture had been the foregrounding of inherent
physical forces, which determined the structure and position of
the sculptural construct. In Gabo's and Pevsner's postwar work,
gravity, weight, and tension were aestheticized as stylistic devices, generating the advanced techno-scientistic appearance of
the gadget, while no longer performing any of the functional tasks
demonstrated by the wire in Tatlin's work or the collapsible, se-
rial, volumetric elements in Rodchenko's *Hanging Constructions.*

The third and final question concerns materials. In many of
Gabo's postwar works (and in almost all of Pevsner's work of that
period), there is a partial or complete return to the traditional
medium of bronze: this categorically rejects all earlier claims associated with the new materiality of Constructivist sculpture, as
defined in the *Realistic Manifesto.* This programmatic falsification of Constructivist thought is best indicated by the discrep-
ancy between the structural and material elements in Gabo's
Bijenkorf sculpture (1956–57): it sits on its black marble base,
with its bronze-wire network faking tension and structural function. Clearly, it had to be impossible to simultaneously *maintain*
the Constructivist legacy and *withdraw* from the program of a
materialist and socialist art production into an emphatic renewal
of a completely abstracted art practice, insisting on its pure spirituality and transcendental beauty. These contradictions were further heightened by attempts to impose such work on the public,
in the guise of monumental sculpture, without having analyzed
the conditions of Western economic and political reality. Thus,

there was no consideration at all of the audiences for whom sculpture would be produced nor for its situation in public space: this issue was excluded from the concerns of the artists, and, most certainly, from those of the new patrons of public sculpture—state agencies of corporate enterprises. Obviously, their art production had systematically detached itself from all questions of concrete specificity, regardless of whether these were questions of production (concerning the discursive and institutional conditions of practice) or of reception (relationship of a work to both its presumed and actual audience and to cultural, political, and economic conditions determining that audience).

Paradoxically, it was precisely this reorientation toward a modernist autonomy that placed Gabo dangerously close to that tradition of abstract art, particularly the European Abstraction-Création and Cercle et Carré and the American Abstract Artists group, which was just about to be displaced by the much-heralded emergence of the New York School aesthetic. As early as 1936, Alfred Barr had concluded his brief (but epochal) study *Cubism and Abstract Art* with these rather astonishing remarks:

> At the risk of generalizing about the very recent past, it seems fairly clear that the geometric tradition in abstract art . . . is in the decline. . . . The non-geometric biomorphic forms of Arp and Miro and Moore are definitely in the ascendant. The formal tradition of Gauguin, Fauvism and Expressionism will probably dominate, for some time to come, the tradition of Cézanne and Cubism.[18]

Just when the geometric reductivist and supposedly "European" legacy was about to be displaced by the emergence of Abstract Expressionism, Robert Goldwater, another pivotal figure of this period, described the same attitude in his "Art Chronicle" of July 1947:

> Here, in art, as elsewhere, this country has a more important international burden to carry. . . . There is a growing inclination to shy away from what is, by now, due to long exposure, our easy acceptance of the compositional and technical virtuosity of pure abstraction, to embrace an art *in which emotion has not been subjugated and uncontrolled feeling breaks through the boundaries of the medium* [my italics]. One tends to say "So what" to the beautifully mastered forms of ab-

Alexander Rodchenko,
Oval Hanging Con-
struction Number 12,
c. 1920. Collection, The
Museum of Modern Art,
New York.

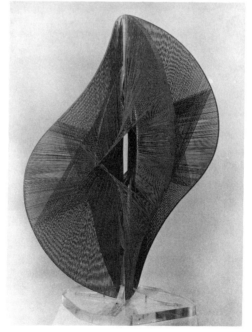

Naum Gabo, Linear
Construction in Space
No. 2 (Variation), *1949/*
1962–64. Collection,
Albright-Knox Gallery,
Buffalo.

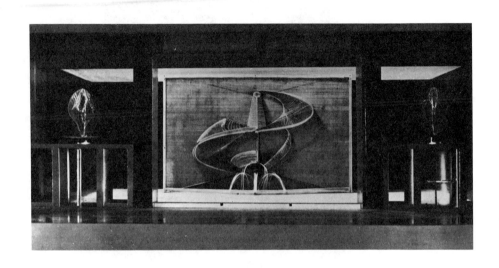

Naum Gabo, Model for
the sculptures for lobby
of the Esso Building,
Rockefeller Center,
1949

straction. . . . This is the effect produced by so many members of the *American Abstract Artists* group.[19]

To complicate matters even further, from this point on Gabo had to define his own position with explicit reference to the actual "threat" (as he surely perceived it) posed by the "deep irrationality and collective politics" of the Surrealist aesthetic, which increasingly dominated the New York sensibility in the late 1940s. Accordingly, Gabo deemed it necessary to voice his critique of the political potential of Surrealism, already withering in its New York School incarnation. In a *New Yorker* piece of 1948, Gabo wrote, "I don't believe in trusting the subconscious. I don't care for the transitional acceptance of the crowd either. Artists are done for, if they go in for effects that attract the man in the street."[20] Once again Gabo had to realign himself and stake out his territory, and once again he was forced to redefine his position in manifest contradiction to those positions he had espoused until that very point. Now, it was no longer a question of his past membership in the Soviet avant-garde, when (as *Time Magazine* put it in 1953), he was "still the darling of the Bolsheviks." Rather, it was his more recent involvement with the relatively progressive Socialist circle in London, grouped around Herbert Read in the late 1930s, that created difficulties for him. While the presence of Surrealism had made itself felt in London as well, the conflicting aesthetic positions had appeared more balanced during that period. Then, Gabo was able to comfortably fend off any critical accusations that might have been leveled against his work. For example, when questioned in 1936 by the so-called "theorists of art" as to whether his work was too rational, ignoring the power and value of imagination and free-ranging fantasy (as Gabo put it, whether "our works lack the mythical element"),[21] he could still reply with references to the architectonic and social dimension of his art. Or, as he wrote one year later, in 1937: "The constructive idea has given back to sculpture its old forms and faculties, the most powerful of which is its capacity to act architectonically. . . . By architecture I mean not only the building of houses, but the whole edifice of our everyday existence."[22] But as we have already seen, shortly after his arrival in New York, this collective dimension had to be obliterated. An interview with the curator of his first retrospective exhibition (a joint exhibition, in 1948, with Pevsner) at the Museum of Modern Art suggests that the social and architectural dimension was already erased from his memory: "In 1923, in Germany, my work hovered on the verge of architecture. But now, it is more mature, self-sufficient, or pure art."[23]

In 1948, however, the New York situation was by no means as homogenous and unified as it would soon be portrayed: the various arguments lodged against the legacy of academicized abstract-geometric art and for the Surrealist liberation were not easily reconciled. These contradictions are most evident in the positions voiced by yet another critic, Clement Greenberg, who at that time was still quite far from being the unequivocal champion/spokesman of Abstract Expressionism he would soon become. His description of the conflicts and paradoxes with which the Americanized Constructivist Gabo was confronted appears to be most accurate. In "The Situation at the Moment" Greenberg assured us that "when it comes to the Zeitgeist we Americans are the most advanced people on earth, if only because we are the most industrialized." Further on he stated:

> After all, the easel painting is on its way out; abstract pictures rarely go with the furniture, and the canvas, even when it measures ten feet by ten, has become a kind of a private journal. . . . Perhaps the contradiction between the architectural destination of abstract art and the very very private atmosphere in which it is produced, will kill ambitious painting in the end. As it is, this contradiction, which lies outside of the autonomy of art, defines specifically the crisis in which painting now finds itself.[24]

Surprising as it may be, this article makes one speculate whether, at least for a short period, Greenberg's position was approximating that of the original Constructivists: for example, when he mentions "the architectural destination of abstract art," El Lissitzky's view of his Proun paintings as "transit stations between painting and architecture" comes to mind.

Further, in an even more explicit essay that year, Greenberg drew even more astonishing conclusions, based on his diagnosis of the end of abstract art in the late 1930s. In distinct opposition to his subsequent beliefs, Greenberg all but declared the end of painting in his essay "The New Sculpture":

> I do not mean to suggest that painting will soon decline as an art. . . . What is to be pointed out is that painting's place as

the supreme visual art is now threatened, whether it is in
decline or not. And I want also to call attention to sculpture,
an art that has been in relative desuetude for several centuries but which has lately undergone a transformation that
seems to endow it with a greater range of expression for
modern sensibility than painting now has. This transformation, or revolution, is a product of Cubism.[25]

In this statement, Greenberg foresaw a future for post-Cubist art
totally opposed to Barr's prognosis: he argued that the logical
evolution of Cubism would inevitably lead into three-dimensional
spatial, sculptural, and (probably) architectural constructs. However, even more astonishing here is Greenberg's historical awareness: when he traced the historical lineage of the new sculpture,
Greenberg did not hesitate to name Dadaists (like Schwitters or
Arp) or Constructivists (like Tatlin, Gabo, or Pevsner), all of
whom would soon disappear from his memory. In fact, this amnesia would become so complete that, when asked why the references to Dadaism and Constructivism had all but vanished from
his later argument, Greenberg simply replied that he did not
think about it because he had not seen enough of it.[26]

However, in 1948, Greenberg wrote:

Thence the new sculpture grew through the bas-relief constructions that Picasso and then Arp and Schwitters created
by raising the collage above the picture plane; and from
there Picasso . . . along with the Russian Constructivists
Tatlin, Pevsner and Gabo . . . at last delivered it into the
positive truth of free space, altogether away from the picture
plane.[27]

What could Greenberg possibly mean when he speaks about "the
positive truth of free space altogether away from the picture
plane"? This is a conceptual and perceptual condition apparently
profoundly at odds with the foundations of Greenberg's later,
neo-modernist aesthetic, with its notorious emphasis on flatness
and opticality.

To clarify this question, we must read further:

This new, pictorial, draftsman's sculpture has more or less
abandoned the traditional materials of stone and bronze in
favor of ones more flexible under such modern tools as the

oxyacetylene torch: steel, iron, alloys, glass, plastics. It has
no regard for the unity of its physical medium and will use
any number of different materials in the same work and any
variety of applied colors—as befits an art that sees in its
products almost as much that is pictorial as is sculptural.[28]

While the first statement addresses the new sculpture's historical
lineage, the second speaks to its production aesthetic. But a few
paragraphs later, there is an important statement dealing with
the reception aesthetic of the new sculpture, defining the requisite cognitive and perceptual conditions of the audience, which
justify the structure and morphology of this new work:

> Sculpture has always been able to create objects that seem
> to have a denser, more literal reality than those created by
> painting; this, which used to be its handicap, now consti-
> tutes its greater appeal to our newfangled, positivist sensibil-
> ity, and this also gives it its greater license. It is now free to
> invent an infinity of new objects and disposes of a potential
> wealth of forms with which our taste cannot quarrel in prin-
> ciple, since they will all have their self-evident physical real-
> ity, as palpable and independent and present as the houses
> we live in and the furniture we use.[29]

But, of course, this is not the Clement Greenberg most of us
would encounter, in 1961, in *Art and Culture*, the widely dis-
seminated first collection of his essays. While "The New Sculpture" essay was included in this collection, it carried two dates
(1948 and 1958), indicating that it had been extensively rewritten
in the intervening decade.

Obviously, to forge the aesthetic of reconstruction modernism, Greenberg had to make several elisions: adaptations had to
be made within the text and outside of it, in actual history, where
participants and criteria would have to be erased and eliminated.
The 1958 revised version of the passages just quoted reads:

> The new construction sculpture points back, almost insis-
> tently, to its origins in Cubist painting: by its linearism and
> linear intricacies, by its openness and transparency and
> weightlessness, and by its preoccupation with surface and
> skin alone, which it expresses in blade or sheet-like forms
> Space is there to be shaped, divided, enclosed, but not to

be filled. The new sculpture tends to abandon stone, bronze and clay for industrial materials like iron, steel, alloy, glass, plastics, celluloid, etc., etc., which are worked with the blacksmith's, the welder's and even the carpenter's tools.[30]

And a few paragraphs later, still in this 1958 version, Greenberg described (apparently affirmatively) the inversion of each and every quality of Constructivist sculpture in the work he was considering, and he provided the ideological legitimation for these inversions of the Constructivist legacy:

To render substance entirely optical and form, whether pictorial, sculptural or architectural, as an integral part of ambient space—this brings anti-illusionism full circle. Instead of the illusion of things we are now being offered the illusion of modalities; namely that matter is incorporeal, weightless and exists only optically, like a mirage. This kind of illusionism is stated in pictures whose paint surfaces and enclosing rectangles seem to expand into surrounding space; . . . but better yet in Constructivist and quasi-Constructivist works of sculpture. Feats of "engineering" that aim to provide the greatest possible amount of visibility with the least possible expenditure of tactile surface belong categorically to the free and *total* medium of sculpture. The constructor-sculptor can, literally, draw in the air with a single strand of wire that supports nothing but itself.[31]

It is immediately apparent that this new perspective on Constructivism implied an almost violent dematerialization and depoliticization of the complex formal and material dialectic of Constructivist sculpture. This literal disembodiment of sculpture, as we might call it, also implied a complete disembodiment of the viewer's perceptual experience, as Greenberg (with no hesitation) phrased it, in 1958:

And even should sculpture be compelled eventually to become as abstract as painting, it would still have a larger realm of formal possibilities at its command. The human body is no longer postulated as the agent of space in either pictorial or sculptural art; now it is eyesight alone, and eyesight has more freedom of movement and invention within three dimensions than within two.[32]

Thus, Constructivism—in the works of Gabo and Pevsner, and most certainly in the words of Greenberg in 1958—finally had reached the stage of the "mirage." What had once been tactile and contingent had become "optical"; what had been rigorously anti-illusionistic in emphasizing weight, physical mass, and process, in foregrounding surface and texture, and in "baring the structural device" had turned into an "illusion of modalities."

If the wire in Tatlin's work orginally functioned as an important element in the contextualization of the sculptural construct in architectual space (revealing mass and weight as essential features of sculptural perception), it then became, through a magic trick of dematerialization, an object that "supports nothing but itself" in Greenberg's vision. Here we witness *in situ nascendi* the construction of the neo-modernist aesthetic, with its requirements and its amazing conceptual and terminological *volte face*. This text seems to have been the first instance in which Greenberg used the concept of "opticality," a term that circulated for at least the next twenty years as a "key term" in the neo-modernist aesthetic, particularly in the criticism of Michael Fried.

Yet, in this case, despite its efforts to transform Constructivism into an idealist and ahistorical aesthetic, that key term was still applied to its complicated relationship with historical avant-garde legacies. But this relationship was eclipsed soon after, and it was ultimately restricted to an almost exclusive reference to Cubism alone.

Apparently yet another type of elision was necessary, and it is also equally evident in the text. This adjustment occurred within Greenberg's own attempt to eliminate all contradictions from the new aesthetic. While in the original 1948 version he could still affirm "our positivist sensibility," in 1958 he modified this to only a mention of a "positivist aspect of the modernist aesthetic." Most importantly, in the original version Greenberg credited sculpture with "a self-evident physical reality," describing it with this astonishing comparison: "as palpable and independent and present as the houses we live in and the furniture we use."[33] Greenberg's emphasis on the positivist dimension of this aesthetic led him to reveal (perhaps involuntarily) the dull and pragmatic dimension of positivism. Clearly, this furniture analogy would have been extremely discordant with the discourse of the tragic, the sublime, and the transcendental that supported Abstract Expressionism in 1958. Accordingly, this surprising statement—which could have easily been misread as an ingenuous anticipation of Minimal sculpture—was deleted from the revised version.

A few years later, such maneuvres were no longer necessary,[34] since Greenberg's reconstruction of the history of modernism (from which some of its most important contributions were deleted) had been thoroughly and successfully institutionalized. In fact, Greenberg's reconstruction had become the *doxa* which, well into the 1960s, was hardly questioned by American and European critics, curators, and audiences.

Notes

1.
The distinction between the post-World War II neo-avant-garde and the historical avant-garde of the 1915–35 period was developed in Peter Burger's Theorie der Avant-garde (Frankfurt, 1974; translated into English as Theory of the Avant-garde (Minneapolis, 1984).

2.
Clement Greenberg, "Irrelevance versus Irresponsibility," Partisan Review, 15:5 (May 1948), p. 579.

3.
Serge Chermayeff, "Naum Gabo," Magazine of Art, 41 (February 1948), pp. 56–59. Michel Seuphor adopted this juxtaposition of Russian and Soviet modernist art to Socialist Realism in the conclusion of his important article "Au temps de l'avant garde," in the French journal L'Oeil (November 1955), pp. 24–39. This first major sketch in postwar France of the history of Russian Constructivism concluded with an unusually large number of color reproductions of Socialist Realist paintings.

4.
Naum Gabo, "The Concepts of Russian Art," World Review (June 1942), pp. 48–53.

5.
Naum Gabo, quoted by Jean Clay, Visages de l'art moderne (Paris, 1969), pp. 70–120.

6.
For a discussion of the relationship of Gabo and Pevsner to the Moscow Free State Art Studios (VKhuTEMAS), see Christina Lodder, Russian Constructivism (New Haven and London), 1983, pp. 34, 109–130.

7.
El Lissitzky, "Neue Russische Kunst," in Sophie Lissitzky-Küppers, El Lissitzky (Dresden 1967), p. 354 (my translation; italics added).

8.
Most notably, Alfred Barr's seminal exhibition Cubism and Abstract Art included and/or reproduced in the catalogue a number of central works from the Russian and Soviet avant-garde, including works by Rodchenko, Tatlin, Popova, and Stepanova. A year later, in spite of its obvious limitations, Carola Giedion-Welcker's study Modern Plastic Art (published in English and German in 1937) was even more developed in its comprehension of the new sculptural phenomena. Both Barr's and Giedion-Welcker's vision of Constructivist sculpture was more advanced in the mid-1930s than virtually every other study to be published during the first two decades after the war. Not only does Giedion-Welcker reproduce Tatlin's counter-reliefs, corner-reliefs and, of course, the Monument to the Third International, but she also documents those sculptural works which, in spite of their seminal position, will soon vanish mysteriously from the art history of twentieth-century sculpture: Rodchenko's Oval Hanging Construction, works by Katarzyna Kobro, and the work of the Laboratory Constructivists Medunetzky and the Stenberg Brothers.

The suspicion that the repression of Russian and Soviet avant-garde material from the art-historical reception process during the period of the reconstruction (which was also that of the reconstruction of modernism), was at least partially determined by such obvious factors as the rabid anti-Communism of the postwar period is corroborated by the fact that this elimination seems to have taken place at a different pace, and to a different degree, in the various geopolitical contexts. While in the West German and the American contexts the elimination of historical memory seems to have been all but complete for many years to come, the French situation seems less distorted in its political relationship with the Soviet Union, and it seems to have also a*l*lowed for a more open and liberal reception of the Constructivist legacy.

As for the actual falsification of (art) history, in the attitudes of postwar scholars toward the Russian and Soviet avant-garde, it is particularly amazing to witness the persistent repetition of these ideological clichés about the prohibition and prosecution of Constructivist art in the Soviet Union after 1921. Not a single study of that period mentions the artistic and political debates among the artists themselves, or the gradual transformation from the Constructivist aesthetic into the Productivist aesthetic, initiated from within the ranks of the artists, critics, and theoreticians of that generation. The typical attitude regarding these phenomena can be

found in every single sculpture history of that period, and it seems that once the ideological cliché had been set up, it was repeated for generations to come. Thus, in 1954, as Eduard Trier phrased it, "The so-called revolutionary masses of Russia [sic] destroyed these hopes [of the Constructivists] already in 1922, when abstract constructivism was prohibited by the state and when it was interrupted or eliminated as undesirable." (Trier, Moderne Plastik [Berlin 1954], p. 74). Ten years later, it was Herbert Read who seemed to have become something like the mouthpiece of Gabo and Pevsner, voicing the ideological clichés with more distinction: "For a few years, the politicians were too busy to interfere in such matters, but five years later they felt compelled to call a halt. The movement was suppressed, its promoters silenced or exiled, but they had already created, not merely a new movement in art, an advance in the evolution of style, but an altogether new kind of art, Constructivist art, and its practice was to spread from Moscow throughout the world" (Read, Modern Sculpture [London, 1964], p. 93). Or, in a

third example from the seemingly inexhaustible repertory of ideological clichés, as late as 1969 in a study by an eminent American scholar: "But in 1922 the government suppressed the movement (of Constructivism), saying it was of no service to the state" (Robert Goldwater, What is Modern Sculpture? [New York, 1969], p. 67).

For an attempt to clarify the actual transformation of aesthetic theory and practice in the Soviet Union after 1920, and a first study to discuss the collaboration between Stalin's propaganda ministry and artists like Alexander Rodchenko and Varvara Stepanova, see Hubertus Gassner, Rodchenko Fotografien (München, 1982) and Hubertus Gassner and Eckhart Gillen's anthology of documents Zwischen Revolutionskunst und Sozialistischem Realismus (Cologne, 1979). As to Lissitzky's work for the same ministry and a first discussion of the transformation of his aesthetic theory and practice, see my essay "From Faktura to Factography," October 30 (Fall 1984), pp. 82–119.

9.
George Heard Hamilton, Painting and Sculpture in Europe

1880–1940 *(London/ New York, 1967),* p. 352.

10.
Naum Gabo, quoted in The Sunday Republican *(Waterbury), June 8, 1947.*

11.
Robert M. Coates, "Naum Gabo," The New Yorker, *February 21, 1948, pp. 43–44. To give another example from 1953: "We started Constructivism in 1915. . . . In the past, my work has been prosecuted—thrown out of Russia, attacked in Germany. The narrow-minded sculptors who are so derogatory, who try to destroy it, believe only in materialist art. . . . When I came to Berlin, as far as I know, there were no Constructivists. Afterwards Constructivism emerged in Berlin, in France, in Holland and in England. They are teaching Constructivism in Yale, Harvard, MIT, N.Y.U. Brooklyn. We have started something which is rolling, something of the human spirit. As yet, Constructivism has not yet reached its full maturity." (Naum Gabo, quoted by A. L. Chanin in "Gabo makes a Construction,"* Art News, *52:7 [November 1953], p. 46). The myth of Gabo*

as the "founder and leader" of the Constructivist movement will be repeated from 1947 on through the next thirty years. Thus, for example, Hilton Kramer in 1966: "Naum Gabo, the Russian sculptor and theorist who founded the Constructivist movement half a century ago. . . . As Alexei Pevsner makes clear in his memoir—Constructivism was the creation of Gabo alone. It was Gabo who formulated the theory, devised the sculptural syntax to realize it and produced the first Constructivist masterpieces" ("Gabo and Constructivism [History Revised]," The New York Times, *No. 3127, 1966). Or, still ten years later: "The work of Naum Gabo, for over sixty years the leading exponent of Constructivism. . . . " (Corinne Bellow, press release,* The Tate Gallery, *London, October 18, 1976).*

12.
Rosamond Bernier, "Propos d'un sculpteur," Antoine Pevsner interviewed by Rosamond Bernier, L'Oeil, *23 (November 1956), pp. 28–35. Bernier concludes: " 'Don't forget, Gabo and I are the only Constructivists,' the artist reminded me when I was about to leave the studio." It is important*

to know that on the occasion of the publication of this interview, even Gabo explicitly corrected the outrageous claims made by his brother and disassociated himself from these remarks. See Naum Gabo, "Statement," L'Oeil 28 *(April 1957), p. 61.*

13.
Naum Gabo, as quoted by Trier, Moderne Plastik, *p. 74 (my translation).*

14.
Boris Arvatov, Kunst und Produktion: Entwurf einer Proletarisch—Avantgardistischen Aesthetik *1921–1930 (Munich, 1972), pp. 11–12 (my translation).*

15.
Alfred Barr, Cubism and Abstract Art *(New York, 1936), p. 138.*

16.
Naum Gabo, Of Divers Arts *(The A. W. Mellon Lectures in the Fine Arts, 1959, Bollingen Series 35: 8 [Washington, 1962]).*

17.
László Moholy-Nagy, quoted in Goldwater, What is Modern Sculpture? *p. 69.*

18.
The statement is astonishing not only because of its prognostic accuracy, but also because

of the fact that Barr's catalogue and exhibition were—and would remain for decades to come—the most comprehensive and exact documentation of the post-Cubist pictorial and sculptural practices of abstraction. This was true, in particular, for its unusually developed documentation of the artists of the Russian and Soviet avant-garde, whose reception in the Western world after 1945 concerns us here.

One of the general questions provoked by Barr's statement asks—and we will not be able to answer it in this context—why his prognosis would turn out to be so accurate. More precisely, why would the legacies of geometric abstraction—in their various forms and formations (Cercle et Carré, Abstraction/Création, and American Abstract Artists)—become increasingly unacceptable toward the end of the 1930s and remain definitely rejected in American art of the 1940s and 1950s, entailing the almost complete obliteration of an entire generation of American abstract artists from the map of modernism.

19.
Robert Goldwater, "A Season of Art," Partisan Review 14:4 (July–August 1947), pp. 414ff.

20.
Naum Gabo, quoted by Robert Coates, The New Yorker, March 20, 1948, p. 25.

21.
Naum Gabo, "Constructive Art," The Listener, November 4, 1936, pp. 846–848.

22.
Naum Gabo, in Circle: International Survey of Constructive Art (London 1937).

23.
Chanin, "Gabo makes a construction," pp. 34–37.

24.
Clement Greenberg, "The Situation at the Moment," Partisan Review (January 1948), pp. 81–84.

25.
Clement Greenberg, "The New Sculpture," Partisan Review (June 1949), p. 641.

26.
In a discussion with the author on the occasion of the 1981 Vancouver conference Modernism and Modernity, see: Modernism and Modernity (Halifax, 1983), p. 271.

27.
Greenberg, "The New Sculpture," p. 640. Greenberg, in 1948, had obviously not quite determined the canon of Abstract Expressionism, nor had he singled out the masters of the movement. Quite the contrary: the list of artists that he mentions at the end of the essay is, with the exception of David Smith, remarkably atypical (it includes Burgoyne Diller, who at that time was still one of the most outspoken defenders of geometrical abstraction). It is also a list of distinctly secondary figures, including Peter Grippe, Adaline Kent, David Hare, Richard Lippold. But most of all it is astonishing because the achievements of Abstract Expressionism would precisely not occur in the field of sculpture; quite the opposite, as Greenberg himself would later admit, this would be the domain of its most obvious weaknesses and failures.

28.
Ibid.

29.
Ibid.

30.
Clement Greenberg, "The New Sculpture" (Revised version), in Art and Culture (Boston, 1961), pp. 139–145. This quotation p. 142. I would like to thank Yve-Alain Bois, who originally brought the differences between

the two versions of the
essay to my attention.

31.
Ibid., p. 144.

32.
Ibid., p. 143.

33.
"The New Sculpture"
(1948), p. 641.

34.
A further example of
the workings of recon-
struction modernism: in
this text, Greenberg can
still mention David
Smith's work in the con-
text of his discussion of
Constructivist sculp-
ture, but soon he will
have to extract him
from any such refer-
ence, in order to start
rewriting modernist
sculptural history—not
only according to the
new terms of a recon-
structed modernist
aesthetic, but also ac-
cording to the particu-
lar interests and
investments of his pres-
ent: the construction of
an autonomous and
hegemonous local neo-
avant-garde. Soon
Greenberg would say,
by contrast, that in
Smith's sculpture "there
is no flavor in it of (de)
Stijl or of the Bauhaus
or even of Constructiv-
ism." See Greenberg,
"David Smith's New
Sculpture," in Garnett
McCoy (ed.), David
Smith *(New York,*
1973), p. 222.

Audience

You mentioned that even before leaving the Soviet Union in 1922, Gabo had been confronted with disputes and aesthetic disagreements with his peers and colleagues. Are you implying that he changed even more so after his arrival in the West?

Benjamin Buchloh

Well, I think that you do have a point by saying that already by the early 1920s, Gabo's conception of Constructivism was unacceptable to his peers. In fact, Gabo refused to participate in the transition from Constructivism to Productivism that was the major shift within the work of Tatlin, Rodchenko, Lissitzky, and many others. So I would agree that the split existed. Furthermore, I think that the split is evident in the work as well because, as you know, in the 1920s Gabo desperately tries to catch up with Tatlin's projects by devising all kinds of airport models or institutes for astrophysics in small-scale designs.

So this incapacity to resolve the schism between a public, socially utilitarian art and a modernist, Constructivist aesthetic that remains within the dimensions of the pictorial frame or the sculptural volumetric body, however transparent it might have become, is at the heart of Gabo's problems. That schizophrenic shifting between the two positions becomes intensified in the postwar period when he confronts the needs of Western European and American audiences. At that point, you can read any two statements by Gabo and you are very likely to find one which says that art is completely devoted to utilitarian functions and another one which insists on the absolute purity, self-sufficiency, and autonomy of art.

Therefore, whereas your point is well taken that a schism exists in Gabo's work in the 1920s, I would argue that it becomes intensified and more manifestly unresolved. Furthermore, due to its confrontation with the actual conditions that surround Gabo in America, that schism becomes more obviously grotesque in its attempts to comply with what is needed.

Thierry de Duve

Would you be able to cite an instance of artists or works that have resolved that schism?

Benjamin Buchloh

Yes, I would argue that Abstract Expressionism resolves that schism very pertinently in 1948. If you read the often contradictory arguments that Greenberg makes for Pollock, they do range from a completely positivist analysis of Pollock's work—to the affirmation of the Surrealist legacy, the Gothic, etc. And I think that it is really relevant in that context to see how Greenberg's attempt to struggle with these contradictions fails: how he fails to read sculpture, even though he tries very much in that critical period to establish the ground for the viability of sculpture when apparently he has doubts about the future of painting, and how this is an irreconcilable problem. I think Abstract Expressionism offers the solution to that schism at that moment.

Audience

Did you come across any relationship between Gabo's work and that of Buckminster Fuller's, and the possibility that his work could have offered in a sense a technological and artistic model for the idea of technological redemption?

Benjamin Buchloh

I do think that the question of technological redemption is an infinitely important subject, but this seems a very complex issue to bring up right now.

Audience

Yes, but it seems to me that Gabo's work is the classic example of such a desire expressed artistically because it always ends up as transcendent and idealist, almost a mystical object.

Benjamin Buchloh

I don't know if one can say almost. I would definitely separate Buckminster Fuller from Gabo. Whatever one has to say about Fuller, that is precisely not his problem. It is the problem of that European generation: it's the problem of Moholy-Nagy as much as it's the problem of Gabo.

It would be interesting to develop a comparison. However, I don't know Fuller's work well enough to say if there could have been a possible connection. As far as I know, Fuller did not insist on being an artist. Pure art was not his subject. He found himself as a productive, working, thinking designer. He never approached the issue of pure art, sculpture, etc.

Marginality as a Political Stance:
The Canadian Painter Jean McEwen

Constance Naubert-Riser

Jean McEwen's position in Canadian painting is more one of discretion that of aloofness. His lack of arrogance is probably responsible for art historians' lack of awareness of the importance
and the significance of his work. Not nearly as well known as his
contemporary Jean-Paul Riopelle, he is too often dismissed as a
mere case of "delayed reaction." This paper will carefully examine his career between 1951 and 1956 to show that he can be
viewed as a kind of paradigm of the manner in which triangular
relationships among New York, Montreal, and Paris shaped the
development of the artist during these crucial years.

Crossroads: Paris—New York—Montreal

McEwen arrived in Paris in September 1951, the product of a
cultural and literary community that was particularly attracted to
the French capital. His first concern was to round out his knowledge of painting. He spent long hours in museums like the
Louvre and the Jeu de Paume, where he was literally fascinated
by the luminous texture of Renoir's blues. For the young artist,
educated by books and the study of reproductions, seeing the
original paintings was no less than a revelation. It was only after
this immersion that he was able to direct his attention to more
contemporary galleries and make contact with his compatriots.
As luck would have it, he did not meet Jean-Paul Riopelle until
December, after the important *Signifiants de l'informel*[1] exhibi-

tion in November at Studio Paul Fachetti. Riopelle wasted no time in bringing McEwen up to date on the controversial issues of the day, which we will briefly review here.

Riopelle had been in Paris since 1946.[2] His mission was to find outlets in Paris galleries for the works of his Automatist friends gathered around Paul-Emile Borduas. Still steeped in Surrealist doctrines, he had succeeded, undoubtedly through the intervention of the Galerie Pierre Loeb, in meeting André Breton, who asked the group to participate in an international Surrealist exhibition.[3] The exhibition took place at the Galerie Maeght in July 1947. Only Riopelle participated, although he later regretted it because "his painting was relegated to a dark corner, surrounded by mediocre works."[4]

Meanwhile, with the help of Fernand Leduc, who was then working in Paris,[5] he organized the *Les Automatistes canadiens* exhibition at the Galerie du Luxembourg in June 1947, in which Borduas, Marcel Barbeau, Roger Fauteux, Fernand Leduc, and Jean-Paul Mousseau participated. What is more interesting for our purposes, however, is that in December 1947 only Riopelle and Leduc participated in the *L'Imaginaire* exhibition, also held at the Galerie du Luxembourg.

An examination of the avowed intentions of this exhibition explains the direction in which Riopelle's work would evolve and, as a result, the one which McEwen would later discover. As Bernard Ceysson has pointed out, " 'L'Imaginaire' was not, however, in keeping with the succession of experiences recommended by Breton. The basic tenets of Surrealism were not accepted for what they were worth by most of the participating artists."[6] In the text that accompanied the exhibition, Jean-José Marchand maintained that "only one tradition is valid: that of absolutely free creation."[7] Riopelle seems to have found himself in a core group of artists who wanted "to dissociate themselves from formal abstraction as much as they wanted to keep their distance from Surrealism."[8] Also represented, aside from Riopelle, was Georges Mathieu, who was, along with the gallery director, responsible for organizing this exhibition. In fact it was Mathieu who invited the two Canadians to join Hans Hartung, Camille Bryen, Wols, Raoul Ubac, Victor Brauner, Solier, and Verroust. The title, *L'Imaginaire*, was tacked on at the last minute by Eva Philippe, the gallery director, who thought it sounded better than the original title selected by Mathieu, the more precise *Vers l'abstraction lyrique*,[9] which would have situated the group historically. Through Riopelle's participation in this exhibi-

tion, we can see that his break from Surrealism and the Automatists would be an inconspicuous one and that he would follow a
more individualist path. This was made possible by the pluralism
of the Parisian art scene.

By the time McEwen made his acquaintance, Riopelle was
already involved in the avant-garde network led by Michel Tapié
and Georges Mathieu, who had both been working for several
years on proposals for a less dogmatic concept of painting. From
these debates, the concepts of lyrical abstraction, free abstraction, and informal art emerged. The purpose of the group was
primarily to destabilize the form of geometric abstraction (Herbin,
Magnelli, etc.) which was then being imposed as the dominant
trend at the Salon des Réalités Nouvelles.

A detailed chronology of the exhibitions held during this period[10] indicates that *L'Imaginaire* was not an isolated event, but
rather the beginning of a rich and complex sequence (which can
only be briefly outlined here) leading to *Signifiants de l'informel*.
Between these two exhibitions, there was a concerted effort by
New York dealers to promote American painting in Paris.[11] A
first exhibition at the Galerie Maeght in April 1947 presented
the protégés of the Kootz Gallery: Romane Bearden, William
Baziotes, Byron Browne, Carl Holty, Robert Motherwell, and
Adolph Gottlieb. Then in January 1949, Maeght went on to exhibit the work of Hans Hoffmann. Mathieu, who was very well
informed about the New York avant-garde, detected some similarities between Parisian "Informel" and New York "Abstract
Expressionism." He contacted some New York galleries to organize an exhibition for both tendencies, but this did not materialize until March 1951.

With the help of Tapié and Alfonso Ossorio, Mathieu organized an exhibition at the Galerie Nina Dausset, rue du Dragon,
with the revealing title of *Véhémences confrontées*, where works
by de Kooning and Pollock, in addition to those by Riopelle,
Bryen, Wols, Hartung, and Mathieu, were exhibited.[12] This impressive list shows not only to what extent Riopelle was involved
in the art scene, but also why he was the ideal person to bring
McEwen up to date on the recent history of French painting and
the stakes involved.

In December 1951 McEwen saw Riopelle's solo exhibition at
Studio Paul Fachetti, rue de Lille. Unprepared, but receptive
and open-minded, since he had received no academic painterly
training, McEwen was quietly taken by surprise by the course
of the artistic problems that had emerged from the Paris-New

York-Montreal triangle. He slowly but resolutely began his painting, a process which was presented to him as a never-ending exploration.

Given the context, the *Signifiants de l'informel* exhibition in November 1951 was unusually important. The variety of trends shown exemplified its attempt to focus attention on the diversity of new solutions—I dare say "healthy" diversity, especially if we situate this exhibition in the Parisian postwar artistic community, which seemed doomed to the perpetual and unoriginal exploitation of post-Cubist formulas. It also attests to "a passion for apparently haphazard textural effects that had taken hold among a number of artists in the early 1950s."[13] The result was not always first-rate, but the intention to make texture as important as color and form was significant, and would later bear fruit. In any case, McEwen made his debut in Paris in December. He participated in a group show at the Galerie Nina Dausset along with Riopelle, Serpan, Sam Francis, and other artists, whose names have been lost.[14]

A careful study of McEwen's 1952 paintings shows that the slow transformation taking place in his work cannot adequately be explained by the mechanistic notion of influence. The transition from his first Paris paintings to his last is unmistakable. At first, his paintings were closely linked to certain works by Borduas (plant-like motifs on an indeterminate background) and then they evolved into a more personal style, in which the field effect is already obvious and where the absence of a focus gives the painting a clearly "all-over" impression. This transition may appear abrupt, especially considering that the new effect obtained in his last Paris painting was performed on the back of a canvas from the previous series. A comparison of these two paintings, one at the beginning and the other at the end of his stay in Paris, illustrates just how crucial this year of work and contact with other artists proved to be for McEwen. An examination of a series of inks on paper done during his summer holiday at Belle-Ile-en-mer (Bretagne) shows that these small works played a decisive role in his abandonment of reference to landscape, or at least to plant-like motifs. A network of black India ink blobs is superimposed on a network of brightly colored ink blobs. Unlike Riopelle's use of black in his watercolors of the same period,[15] McEwen's is in no way linear. McEwen creates instead a rhythmical reunion of the two networks. This rhythm is here purely formal, since the artist no longer felt the desire to transcribe the movement of waves.

Starting with this discovery, the ability to find a rhythmical expression for colored pigment, McEwen began a series of canvases in Paris that fall, the last of which was the blue *Sans Titre*. He worked on four coats of superimposed pigment—first white, then yellow, red, and finally blue. Using a palette knife, he imprinted a direction on the thick colored pigment. These paintings were the first of McEwen's works in which he achieved an all-over composition. Unlike Riopelle's works of the same year, they are not covered with splashes and drips. McEwen had no affinity for this form of controlled yet apparently haphazard work, although he did see Pollock's first exhibition in Paris, organized by Tapié at Studio Paul Fachetti, which ran from March 7 to 31.[16] It presented a group of fifteen works painted between 1948 and 1951, including the very large *One: Number 31*, now in the collection of the Museum of Modern Art in New York. Obviously, contact with a body of work does not necessarily result in adoption of all of its elements. The only similarity in the work of McEwen, Riopelle, and Pollock was the importance they accorded to large scale for obtaining the desired field effect.

Other exhibitions in 1952 contributed to an understanding of the importance of format. In January, also at Studio Paul Fachetti, Mathieu showed five very large canvases, which he painted right in the gallery the night before the *vernissage*—in less than forty-five minutes.[17] Despite assertions to the contrary, McEwen never actually met Mathieu. The role he might have played in McEwen's development must therefore be minimized.

Such was not the case, however, with Sam Francis. Francis was introduced to McEwen by Riopelle in February 1952 at his first solo exhibition in Paris, held at the Galerie Nina Dausset.[18] Francis showed some of the works he had done since his arrival in Paris in 1950: *Red and Pink*, in which the use of pastel tones is indicative of a radical change from the bright colors of his Berkeley period and a transition to the use of a more subdued light; and the *White Paintings* series, which are not monochromes, although they are often described as such. A more careful examination of their surface reveals the presence of light browns, grays, and pale yellows. The overall whiteness is, however, predominant.

Francis came not from the New York scene, but directly from the West Coast, where he had studied under Mark Rothko and Clyfford Still at the California School of Fine Arts from 1947 to 1950.[19] His early Paris canvases already present some very advanced proposals regarding tensions between

Jean McEwen, Untitled
*(*Dernière toile de
Paris*), 1952, oil on*
canvas, 37¾ x 50¼ in.
Private collection.

the framing edge and a central surface composed of translucent "cellular" elements. As explained by Robert Buck:

> Francis'[s] early works were harbingers of American color field painting in Europe. These paintings appear to be a window onto another, more vast world of which we are only seeing a detail. Movement beyond the borders of the canvas is implicit in each of them, for the loose, stained forms moving across the surface at their own strange cadence do not react to the arbitrary limits set forth by the size of the canvas. Francis shows an early interest in activity at the edge and sometimes, pockets of intruding color ranging from soft blue to red appear to hover at the edge of the composition.[20]

McEwen was being drawn into a complex network, through which he was introduced to the different possibilities inherent in modernist painting: the field effect in large-scale work, dripping, and, most importantly, painting reduced to its component elements: color, surface, frame, size. McEwen was on friendly terms with Riopelle and often met with Sam Francis, who was glad to discuss his painting, and Georges Duthuit, a common friend of both artists. Although Duthuit, the son-in-law of Matisse, was one of the most demanding art critics in Paris, this did not prevent him from being one of the first defenders of North American painting in France.[21] The small group met at the Café du Dragon, opposite the Galerie Nina Dausset.

If we now reexamine overall pictorial production in 1952, we cannot but notice that McEwen's Paris paintings have little in common with any he may have seen. We are therefore faced with a problem more complex than the establishment of artistic relationships. After his return to Montreal, it took him three years to fully assimilate his Paris experience. Strangely enough, this led him back to Borduas's style between 1953 and 1955.[22] In other words, he still had to fully explore the extent of his own painterly problems, until he was able to come to terms with them. It was not until this realization that the cultural concepts that had permeated his work were able to resurface. Paul Klee once wrote about the "difficulty involved in converting *nature* into one's own style."[23] In the context of modernist painting, McEwen may well have talked about the difficulty involved in converting *painting* into his own style. This is what he attempted in a series of colored inks presented at the *Espace 55* exhibition at the Montreal

Jean McEwen, Prin-
temps, *1952, oil on
canvas, 29¾ x 24¾ in.
Private collection.*

Museum of Fine Arts in February 1955. In these works, he recaptured the all-over composition of his last Paris paintings. The digression into the style of Borduas was definitely over.

Rupture: The Monochrome Series

In the summer of 1955, McEwen abandoned the palette knife to paint directly with his hands. For two years, his attitude was destructive. He covered his earlier paintings with white or pale yellow paint. Few works escaped this process. By comparing *La Corrida* (1954) with *Pierres du moulin no. 1* (1955),[24] both exactly the same size, we can appreciate the gap between the two procedures. The application of white to the whole surface suppresses the figure/ground relationship, while allowing the colors in relief to show through. They are then recomposed in a fine network of lines, dividing the surface into discrete rectangles. A light yellow is then applied to balance the composition.

It was also in 1955 that he produced an isolated canvas whose conception was astonishing for the period: *Blanc marges orangées*, now in the collection of the Musée du Québec. With its rectangles concealed beneath a thick coating of grayish and greenish white, it resembles *Pierres du moulin*. However, it is the presence of the orange margins, never before seen in his work, that mark this painting as a turning point. They introduce *verticals*,[25] which became a recurrent pictorial element, work on the framing edge and its visual tension with a central plane, and the potential for the underlying layers of color to show through.

The next series, *Jardin de givre* (1956), represents a real breakthrough in McEwen's progression toward a more resolutely North American style of painting. This would undoubtedly have been impossible without the now-distant memory of the exceptional circumstances that allowed him to simultaneously discover the all-over style, large-scale work (Pollock, Riopelle), and the luminous effect of Sam Francis's *White Paintings* when he was in Paris. After a four-year interval, *Jardin de givre* is evidence of McEwen's newly acquired pictorial maturity, which allowed the artist to establish his *own*, completely personal style of painting, which fits in somewhere between the two main groups of nonfigurative painters on the Montreal art scene at the time: the Automatists and the Neo-Plasticians.

In the spring of 1956 Molinari showed a series of ten small black and white paintings at his new gallery, L'Actuelle,[26] as evi-

Jean McEwen, Jardin de givre, *1955, oil on canvas, 82½ x 54½ in. Private collection.*

dence of his adoption of a "hard-edge" style. The next exhibition was the series of large-scale *Panneaux* in pure unmodulated colors by Claude Tousignant.[27]

In November 1956 McEwen had his first one-man show at L'Actuelle. He presented a group of paintings that were extremely significant because of their size structure, and monochromatic nature. The exhibition included *Les Pierres du moulin* (1955), *Jardin de givre* (1956), *Rouge sur blanc* (1956), and *Blanc marges orangées* (1955). In nonfigurative art circles in Montreal, the importance of these works stemmed from the use of large-scale canvas, the all-over treatment of a modulated color (white or red), and the presence of fine, flowing, fragile vertical lines, creating an alternative to the rectilinear works of the Neo-Plasticians.

The difference between his works and those of the Automatists was immediately perceived by the critic Rodolphe de Repentigny:

> Since his last solo exhibition, the painting of Jean McEwen has, in appearances at least, undergone a radical change. Unquestionably, his work is no longer a reflection of Borduas'[s] style, which inspired many of his earlier paintings. His paintings and watercolours presently being shown at the Galerie L'Actuelle all exhibit the same approach— both more disciplined and less conventional than any other Montreal artist. The paintings contain few traces of the improvised structures so dear to contemporary artists.[28]

This is quite a compliment, considering that de Repentigny was one of the Plasticians' theoreticians. The rupture with Automatist painting was so radical that Agnes Lefort refused to exhibit McEwen's works, considering that his concept of painting went well beyond what she wanted to defend.

Lefort's attitude may be surprising, especially since she exhibited Borduas's work, but it is indicative of the insecure position of abstract art in the Montreal cultural milieu. Before passing judgment on the forms of nonfigurative art that appeared in the 1950s, and especially before reducing them to mere imports of issues developed by American artists, it is important to situate them in the social, cultural, and political context of Quebec at the time.

Maurice Duplessis and his Union Nationale party had been in power since 1944. Their policies were extremely conservative, including those regarding art and culture. According to Marie Carani:

> The Duplessis officialdom did not encourage nonfigurative pictorial research. In the early 1950s, the representational dictatorship was still victorious, refusing to have anything to do with any form of abstract painting. Louis Belzile recalls this period: "All public places, all official places, like museums, galleries, everything that was art, everything that was associated with the arts, was inaccessible to us."[29]

We must also clarify the position of the left, because since the publication of Max Kozloff's article "American Painting During the Cold War" in 1973, denunciations of the apparent neutrality of American painting in the 1950s by representatives of social art history escalated.[30] As Lintel and others note:

> The postwar period was a very difficult one for the Quebec left. Since many of their positions and demands had been adopted by neo-liberals and reformist neo-nationalists, they were forced to either become more radical or to ally themselves with reformist groups. The left viewed both possibilities as a form of marginalization. The international situation also worked against them. The Progressive Labour Party was particularly hard hit by the new wave of anti-Communism that occurred as a result of the Cold War (1946–56) and the Korean War (1950–53). In Canada Communists were tried and convicted for espionage after the Gouzenko affair in 1946. In Quebec the Duplessis government renewed its all-out offensive against "agents of Moscow," joined by the clergy, nationalist groups, and trade unions. At the same time, Quebec Communists were divided in their reaction to the position taken by their federal party, which, in its struggle against American imperialism, wholeheartedly supported centralism, federalism, and Canadian nationalism. . . . Finally, in 1956, Khrushchev's revelations about the horrors of Stalinism and the invasion of Hungary by the U.S.S.R. demoralized party activists and marked, for all intents and purposes, the suspension of Communist activities in Quebec for a decade.[31]

Under these circumstances, merely producing or defending nonfigurative painting placed people in a marginal position, no matter what their political allegiance. One must never lose sight of this fact when discussing painting in Quebec. In fact, Pierre Théberge's comment about Molinari's involvement in L'Actuelle can be extended to cover all nonfigurative artists in Montreal:

> Even at that time, the opening of a gallery would not have been an exceptional event, except that Molinari committed himself to exhibiting nonfigurative paintings exclusively. This was an important commitment for the circle, at a time when nonfigurative art was a culturally progressive force and served as a manifesto against oppressive traditions. The conditions described in the *Refus global* had not changed fundamentally.[32]

In 1956 there was also a particularly animated debate between Noel Lajoie and Rodolphe de Repentigny, the art critics for *Le Devoir* and *La Presse*. Lajoie systematically rejected the Plasticians' painting; de Repentigny defended it.[33] In retrospect, this debate seems to have preoccupied art historians so much that they missed the importance of McEwen's 1956 exhibition at L'Actuelle. He is usually relegated to the catch-all category of "Post-Automatists." An important point to note is that critics at the time were familiar with American painting. Lajoie, for example, commenting on a group exhibition at L'Actuelle in February 1956, viewed the works of Sam Francis as exemplary, for " 'the strictly abstract function' of the various pictorial elements allows the artist to achieve 'pure painting' i.e. the 'most avant-garde' forms of painting."[34] It must also be pointed out that the possibility of comparing the artistic trends of Montreal and New York was a *positive* factor, since it was the best means of determining the *avant-garde quality* of a painting. As Lajoie commented about the group exhibition organized on Saint Helen's Island by l'Association des artistes non-figuratifs de Montréal, "One of the most pleasant surprises in the exhibition . . . is to see the growing importance of American painting in the eyes of our young painters. There isn't a single famous New York painter who does not have a disciple here."[35]

What can one say about the incongruity of such a position— needing the American art world as a model of avant-garde art, to use it against the oppressive conservatism in Quebec at the time? The ideology of nonfigurative painting in Montreal was one of liberation, not one of neutrality or anguish. It must always be seen as implicitly political, because of the context in which it emerged. But the nature of this political position is specific to Montreal and the way in which the artists viewed their relationship to the New York art world. Paradoxically, it was considered more important to be liberated and avant-garde than to be critical of American ideology. Being marginal within the Quebec social and cultural milieu was the apex of a political stance on art.

Translated by Helena Scheffer

Notes

1.

This exhibition, organized by Michel Tapié, included Jean Fautrier, Jean Dubuffet, Henri Michaux, Georges Mathieu, Jean-Paul Riopelle, and Jaroslav Serpan. The importance of this exhibition will be discussed elsewhere in this paper.

2.

Before going to Paris, Riopelle made a trip to New York with Claude Gauvreau and Françoise Lespérance, possibly in 1945. François-Marc Gagnon suggests that the trip took place in 1944, in which case they would have seen the Motherwell exhibition at the Peggy Guggenheim Gallery. He also reports that Riopelle visited Ozenfant and the Galerie Pierre Matisse, where he saw the Chagalls, and that he also offered his own works. The offer was declined (F.-M. Gagnon, "New York as Seen from Montreal by Paul-Emile Borduas and the Automatists, 1943–1953," this volume). Contrary to what D. Burnett wrote in Contemporary Canadian Art (Edmonton: Hurtig, 1983, pp. 26–27), Riopelle was unable to see any Pollocks during his trip to New York.

3.

F.-M. Gagnon, P.-E. Borduas (Montreal: Fides, 1978), pp. 205–206.

4.

Letter from F. Leduc to Borduas, cited by Gagnon, ibid., p. 219.

5.

Fernand Leduc worked in Paris from 1947 to 1953.

6.

Bernard Ceysson, "À propos des années cinquante: tradition et modernité," in Vingt-cinq ans d'art en France, 1960–1985 (Paris: Larousse, 1986), p. 50.

7.

Cited by Jean Laude, "Problèmes de la peinture en Europe et aux Etats-Unis, 1944–1951," in Art et Idéologies (Université de Saint-Etienne, 1978), p. 54.

8.

Ibid., p. 57.

9.

Georges Mathieu, De la révolte à la renaissance (Paris: Idées/Gallimard, 1972), pp. 47–49).

10.

For this detailed chronology, see the Paris-Paris 1937–1957 exhibition catalogue (Paris: Centre Georges Pompidou, 1981), pp.

220–233. Also pertinent are Laude, "Problèmes," pp. 9–87; Mathieu, De la révolte, pp. 47–86, and Ceysson, "A propos," pp. 9–62.

11.

Serge Guilbaut, How New York Stole the Idea of Modern Art (Chicago: University of Chicago Press, 1983).

12.

See the Paris-New York exhibition catalogue (Paris: Centre Georges Pompidou, 1977), pp. 514–517. Meanwhile, Riopelle profited by a one-man show, also at the Galerie Nina Dausset, in March 1949. It is important to mention that the Pollock painting he was able to see in 1951 was Number 8, done in 1950. It would also be interesting to verify the following apparently innocuous statement by Pierre Schneider in the Jean-Paul Riopelle, 1946–1977 exhibition catalogue (Paris: Centre Georges Pompidou, 1981), p. 88: "Two brief encounters in 1955 with Jackson Pollock, whose works he did not know until 1949, when he saw them reproduced in Life magazine." (I would like to thank F.-M. Gagnon for having brought this text to my attention.) Schneider strives, no

doubt correctly, to
prove the difference in
the intent of the works
of the two artists. But
has he not unwittingly
given us the key to the
mystery? In its August
8, 1949, issue, Life
magazine published an
article, accompanied by
a number of photo-
graphs of the artist at
work, entitled, "Jack-
son Pollock: Is he the
Greatest Living Ameri-
can Painter?" Annette
Cox, in her thesis Art
as Politics (Ann Arbor:
UMI Research Press,
1982) provides a de-
tailed analysis of these
photographs and this
article on pages 83–94.
She writes: "Despite
these public misconcep-
tions about Pollock's
art, the photographs
and written descriptions
of Pollock's personality
clearly captured the at-
tention of writers and
other artists. It is per-
haps with this narrow
audience that Pollock's
photographs had the
greatest impact"
(p. 90). The fact that
Riopelle may have bor-
rowed from Pollock's
techniques in no way
lessens the merit of his
painting. But in the
context of our examina-
tion of the circulation
of ideologies between
New York, Paris, and
Montreal, a closer
analysis is surely called
for, especially since
McEwen recalls having

seen sticks, cans of
paint, and drips on
the walls around the
canvases drying in
Riopelle's Paris studio.

13.
H. Damisch, Fenêtre
jaune cadmium (Paris:
Seuil, 1984), p. 135.

14.
According to McEwen,
the two paintings shown
at this exhibition were
lost or destroyed.

15.
McEwen spent his vaca-
tion at Belle-Ile-en-mer
with Riopelle and his
family. These inks owe
their inspiration to ab-
stract motifs at the bot-
tom of the sea. The
differences prove that
the proximity of the two
artists was not enough
to justify formal anal-
ogies (superficial ones
in any case) that some
critics have found in
their work.

16.
See the Paris-New
York exhibition cata-
logue, pp. 537–541,
which includes a list of
the paintings exhibited
and Tapié's explana-
tory text.

17.
Ibid., p. 226.

18.
An exhibition entitled
Regards sur la peinture
américaine was being
held at the same time at
the Galerie de France
(ibid., p. 227). The list

of works is impressive,
but, oddly enough, few
art historians mention
it.

19.
Critics have the habit of
maintaining, a little
hastily perhaps, that
Rothko and Still "in-
fluenced" McEwen. It is
therefore important to
note that this influence,
if in fact there was any,
was indirect, in that it
went through the paint-
ing of Sam Francis,
which was free of these
"influences" by the
time McEwen saw it.
McEwen had no direct
contact with Rothko's
painting until much
later, at MoMA in the
early 1960s.

20.
Robert T. Buck Jr.,
"The Paintings of Sam
Francis," in Sam
Francis Paintings,
1947–1972 (Buffalo:
Albright-Knox Gallery,
1972), p. 17.

21.
See Georges Duthuit,
L'Image en souffrance
(Paris: G. Fall Ed.,
1961).

22.
In 1953, when Mc-
Ewen's works were ex-
hibited at the Foyer de
l'art et du livre, an
Ottawa bookstore, critic
Carl Weiselberger
wrote, "My immediate
reaction to Mr. Mc-
Ewan's [sic] oils was
a one word explo-

sion too: 'Borduas',"
Ottawa Citizen,
November 4, 1953.
R. *de Repentigny's com-*
ments in 1954 were in
the same vein: "It is
rather strange to see
that his art is evolv-
ing in the same direc-
tion as Borduas," in
"Jean McEwen redou-
ble d'audace," La
Presse, *Montreal,*
March 31, 1954.

23.
Paul Klee, Journal
(Paris: Grasset, 1959),
p. 198.

24.
In this period, all of his
paintings were untitled.
It was not until later
that McEwen named
this first series, to com-
memorate the place
where they were
painted, the Vieux
Moulin in Saint
Eustache. The title of
the Jardin de givre
series was inspired by
the title of a poem by
Nelligan.

25.
McEwen recalls having
previously introduced a
unique central vertical
in one of his Pierres du
Moulin *paintings, and*
having subsequently
painted over it. At that
time in Montreal, he
could not have heard of
Barnett Newman, who
did not exhibit his work
between 1951 and 1958.

26.
Molinari opened this
gallery in May 1955,
with the help of
Fernande Saint-Martin.

27.
F.-M. Gagnon,
"Quebec Painting,
1953–56, a Turning
Point," Arts Canada
(February–March
1973), p. 50.

28.
Rodolphe de Repen-
tigny, "La peinture de
Jean McEwen: discre-
tion, audace, rafinne-
ment," La Presse,
Montreal, November 16,
1956.

29.
Marie Carani,
"L'Oeuvre critique et
plastique de Rodolphe
de Repentigny," M.A.
thesis, "Université du
Quebec à Montréal,
1984, p. 56. This thesis
should be required
reading for anyone
studying the Montreal
intellectual community
during the 1950s.
Carani also examines
the art magazines, crit-
ics, the debates at the
time, etc.

30.
The article by Kozloff,
as well as the principal
articles on this debate,
are reprinted in Pollock
and After, *ed. Francis*
Frascina (New York:
Harper & Row, 1985).

31.
Paul André Linteau,
René Durocher, Jean-
Claude Robert,
François Ricard, Le
Québec depuis 1930
(Montreal: Boréal Ex-
press, 1986), pp. 334–
335.

32.
Pierre Théberge, Guido
Molinari *(Ottawa:*
Galerie nationale du
Canada, 1976), p. 18.

33.
Carani, "Rodolphe de
Repentigny," pp.
101–109.

34.
Ibid., p. 98. The paint-
ing by Francis shown in
this exhibition belonged
to Gilles Corbeil. It now
hangs in the Montreal
Museum of Fine Arts.

35.
In Le Devoir, *March*
1956, cited in ibid.,
pp. 98–99.

New York as Seen from Montreal by Paul-Emile Borduas and the Automatists, 1943–1953

François-Marc Gagnon

In this paper I would like to show how New York was perceived by the French-Canadian painter Paul-Emile Borduas and his group, the Automatists, from 1943 to 1953, that is to say, from Borduas's first brief visit to the city in 1943 to his final departure for New York in 1953. It is clear that, during this period, Paris remained for everybody, including Borduas and his friends, the only center of modern art. But New York was more accessible, had the lure of the French *exilés'* presence during the war, and was certainly visited more often by Montrealers than Paris.

Borduas visited New York at the beginning of May 1943. It is difficult to be more specific. The pretext of the trip was probably academic, since Jean-Marie Gauvreau, the director of the Ecole du Meuble where Borduas taught, wrote a letter of introduction on his behalf.

If we do not know the exact dates of the sojourn in New York, at least, and this is more important, we have an idea of what Borduas saw (or wanted to see?) from the exhibition catalogues he brought back, which are preserved in his papers.[1] Of course, one has to be prudent with this kind of assumption. For instance, he had in his papers the catalogue of Matta's *Drawings* show at the Julien Levy Gallery, but I doubt that he actually saw the show, scheduled from March 16 to April 5, since we can establish that Borduas was still in Montreal on April 19. It is at that date that he sold the famous *Viol aux confins de la matière*, (1943) to Dr. Albert Jutras.[2] At least we can imagine that he entered the gallery, which was then at 42 East 57th Street. And, I think, we can establish that his visit to the gallery coincided with the opening, on May 5, of an exhibition of Max Ernst's collages and recent drawings. Borduas had in his library an English translation by Hugh Chisholm of *Les Malheurs des immortels* (1943), a collaborative volume with collages by Max Ernst and poems by Paul Eluard, originally published in 1922. Now, we learn in *Art News* that "coincident with the publication of *Misfortunes of the Immortals* by [Max Ernst] and Paul Eluard . . . [there was] a presentation of his celebrated *collages* and latest drawings at the Julien Levy Gallery."[3] It is tempting to think, of course, that Borduas was there at the right time and purchased his copy of *Misfortunes of the Immortals*, with the Matta catalogue, at the gallery.

If he saw Ernst's show at Julien Levy, he could very well have seen the Dali show of *Portraits* presented at Knoedler, 14 East 57th Street, from April 14 to May 5. At least he had the catalogue in his papers. He knew of Dali, of course, but he did not much appreciate either his art or his personality. This completely venal show must have confirmed his doubts about the painter.

From there it was no problem to see an Abraham Rattner show at Paul Rosenberg's Gallery, since the two galleries were neighbors. The show was scheduled from May 3 to May 29, 1943.[4] At this time Rosenberg also represented Marsden Hartley and Max Weber, according to Sam Kootz,[5] who nevertheless chose Rattner for the cover of his 1943 book, *New Frontiers in American Painting.*

On that side of the street, Borduas also entered the Gallery of Modern Art, 18 East 57th Street, but was disappointed by what he saw there: a first one-woman show of a pupil of Kuniyo-shi, Helen Ratkai, scheduled May 3–22, 1943. Her main subject matter was "girls and flowers," according to *Art Digest*,[6] or "acrobats and . . . rather *outré* young women," according to *Art News.*[7] "Faible" wrote Borduas on the catalogue. It is curious that in her "Fifty-Seventh Street in Review," Helen Boswell of *The Art Digest* entitled her article "Strength of Helen Ratkai."

Borduas then crossed the street and saw at André Seligmann Gallery, situated at 15 East 57th Street, an exhibition by a Robert T. Francis, scheduled May 5–31, 1943, that was not much better. "Pas intéressant," he noted on the catalogue. Maude Riley, in her "Fifty-Seventh Street in Review" article,[8] tells us that "Robert T. Francis is a textile manufacturer who, at an advanced age, found great happiness with paints." It seems that he did not

made to New York with Jean-Paul Riopelle and his fiancée Françoise Lespérance: "When I came to the Museum of Modern Art in New York, I felt as if I was entering the Garden of Eden. At that time, one could not see in New York works as progressive as Riopelle's; Motherwell, for instance, was painting then some kind of floor tilings that looked to me very *dépassés*."[18] Gauvreau was not sure of the date of the trip, recalling only "in 1945, I believe." Could it have been in November 1944? If so, they could have seen Motherwell's first mature one-man show at Peggy Guggenheim's gallery (October 24–November 11, 1944).[19] *Robert Motherwell: Paintings, Papier Collés, Drawings* was accompanied by a catalogue, prefaced by James Johnson Sweeney, a name more known in Montreal than Motherwell's because of his involvement in the book on Fernand Léger published in Montreal in 1945.[20] What Gauvreau called *carrelages* (tiling, tile pavement, flooring) were probably paintings like *The Little Spanish Prison* (1941) or collages like *Pancho Villa, Dead and Alive* (1943), in which the Cubist grid is indeed important.

Gauveau also mentioned a visit to Amédée Ozenfant, for whom Le Corbusier had built a studio in Paris in 1922–23 and who had opened his own School of Modern Art in New York in 1938. How did Riopelle and Gauvreau know about the Purist painter? Probably through his book, *Foundations of Modern Art*, the French edition of which dates from 1928 and was circulated in Montreal during the war. They were sorry to have met him. Ozenfant looked at some inks that Riopelle had brought along and told him that since his works reflected no precise intention, it was impossible to comment on them. It is not surprising then that Claude added, "His comments seemed to me singularly poor in comparison to the ones I was used to hearing from Borduas."

Riopelle went finally to Pierre Matisse Gallery, apparently less to see the *Chagall. Recent Works. Paintings & Gouaches* exhibition, his second show since his arrival in America (to November 30, 1944), than to show examples of his own works to the owner. Matisse was not impressed. (I have often thought that this first rejection has figured in Riopelle's decision to settle in Paris instead of New York.)

Though we cannot be sure when Riopelle went to New York with Gauvreau, the fact that Fernand Leduc met Breton in New York on Easter morning, "à l'heure de la messe," notes Teyssèdre devilishly,[21] April 1, 1945, is much better established. In other words, what neither he nor Borduas had succeeded in doing in 1943 was accomplished two years later.[22] According to Teyssèdre,[23] in this trip Leduc visited the Museum of Modern Art and a few exhibitions, including those of Gorky, Matta, Donati, and Tanguy.

The Gorky exhibition at the Julien Levy Gallery from March 6 to March 31, 1945, is well known. It was Gorky's first one-man show at this gallery. According to one recent scholar, "In his 1945 show Gorky exhibited mainly his 'veiled' paintings of 1942–1944, including *Water of the Flowery Mill, How My Mother's Embroidered Apron Unfolds in My Life, The Pirate I, One Year of the Milkweed, Love of the New Gun* and *The Sun, the Dervish in the Tree.* Although these paintings are today considered among Gorky's most original and provocative works of the period, they met with negative and even hostile criticism at this show."[24] The catalogue carried a preface by André Breton.

Matta was showing at the same time (March 12–31) at the Pierre Matisse Gallery. His show was entitled *1944–Matta–1945,* indicating that he presented only new paintings, among which *Onyx of Electra* (1944), *Le Poëte* (1944–45), and *X Space and the Ego* (1945) are the best known. It is with this exhibition that it became clear that Matta had "reintroduced the human figure" into painting, a thing for which Breton was to reproach him later.[25]

Enrico Donati was showing at Durand-Ruel, 12 East 57th (to March 31). *Art News* reproduced *Le Feu Saint-Elme et le feu follet* and mentioned *Oracle* and *La Métamorphose* as being in the show.[26] I do not, however, know what Tanguy show Leduc could have seen at that time, unless he saw the Tanguys included in a group show through April 11 at the Whitney devoted to *European Artists in America.*

For Leduc, no doubt, the better painter of the lot was Matta. He could not understand Breton's enthusiasm for Gorky. Breton told him that Gorky was the first Surrealist to go back to nature, "treating her as a cryptogram," revealing "the very rhythm of life," but to no avail. Leduc still asked how nature could even be considered in a Surrealist perspective. Was it not rather Matta, probing the inner self, who had the genuine Surrealist approach? Leduc was right. One knows that, except for his friendship with Breton, Gorky had not much to do with Surrealism. He finally rejected it, as the idea of great art coming from the unconscious was competely alien to him. Among the Automatists, Françoise Sullivan had the most successful contact with New York. She was also in New York in the spring of 1945, and she was staying at Louise Renaud's apartment. As a ballet dancer, she was interested in finding in New York a studio that offered training more akin to her aspirations than the classical ballet she had learned up to then. She finally found the Franzisca Boas Studio and decided to enroll for the next season. In the meantime, she spent the summer with the other members of the group on the Charbonneau farm in Saint-Hilaire. She returned to New York in the fall, and in January 1946 she even exhibited the works of Borduas, Leduc, Mousseau, Riopelle, Pierre Gauvreau, and Guy Viau at the studio. (It was in fact the first group show of the Automatists. It preceded by a few months the one on Amherst Street in Montreal, April 20–29, 1946.) With the help of Louise Renaud, she contacted Pierre Matisse (he must have been fed up with "ces Canadiens") and showed him the paintings of her friends. Once again, he was not impressed.[27] In fact, Sullivan seems to have been more eager to make her friends known in New York than to get informed about the New York scene.

To tell the truth, Montreal artists thought very little of American art at the time. In fact, when Borduas had a new occasion to express an opinion on American art in general, it was a negative one. The occasion was provided by Josephine Hambleton, who initiated, on December 4, 1946, an exchange of letters that was to last many years. At the time Hambleton was working for the Canadian Information Service (Latin America Section) and wanted to write articles on Canadian artists to be published in South America. When she contacted Borduas, she had already visited Henry Eveleigh, Marian Scott, and a few teachers from the Art Association of Montreal[28] (she mentions Moe Reinblatt in a subsequent letter to Borduas).

She had discovered Borduas's work at the Contemporary Arts Society exhibition at the Dominion Gallery, Montreal, November 16–30, 1946. At that show Borduas presented *La Fustigée* (1941–46) and another painting less easy to identify: a *Composition*, says Emile-Charles Hamel,[29] which is probably *6.46* or *Sous l'eau* (1946), whose location is unknown.[30] She was fascinated by what she saw and would even acquire a Borduas the year after: *7.47* or *Quand mes rêves partent en guerre*.[31] She was also perplexed. She thought Borduas stood for "abstraction pure," for "estétique pure," in contrast to Eveleigh and Scott, who, she said, used abstract shapes to express ideas. Borduas evidently missed her point and simply replied that he was striving for the "purest automatism possible."

In her first letter, she had made a curious remark about veterans not liking abstract painting. Borduas did not pay it much

attention; but, in a letter of December 13, she returned to the
subject more insistently:

> When I asked you why the veterans seem to feel no sym-
> pathy with abstract painting, it was because I wanted to
> know if the reason was that this group, who more than any
> other has felt the shock of the social problems of our time,
> could not find in abstract painting any reflection of their
> anxieties.

This is certainly a less banal question, and Borduas's answer is
much less whimsical than his earlier ones.[32] After a few lines
on the necessity of distinguishing between art and politics, he
remarks:

> Their anxieties are social, not pictorial. This is why, per-
> haps, I witness among them a political evolution, not a
> plastic one. . . . The wish to see in art the expression of an
> immediate social concern is felt more by British intellectuals
> to Socialism than by veterans. To be more specific, I have
> also noted this tendency in Diego Rivera, and, after him, in
> several Mexican painters. I have also found the same desire
> in publications about Russian painting and, generally, in the
> whole of American art. Needless to say, I have never felt in
> all this the rich sensation of the new. I consider all these
> works as futile, delusive, and unrefined. The pretensions of
> their producers are indefensible.

This long quotation reveals better than anything else what was
the perception of American art in Montreal, despite all the contacts with New York: not much better than Socialist Realism, a
little worse than the art of the Mexican muralists. Some of the
latter's works Borduas could have seen at the AAM in the show
Mexican Art Today.[33] He had the catalogue in his papers. I do
not know if he could (or did) read the introduction by Señor Luis
Cardoza y Aragón (written in Spanish but translated in English).
If he did, he would probably have been amazed by the "preten-
sion" of modern Mexican art to be the only actual alternative to
the "Escuela de Paris": "We may state that at the moment, there
are two universal movements in the field of plastic art, one in the
western world and one in the Americas, the former represented
by the School of Paris, the latter by the art of Mexico."[34]

While it is impossible to say in which publications Borduas

saw examples of Soviet art, publications on American art were quite accessible in Montreal. One could buy *Art News* or *The Art Digest* without problems at Eaton's in Montreal, and Borduas's close friends, such as Robert Elie, mention having purchased these magazines at the time. And, of course, the image of American art carried by these magazines was rather heavily weighted, if not toward Social Realism, at least toward American Scene paintings. Borduas probably lumped the two trends together.

Social Realism—in America, in Mexico, or in Russia—was spurned by Borduas because it rejected art as an end in itself and wanted to make it serve a cause. For Borduas, this was just a way to reduce art to mere illustrations of old political ideas, instead of granting it the power to transform human sensibilities and therefore making it the starting point in the chain reaction that ultimately brings political change. Art does not follow revolution; it foreshadows it. Politics is just the translation at the level of institutions of the profound "spiritual" transformation worked by art in the first place.[35] According to Borduas:

> One can follow in the French arts the premonitory signs of the French Revolution, becoming more and more evident from one century before its political realization. One finds the same clear signs à propos the Russian Revolution, much before its realization: in Russian art and in the creation of Marxism in 1857.[36] I have no doubt that the plastic revolution initiated by the School of Paris is the sign of a future revolution, which I ignore.[37]

By comparison, of course, Social Realism and American art were foreshadowing nothing of consequence. In Montreal then, light did not come from the south, but from the east!

Then, there was *Refus Global*, the manifesto Borduas wrote and published in 1948. The anti-Catholic stand of the manifesto led to Borduas's dismissal from the Ecole du Meuble. Quebec was no longer a good place to be, a good place to fight for new ideas. Everybody dreamed of exile. The luckier ones, like Leduc, Riopelle, and Marcelle Ferron, went to Paris. The less fortunate ones, like Borduas and Marcel Barbeau, dreamed of going less far and started to think of New York as a place to exhibit, if not yet to live.

One would think that in this new climate a certain openness to American art would develop. It was not the case. One sees Borduas, for instance, more and more eager to be in contact with

New York—he will finally go to live there in 1953—not as a place where great art was produced, but as a fantastic marketplace, where one could sell one's works without problems. All his contact after 1948, with Sweeney, with the officials of the Guggenheim Foundation, with Rose Fried of the Pinatotheca Gallery, had only one purpose: to find a way to show and see his work in New York. That is why when, at last, American art came to Montreal, nobody paid attention to it.

Laurier Lacroix[38] and Dennis Reid[39] have mentioned an exhibition entitled *Contemporary Paintings from Great Britain, the United States and France with Sculpture from the United States,* organized by the Art Gallery of Toronto (it was first shown there in November–December 1949), but shown at the Montreal Museum of Fine Arts, January 7–31, 1950. The list of works exhibited has to be handled with care. A photocopied note inserted in the catalogue indicates that many works were not presented in Montreal, "in this somewhat abbreviated travelling exhibition." For instance, no sculpture was included in the Montreal show. We can confirm, however, that Jackson Pollock's *Cathedral,* 1948 (no. 116 in the catalogue), Gorky's *The Calendars,* 1946–47 (no. 76), Gottlieb's *Amulets of Phoebus,* 1948 (no. 77), Rothko's *Vessels of Magic,* 1946 (no. 120), and Tomlin's *Tension by Moonlight,* 1948 (no. 134) were part of the show.

We are told in the "Foreword" to the catalogue[40] that the American works were chosen by a committee chaired by Lloyd Goodrich (of the Whitney) and composed of Dorothy Miller (of the MoMA), John I. H. Baur (of the Brooklyn Museum), and Douglas MacAgy, Director of the California School of Fine Arts in San Francisco. (An excellent committee, by the way. It is no surprise that their choice was so good.)

Reid seems to think that Borduas could not have missed the show and, if he saw it, could not have but been much impressed by it. I doubt both assumptions. In January 1950 Borduas was recovering from an appendectomy and an ulcer operation. He lived a rather secluded life in Saint-Hilaire, lacking, since his dismissal from the Ecole du Meuble, the incentive to go into Montreal as often as before.

More, I believe that his sympathy (not to say his prejudices) would have gone spontaneously to the French work, although the selection was much poorer, as France was represented, for instance, by Léger's *Papillons jaunes* (no. 176), an oil on canvas of modest size (36¼ x 28¾ in.), by *Femme, oiseau, étoile,* a watercolor by Míro (no. 184), *Le Faune au maillot violet,* a work on paper dated 1946 by Picasso (no. 187), and *La Sybille* by Rouault (no. 192), not to mention the Matisse of the MMFA, which was also part of the show. Big names, but. . . .

One thing is sure. When Borduas had already settled in New York and had exhibited his recent production at Agnès Lefort's Gallery in Montreal (October 12–26, 1954), Pierre Gauvreau, the brother of Claude and himself a painter belonging to the Automatist group, deplored his own ignorance of avant-garde American painting, feeling rightly that it could be the key to the visible change in Borduas's paintings since his move to New York. "We have completely ignored American avant-garde painting," Gauvreau wrote in 1954, and, he added, "Despite the proximity of the American metropolis, no valuable exhibition has come from New York."[41] If Gauvreau had seen *Contemporary Paintings* at the MMFA in 1950, he was not impressed enough to remember it four years after. He may, for all I know, not even have seen it.

It is when one attempts to reconstruct precisely the itineraries, the readings, the prejudices, of the French Canadian painters that one can give a factual basis to the problem of their perception of the New York School. As we have seen, this perception was negative. It was also misinformed—not only because it was negative, but also because of all the contingencies that we have tried to retrace in some details. To be appreciated, an art movement has not only to be regarded as important, but the works it has produced have to be seen.

Notes

1.
Borduas Archives,
Musée d'art contempo-
rain, Montreal, no. 47.
Will be referred to sub-
sequently as AB.

2.
See Borduas's Account
Book, item 73. AB no.
39.

3.
S.N., "Closeup of the
Dali Technique; or,
What Sitters Get for
Their Money," Art
News 42:5 (April 15–
30, 1943), p. 11, where
The Portrait of Marquis
George de Cuevas and
The Portrait of Mrs.
Ortis de Linares are re-
produced, with details;
this last painting is
noted as "included in
the show at Knoed-
ler's." Royal Cortissoz
in his review of the
show for The Herald
Tribune also mentioned
that "the tiny Geode-
sical Portrait of Gala
was part of the show."
Cortissoz's paper is
quoted in the next issue
of Art News, p. 20.

4.
[Maude] [Riley], "Re-
cent Paintings by Abra-
ham Rattner," The Art
Digest 17:16 (May 15,
1943), p. 16, illustrated
by Should One Paint
the Sky Muddy and
Black (if it really is the
title of this work!). The
reviewer also mentions
There Was Darkness

Over All the Land, A
Place Called Golgotha,
Hallucinations, Family
Wedding Day Portrait,
Springtime, and April
Showers among the
twelve paintings in this
show.

5.
Sam Kootz, New Fron-
tiers in American
Painting (New York,
1943).

6.
The Art Digest 17:15
(May 1, 1943), pp. 18–
19, with a black-and-
white reproduction of
Acrobats.

7.
Art News 42:7 (May
15–31, 1943), p. 22,
also illustrated with
Acrobats.

8.
The Art Digest 17:16
(May 15, 1943), p. 19;
no reproductions.

9.
Art News 42:7 (May
15–31, 1943), p. 23; no
reproductions.

10.
M[aude] R[iley],
"Zadkine, Sculptor,"
The Art Digest, 17:16
(May 15, 1943), p. 17;
The Maenades are re-
produced. Three other
pieces are mentioned:
Tatooed Dreamer,
Pomona, Juglers, all of
them declared to be re-
cent, "less than two
years—Zadkine having
come here from Paris

with no more to show
for his years of work
than a portfolio of
gouaches."

11.
B. Teyssèdre, "Fernand
Leduc, peintre et théori-
cien du surréalisme à
Montréal," La Barre du
jour (January–August
1969), pp. 224–270.

12.
See A. Beaudet, Fer-
nand Leduc. Vers les
îles de lumière. Ecrits
(1942–1980) (Montreal:
Hurtubise HMH, 1981),
pp. xxix–xxx. Teyssèdre
does not mention this
New York trip in the
summer of 1943. His
chronology of this sum-
mer (pp. 232–233) is
hard to reconcile with
the one proposed by
Beaudet and by Laurier
Lacroix, "Chronologie
des évènements reliés
au mouvement auto-
matiste: 1942–1955,"
Borduas et les automa-
tistes. Montréal. 1942–
1955 (Paris: Grand
Palais, 1971), p. 22,
who both state cor-
rectly, I believe, that
Leduc spent the months
of July and August with
Guy Viau in Saint-
Hilaire, after his trip to
New York. I suspect
Teyssèdre has given too
much weight to Viau's
souvenirs for this
detail.

13.
Beaudet, Leduc, p.
226.

14.
Ibid., where the answer to Breton is reproduced in toto.

15.
No one knows how she made this connection with Matisse. In her Une mémoire déchirée. Récit (Montreal: L'arbre HMH, 1978), she mentions that her father made frequent visits to New York and had connections with Columbia University. Could it be one piece of information useful to solve the problem?

16.
B. Teyssèdre, "Leduc," p. 250.

17.
Claude Gosselin, Françoise Sullivan. Rétrospective (Montreal: Musée d'art contemporain, 1981), p. 12.

18.
Claude Gauvreau, "L'épopée automatiste vue par un cyclope," La Barre du jour (January–August 1969), p. 58.

19.
See reviews by Clement Greenberg, The Nation 159:20 (November 11, 1944), pp. 598–599; Jon Stroup, Art Digest 19:3 (November 1, 1944), p. 16.

20.
M.-A. Couturier, Maurice Gagnon, S.

Giedion, François Hertel, S. M. Kootz, Fernand Léger and J. J. Sweeney, Fernand Léger. La Forme humaine dans l'espace (Montreal: Les Editions de l'arbre, 1945).

21.
Teyssèdre, "Leduc," p. 250.

22.
The paradox of course is that Breton himself was in Canada in the meantime—from August to October 1944—but he met neither Borduas nor any members of his group.

23.
B. Teyssèdre, p. 250.

24.
Melvin P. Lader, Arshile Gorky (New York: Abbeville Press, 1985), pp. 85, 89.

25.
See Dominique Bozo, Matta (Paris: Centre Georges Pompidou, Musée national d'art moderne, October 3– December 16, 1985), p. 278.

26.
Art News 44:3 (March 15–31, 1945), pp. 18–19.

27.
Gosselin, Sullivan, p. 13. In fact, Matisse was to open his door to Riopelle (and to Riopelle only) in 1953, after he managed to get

the backing of Breton and to exhibit in Paris, at Nina Dauset in 1949, at Facchetti in 1952, and at Pierre Loeb in 1953.

28.
Josephine Hambleton to Borduas, December 4, 1946. AB no. 130.

29.
Emile-Charles Hamel, "Grande variété de l'exposition de la SAC," Le Canada (Montreal), November 21, 1946.

30.
See F.-M. Gagnon, Paul-Emile Borduas. (1905–1960). Biographie critique et analyse de l'oeuvre (Montreal: Fides, 1978), pp. 196–198.

31.
Account book, item 128. AB no. 39.

32.
Letter not dated. At least, his first draft was not. The final copy, the one received by Hambleton, must have been. It is still in her possession, and all the efforts of Georges-André Bourassa to get it from her were vain.

33.
September 9 to October 3, 1943. The show originated in Philadelphia.

34.
Mexican Art Today (Philadelphia, 1943), p. 21.

35.
Combat, *the official journal of the Communist Party in Quebec at the time, should be examined with this problem in view.*

36.
Where did he get this date? The Manifesto, as everyone knows, is of 1848, not 1857. . . . Maybe it is a lapsus calami *for 1867, date of the publication of volume 1 of* The Capital.

37.
Borduas to Josephine Hambleton, AB no. 130.

38.
Lacroix, "Chronologie des évènements," p. 41.

39.
Dennis Reid, A Concise History of Canadian Painting *(Toronto: Oxford University Press, 1973), p. 231.*

40.
Contemporary Paintings from Great Britain, the United States and France *(Toronto, 1949), p. 3.*

41.
Pierre Gauvreau, "Borduas et le déracinement des peintres canadiens," Le Journal musical canadien *(November 1954), p. 6.*

Greenberg's Matisse and the Problem of Avant-Garde Hedonism

John O'Brian

On a rereading of the earlier essays I am struck again by the excellence of Eliot's prose—not so well maintained nowadays—and at the same time by the great amount of personal insecurity that was both concealed and revealed by the tone he established for himself.

Clement Greenberg, "T. S. Eliot: The Criticism, The Poetry," 1950[1]

This paper takes as its subject the place of Matisse in the criticism of Clement Greenberg, with emphasis on the decade from 1944 to 1954. The starting point of the investigation—as it must be in any serious investigation of Greenberg's thought—is the two early essays "Avant-Garde and Kitsch" (1939) and "Towards a Newer Laocoon" (1940). T. J. Clark has argued at length that it was in these essays that Greenberg established the main lines of his theory of art and of his critical practice.[2] If this is true, and the evidence is convincing, then we should expect the implications of those essays to be apparent in the criticism of the 1940s, the decade of Greenberg's greatest activity as a critic and the decade immediately subsequent to the essays' publication. In some of the most pointed and sustained criticism of the modern era, we find Greenberg in the 1940s attempting to measure his response to contemporary art while at the same time trying to reconcile that response with the political and aesthetic assumptions of the essays. That he was conscious that reconciliation

must often elude him only emphasizes the difficulty and
seriousness of his endeavor. It also underscores the note of uncertainty that one finds in his criticism of the period—an uncertainty, it may seem, comparable to the "personal insecurity" he
detected and admired in Eliot—as he struggled to judge and to
establish relative values for the art that confronted him.

Matisse's art played a pivotal role, I shall argue, in the establishment of those relative values. He became for Greenberg
"the greatest painter of our time,"[3] the one who reflected "the
most profound mood of the first half of the twentieth century."[4]
That Matisse came to hold this position for Greenberg is clear
from the most cursory reading of his criticism in any single year
from 1946 on. What also is clear, or seems so to me, is that
Greenberg's choice of Matisse as a paradigm for what contemporary art ought to hold valuable was, at least initially, contrary and
idiosyncratic. Notwithstanding the interest in Matisse reflected
by the mass media, by dealers and collectors, and by growing
numbers of museums and curators, the artists who would come
to be known as the Abstract Expressionists mostly held Matisse
in 1946 to be *passé*. Thus, not only were Greenberg's reasons for
elevating Matisse to a position of dominance in avant-garde culture supported, as I hope to show, by a more questioning and
complex appraisal of his art and its place in that culture than
those offered elsewhere, but in reaching his conclusions—conclusions notably at odds with prevailing critical views before and
during the war—he stood in opposition to the views of those
American artists he valued most highly.

For the sake of clarity, I will work through Greenberg's references to Matisse more or less chronologically. I will also try to
do justice to the complexity of his critical thought by incorporating longish passages from his writings into the text before sub-
jecting them to scrutiny.

Art in the Pastoral Mood

The first time Greenberg singles out Matisse for special mention
occurs in 1944. In a review of *Art in Progress*, the exhibition
mounted at the Museum of Modern Art to celebrate its fifteenth
anniversary, Greenberg writes with just a suggestion of surprise
that "Matisse is shown at his best, and the spectator is reminded,
as he needs to be, that the old Frenchman is the only living
painter to offer Picasso any competition as a dominating force."[5]
That is all. There is no discussion of what paintings represent

Matisse at his best or why the spectator needs to be reminded that "the old Frenchman" offers competition to Picasso. We do not have to go far, however, to discover the paintings Greenberg admired, for the exhibition catalogue informs us that Matisse's *Blue Window* (1913), *Window: Interior with Forget-Me-Nots* (1916), and *Odalisque with a Tambourine* (1926) were those exhibited.[6] It may be inferred then—an inference borne out by later criticism—that the work Greenberg admired included both the austere, architectonic paintings from 1913 to 1917 and the paintings of strongly modeled nudes in ornamented interiors from the mid-1920s.[7]

Greenberg's reason for declaring Matisse almost on a par with Picasso is not so easily discovered. True, in "Avant-Garde and Kitsch" he had included Matisse among a select few of twentieth-century artists who had to be recognized for "deriv[ing] their chief inspiration from the medium they work in" and who for that reason must elicit our admiration.[8] But in the interim, during which Picasso's lesson for contemporary art loomed large in Greenberg's eyes (as it loomed large in the eyes of so many American artists and critics), Matisse's lesson diminished to the point that he vanished from mention. Earlier in 1944 Greenberg rehearsed some ideas about the European modernist canon, stating that "Picasso, Miró, Braque, Arp, Lipchitz, Brancusi, the 'inhuman' Mondrian, and the 'intellectual' Gris have given the 'romantic' as well as the 'classical' aspects of contemporary life their most intrinsic expression in visual art."[9] Given the absence of Matisse from this list, the question then arises as to the circumstances that catapulted Matisse above all others save Picasso in Greenberg's pantheon. The leap cannot be attributed to the exhibition of new work by Matisse, for the war prevented any from being seen. Is it possible, then, that it stemmed from an encounter with only three paintings, albeit three remarkable paintings, seen at a single exhibition?

The answer is not clear. Certainly Hans Hofmann, whom Greenberg has credited with influencing his understanding of modern art, may have helped to animate, or reanimate, Greenberg's enthusiasm for Matisse.[10] However, Matisse remains a shadowy figure in Greenberg's criticism until the winter of 1945–46. It was not until an article on an exhibition of landscape painting at the Brooklyn Museum that Greenberg offered an inaugural description of a painting by Matisse. The impact of *Large Landscape: Mont Alban* (1918), he writes, is achieved "not only by design but also by color, green being summarily transposed into

Henri Matisse, Large
Landscape, Mont Al-
ban, *1918, oil on can-
vas, 28³⁄₄ x 36¹⁄₄ in.
Collection of Alexina
Duchamp.*

black, umber, and gray, and the trunks of saplings dealt with in cerulean blue."[11] As far as descriptive formal analysis goes it is not much. This reluctance to write about formal matters, however, may serve to remind us that before Greenberg was a critic of art, he was a critic of the *conditions* that had given rise to certain kinds of art—notably to that art in Western capitalist societies which we call avant-garde.

The passage on *Large Landscape: Mont Alban* was followed some weeks later (January 1946) by a curious article relating more directly to Matisse than to any other painter, though it does not refer to Matisse by name. It is on the pastoral mood in modern painting and announces a fresh inflection in Greenberg's aesthetic that predicts certain critical stances that will shortly become evident. For that reason, it seems worthwhile to excerpt from it at some length.

What characterizes painting in the line Manet to Mondrian—as well as poetry from Verlaine through Mallarmé to Apollinaire and Wallace Stevens—is its pastoral mood. It is this that is mistaken for the "classical." And it is away from the pastoral, the preoccupation with nature at rest, human beings at leisure, and art in movement, that so much painting has turned of late. . . .

Now the pastoral, in modern painting and elsewhere, depends on two interdependent attitudes: the first, a dissatisfaction with the moods prevailing in society's centers of activity; the second, a conviction of the stability of society in one's own time. One flees to the shepherds from the controversies that agitate the market-place. But this flight—which takes place in art—depends inevitably on a feeling that the society left behind will continue to protect and provide for the fugitive, no matter what differences he may have with it.

This feeling of pastoral security has become increasingly difficult to maintain in the last two decades. It is the dissipation of this sense of security that makes the survival of modern avant-garde art problematical. The first impulse is to rush back to the market-place and intervene in or report its activities. Here political art, some forms of expressionism, popular surrealism, and neo-romanticism complement one another in their anxiety to relate art to the current crisis of our civilization. What is wrong, however, with surrealism and neo-romanticism in particular is that they stay falsely pastoral in resorting to styles of the past in order to make

emotions about the present plain and explicit. Genuinely
pastoral art never turns to the past; it simply rejects one
present in favour of another—and without escapism. Even
today one must look still to avant-grade pastoral art to see
revealed the most permanent features of our society's
crisis.[12]

There we have it: the art of the avant-garde which deals most
honestly and intelligently with "the most permanent features of
our society's crisis"—a crisis, it needs saying, that in Greenberg's opinion is the crisis of capitalism, of the enervating
"controversies that agitate the market-place," of a culture that
cynically manufactures *Kitsch* for the urbanized masses—is art
in the so-called pastoral mood.

There are a number of observations to be made about Greenberg's formulations about avant-garde pastoral art. First, the pe-
culiarity of the application of the term pastoral itself; it is not a
category that Greenberg had firmly attached to visual art before,
or that he would insist on in the future. Indeed, one may wonder
why it was used at all unless to bring to mind William Empson's
group of essays published as *Some Versions of Pastoral* (1935). It
may be recalled that the title of the first essay in Empson's book
is "Proletarian Literature" and that the stated purpose of the
essays was to show "the ways in which the pastoral process of
putting the complex into the simple (in itself a great help to the
concentration needed for poetry) and the resulting social ideas
have been used in English literature."[13]

Here, it may seem, is the telling point of contact between
Greenberg's enterprise and Empson's. Greenberg's conception of
the place of "medium" in modern art is nothing if not a "process
of putting the complex into the simple" for the purpose of what
Empson calls "concentration" and Greenberg calls "expression."
In "Towards a Newer Laocoon," the historical fact and necessity
of the conscious separation of the means of visual art from those
of the other arts for the purpose of purer expression is the main
burden of the argument.

However, Greenberg's indebtedness to *Some Versions of
Pastoral* ought not to be pressed too hard, any more than his
indebtedness to Hofmann ought to be overemphasized, strong
though both seem to have been. Instead, it is more germane to
see how Greenberg's notion of pastoral in 1946 looks back to his
articles of 1939–40 and at the same time ahead to his accounts of
Matisse. In 1940 he had written that it was "the task of the avant-

garde to perform in opposition to bourgeois society the function of finding new and adequate cultural forms for the expression of that same society, without at the same time succumbing to its ideological divisions and its refusal to permit the arts to be their own justification."[14] It might well be asked what kind of avant-garde could accomplish this. What art in postwar Western society could "perform in opposition to bourgeois society" but still find forms that express that society? Certainly not Surrealism, political art, and certain forms of expressionism, we are told by Greenberg in 1946, because these manifestations in contemporary art, in their "anxiety" to relate themselves to the crisis of modern civilization, have resorted to means from the past, to worn-out stylistic orders that have no place in the new cultural context.

In avant-garde pastoral art, however, Greenberg claims to find a positive and authentic reaction to the plight of contemporary culture, a reaction adding up to more than just an insistence on attention to medium. This reaction is demonstrated by, and one must quote precisely here, its "preoccupation with nature at rest, human beings at leisure."[15] The claim is calculated and would seem to refute an objection raised by Clark in his essay on Greenberg. Clark argues that Greenberg, in placing so much emphasis on the role of medium in avant-garde art (an emphasis, as Clark says, that is not in a historical sense misguided) at the same time that he emphasizes the consequent separation of that art from the concerns of the society it purportedly serves, gives aid and comfort to an art that proposes to "substitute *itself* for the values capitalism has made valueless."[16] Is Clark correct to assume that in these years (I make no claims for the later criticism) Greenberg proposed an unqualified substitution of the values of art for the counterfeits of society? The charge seems too strong. Here, at least, Greenberg's attempt to isolate a pastoral mood in modern art and his determination to find in it an art relevant to the crises afflicting society belie the thrust of the criticism.

Greenberg does not persist with the 1946 notion of a pastoral art, however, and modifies the claims made for that art's constructive place in society. From positing that the best and most characteristic avant-garde art had been preoccupied with "nature at rest, human beings at leisure," his stance had shifted by 1949 (in "The Role of Nature in Modern Painting") to the assertion simply that the best modern art was grounded in nature. It was as if he had come unexpectedly across the letter written by

Matisse to Henry Clifford—published in English in 1948 in the
Philadelphia Museum of Art retrospective catalogue[17]—in which
Matisse insisted that the artist "must possess nature," that he
must identify with nature's rhythm; and as if Greenberg accepted
the proposition on the strength of Matisse's say so. Still, and
there should be no mistake about this, the crux of the argument
remains the same—that the claims of medium, no matter how
strong, must be accommodated to something beyond medium itself. Greenberg continues:

> As it turned out, the movement that began with Cézanne
> eventually culminated in abstract art, which permitted the
> claims of medium to override those of nature almost entirely.
> Yet before that happened, nature did succeed in stamping
> itself so indelibly on modern painting that its stamp has re-
> mained even in art as abstract as Mondrian's. What was
> stamped was not the appearance of nature, however, but its
> logic.[18]

Thus the logic of nature, Greenberg is saying here, its integrity
and coherence, are what give medium its ultimate *raison d'être*.

But Greenberg's argument, in becoming more general, becomes less cogent. Are we not entitled to ask of fully abstract
images what it means for them to be "stamped" by the logic of
nature? When Greenberg concludes the 1949 article with the
statement that "the best modern painting, though it is mostly
abstract painting, remains naturalistic at its core, despite all
appearances to the contrary,"[19] is he making sense? The doubt-
ful logic of the proposition, I think, masks a ruse. Greenberg is
employing an outwardly plausible (though specious) argument to
justify a predilection for a kind of avant-garde art that is ordered,
cool, and detached; in other words, to justify an art like Matisse's
as opposed, say, to an art like Dubuffet's, Pollock's, or even
Picasso's.

Conflicting Paradigms

Greenberg's growing predilection for Matisse over Picasso is
clarified in an article from mid-1946. The event that occasions his
remarks is an exhibition of several paintings by Matisse, Picasso,
Dubuffet, Rouault, and Bonnard at the Pierre Matisse Gallery.
The paintings are among the first new oils by these artists to be
seen in New York since the war, Greenberg tells us, and for that

reason bear close scrutiny. "The School of Paris," he writes, "remains still the creative fountainhead of modern art, and its every move is decisive for advanced artists everywhere else—who are advanced precisely because they show the capacity to absorb and extend the preoccupations of that nerve-center and farthest nerve-end of the modern consciousness which is French art."[20] We may be sure, then, that Greenberg weighed his words carefully when writing on the works exhibited.

Picasso, who only a short time earlier was seen to be the standard around which so much contemporary painting revolved, is found wanting. Greenberg criticizes his *Still Life with Candle* (1944) in this exhibition for striving toward the same *terribilità* as his figure paintings. "This picture fails," Greenberg writes, "as sadly as does all of Picasso's recent work that I have seen in reproduction. He insists on representation in order to answer our time with an art equally explicit as to violence and horror."[21] The judgment is in marked contrast to Greenberg's opinion of Matisse's two still lifes in the exhibition (one of them, *Still Life with Christmas Roses and Saxifrages*, is reproduced here). Greenberg sees in Matisse's paintings no violence and horror, but rather a "controlled sensuality" and a "careful sumptuousness" which, he states with a touch of hyperbole, place the paintings among Matisse's highest achievements.[22]

The antipathy between the aesthetic manifested in Matisse and the one found so much less palatable in Picasso haunts Greenberg's criticism for the last part of the 1940s and the early part of the 1950s. It is necessary, therefore, to inquire into its source. Certainly, it reflects partly a personal bias for a kind of art that is "bland, large, balanced, Apollonian," as Greenberg himself puts it a year later.[23] But to take that as the sole reason would be to misunderstand the seriousness of Greenberg's project in the 1940s. Instead, we must turn back to his notion of "avant-garde pastoral" to see how, without much difficulty, it is transformed into the notion of an "avant-garde hedonism," the chief exemplar of which is Matisse.

Initially, Greenberg argues, both Matisse and Picasso were engaged in the necessary pursuit of an art that was, above all things, "physical." A propos the development of modern art after 1920, Greenberg writes:

> Artists like Matisse and Picasso also appear to have felt that unless painting proceeded, at least during our time, in its exploration of the physical, it would stop advancing alto-

gether—that to turn to the literary would be to retreat and repeat; whether the physical was exhausted or not, there was no ambitious alternative. . . .

Materialism and positivism when they become pessimistic turn into hedonism, usually. And the path-breakers of the School of Paris, Matisse and Picasso, and Miró too—no less than the surrealists and the neo-romantics, whose pessimism rests on cynicism rather than on despair—began during the twenties to emphasize more than ever the pleasure element in their art. The School of Paris no longer sought to *discover* pleasure but to *provide* it. But whereas the surrealists and the neo-romantics conceived of pleasure in terms of sentimental subject matter, Matisse, Picasso, and those who followed them saw it principally in luscious color, rich surfaces, decoratively inflected design.[24]

In short, Greenberg is saying, the purpose of painting in the positivist age of bourgeois industrialism is to provide pleasure as a response to the shrinking possibilities of the age.[25] (Matisse expresses much the same view in his writings, though his choice of language is much less obviously pessimistic.) What is more, this pleasure is reflected not so much in subject matter—though presumably "nature at rest, human beings at leisure" would be appropriate subject matter for those artists who would paint other than abstractly—but in a hedonistic alignment with medium.

If this sounds prescriptive, it is. Yet contradictorily, or apparently so, Greenberg also recognizes that some of the most compelling painting around him does not submit to being described as hedonistic and that it consciously opposes such an epithet. Moreover, he is prepared to deal with this art largely (though not entirely, as we shall soon see) on its own terms. To this extent there is a paradox in Greenberg's prescription, a paradox with enough leaven to prevent it from hardening into dogma. A nearly contemporaneous account of Pollock's third exhibition at the Art of This Century gallery illustrates the point:

It is possible to accuse the painter Jackson Pollock, too, of bad taste; but it would be wrong, for what is thought to be Pollock's bad taste is in reality simply his willingness to be ugly in terms of contemporary taste. In the course of time this ugliness will become a new standard of beauty. Besides, Pollock submits to a habit of discipline derived from cubism; and even as he goes away from cubism he carries with him

Pablo Picasso, Nature
Morte à la Bougie,
1944, oil on canvas,
35¾ x 23½ in. Private
collection.

Henri Matisse, Still
Life with Christmas
Roses and Saxifrages,
1944, oil on canvas,
19¾ x 25¾ in. Private
collection.

the unity of style with which it endowed him when in the beginning he put himself under its influence. Thus Pollock's superiority to his contemporaries in this country lies in his ability to create a genuinely violent and extravagant art without losing stylistic control. His emotion starts out pictorially; it does not have to be castrated and translated to be put into a picture.[26]

The paintings included *Water Figure* (no. 2 in the exhibition), *Troubled Queen* (no. 3), *Moon Vessel* (no. 9), and *Direction* (no. 8), all dating from 1945. Greenberg offers no specific analysis of any of these paintings, saying only that none seems to him the equal of the two large canvases *Totem Lesson I* (1944) and *Totem Lesson II* (1945) exhibited the previous year. Although Greenberg's reluctance to analyze individual works may be an act of caution and to his credit—as he explains, "One has to learn Pollock's idiom to realize its flexibility. And it is precisely because I am, in general, still learning from Pollock that I hesitate to attempt a more thorough analysis of his art"[27]—there is a rather different point to be made here. It is that Greenberg is prepared to countenance Pollock's art at all; that despite his distaste for art that risks incoherence and nihilistic excess, he sees in works like *Totem Lesson I* qualities that cannot be dismissed merely on the grounds of taste. It will have been noted that the adjective "violent" that Greenberg attaches not disapprovingly to Pollock's art is exactly the one he employs as a term of opprobrium in describing qualities of Picasso's still life. What, then, distinguishes the violence in Pollock's work from that in Picasso's? Greenberg's answer is "stylistic control." According to his lights, Pollock does not relinquish control of the pictorial elements of his paintings whereas Picasso does. Where Pollock insists on maintaining a "unity of style," Picasso in his still life presents for our contemplation a vulgarly drawn jug and a painting surface without unity.

What, it might be asked, does Greenberg think is the cause of Picasso's loss of pictorial control? A revealing answer is offered in a somewhat earlier article dating from 1944. By way of contrast to Miró's supposed willingness to stay within "the limitations of his medium," Greenberg finds in Picasso—"a more profound artist . . . more ambitious, more Promethean"[28]—an insistence on *not* being restrained by medium. Picasso, writes Greenberg, demonstrates "a dissatisfaction with the resources of his medium; something beyond painting yearns to be expressed,

Jackson Pollock, Totem
Lesson I, *1944, oil on
canvas, 70⅛ x 44 in.
Collection of Mr. and
Mrs. Harry W. Anderson.*

something which color and line laid on a flat surface can never quite achieve."[29] Picasso's yearning and ambition to transgress the restraints of the flat picture surface, then, would seem to be at the root of his difficulties.

A parallel yearning (but far less admirable in Greenberg's eyes) is observed in the art of the Surrealists. The Surrealists also are dissatisfied with the limitations of medium, they too exhibit "a yearning to put their art into a more explicit relation with the rest of their lives than post-cubist painting and sculpture seem to allow." He continues:

> Cubism, or abstract art, gives the artist no room to express his *immediate* feelings about sex, for instance. They must first be transposed. [There] is impatience with the thought and feeling involved in the transposition of the aesthetic to and from the rest of experience.[30]

These criticisms are explicit. It must be clear that there is a relation between the two, between Greenberg's rejection of Surrealism on the one hand and his doubts about an art of "violence" on the other. The issue of violence in the art of Pollock and Picasso, therefore, is informed by Greenberg's attitude toward Surrealism. His position (as well as his dilemma) is made strikingly evident when he is called upon to write an article for the October 1947 *Horizon* ("The Present Prospects of American Painting and Sculpture"). Here, in concert with the tone of the June 29, 1946 article, Greenberg expresses his desire to see America as a place for art and artists not given to extremes. "We have had enough of the wild artist," Greenberg writes, "—he has by now been converted into one of the standard self-protective myths of our society: if art is wild it must be irrelevant."[31] But the difficulty, of course, lies in his recognition that the most powerful painter in contemporary America is Jackson Pollock—Pollock, who is a "morbid and extreme disciple of Picasso's cubism and Miró's post-cubism"[32] and who, Greenberg cannot have failed to recognize, was contributing to the very myth that he wished to see laid to rest.

Therefore we may guess at Greenberg's pleasure (even though it comes close to being tongue-in-cheek) in being able to report early in 1948, on the occasion of Pollock's 1947 48 exhibition at the Betty Parsons Gallery, that "Pollock's mood has become more cheerful these past two years."[33] He deduces the elevated cheerfulness from the higher-keyed color that Pollock is using. Indeed, the new and pervasive use of aluminum paint, as in the canvas *Cathedral* (1947), "runs the picture startlingly close to prettiness" in several instances. But we do not sense in the article that Greenberg is deeply disturbed by the aluminum phenomenon or the near-prettiness of the paintings, for he finds in the best of the paintings qualities he most admires in art: "style," "harmony," and "logic." If anything, his worry is that the paintings will be misunderstood by an uninformed public as being too decorative, as being merely "wallpaper patterns." His worry was not unfounded. As early as 1948 the apparent facility of Pollock's work was an issue for spectators. At a round-table discussion sponsored by *Life* magazine, in which Greenberg participated, Francis Henry Taylor, Director of the Metropolitan Museum of Art, New York, describes *Cathedral* as reminiscent of a "panel for a wallpaper which is repeated indefinitely around the wall."[34] And Leigh Ashton, Director of the Victoria and Albert Museum, London, finds it "exquisite in tone and quality. It would make . . . an enchanting printed silk."[35]

These half-baked responses to Pollock's art, Greenberg understands, are found in public reaction to some work that is not even abstract—including the work of Matisse and Miró. "The same charge of frivolity and superficiality has been made against Matisse," Greenberg writes in an article about Miró.[36] However, he also expresses the opinion that "Matisse's cold hedonism and ruthless exclusion of everything but the concrete, immediate sensation will in the future, once we are away from the present *Zeitgeist*, be better understood as the most profound mood of the first half of the twentieth century."[37] Apart from the force and conviction of Greenberg's enunciation of Matisse's "cold hedonism," as he chooses to term it, the statement is revealing for what it implies about Greenberg's impatience with the nature of the prevailing *Zeitgeist*. I take this impatience to be of a rather different order from the pessimism expressed in the 1939–40 articles about the general decline of modern civilization. For the latter, Greenberg held out little hope. But the *Zeitgeist* of 1947, I think, is seen as a moment of shorter duration, reflecting an apprehension brought on by conditions in a world that has suddenly found itself in possession of nuclear weapons, and to which the world would adjust itself. Although this world might never be the same again, Greenberg seems to imply, sooner or later the avant-garde will come to its senses and appreciate that the atomic bomb cannot be painted and that the enduring purposes of its existence remain as before.

Jackson Pollock, Ca-
thedral, *1947, enamel
and aluminum paint on
canvas, 71½ x 35⅛ in.
Dallas Museum of Art.
Gift of Mr. and Mrs.
Bernard J. Reis.*

The theoretical basis for Greenberg's impatience lies in Kant's notion of disinterestedness, of aesthetic distance as a guarantee of quality in art.[38] Greenberg gives full vent to his exasperation with the failure, in his opinion, of so much contemporary art to cultivate the proper degree of disinterestedness. He writes:

> In the face of current events painting feels, apparently, that it must be more than itself: it must be epic poetry, it must be theatre, it must be rhetoric, it must be an atomic bomb, it must be the Rights of Man. But the greatest painter of our time, Matisse, preeminently demonstrated the sincerity and penetration that go with the kind of greatness particular to twentieth-century painting by saying that he wanted his art to be an armchair for the tired businessman.[39]

The grim counterpoint between art as an atomic bomb and art as an armchair for the tired businessman—or at least the implications of the counterpoint—did not pass unchallenged. George L. K. Morris, both a critic and a painter like Greenberg, took Greenberg to task in the pages of *Partisan Review*. Responding specifically to an article of March 1948, "The Decline of Cubism," Morris contested what he perceived to be Greenberg's main thesis, "that in times of disaster the radical artists lose their nerve, and through demoralization become less radical."[40] But what really exercised Morris, it turned out, was Greenberg's critical judgments of certain individual artists:

> The field of contemporary art is given the semblance of a tournament. Umpire Greenberg charts the last rounds somewhat as follows: the expected champions (Picasso, Braque, Arp, etc.) have lost their punch, and no new blood is coming along—so to everyone's surprise, a couple of Old Timers (Matisse, Bonnard), who have been relying all these years on poky lobs and drop shots rather than spectacular rushes to the net, were the ones to reach the finals after all. I do not feel that anything as elusive as the ultimate values of contemporary art can be graded as simply as this, certainly not without considerable substantiation. And such a prearranged result might prove highly irritating to a different referee, who thought he saw Matisse pass out of the tournament in love sets around 1917.[41]

While Morris's mapping of modern art on to a tennis court may seem an unfortunate choice of arenas in which to conduct the debate, we can appreciate the thrust of his objections. Do Matisse's private and mannered paintings after 1917 really fulfill the claims that Greenberg wants to make for them?

We are not reassured by Greenberg's reply to Morris in the same issue of *Partisan Review*. In defense of his position he singles out *Woman Before an Aquarium* (1923, Art Institute of Chicago) and *Lemons on a Pewter Plate* (1926, Collection of Mrs. Joan Toor Cummings), two paintings included in the Matisse retrospective earlier that year at the Philadelphia Museum of Art. Greenberg describes them as works "painted in a style whose elements were formed by 1907" but whose "intrinsic merits" are as great as "the much more historically important pictures Mondrian and Picasso were turning out around the same time."[42] This is a strange argument. Just how, it may be wondered, are the intrinsic merits of these Matisses of 1923 or 1926 to be compared with, let us say, "the much more historically important" *Composition in White and Black* by Mondrian (1926, Museum of Modern Art) or *The Studio* by Picasso (1927–28, Museum of Modern Art)? And what purpose would be served by such a comparison? Greenberg does not say, leaving us to conclude that if all his accounts of modern painting were this flaccid we should have little option but to grant victory to Morris—in, to stay with Morris's terminology, love sets.

Greenberg, however, was not often so uncritical of his own writing in the 1940s. Moreover, he had subsequent doubts about what he had written, demonstrated by an article from early 1949.[43] The occasion for the article was an exhibition of recent work by Matisse at the Pierre Matisse Gallery, New York. Here Greenberg owns up more honestly than he has before to certain difficulties Matisse presents for him, admitting that his choice of Matisse as the preeminent painter of the contemporary era on the basis of his sensuous facility with medium offers a "peculiar problem." A revealing passage in the article begins with a nod to Morris that indicates more than a modicum of contrition:

It is held by some people of informed taste in modern art that Matisse's contribution was exhausted by at least 1920. Though I could not agree that exhaustion was the term to apply to an artist capable of the still lifes Matisse turned out in the twenties, it did seem until recently that his ambition had slackened in the last three decades and that, if he still

handled paint as paint better than Picasso did, his art had
become far less relevant than Picasso's, or even then Miró's,
to the highest aims of painting. However genuine the pleasure received from Matisse's later canvases, it had to be
conceded that this pleasure had begun to thin out and that
the emotion which had moved us in his masterpieces of the
years before 1920 was being replaced by virtuosity.[44]

The passage highlights Greenberg's difficulty. On the one hand,
he wants to declare that a sensuous handling of medium for rigorously hedonistic ends (Matisse) gives rise to the best that art can
hope for in the mid-twentieth century; on the other hand, he recognizes that the line between an art of sensuous certainty and
one of mere virtuosity is a tenuous one, and that even Matisse
produces canvases in which what is most to be wished for is little
in evidence. This forces him to admit that perhaps the painting of
Picasso, or Miró, has been, after all, more relevant to the most
serious aims of painting than that of Matisse.[45]

However, Greenberg's confession of doubt, and his atone-
ment for past sins against Morris, are shown to be *pro tem*. They
are only prolegomena to Greenberg's most concerted effort yet to
install Matisse at the apex of avant-garde painting. The work
shown at the Pierre Matisse Gallery, he decides, almost none of
which had been seen in Philadelphia, offers a "refutation of those
who may still doubt that Matisse is the greatest living painter."[46]
In Greenberg's opinion, the canvases of 1947–48 represent a
"glorious final statement, such as those Titian, Renoir, Bee-
thoven, Milton had issued," and rank of a level with Matisse's
large works from 1911–18.[47]

Large Interior in Red (1948) is selected as the best painting
on hand. Not only is it fully "felt through" in terms of design and
color, in Greenberg's opinion, but it owes its success to Matisse's
decision to absent the human figure. Indeed, "Matisse's chances
of complete success are [greater] when he stays away from the
human figure."[48] This is a curious assertion, and we should want
to know what Greenberg means, particularly when we recall that
throughout his life Matisse was at pains to insist on the primacy
of the human figure in his painting. In the early "Notes of a
Painter" (1908) he had written: "What interests me most is
neither still life nor landscape, but the human figure. It is that
which best permits me to express my almost religious awe towards life"[49]; and in the late "Exactitude is Not Truth" (1947),
dealing with four self-portrait drawings chosen by the artist for

Henri Matisse, Large Interior in Red, *1948, oil on canvas, 57 x 37¾ in. Musée National d'Art Moderne, Paris.*

the Philadelphia retrospective, he approvingly quoted Rembrandt
as having said, "I have never painted anything but portraits."[50]

Greenberg did not elaborate at the time on why he considered the human figure problematic in Matisse's art. However, his
1953 book on Matisse makes enough references to the subject for
us to learn exactly what he had in mind. The matter is presented
most bluntly in an analysis of *White Plumes* (1919):

> Responding to a subject attractive in itself and gotten up
> attractively, Matisse does not enhance the attractiveness
> in representing it, but creates an independent beauty. An-
> toinette's sex appeal is so solemn as to contradict itself,
> what with the fixed stare of her eyes and the rigid set of her
> features that make her more effigy than seductive woman.
> What is really seductive are the appurtenances, the Indian
> red background, the pearly whites and grays in the feath-
> ers—that is, the paint, the disinterested paint.[51]

The danger of dealing with the human figure in painting, then,
is nothing less than the danger of failing to dehumanize it. For
Greenberg is insisting here on the ruthless hegemony of medium
over the objects it represents, on the possibilities of paint over
the presence of the sitter, in this case the model Antoinette.
Hence the conclusion that Matisse does better not to tamper with
the human figure at all. It is a drastic conclusion, one might almost say preposterous—and it has the air of having been invented in order to insist upon that side of Matisse's endeavor that
is abstract, serene, Apollonian.

There exist, however, passages on the same subject in the
same book that demonstrate a less easy and a more dialectical
play of mind. It is this dialectical quality, I think, a questioning
give-and-take for the purposes of relating practice to idea and
idea to practice, that distinguishes Greenberg's most valuable
criticism on Matisse. "His detachment lets him view the female
body as a consumer's article," Greenberg writes of a painting in
which Matisse represents himself in front of his model, "but it
also enables him to convert into a masterpiece a subject and an
arrangement others could use only to decorate a candy box."[52]
This, briefly, is the kind of commentary I mean, observations in
which complex and contradictory ideas cohere in ways that do
not foreclose on other possibilities. From it, and passages like it,
we can understand better Greenberg's comprehension of the relation of Matisse's "cool hedonism" to the conditions of the pro-

Henri Matisse, White
Plumes, *1919, oil on
canvas, 28¾ x 23¾ in.
The Minneapolis
Institute of Arts, The
William Hood Dun-
woody Fund.*

duction of his painting. At the same time, we can realize that Greenberg's perception of Matisse as first among living painters and his insistence that Matisse expresses the most profound mood of the twentieth century has a provisional status. Clearly, Greenberg does not hold that the example of Matisse is easy to learn from—at least if an art of confection is not to be the result. As much as he might desire with Matisse an art of serenity and balance, it is a mark of his criticism in the decade after the war that he recognizes the necessity for its antidote, for an art of violence and indeterminancy which, if nothing else, questions and keeps vital the premises of its obverse.

Notes

1.
Clement Greenberg, "T. S. Eliot: The Criticism, The Poetry," The Nation *(December 9, 1950), p. 531; a substantially changed version of the article, from which the passage cited above was expunged, is published in* Art and Culture *(Boston: Beacon Press, 1961), pp. 239–244.*

2.
T. J. Clark, "More on the Differences Between Comrade Greenberg and Ourselves," Modernism and Modernity: The Vancouver Conference Papers, *eds. Benjamin H. D. Buchloh, Serge Guilbaut, and David Solkin (Halifax: Press of the Nova Scotia School of Art and Design, 1983), pp. 169–87, followed by an exchange with Greenberg himself, pp. 188–93. Clark's paper has been republished as "Clement Greenberg's Theory of Art," in* The Politics of Interpretation, *ed. W. J. T. Mitchell (Chicago: University of Chicago Press, 1982–83), incorporating a response to it by Michael Fried and a riposte to Fried by Clark. In the same conference volume Thomas Crow, "Modernism and Mass Culture in the Visual Arts," pp. 215–264, discussed* Greenberg's theories in light of the later criticism, particularly as they reflect on issues relating to high and low culture. Donald Kuspit, Clement Greenberg: Art Critic *(Madison: University of Wisconsin Press, 1979) glossed over the differences between Greenberg's early and late writings by choosing to treat the writings as all of a piece.*

3.
Greenberg, The Nation *(March 8, 1947), in* The Collected Essays and Criticism, *volume 2,* Arrogant Purpose, 1945–1949, *ed. John O'Brian (Chicago: University of Chicago Press, 1986), p. 134. The two volumes of* Collected Essays *will hereafter be cited as* CG.

4.
Greenberg, The Nation *(June 7, 1947), in* CG, 2, p. 155.

5.
Greenberg, The Nation *(June 10, 1944), in* The Collected Essays and Criticism, *volume 1,* Perceptions and Judgments, 1939–1944, *ed. John O'Brian (Chicago: University of Chicago Press, 1986), p. 212.

6.
Art in Progress: A Survey Prepared for the Fifteenth Anniversary *(New York: Museum of Modern Art, 1944), pp. 40–41. The Blue Window was reproduced in color as the frontispiece.*

7.
In concluding that "Matisse is shown at his best" in the work of 1913–17, Greenberg was singling out the same period that had gained Alfred H. Barr's particular admiration as early as 1931 ("Introduction," Henri-Matisse *[New York: Museum of Modern Art, 1931], p. 18) and that Barr was to continue to champion in his writings on the artist (e.g.,* Matisse: His Art and His Public *[New York: Museum of Modern Art, 1951], pp. 177–94) and in his acquisitions for the Museum of Modern Art.*

8.
Greenberg, Partisan Review *(Fall 1939), in* CG, 1, p. 9.

9.
Greenberg, The Nation *(January 1, 1944), in* CG, 1, pp. 172–73. No account of Matisse in America in the 1940s can proceed without some kind of parallel investigation of Picasso in the 1940s. The two artists continued to be contrasted and compared, by every kind of audience, as they had been in the 1920s and 1930s.

10.
Hofmann was an admirer of Matisse and had worked briefly in the same atelier with him in Paris in the early years of the century. It had been Hofmann, we are informed in a footnote to "Avant-Garde and Kitsch" (n. 2, p. 9), who disclosed to Greenberg the conception of the place and function of medium in modern painting. And some years later Greenberg offered the opinion that "Hans Hofmann is in all probability the most important art teacher of our time. . . . Hofmann has not yet published his views, but they have already directly and indirectly influenced many, including this writer—who owes more to the initial illumination received from Hofmann's lectures than to any other source" (The Nation [April 21, 1945], in CG, 2, p. 18).

11.
Greenberg, The Nation (December 15, 1945), in CG, 2, p. 44. A fuller analysis of Large Landscape: Mont Alban was offered by Greenberg eight years later in Matisse (New York: Abrams, 1953), n.p. The later description demonstrates a change of emphasis in Greenberg's writing, a change by which theory is made to function hand-in-hand with a consideration of individual paintings. At the same time, the theory seems to have become less explicit.

12.
Greenberg, The Nation (January 26, 1946), in CG, 2, pp. 51–52.

13.
William Empson, Some Versions of Pastoral (1935) (New York: New Directions, 1968), p. 22. For an account of the pastoral tradition in Western landscape painting, see Robert C. Cafritz, Lawrence Gowing, David Rosand, Places of Delight: The Pastoral Landscape (Washington, D.C.: Phillips Collection, 1988). For a sustained analysis of Matisse's early work in relation to the pastoral idiom, see Margaret Werth, "Engendering the Imaginary Genre: Matisse's Bonheur de Vivre," Ph.D. qualifying paper, Department of Fine Arts, Harvard University, 1987.

14.
Greenberg, "Towards a Newer Laocoon," Partisan Review (July–August 1940), in CG, 1, p. 28.

15.
Greenberg, The Nation (January 26, 1946), in CG, 2, p. 51.

16.
Clark, "More on the Differences Between Comrade Greenberg and Ourselves," p. 184.

17.
"Letter from Henri Matisse to Henry Clifford," Henri Matisse: Retrospective Exhibition of Paintings, Drawings and Sculpture (Philadelphia: Philadelphia Museum of Art, 1948), p. 15.

18.
Greenberg, "The Role of Nature in Modern Painting," Partisan Review (January 1949), in CG, 2, p. 272.

19.
Ibid., p. 275.

20.
Greenberg, The Nation (June 29, 1946), in CG, 2, p. 87.

21.
Ibid., p. 89.

22.
Ibid., p. 89. It is likely that Greenberg would have known Still Life with Christmas Roses and Saxifrages in reproduction. The painting was illustrated in color in Verve 4: 13 (1945), pp. 11–12.

23.
Greenberg, "The Present Prospects of American Painting and Sculpture," Horizon (October 1947), in CG, 2, p. 167.

24.
Greenberg, The Nation (June 29, 1946), in CG, 2, pp. 88–89.

25.
Greenberg's insistence that art should provide pleasure as a response to the dwindling expectations of twentieth-century experience has as its dark side his rejection of "the world-hating attitudes revealed by French Existentialism in such works as Jean-Paul Sartre's La Nausée" (The Nation [July 13, 1946], in CG, 2, p. 91). This willful misreading of Sartre finds an ironic parallel in an account of Matisse written by Louis Aragon, in which Aragon also wants to contrast Matisse with Sartre but in which Matisse's work is made to stand for some kind of mindless "happiness" ("Henri Matisse or the French Painter," in Henri Matisse: Retrospective Exhibition of Paintings, Drawings and Sculpture, p. 31).

26.
Greenberg, The Nation (April 13, 1946), in CG, 2, pp. 74–75.

27.
Ibid., p. 75.

28.
Greenberg, The Nation (May 20, 1944), in CG, 1, p. 207.

29.
Ibid.

30.
Greenberg, The Nation (January 1, 1944), in CG, 1, p. 172.

31.
Greenberg, "The Present Prospects of American Painting and Sculpture," in CG, 2, p. 168. One may wonder in passing if there is not a parallel between Greenberg's attitude toward the "wild artist" in American society and the Cold War attitudes identified by Lary May in his essay in this volume.

32.
Ibid., p. 166. It may be noted that Clark, "More on the Differences Between Comrade Greenberg and Ourselves," draws somewhat different and larger lessons from this and other articles in which Greenberg contrasts Pollock's achievement with Matisse's.

33.
Greenberg, The Nation (January 24, 1948), in CG, 2, p. 202.

34.
"A Round Table on Modern Art," Life (October 11, 1948), p. 62. Matisse's Goldfish and Sculpture (1912) in the Museum of Modern Art, New York, was also among the paintings presented for discussion at the round-table. Apart from Georges Duthuit's observation that it was "one of the acknowledged classics of modern art" (p. 61), it excited little comment. For more on the contemporary reaction to Pollock's painting, see T. J. Clark's essay in this volume.

35.
Ibid., p. 62.

36.
Greenberg, The Nation (June 7, 1947), in CG, 2, p. 155.

37.
Ibid.

38.
The question of the place of Kant in Greenberg's criticism has led to several articles, among them Paul Crowther, "Greenberg's Kant and the Problem of Modernist Painting," British Journal of Aesthetics 25:4 (1985), pp. 317–325; and Ingrid Stadler, "The Idea of Art and Its Criticism: A Rational Reconstruction of a Kantian Doctrine," in Essays in Kant's Aesthetics, eds. Ted Cohen and Paul Guyer (Chicago: University of Chicago Press, 1982).

39.
Greenberg, The Nation (March 8, 1947), in CG, 2, pp. 133–34. The is-

sue raised by Greenberg was a major topic of debate and remained so into the 1950s. In 1951 de Kooning observed with irony: "Today some people think that the light of the atom bomb will change the concept of painting once and for all. The eyes that actually saw the light melted out of sheer ecstasy. For one instant, everybody was the same color. It made angels out of everybody" ("What Abstract Art Means to Me," Museum of Modern Art Bulletin 18 [Spring 1951], p. 7). Even Matisse had his say; he apparently referred to Jazz as "my atomic bomb" (Newsweek [April 12, 1948], p. 52).

40.
George L. K. Morris, "On Critics and Greenberg," Partisan Review (June 1948), p. 684. Benjamin H. D. Buchloh, "Figures of Authority, Ciphers of Regression: Notes on the Return of Representation in European Painting," in Modernism and Modernity: The Vancouver Conference Papers, pp. 81–115, takes up the question at length. Buchloh arrives at the conclusion that there are direct causal connections between the rise of political oppres-

sion in Europe during certain periods of the twentieth century and the reversion by artists to traditional modes of representation.

41.
Morris, "On Critics and Greenberg," p. 682.

42.
Greenberg, "Reply to George L. K. Morris," Partisan Review (June 1948), in CG, 2, p. 243.

43.
Greenberg, The Nation (March 5, 1949), in CG, 2, pp. 292–294.

44.
Ibid., p. 292.

45.
Greenberg's desire to distinguish between "major" art and that which was not major despite (or because of) its virtuosity, is particularly evident in an article on Bonnard (The Nation [June 12, 1948], in CG, 2, pp. 246–248). Matisse's virtuosity was also a source of concern for Barr in his work on Matisse; it has remained a vexing issue in most serious commentaries on the artist.

46.
Greenberg, The Nation (March 5, 1949), in CG, 2, p. 293.

47.
Ibid., p. 292.

48.
Ibid., p. 293.

49.
Matisse, "Notes of a Painter" (1908), in Matisse on Art, ed. Jack D. Flam (New York: E. P. Dutton, 1978), p. 38.

50.
Matisse, "Exactitude is Not Truth," Henri Matisse: Retrospective Exhibition of Paintings, Drawings and Sculpture, pp. 33–34.

51.
Greenberg, Matisse, n.p. Barr was less prepared than Greenberg to accept that the "paint, the disinterested paint" in White Plumes transcended the painting's subject matter. Barr reportedly described the painting as "cheesecake" and refused to accept it as a gift to the Museum of Modern Art (Russell Lynes, Good Old Modern: An Intimate Portrait of the Museum of Modern Art [New York: Atheneum, 1973], p. 245).

52.
Ibid., n.p. The painting referred to by Greenberg is The Painter and His Model, Studio Interior, 1919, Collection of Mr. and Mrs. Donald B. Marron, New York.

Jackson Pollock's Abstraction

Timothy J. Clark

For Serge Guilbaut

Farai un vers de dreit nien:
non er de mi ni d'autra gen,
non er d'amor ni de joven,
ni de ren au,
qu'enans fo trobatz en durmen
sus un chivau.

(I shall make a poem out of/about nothing at all:
it will not speak of me or others,
of love or youth,
or of anything else,
for it was composed while I was asleep
riding on horseback.)

William IX of Aquitaine, *Poesie*, no. 4[1]

Take Flaubert, for instance, in 1852, toward the start of work on *Madame Bovary*, already chafing at the bit of reference in the novel and playing with the idea of "a book about nothing, a book dependent on nothing external, which would be held together by the internal strength of its style . . . . a book which would have almost no subject, or at least where the subject would be almost invisible, if such a thing is possible."[2] Or William himself, ninth Duke of Aquitaine and fourth Count of Poitou, writing sometime around 1100 and likewise dreaming of an art uncluttered (unso-

phisticated) by otherness—an art come literally out of the unconscious and therefore blessedly empty. Or Pollock in 1947,
making the first group of pictures done with his new technique of
poured and thrown paint and calling two of them *Sea Change* and
Full Fathom Five. The titles were both taken from Ariel's song in
The Tempest, one of the play's most glittering, masque-like moments; and being so grandly, deliberately literary in his titles—it
was not a tactic Pollock often allowed himself—was presumably
meant to establish the basic tenor or register of the new paintings
and encourage his viewers to look at them through Ariel's eyes.
Which is to say, look through their superficial roughness and materialism and see them as magic—spells or disguises of some
sort, fanciful, filigree, even a bit gaudy:

> Full fadom five thy father lies;
> Of his bones are coral made;
> > Those are pearls that were his eyes:
> Nothing of him that doth fade,
> But doth suffer a sea-change
> Into something rich and strange.

These examples are meant to suggest that an art of high
negativity is not necessarily anarchical, scabrous, or otherwise
low. It has often consorted with a courtly atmosphere; dukes
have gone in for it, as part of a general, lordly "balance, largeness, precision, enlightenment, contempt for nature in all its
particularity"[3]; the negative can very well be one arm of aristocracy, whether the aristocracy be real or ersatz.

So it proved in Pollock's case. On March 1, 1951 *Vogue* magazine published four pages of photographs by Cecil Beaton, in
which Irene and Sophie showed off the latest creations in front of
Lavender Mist—the picture still had the title *Number 1, 1950*—
Number 28, Number 27, and *Autumn Rhythm*. Hedging his bets
just a little, the *Vogue* subeditor informed readers that "the
dazzling and curious paintings of Jackson Pollock, which are in
the photographs on these four pages, almost always cause an intensity of feelings." *Vogue* in the 1940s and 1950s was not to be
sniffed at: it sold copies and it was on Pollock's side. It had
printed a full-color photo of *Reflection of the Big Dipper* as early
as April 1948, the first time a drip painting was reproduced in
color—beating *Life* with *Cathedral* by a full six months. Financially, 1951 was not a very good year for Pollock: he was waiting
for his contract with Betty Parsons to expire, and broke with her

Cecil Beaton, Model in front of Number 1, 1950, *photograph in* Vogue, *March 1, 1951*

Cecil Beaton, Model in front of Number 28, 1950 and Number 27, 1950, *photograph in* Vogue, *March 1, 1951*

Cecil Beaton, Model in
front of Autumn
Rhythm, *photograph in*
Vogue, *March 1, 1951*

once it did; nobody seems to have made much money out of the 1950 show—the one that Beaton photographed—and in any case Pollock had a reputation for working the media (Rothko to Newman in 1946: "Pollock is a self contained and sustained advertising concern").[4] His tone when he wrote to Ossorio in February was matter-of-fact: "The issue of Vogue has three pages of my painting (with models of course) will send a copy."[5] These things happen. They help a bit. Is there anything more to be said?

The photographs in *Vogue* have become a bit notorious lately; and in the present state of things, that means they are likely to lead a double life, making their way into a certain Left art-historical canon and being cold-shouldered by most everybody else. The model in front of *Autumn Rhythm*, for example, appeared in a lecture by Serge Guilbaut I heard some time ago in Boston. It made a powerful point, I thought at the time. But I gather that not everybody thought so. The comment came back to me—at second hand, as tends to happen in these cases—"So the Pollocks got used as background in a fashion magazine. We all know that by now. So what?" There is a phrase that sticks in my mind from another conversation about Guilbaut's work, to the effect that his account of Pollock and the New York School amounted in the end to an exercise in "guilt by vague association." For is not any art of real complexity fated to be used, recruited, and misread? What are we supposed to say, for example, about a photo of Mussolini's shocktroops marching through the Arch of Constantine? Put the blame on the Arch somehow? Pretend that Mussolini got Roman architecture right? (To which the reply might reasonably be, in fact: Are you saying he got it wrong? What else, after all, was the Arch of Constantine for?)

None of these questions are open and shut. This essay is meant as an answer to some of them in Pollock's case—in particular to the baldest, most pugnacious question put to the *Vogue* photos, the "So what? Do they matter?"

A first stab at an answer would be this. The photographs matter because they raise the question of Pollock's paintings' public life, which is very far from being an extrinsic, *ex post facto* issue. They raise the question of what possible uses Pollock's work anticipated, what viewers and readers it expected, what spaces it was meant to inhabit, and, above all, the question of how such a structure of expectation entered and informed the work itself, determining its idiom. This is difficult territory, and

not much explored; the best map we have of it still seems to me
that offered by Mikhail Bakhtin, in particular in the essay called
"Discourse in the Novel," written sometime during the early
1930s. Any particular utterance, Bakhtin tells us (and it is not at
all forcing things to treat a Pollock painting as an utterance in
Bakhtin's sense), "finds the object at which it was directed already as it were overlain with qualifications, open to dispute,
charged with value, already enveloped in an obscuring mist—or,
on the contrary, by the 'light' of alien words that have already
been spoken about it. It is entangled, shot through with shared
thoughts, points of view, alien value judgements and accents."[6]
Not only the object of the utterance—and it goes without saying
that Bakhtin constantly plays on the ambiguities of the word *object* in such a case—but the utterance's very material is always
"already bespoken."[7] "The word in language is half someone
else's," Bakhtin says[8]; the so-called context of a work of art is
therefore not a mere surrounding, separable from form; it is what
the speaker or maker has most concretely to work with: context
is text, the context is the medium, and thus the whole idea of
having and sustaining "one's own word"—an idea basic to Pollock's view of art—is fragile and paradoxical. "Discourse lives,
as it were, on the boundary between its own context and another,
alien context,"[9] which means that any speaker "strives to get a
reading on his own word, and on his own conceptual system that
determines this word, within the alien conceptual system of the
understanding receiver."[10] All utterances anticipate *answers*, pro-
voking them, eluding them, orienting themselves toward an imagined future in which something is said or done in reply; and
works of art, being specially elaborate, pondered cases of utterance, are most of all shot through with such directedness.

The future that works of art envisage is very often, at least
in the modern period, one of misuse and misunderstanding, and
they may either try to contain and figure that future in an effort to
control it, or attempt instead—as certain of Pollock's do—to an-
nihilate the very grounds of misreading and shrug off past and
future alike, making the work turn on some impossible present,
thickened to the point where it can dictate its own (unique)
terms. Not that Pollock was incapable of pragmatism on this subject, or even optimism of a kind—at least when writing grant
proposals. "The pictures I contemplate painting would constitute
a halfway state, and an attempt to point out the direction of the
future, without arriving there completely."[11] "Well, yes, they're

an impractical size. . . ." "I think the possibilities of using painting on glass in modern architecture—in modern construction—
terrific."[12]

Let me put it another way. The *Vogue* photographs matter
because they bring to mind—or stir up in us—the most depress-
ing of all suspicions we might have about modern art: the bad
dream of modernism, I shall call it. For better or worse, this
dream is associated in my thinking with those two rank pessimists, Manfredo Tafuri and Michel Foucault. I cannot quite bring
the suspicions into focus without imagining them spoken by the
two of them, the sardonic glumness of the one serving as foil for
the other's grim exaltation; and yet the two only give voice to a
nightmare we all may have had and chosen to forget. It goes as
follows. Just as the early twentieth-century vision of Utopia
comes to seem in retrospect—this is Tafuri speaking—not much
more than an idealization of capitalism and *its* representations,
putting the best face on rationalization and imagining a world
where capital would finally have disposed of the inconvenient
"subject" (imagining it mostly with sanctimonious glee), so too
does the modernist exploration of the Other to bourgeois experience—its dream of discovering the "outside," the "before," the
opposite of consciousness—more and more seem part of a general policing of spaces hitherto useless, and therefore uncharted,
but which capital now thinks it can profit from and wants brought
into the realm of representation. By the end of that sentence, you
will have realized, the voice has changed from Tafuri's to Foucault's, but in any case the two voices overlap; the bad dream
of Utopia is only the other face of the bad dream of Nameless
Wildness.

In the case of Pollock, it is Foucault's charge that seems
closest to home. Pollock, for sure, had truck with the dream of
Nameless Wildness: his art was very often, as Clement Greenberg put it in 1947, one of "Gothic-ness, paranoia and resentment," of "violence, exasperation and stridency."[13] It was "an
attempt"—this is Greenberg again—"to cope with urban life; it
dwells entirely in the lonely jungle of immediate sensations, impulses and notions, therefore is positivist, concrete."[14] "Cette
oeuvre . . . fait penser à Poe et elle est remplie d'une sensibilité
sadique et scatologique."[15] Of course there is a sense in which
Foucault would have felt more at home with such a sensibility
than Greenberg ever did, but all the same he would have had
some unforgiving things to say about it. I fancy them taking the
following form.

These impulses in modern art were genuine, and perhaps unavoidable, and it may even be that they added up to "contesting bourgeois hegemony in the realm of consciousness." (This last phrase would not have tripped lightly off Foucault's tongue, but he can nonetheless be pictured using it, especially toward the end.) The point is this, however: contesting bourgeois hegemony in the realm of consciousness meant appropriating a set of representations which were already there in the culture, but which up till then had been thought of as "primitive," childish or deviant, lunatic, chaotic, otherwise beneath contempt. And in a sense they *were*, they *are*. Bourgeois hegemony is not an empty phrase: it describes a complex previous mapping and extension of experience over the centuries, and all that that hegemony left outside itself was the dislocated, the inarticulate, the outdated, the lacking in history, the solipsistic, the *informe*. These areas have provided art with raw material, but they are no kind of basis for conflict with or criticism of the bourgeoisie, which possesses descriptions far and away more powerful, because more differentiated, than anything modernism can offer. True, this search for the "outside" of bourgeois consciousness has sometimes gone hand in hand with an immanent critique of established forms of representation, and has been effective in a limited way. But insofar as these margins have been posited and organized as new territories on which representation could take place—territories with their own richness—what resulted was to the bourgeoisie's advantage rather than otherwise. On the one hand, for example, "primitivism": which is to say, a largely parasitic and second-rate imitation of a set of tribal objects, lacking the skills needed to do the job properly, not having so much as the beginnings of an understanding of what was being imitated—not thinking such an understanding *necessary*. On the other hand (and here we steer back to Pollock and *Vogue*), a kind of softening-up process: art preparing the ground for the real, ruthless appropriation of all those marginal and underdeveloped states which was to be effected, in the end, by the central organs of bourgeois culture itself. What *became* of *Völkischness*, finally? Who made best use of the forms art provided for celebrating the irrational? In whose interests was atavism?

This is the bad dream of modernism: that however urgent the impulse had been to alter the aesthetic and move out into uncolonized areas of experience, all that resulted was a thickening—a stiffening—of the same aesthetic mix. I take this to be

Pollock's own suspicion of his work, a bad dream he had, built into his practice. I shall give my reasons for thinking so in what follows. But for the moment let us look again at the *Vogue* photographs and approximate Foucault's verdict on them.

What else, he might say, did modernism expect from the public realm? What else did it think art was *for*? What Pollock invented in 1947–50 was a set of forms in which previously disorganized aspects of self-representation—the wordless, the somatic, the wild, the self-risking, spontaneous, uncontrolled, "existential," the "beyond" or "before" the conscious activities of mind—could achieve a bit of clarity, get themselves a relatively stable set of signifiers. A poured line with splatters now *equals* spontaneity, etc. A certain kind of painted interlace now can be taken to stand—taken quite casually—for states of mind like rage or elation, another kind of interlace for "pure harmony, an easy give and take,"[16] and so on. These are aspects of experience that the culture wants represented now, wants to make use of, because capitalism at a certain stage of its development *needs* a more convincing account of the bodily, the sensual, the "free," in order to extend—perhaps to perfect—its colonization of everyday life. Of course the *Vogue* photos give that process of recuperation a somewhat glib, somewhat superficial form; we think we can condescend to the models' outdatedness; fashion changes and art endures. But the process these photos glamorize is not glamorous, in fact, and not incidental; it is one that the practice of modernism knows lies in wait for it and may be its truth; that fact or fear is internalized by modernism and built into its operations; it is part, perhaps even cause, of modern painting's peculiar way with its medium. It is certainly part of Pollock's way with *his*.

I realize that the last flurry of assertions does not necessarily follow from the account of modern art I have outlined, and that for the present purpose it is the last assertion of all—the one about Pollock—that has to be argued for. That is what the rest of the essay tries to do: it lays out the reasons for my thinking this—*Vogue* photos and all—the right frame of reference in Pollock's case.

What I am looking for—not to seem to load the dice from the beginning in Foucault's favor, or even Cecil Beaton's—are ways into Pollock's achievement, particularly in 1947–50; ways in which we could ask the question of Pollock's intentions in, say, *Number 3, 1949*, the possible manner in which a picture like this would have been scanned and adjudged by its maker, its possible purposes. This cannot be done directly. It will involve a fair amount of toing and froing, overlay and overstatement, repetition, monotony, big pronouncements followed by long-winded qualifications, backtracking, mess; all of it unavoidable given the subject: "that wild whaling life," to quote one of Pollock's sacred texts, "where individual notabilities make up all totalities."[17]

But this immediately has too much the flavor of an excuse, and not even strictly the right one. The indirection of what follows does not derive so much from the wild uniqueness of the object of study as from its ordinary, entirely representative distance from the world it is part of. There is a real difficulty involved, is there not, in thinking at all of *Number 3, 1949* as belonging to the social body, beyond, that is, the mere brute fact of its being produced at such and such a time by such and such a member of the bourgeoisie? That difficulty ought to be admitted and made into the motor of the argument. This picture wishes to *efface* the "social" in itself; which is not to say that it succeeds in doing so, or even that such a project makes sense, but that the social will be found here, if at all, very thoroughly "absorbed into the work by implication or articulation."[18] Nobody wants to write a history of Pollock's painting which works by "vague association," whether it ends up proving the artist guilty or innocent of his class; nobody wants the social history of art to be, in Hegel's words, "an external activity—the wiping-off of some drops of rain or specks of dust from the [artistic] fruit, so to speak—one which erects an intricate scaffolding of the dead elements of their outward existence—the language, the historical circumstances, and so on"[19]; but to do more than this is difficult, especially with fruit of this kind. "Collective actions and ritual gestures," writes a literary historian about Shakespeare's *King Lear*, "paradigms of relationship, and shared images of authority penetrate the work of art and shape it from within."[20] Perhaps they do; some such assumption informs what follows; but the fact that straightaway in Pollock's case we should have to negate all the great social positives that give *Lear* its form—put "modes of privacy and privation" in place of collectivity, and histrionics instead of ritual; put non- in front of relationship; delete "shared images of authority" altogether; and all this in the face of the culture's continuing, voracious appetite for value of *some* kind, for imagery

Jackson Pollock, Number 3, 1949: Tiger, *oil, enamel paint, metallic enamel, string, and cigarette fragment mounted on fiberboard,* 62⅛ x 37¼ *in. Hirshhorn Museum and Sculpture Garden, Smithsonian Institution, Gift of Joseph H. Hirshhorn, 1972.*

of some sort, for the faint trace of authority somewhere—these things should suggest what the "social" will look like, in Pollock's work, when it is finally unearthed.[21]

If there is to be a positive moment at all to an account of Pollock's abstraction, then again it is suggested by Bakhtin's "Discourse in the Novel." I have in mind those moments in the essay (they are sometimes seen as weaknesses) when Bakhtin reflects not just on the otherness of language—its being always "already bespoken," its being "populated—overpopulated—with the intentions of others"[22]—but on the possibility, nonetheless, of some form of dialectical retrieval of the word by the speaker. For the word, in Bakhtin's view, is very much more than something possessed at random by individual monads, each wishing to make a way of speaking their private property. "Discourse lives, as it were, beyond itself, in a living impulse [*napravlennost*] towards the object,"[23] and it is in relation to this overall movement of construction—this continual opening of discourse toward the object, this effort to tie word to world, this wish for agreement and grounding—that the possibility of Truth arises. "The speaker breaks through the alien conceptual horizon of the listener, constructs his own utterance on alien territory, against his, the listener's, apperceptive background."[24] Which possibility—of a dialogue other than of the deaf—seems connected in Bakhtin's essay to yet another, more uncompromising image of movement beyond and toward: "The word, breaking through to its own meaning and its own expression across an environment full of alien words and variously evaluating accents, harmonizing with some of the elements in this environment and striking a dissonance with others, is able, in this dialogized process, to shape its own stylistic profile and tone."[25] Put "sign" or "mark" or "metaphor" in place of "word" in the previous sentence, and I think you have a good image—good *because* convoluted—of Pollock's Utopia.

Let me start with matters of vocabulary. If we want to reconstruct Pollock's intentions in 1947–50, are there words and phrases we could put in Pollock's mouth without thinking we were forcing things too much—beyond the unavoidable forcing involved in making Pollock talk at all, when he mostly preferred not to? How far, for example, do the terms of Pollock's best and closest critic at the time, Clement Greenberg, still prove of help? The question presents itself not simply because of the cogency and force of Greenberg's writing, but also because of evidence

Jackson Pollock,
Gothic, *1944, oil on*
canvas, 84⅝ x 56 in.
Collection, The
Museum of Modern Art,
New York. Lee Krasner
Bequest.

we have of some real closeness between the two men—difficult closeness, it looks like, no doubt a bit wary and ironic, but all the same operative, in ways other people recognized and even resented. "You must understand," writes Baziotes to his brother in March 1947, that "Clem Greenberg boosts Pollock and considers me in a slump."[26] "Dear Clem," writes Peggy Guggenheim the same year, "I am so happy you are carrying on the battle of Pollock."[27] It is a figure of Pollock journalism all through the later 1940s how certain unnamed arbiters of taste have already decreed that this is the great American painting of our day; so that Douglas Macagy in the *Magazine of Art* for March 1949, writing in general terms of the divorce between painters and writers, can first of all describe the usual state of affairs, that "only a few [American painters] have found the company of American writers congenial," and then run on quite confidently, as if his audience will know what he means, to two chosen exceptions, Benton and Thomas Craven, and Greenberg and Pollock: "Clement Greenberg's espousal of Jackson Pollock's work must have been useful to that artist."[28]

The relation of Greenberg and Pollock is all the more interesting because it was so clearly not, at the level of basic aesthetic preferences and commitments, an easy one. Pollock was doing the best painting in America, Greenberg thought, but a lot of the time he wondered *how*. All of those qualities that Greenberg rightly found in Pollock's painting in 1947—the "Gothic-ness, paranoia and resentment," the "morbid" atmosphere, the wish to be "wild and extravagant," the "pretentious" American "exasperation and stridency"[29]—all these are the opposite of what Greenberg believed the real strength of the modern tradition, and what he hoped for "in this country, the development of a bland, large, balanced, Apollonian art in which passion does not fill in the gaps left by the faulty or omitted application of theory but takes off from where the most advanced theory stops, and in which an intense detachment informs all."[30] The proof of the pudding, though, was in the eating. Pollock was a great painter; the inessential, boring qualities worked for him, even the ones Greenberg despised most. ("Gothic-ness," for example, in Greenberg's lexicon is a code word for Surrealism, than which art can sink no lower. "Surrealism has revived all the Gothic revivals," he writes in 1944, "and acquires more and more of a period flavour, going in for Faustian lore, old-fashioned and flamboyant interiors, alchemistic mythology, and whatever else is held to be the excesses in the tastes of the past."[31] What price Pollock's *Moon Woman* or *Pasiphäe* or, come to that, his *Alchemy* and *Lucifer?*)

Does it come down, then, to the simple fact of recognition and support on Greenberg's part, and to Hell with shared points of reference? In which case Greenberg's writing would be of precious little use, at least from the present point of view. I do not quite think so.

It is clear, for example, from various things Pollock said, that the painter subscribed to a fairly straightforward notion of the root cause of a work of art's quality; that he would have agreed with Greenberg in 1946—he is working up to declaring Pollock's *Two* the only major picture in the Whitney Annual— that "Everybody knows what has *already* made painting great. But very few know, feel, or suspect what makes painting great anywhere and at any time—that it is necessary to register what the artist makes of himself and his experience in the world, not merely to record his intentions, foibles and predilections."[32] In its very simplicity, this seems to tally with Pollock's view of what was at stake. And it seems to me also that Pollock would have understood—and in large measure responded to—the accompanying stress in Greenberg's account of art and experience: the stress on positivism, the materialism, the call for concreteness at all costs. It may even have been that this was a stress that came to mean more to Pollock as the late 1940s went on, and was part of the reason his painting changed. Certainly I think that Pollock would have sympathized, reading the long comparison between himself and Dubuffet that Greenberg mounted in February 1947 —in the end the comparison is to Pollock's advantage, but a lot of time is spent insisting on what the two painters share—with this sort of cutting and slashing: "Where the Americans mean mysticism, Dubuffet means matter, material, sensation, the all too empirical and immediate world—and the refusal to be taken in by anything coming from outside it. Dubuffet's monochrome means a state of mind, not a secret insight into the absolute; his positivism accounts for the superior largeness of his art."[33] (By "the Americans" in this passage, Greenberg means Rothko, Gottlieb, and Barnett Newman.)

In other words, I believe that Pollock in some sense responded to the pressure of Greenberg's argument; not of course because it was a good argument (though it was) but because it framed a real set of tensions inherent in Pollock's practice—it saw where Pollock was going. "Unless American art reconciles

itself," this is Greenberg in 1946 in *Les Temps Modernes*, "with
that minimum of positivism on which rests . . . the force of modern art . . . unless we integrate our poetry into the art's immediate physical dimensions," we shall go on producing limited,
fitful, discontinuous work; all this in spite of the fact, which
Greenberg acknowledges once again, even to his Paris readers,
that Gothicness has been and is "at the root of most of the best
works of American literature and painting."[34]

I take this to be a doubleness of mind that Pollock shared,
and out of which he acted in 1947, making *Galaxy* and *Full
Fathom Five*. It was not, of course, that the new way of painting
presented exactly a solution—though for a time it may have
seemed that way; there is an elation to the titles in 1947, and a
richness to the imagery, that suggest as much. But the nature of
the problem was clarified, so to speak, or brought into the open.
What was Pollock's art to be—after all, this question had
haunted Greenberg's criticism for the past four years—if *not*
"Gothic, morbid and extreme"? Perhaps it was true that an imagery of rage had proved itself unworkable in the end, the picture
space stuffed to the point of ludicrousness with shrieking, plan-
gent bits and pieces of emotion, each buttonholing the viewer and
talking at once. What painter would not retreat from *Something
of the Past*—this painting, remember, was in the show that
Greenberg preferred to Dubuffet's in 1947? Some kind of balance
had now to be struck—struck in the act of painting as opposed to
the imagery, built into the picture's positivity, its "handling"—
between nameless wildness and "the high impassiveness of true
modern style." *Some kind of balance*; one struck by the painter
of *Something of the Past*. I do not believe, in other words, that
Pollock envisaged his new way of doing things—getting paint on
canvas, I mean—as simply putting an end to the previous
violence, exasperation, and stridency. For these qualities were,
as Greenberg knew, what "the artist [made] of himself and his
experience in the world"; without them Pollock's art would most
likely decline to a record of "his intentions, foibles and
predilections."

A great deal depended, therefore, on technique. I shall take
it for granted that most of us approximately know how pictures
like *Full Fathom Five* were done; and the things we do not understand about the process—how many sessions, usually, went
into a painting like this? were there many paintings, even multi-
colored ones, that Pollock did at one fell swoop and never returned to? how long were pictures left hanging round the studio,

Jackson Pollock, Something-thing of the Past, *1946, oil on canvas, 56 x 38 in. Private collection.*

in some kind of unfinished state, or while Pollock decided if they *were* unfinished? what proportion of pictures was discarded?— these questions never will get answered now, though there are things in Namuth's testimony or Krasner's that give hints of answers.[35] Nor do I think that the privileged witnesses are holding out on us: the process was partly a secret at the time, for all Pollock's release of bits of it into the public realm as part of his "self contained and sustained advertising concern"; some of these questions did not occur to Pollock's first onlookers, and cannot be decided in retrospect.

In any case, the questions that matter most about the technique are interpretative. What was it precisely that Pollock's new way of painting allowed aesthetically and, even more, what did it disallow? There are at least two aspects to this, which I should like to keep partly separate: matters of physical procedure on the one hand, and issues of perception and judgment on the other. In the first place, as has often been pointed out, the technique disqualified certain kinds of painterly habits and know-how, or made them damn difficult; it put the painter literally out of reach of his skills, his "touch," his distinctive handling.[36] This was important because Pollock *was* skillful, perhaps even facile, and facility was the enemy. One critic in 1946 quoted Arthur B. Carles against Pollock—a remark Carles was supposed to have made when asked why he did not do more watercolors: "They terrify me . . . . they get beautiful so quick." Pollock suffered, so this critic thought, from the same "ability to achieve surface virtuosity."[37] This was not altogether a cheap shot, at least by comparison with the general run of criticism Pollock received at the time; or rather, cheap or not, it may well have chimed in with some of Pollock's own doubts—and Greenberg's. "Facility has a stubbornness of its own and is loath to abandon easy satisfactions."[38] This is Greenberg on De Kooning in 1948; it is a leitmotif of his writing on art in the 1940s, and I have no doubt that it translates, partly, the common talk of the studios of the time. It is, after all, a basic modernist trope.

But the method did more than disallow Pollock's normal ways of drawing a line or working up that "thick, fuliginous flatness" which had previously been his trademark.[39] It interfered with his whole perception of the pictures he was making, his "reading" of them, upsetting most of the habits of scanning and understanding he had acquired from twenty years at the easel or on the wall. Standing over the canvas, coming at it from all four sides, throwing and pouring from sticks and cans: the new technique set Pollock at a distance from his own sense of the "aesthetic," and made it peculiarly hard again to decide when the work had reached a proper "state of order" and "organic intensity."[40] (The phrases are Pollock's; they seem to be his preferred terms of aesthetic judgment.)

Something very odd and specific is being tried for here. Technique is altering judgment or dispersing it, or at least grating against it. It seems that if we could fully understand Pollock's actual, physical ways of doing things in 1947–50, we might have the key to his sense of what abstraction was in painting, and what it was for. Hence the temptation to have the bits and pieces of evidence in this area add up, where in fact they are mostly ambiguous. We know, for example, from Lee Krasner, that an amount of time and effort went into dragging the drip paintings up from the floor and hanging them provisionally—leaving them around on the wall, deciding whether they worked there or not.[41] It would be easy to make too much of this. When Rosalind Krauss decides on the basis of it that "there was a caesura, a very great one, between the state in which [Pollock] worked the painting itself, and the one in which he 'read' it; the painting itself, in order to be read, had to be transferred to the wall," this will just about do, it seems to me, as (slightly overcolored) metaphor.[42] A lot depends on the meaning of the word "read." Certain kinds of reading were no doubt made difficult, or next to impossible, by the fact that the field Pollock was working on "was so large that the painting, as a whole image or configuration, could not be seen by him from the position in which he was working on it." But the same had been true for Tintoretto or Tiepolo at work on a ceiling; and only a few of Pollock's pictures, in fact, were monsters swallowing the whole studio floor.

Even of these I think we can say the following. Pollock did "read" the totality of his painting as he worked on it; he synthesized an image of the whole picture from the various partial views he had of it. He was reading his pictures and acting upon the reading; but what he seemed to want in his practice was a situation where the synthesis of aspects—the reading—came about as part of a sequence of *movements*; it took place, but was never entirely arrested and fixed. Not that such arrest and deliberation was simply left out of the process of picturemaking. It happened; the photos of the studio show us that. There are at least two of Burckhart's photos, for instance, that show what I take to be the picture *Silver Plaques*—its strict title is *Number 9, 1950*—still in transit, without its final, erasing smudges of aluminum: at first propped against the wall, next to a picture on the floor that is hard to identify—perhaps a discard, possibly an unfinished state of *Number 3, 1950*—and then hung at the head of the same painting, three feet or so off the ground.[43] The process seems to have been elaborate sometimes, and not one Pollock relished; the picture was hung, subjected to judgment, often returned to the floor for further work; but all the same, in the process of actual manufacture, it seems there had to be a series of obstacles to aesthetic freezing and framing; aesthetic decison-making had somehow to be *ingested into* the act of manufacture, the deskilled address to the surface from above, "the positive moment of practising what it does not understand"—Hegel's phrase on the Unhappy Consciousness.[44]

"The positive moment of practising what it does not understand": I do not want to offer that as a catchphrase for Pollock's procedure. As I said, judging and understanding did get done; the question is *how*, under what set of constraints, as part of what physical process? Nonetheless the phrase from the *Phenomenology* does point to something in Pollock's method, especially if we give the words "positive" and "practising"—a bit willfully, of course—the flavor of concreteness they might have in a piece of Greenberg criticism from the time.

Questions about method cannot be disentangled, in other words, from more contentious ones about aesthetic and intention. What kinds of configuration were thrown up, after all, by this unlikely way of doing things? What kinds of work on the language? Answers to these questions are not exactly in short supply; the best have come from the modernist writers who looked at Pollock's work in the 1960s. Their account has got a bit inert and tedious since, from repetition, but it is obvious that any description of Pollock has to work out of them, and my descriptions proceed accordingly.[45]

The main thing the modernist critics got right, I think, about the paintings from 1947 to 1950 is their fierce, almost doctrinaire quality, their quality of renunciation; which is not to say, of course, that they renounce sensuality or do not often have beauty, even charm, in view. But if a painting is to be abstract at all—this seems to be the pictures' logic—then it has to be so through and through, down to the last detail or the first gestalt; it has to be made into the *opposite* of figuration, the outright, strict negative of it. There is work going on in 1947–50 to free the most rudimentary elements of depiction—line, color, handling—from their normal associations with the world we know, or at least the

Jackson Pollock, Num-
ber 1, 1948, *oil on can-*
vas, 68 x 104 in.
Collection, The
Museum of Modern Art,
New York.

world of objects, bodies, and spaces between them. Line, to
quote the *locus classicus* of this discussion in Michael Fried's
Three American Painters, "has been freed at last from the job of
describing contours and bounding shapes." He goes on:

> It has been purged of its figurative character. Line, in these
> paintings, is entirely transparent both to the non-illusionistic
> space it inhabits but does not structure, and to the pulses of
> something like pure, disembodied energy that seems to move
> without resistance through them. Pollock's line bounds and
> delimits nothing—except, in a sense, eyesight. . . . In these
> works Pollock has managed to free line not only from its
> function of representing objects in the world, but also from
> its task of describing and bounding shapes or figures,
> whether abstract or representational, on the surface of the
> canvas. In a painting such as *Number 1, 1948* there is only a
> pictorial field so homogeneous, overall and devoid both of
> recognizable objects and of abstract shapes that I want to
> call it *optical*, to distinguish it from the structured, essen-
> tially tactile pictorial field of previous modernist painting
> from Cubism to de Kooning and even Hans Hofmann. Pol-
> lock's field is optical because it addresses itself to eyesight
> alone. The materiality of his pigment is rendered sheerly vi-
> sual, and the result is a new kind of space—if it still makes
> sense to call it space—in which conditions of seeing prevail
> rather than one in which objects exist, flat shapes are jux-
> taposed or physical events transpire.[46]

There is a lot here that strikes me as debatable, especially in
the last three sentences. I do not agree—this will emerge more
clearly later—with what gets said in passing about the materiality
of Pollock's pigment and the viewer's perception of it; and for all
that the remark seems incidental to Fried's argument, a great
deal will turn out to depend on it. "Optical," a few lines earlier,
is a word called on to do an immense amount of rhetorical work,
as the text freely admits. (Fried's "wanting to call it" optical, and
putting the concept in anxious italics, makes one feel churlish at
not wanting to do the same.) The phrases that follow—"addresses itself to eyesight alone," "rendered sheerly visual,"
"conditions of seeing prevail"—are fine as long as they are not
meant to conjure up some bogus ontological threshold which Pollock's line magically crosses. (A lot of rotten modernist criticism
thrived on this kind of thing.)

In any case the main point of Fried's description seems to me to stand. It could easily be extended, in fact, to other formal elements about which he has less to say. Color, for instance, does not *behave* in the drip paintings, at least when the process of pouring is successful. It takes on none of its normal states or relations: it is no longer seemingly present as the attribute of a surface, as a covering or a substance, and yet it is equally far from having the look of a film or an atmosphere, a no-thing, a disembodied property; color in Pollock is too much a matter of fact for that to happen, too much aluminum as opposed to "silver." There is the thickness and obtrusiveness of the paint in detail, the matter it is and the matters that are crushed or folded into it; and there is the evenness and openness of the final thing, helped on by swathes of white or aluminum. There is the mud and the sheen; color ought to be one or the other, and is not.

Likewise handling. Handling in a work of art—traces of making, demonstrations of the artist's touch—has normally functioned as a kind of descant to the main line of figuration. It has been an overtone or undertone to an image; something in which the spectator was meant to "see" the artist, but see him as it were *behind* the image, in the adjustments and nuances which lent the picture its consistency and made it a unity of sorts. Handling in *Number 3, 1949*, or *a fortiori* in the gargantuan *Number 32, 1950*, is not like this anymore. It is not simply that the pictures have become in a sense *all* handling, nor even that handling is no longer the embodiment of touch or "skill"; rather, that handling is not the sign anymore of unity, whether the pictures' or the picturemaker's. The marks in these paintings, it seems to me, are not meant to be read as consistent trace of a subject, a controlling presence, but rather as a texture of interruptions, gaps, zigzags, arhythms and incorrectnesses, which all signify a making, no doubt, but one that enacts precisely the absence of a singular maker, an "artist"—a central continuous psyche persisting from start to finish. Of course this enactment of absence may also be a fiction, but it seems the fiction Pollock wanted.

This is what I meant before by pointing to the fierceness of Pollock's abstraction, its quality of renunciation. If a painting was to be abstract at all—if it no longer could depend on likeness to specify its relation to other matters in the world—then everything in the painting, or in Pollock's painting anyway, should take that fact as the great one. The picture had to be rid of resemblance, rid of it utterly, emptied of all those mere forms that resemblance brought in its wake.

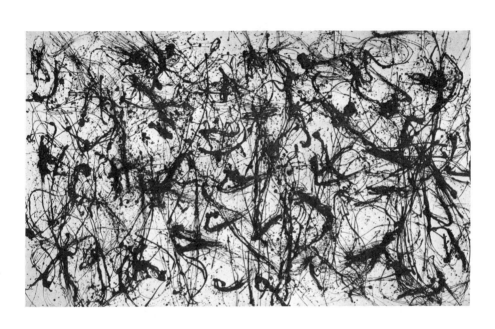

Jackson Pollock, Number 32, 1950, *enamel paint on canvas, 8 ft. 10 in. x 15 ft. Collection, Kunstsammlung Nordrhein-Westfalen, Düsseldorf.*

Jackson Pollock, Detail
of Number 1, 1948, *oil
on canvas, 68 x 104 in.
Collection, The
Museum of Modern Art,
New York.*

Frieze of horses with
hands, *upper
Paleolithic, rock paint-
ing in cave at Pech
Merle, Lot.*

Why? Oh, for many reasons—though of course we are here on speculative ground. Because painting had now to find its way back to the ground of representation, to the moment when marks first stood for things other than themselves—the moment when the handprint was no longer an index of presence but "seen as" a hand, a hand out there, someone else's. (Not that I believe for an instant that Pech Merle came out of any such moment, or even that such a moment ever took place, at least punctually. It may have been that Pollock thought so; it may not.) Because abstraction seemed to mean *priority* in Pollock's case: the possibility of making the first painting again. Numbering paintings, as Jonathan Weinberg suggested, was most of all attractive because it allowed Pollock to call certain paintings One, an opportunity he made use of four times in three years.[47]

Because if abstract painting could finally dispose of its parasitic relation to likeness, then it might discover—here the ground is firmer—some other means of signifying experience. It might put itself in a different *sort* of relation to the world.

It seems to me clear that Pollock believed this, and said it. But as it stands the belief is too general to be of much help in construing his practice: it leads to too many further questions. What world? What kind of experience? Signified how?

Experience, I have said already, is a key word in Pollock's lexicon. "The self-discipline you speak of—will come, I think, as a natural growth of a deeper, more integrated, experience."[48] There are the ghosts of the psychoanalytic institution here, as Pollock repeatedly encountered it. "The source of my painting is the unconscious."[49] The two concepts seem at times to overlap. Neither is clear. Both are probably mediated—I am convinced by Michael Leja—by all manner of popular and semipopular philosophies of mind; books like Harvy Fergusson's *Modern Man, His Belief and Behavior*, in Pollock's library at his death, whose very phrasing seems to crop up in the statements of 1947 or 1950; or James Harvey Robinson's *The Mind in the Making*, whose account of induction—it is not a very brilliant one—is there in note form, in Pollock's handwriting, on the back of a drawing from the thirties.[50] These sources are not impressive, and not surprising. Mediated versions of Freud, as Leja dryly puts it, are often more useful than the real thing; their "very shortcomings . . .—ambiguity, eccentricity, metaphorical extension, or over-simplification"—are what render them tractable, make them stick to a practice or suggest one.

This line of thought cannot be pressed too far. "When you're

painting out of your unconscious. . . ."[51] "The modern artist, it
seems to me, is working and expressing an inner world—in other
words—expressing the energy, the motion, and other inner
forces."[52] "[I]t doesn't make much difference how the paint is
put on as long as something has been said."[53] "I just can't stand
reality."[54] "We're all of us influenced by Freud, I guess."[55] "I
saw a landscape the likes of which no human being could have
seen."[56] A proper account of Pollock has to respect these statements' banality, as well as their deadly earnest, while bearing in
mind that the images they accompanied were not banal in the
least.

"When you're painting out of your unconscious. . . ." One of
the things Pollock was aiming for in 1947–50, and surely thought
he had obtained, was a kind of orderliness in painting, after the
previous shrieking clutter. These paintings were *"One,"* there
was a grand evenness and seamlessness to them. What was to be
signified, no less, was the logic of a certain way of dealing with
the world; and it had to be clear that this was a *kind* of dealing
which, given its tangential relation to our normal categories,
could only be pictured this way. What shall we call it, this experience? Vestigial, immediate, unfigured, "unfounded"? (That last
word crops up in Parsons' records as the title of two of Pollock's
first drip paintings, which later got called *Vortex* and *The Nest*.[57]
One of them was used as the signature image on the announcement for the 1948 show. *Unfounded* is a good, overdetermined
title, and I have a feeling that the word was salvaged from Pollock's reading, from *Moby Dick* or *Finnegan's Wake*, though I
still cannot find the source. It is a good companion, also, to Pollock's other, later title in the negative, his *Unformed Figure* of
1953.)

Unfounded, maybe, but perhaps for that reason rich. There
is a kind of experience, these pictures propose, which is vestigial, no doubt—unusable, uncanny in the limiting sense of that
word—but which at least the culture leaves alone. It is the kind
of experience modern painting has often been forced back on; the
only kind, so it believes, not colonized or banalized by everyday
life. The proposal here is double-edged and registers as such in
Pollock's painting. This experience is not occupied by the parent
culture because it is a wilderness; there are spaces where the
mechanics of "making ordinary" does not get under way because
there is nothing much for it to work on. Does that make such
spaces interesting? Is not openness also emptiness in this case,

finding one's own voice pretending to be inarticulate, and freedom a lot like confinement?

Let me try to draw the threads of this description together. The drip paintings of 1947–50 were intended to signify a certain order to experience; they were, in Parker Tyler's words—it is a piece of criticism that Pollock seems to have valued—to be "made to represent."[58] Yet whatever else had to happen, a necessary preliminary to such "making to represent" was precisely to pulverize any single, unequivocal *belonging* to one space, one part of the world, one kind of Nature. Not that Pollock saw what he was doing in the drip paintings in precisely these terms from the start. In the beginning, in the first flush of discovery—over the last few months of 1947—the world was overridden and transformed but that very transformation was "figured" in terms of a stable, dominant metaphor. The metaphor was of substance: richness, incrustation, sea change, release from mere terrestrial existence. The titles and pictures spoke the same language: *Magic Lantern, Phosphorescence, Alchemy, Enchanted Forest, Comet, Shooting Star, Shimmering Substance, Galaxy, Reflection of the Big Dipper*. The world was a world of delight, of fullness and strangeness, the transmuting of base metals into gold, the suspension of weight and gravity, the slow turn of things in a green sea, the impossible gray fire of phosphorescence on the ocean surface. "Sitting on a bank,/Weeping again the King my father's wrack,/This music crept by me upon the waters,/Allaying both their fury and my passion,/With its sweet air."[59]

The mood was powerful but it did not last. Titles like these persisted for a few months, and then the painter put an end to them. Numbers replaced names, and the picture began to stand in a more difficult, contradictory relationship to any world we might recognize or imagine.

In order to represent at all, I suppose, a series of marks in a picture have to be seen as standing for something besides themselves; they have to be construed metaphorically. (This is true even of indices, if that is what we believe Pollock's marks to be: the moment a character or quality is attributed to an index, we are making it into a metaphor of sorts—of its maker, or of that which gave rise to it.) Metaphor is inescapable, and what in any case would an exit from it be like? Pollock's work in 1948–50, it seems to me, moves between two metaphoric poles. On the one hand, there are those figures of totality I have already referred to: that One-ness, that "pure harmony, easy give and take," *Prism*,

Vortex, Lavender Mist. On the other, a set of metaphors I shall call, a bit warily, figures of dissonance. I mean by this those aspects of Pollock's art which do *not* partake of the One-ness and are neither seamless nor all-over: the quality of "handwriting" to the thing, and of handwriting often become hopeless palimpsest; the figures of obstruction, undergrowth, uncertainty, randomness, of a kind of peremptory violence done (still) with the sticks and cans; the persistence in the markmaking of Gothicness, exasperation, and stridency.[60] It is hard not to melodramatize this side of Pollock's painting, but running that risk seems preferable to what the modernist critics do, which is mostly look through it as if it were a bit embarrassing. (Pollock's "concern in his art was not with any fashionable metaphysics of despair but with making the best paintings of which he was capable": thus Fried.[61] A false distinction propped up nicely by the scareword "fashionable.")

What are we supposed to do, as viewers, with the marks in the picture of discontinuity and aimlessness, improbable roughness and dishevelment, abrupt reversals of direction, inconsistencies, scrawling, episodes of rhetorical excess—crushed glass, chicken wire, whorls of paint squeezed convulsively from tubes, handprints, spatter and clotting, glaring industrial color—all those elements in the work that leave behind the signs of discomposure, which insist that these pictures obey no rules, or none we'll know, no horizon lines, no space, no sense of the whole preceding its parts? Pretend these aspects are not there, that they do not signify, that they disappear into the totality?

I do not think so. But nonetheless "dissonance" is a difficult word on its own. It sounds too dark. Adorno is helpful here. "Dissonance (and its counterparts in the visual arts)," he says, "—the trademark, as it were, of modernism—lets in the beguiling moment of sensuousness by transfiguring it into its antithesis . . . pain."[62] "Dissonance is the truth about harmony. Harmony is unattainable."[63] Dissonance is on the side, always, of mimesis: "Dissonance is the same as expression; whereas consonance and harmony seek to do away with expression . . . . Expression cannot be conceived except as expression of suffering. Delight has shown itself to be inimical to expression (perhaps because there never was such a thing as delight), to say nothing of beatitude, which is completely expressionless."[64] Compare the world of *"One"* with that of *Lucifer*, or *Lavender Mist* (*Number 1*, again) with *Number 32, 1950*.

Dissonance—do not misunderstand me—is not the truth of Pollock's art; it is one moment of it, one aspect of its sensuousness, the means of mimesis it carries within it. Pollock's project, as I see it, is exactly *not* to allow the figures of dissonance to hold sway, any more than the figures of totality. His painting is a work *against* metaphor, against any one of his pictures settling down inside a single metaphorical frame of reference. He wishes to cross metaphors, to block connotation by multiplying it. He intends so to accelerate the business of signifying that any one frame of reference will not fit. Figures of dissonance cancel out figures of totality; no metaphor will get hold of this picture's standing for a world, though we think the picture does somehow stand for one: it has the requisite density. As Don Judd had it later, "The elements and aspects of Pollock's paintings are polarized rather than amalgamated."[65] "Something," as Parker Tyler said, "which cannot be recognized as any part of the universe is made to represent."[66] That is a paradoxical achievement.

One thing that needs to be established straightaway is how these points about metaphor in Pollock connect with the kind of modernist reading rehearsed earlier on. They do and they don't. A painting could be freed of all traces and afterimages of likeness and still not do the kind of work against metaphor I have just been describing. We could have—no doubt we do have—a strictly "optical," nonfigurative abstract painting that nonetheless stood in a *confirming* relation to a world we might recognize —an inert relation—a relation to "Nature," say, in which nothing of that dismal category was in the least negated.

And does not this last possibility loom, for Pollock's painting, the better he gets with his new techniques? Nature, in 1948 and 1949, had been kept at bay, erased by its opposite—by the anti-nature of aluminum and duco enamel, by the brashness and tawdriness of the color scheme in a painting like *Number 1, 1949*. This painting stood sentinel over Pollock's efforts the following year: it is propped up vertical against the partition in one of Hans Namuth's photos, with what looks like *Autumn Rhythm* under way on the floor; and in another it is hung on the inner studio wall, with *"One"* being worked on directly beneath it.[67] The paintings that were done in 1950 seem to me different from the two previous years. The poles of metaphor tend to split apart and simplify. On the one hand, the figures of dissonance become schematic, black-and-white: dissonance becomes mimesis, handwriting, a theater of some sort; it is extracted from the mix of

Jackson Pollock, Number 1, 1949. *Duco and aluminum paint on canvas, 63⅛ x 102⅛ in. The Museum of Contemporary Art, Los Angeles. The Rita and Taft Schreiber Collection, given in loving memory of my husband, Taft Schreiber, by Rita Schreiber. (Photo: Tom Vinetz)*

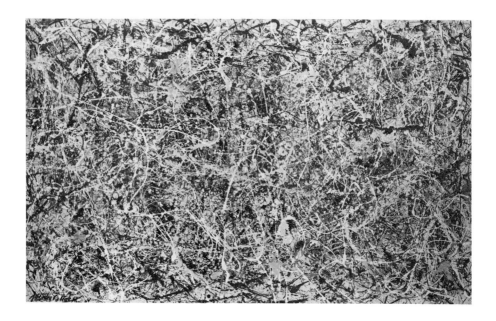

Hans Namuth, Pollock
at work on One (Num-
ber 31, 1950), with
Number 1, 1949 on
studio wall, *photo-
graph. Courtesy Hans
Namuth.*

sensuousness. And on the other, Nature returns—*Lavender Mist,
Autumn Rhythm, "One"*—metaphors whose very breathing *completeness* carries within it the sign of a practice coming to an end.
As usual with Pollock, the sequence of pictures in 1950 and
the amount and duration of work on each are largely matters of
speculation, despite the wealth of what ought to be hard evidence—photographs, title numbers, film sequences, Namuth's and
Krasner's say so.[68] *Lavender Mist* seems to have been the year's
first big picture: Pollock originally called it *Number 1, 1950*, before Greenberg came up with the lusher title.[69] That title is ingenious but a bit misleading. No doubt the great loops and
splashes of pale pink do just about hold the picture together,
abetted as they are by a layer of aluminum gray, very similar in
tone, put on toward the end; the two give the picture an atmosphere, a softness. But *Mist* does not seem quite right. What
kind of mist would it be that contained or extruded this thicket of
blacks, fibrillated and staccato, as if made from some razor-thin
and razor-sharp material? If this is atmosphere, it is one folded
up in barbed wire; if this is Nature, it is a generality (a continuity)
evoked only to be interrupted—almost choked—by the to and fro
of Events.

Nonetheless Greenberg's title does point to something real.
Lavender Mist is sulphurous and tense, but also charming; one
could easily imagine the blacks receding a little further into the
haze, and totality holding the field altogether, almost sweetly.
Greenberg might have welcomed that; Pollock for the moment
did not. *Number 32, 1950* came next, *Lavender Mist*'s violent antithesis, with totality established now by nothing but the centrifuge of line. And then *Number 31, 1950*, the picture that was
subsequently called *"One."*

We know from Namuth that this painting was worked on at
more than one session and changed its appearance radically
along the way. Namuth remembers it having a first stage of
"white, black and maroon," where presumably the oppositeness
of the picture's elements was still pronounced, or more pronounced than it became. "There was more work to be done."[70]
What that seems to have amounted to, visually, was softening,
pulverizing, sewing together; the same kind of work that had
been done in *Lavender Mist*, though this time pushed further
still. After the exacerbation of *Number 32* there was going to be
calm. The undergrowth became exquisite; lines congealed into
atmosphere—even, cool, rich, unassertive, surface-like, suggest-

Jackson Pollock, Number 1, 1950 (Lavender Mist), *oil, enamel, and aluminum paint on canvas, 87 x 118 in. National Gallery of Art, Washington, D.C.*

Jackson Pollock, One
(Number 31, 1950), *oil
and enamel paint on
canvas, 8 ft. 10 in. x
17 ft. 5⅝ in. Collection,
The Museum of Modern
Art, New York. Sidney
and Harriet Janis Col-
lection Fund.*

ing nothing so much as landscape, a kind of ethereal, rain-sodden foliage, "the likes of which no human being could have seen."

And last—by now we are fully back in *Vogue* territory— there is *Autumn Rhythm*. The title seems to have been Pollock's own. The "white, black and maroon" that Namuth remembers from *"One"* have become white, black, and brown, which can be left as an open play of opposites just because the opposition is strictly formal. The painting is a dance, a choreography, measured and repetitive and even a bit florid (compare the jerking, histrionic stops and starts of *Number 32*); all of its movements superintended now by a category drawn from Nature—one evoked quite matter of factly by color. Dry leaves, bare branches, air reappearing where earlier it had been smothered in green: are we meant to be embarrassed by these equations or to revel in them? The picture is an instance of Autumn, is it not; it makes the natural category vivid, gives it the space and stateliness it calls for.

None of these remarks are meant to demote or decry the paintings of 1950 (how tedious that this needs to be said). They are meant as description of the kind of finality they possessed— the terms in which they may have appeared to Pollock himself to put an end to a practice. It seems they did.

What was it, after all, that Pollock had expected of painting in 1947–50? Nothing very realistic. That it be abstract, first of all; that every last trace of likeness be harried out of it, in the hope that the great work of representing could be done differently; that the picture eventually be put in another relation to the world. One further dimension to that project, which I shall mention only in passing, was Pollock's interest at this time in abstract painting's literal, physical "relation to the world." A question that keeps recurring in his statements is whether painting might be on its way to occupying a different space altogether in the culture, and as a result might have to be conceived with different conditions of viewing in mind—seen as part of a Miesian architecture, perhaps, as wall or window or some new built element partaking of the qualities of both. Not quite painting any longer, in other words. It may even be that Pollock never thought the project of abstract painting would succeed without it becoming part of some such general reordering of space. "I believe the time is not ripe for a *full* transition from easel to mural. The pictures I contemplate painting would constitute a halfway state, and an attempt to point out the direction of the future, without

Jackson Pollock, Autumn Rhythm, *1950, oil on canvas, 8 ft. 10 in. x 17 ft. 8 in. The Metropolitan Museum of Art, George A. Hearn Fund, 1957, 57.92.*

arriving there completely."[71] In the studio in 1950, next to the
skulls and the paint cans, was the model of Peter Blake's Miesian
museum, with Pollock's pictures used as dividers of its empty
rectangle.[72] It was a first sketch of how abstraction might go beyond the halfway.

There is still one component to Pollock's practice I have
given short shrift; and if I pull it out of the hat after the others it
is not because I want it to upstage them, or to seem like the truth
of the matter, finally. All the same it has its own determinate
weight.

Painting in Pollock's case had ended up being abstract for a
reason: because figuration had proven, in practice, impossible.
The old forms were flyblown, the new too much the possession of
their particular makers; the attempt to remake them "out of the
unconscious" had led, as it often did, to amateur theatricals, por-
tentous, overstuffed, and overwrought.[73] Abstract painting was a
way out of the mess; but it was also a means of signifying what
had stood in the way of the figure in the first place, and left it
"unformed," "unfounded," *Something of the Past*. Pollock never
seems to have made up his mind for certain, in 1947–50, whether
that signifying could get done *without* the figure reappearing in
the abstract in some readable form. The problem was, of course,
to find a way to reconcile the second coming of the figure with the
work against likeness being done at the same time. The figure, if
it was to appear at all, would have to do so *out of* or *against* that
work, as the strict contrary of it, as the negation of the negation.

This is a topic in its own right. All I want to do in the present
context is point to the effort persisting in 1947–50 and renovate
the sense of uncertainty that some of the best, closest critics had
at the time as regards Pollock's general direction. Here, for instance, is Clement Greenberg's reaction to Pollock's one-man
show at the Betty Parsons Gallery in November and December
1951. The pictures in the show—*Number 14, 1951* is a fair example, and one Greenberg singled out for praise—were not abstract any longer. Masks, fingers and faces, the shapes of
animals and demons, bits and pieces of a half-human world were
now thrown up by the flow of black enamel, or only partly erased
by it. But Greenberg did not seem to see this as marking any
great sea change in Pollock's purposes as an artist, and certainly
not a fall from grace:

Jackson Pollock, Number 14, 1951, *enamel paint on canvas, 57⅝ x 106 in. The Tate Gallery, London. Lee Krasner Bequest.*

Jackson Pollock's problem is never authenticity, but that of finding his means and bending it as far as possible toward the literalness of his emotion. Sometimes he overpowers the means but he rarely succumbs to it. His most recent show, at Parsons', reveals a turn but not a sharp change of direction; there is a kind of relaxation, but the outcome is a newer and loftier triumph. . . .

Contrary to the impression of some of his friends, this writer does not take Pollock's art uncritically. I have at times pointed out what I believe are some of its shortcomings—notably, in respect to color. But the weight of the evidence still convinces me—after this last show more than ever—that Pollock is in a class by himself. Others may have greater gifts and maintain a more even level of success, but no one in this period realizes as much and as strongly and as truly. He does not give us samples of miraculous handwriting, he gives us achieved and monumental works of art, beyond accomplishedness, facility, or taste. Pictures "Fourteen" and "Twenty-five" in the recent show represent high classical art: not only the identification of form and feeling, but the acceptance and exploitation of the very circumstances of the medium of painting that limit such identification.[74]

The masks and figures, that is to say, were part of this painter's meditation on medium. They *were* "the literalness of his emotion"; and in this case at least the literalness did not interfere with the harder task (for Pollock), that of making his native violence and exasperation part of the painting, part of the pictorial order, not an addition to or an interruption of it.

This judgment on *Number 14, 1951* may seem strange, coming from Greenberg. But it is not an aberration. Greenberg had known all along that the figure—the place of the figure—was a question that Pollock's abstraction kept open. "Pollock," says Greenberg in 1947, "again like Dubuffet, tends to handle his canvas with an over-all evenness; but at this moment he seems capable of more variety than the French artist, and able to work with riskier elements—silhouettes and invented ornamental motifs—which he integrates in the plane surface with astounding force."[75] Those riskier elements did not disappear subsequently, nor did Greenberg pretend they had. Among the paintings he put second in quality to *Number 1, 1948* in his review of Pollock's show the following year was *Number 2,* "the one," as he put it, "with the black cut-out shapes."[76] In the sales records it is already called *Shadows*. That painting connects with several others in which drip and figure are put down—sometimes with the utmost of contrivance, and sometimes with a kind of jubilant naivety—as positive and negative, presence and absence, both poles likely to reverse their charge at a moment's notice.

There is a pair of pictures from 1948, the first of them in oil paint built up thickly on paper, with two spindly dancers cut out of the crust, and the second with the two figures stuck on masonite and teetering about unstably underneath a final flurry of thrown paint.[77] There is *Cut Out*, the fully developed state of this idea, in which the figure appears precisely *in the negative*, as that which is absent from the incrusted field. If there is to be a figure at all, in other words, it will be that which the activity of markmaking has excluded. The abstract will displace the figurative, cut it out, put it nowhere; and then give the weightless, placeless homunculus just enough substance for it to be body after all—a few splatters, enough of a physiognomy.[78]

Greenberg was right to say that the elements in this kind of game were risky. The last thing Pollock wanted, after all, was to end up redoing Paul Klee. The whole idea of *Cut Out* was potentially *kitsch*, with its "little man," *Child-Proceeds* mannequin stepping out bravely into the wide world. Was there a way to prevent this basic scenario showing through the splatters, so to speak, and acting as palliative to the play of negation? Pollock was not sure. *Cut Out* can be seen in one or two of Namuth's photos from 1950, still hanging around the studio—it was begun, by the look of things, two years earlier—as cut-out pure and simple, the figure existing as literal *nothing* in the middle of the paint.[79] It took time to decide what to do with that nothing—to give it just enough of positivity to make it coexist with the crust of paint (the evidence of art work) all round. And to take what had been extruded and make a second painting out of it: endow it in turn with a parody of presence, of cocksure, jaunty, material being-there—lend it an absolute dead void as surrounding, and the flash of random energy to set off the figure's incrustation all the better.

These pictures mostly have a one-off, hit-or-miss quality to them. They strike one as prototypes that never went into production. There is a picture called *Triad*, the smallest of the lot, which is the negative again to the negative of *Cut Out*, and even less successful. What is cut out and painted over now is the field itself, the traces of white handwriting which look as though they

Jackson Pollock, Number 2, 1948 (Shadows), *oil and cut-out on canvas (?), 53¾ x 44 in. Private collection.*

Jackson Pollock, Cut Out, *c. 1948–50, oil on cut-out paper mounted on canvas, 30½ x 23½ in. Collection, Ohara Museum of Art, Kurashiki, Japan.*

Hans Namuth, Pollock at work on Autumn Rhythm with Number 32, 1950 on studio wall and Cut Out and Number 4, 1950 visible, *photograph. Courtesy Hans Namuth.*

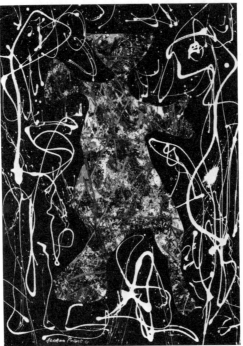

Jackson Pollock, Cut-Out Figure, *1948, oil on paper adhered to masonite, 30 x 22 in. Private collection, Montreal. (Photograph courtesy National Gallery of Canada)*

originally filled the whole rectangle. The void is void, and the flashes of random energy have ended up almost well-behaved, going to and fro across the three figures like hatching produced by a fairground machine. And finally there is *Number 7, 1949*, which Pollock afterward titled *Out of the Web*. It was done later than the other pictures—perhaps as much as a year later—and is three or four times as big. (Eight feet long to *Shadows'* forty-four inches, four feet high to *Cut Out*'s two feet six.) The mannequins are slightly less substantial now, or at least less obtrusive. A great deal of care (almost of fuss) has gone into folding and slid-ing them into the general blur of white and aluminum; they are dancing much the same quadrille as *Shadows*, but more deliber-ately, as if the figures were obliged to own up to the old demon Facility and positively *use* it. Their outlines—in contrast to *Shadows*, say, or even *Cut Out*—are cursive, rhymed, "ornamen-tal" in Greenberg's sense (which is not in any simple way pejora-tive). Pollock was as capable of whimsy as the next man. There were plenty of good modernist precedents for it. Why not go in for glib biomorphic comedy, Miroesque and Chaplinesque, with the dancers all giving a last wave of their club feet and fishtails before disappearing into the shallows? Why should not figurative painting be lighthearted? (By and large Pollock knew very well why not.)

Putting these pictures with figures into a sequence is not meant to seal them off from the general run of work Pollock was doing. They are all pictures *made out of* drip paintings, pictures the new technique gave rise to. Other tactics intersected. Under the influence of Michael Fried and the modernists, we tend to overlook those many paintings from 1947–50 in which the inter-lace of poured line is exactly *not* even and all-over, but centered, vertical, giving rise to the figurative. This is sometimes wild and approximate, as if the intention was to conjure up the shadow of figurative expectations in order to do violence to them more ef-fectively. (I have in mind a picture like *Number 10, 1950*, but there are others.)[80] Sometimes the mood seems parodic or fanci-ful, as it was in the *Cut Out* series.[81] And at others the comedy gets overtaken, more or less, by an access of the old exasperation and stridency.

That much is certainly true of *Number 10A, 1948*, a picture that stayed in Pollock's studio until his death and, according to Lee Krasner, was called *The Wooden Horse*. It is a collage: brown canvas mounted on board, a mixture of oil paint and duco enamel, and a stuck-on head off a hobby horse, two or three

Jackson Pollock, Out of
the Web (Number 7,
1949), *oil and enamel
paint on masonite, cut
out, 48 x 96 in. Collec-
tion, Staatsgalerie,
Stuttgart, Germany.*

Jackson Pollock, Number 10A, 1948 (The Wooden Horse), *oil, enamel paint, and wooden hobbyhorse head on brown cotton canvas, mounted on board, 35½ x 75 in. Collection, Moderna Museet, Stockholm.*

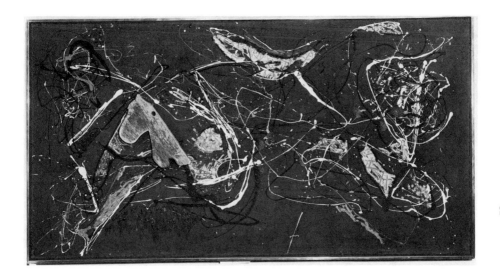

inches deep. The picture inevitably turns on the issue of like-ness, and in a sense its tactics are the same as *Cut Out*'s: there is the field and the figure, the found object and the object-not-being-found, and the two only make sense—conceptually and vi-sually—as negations of one another. The tone, however, seems to me different.

"Likeness is easy," says the hobby-horse head. "It happens without us even meaning it." (One of the reasons Pollock chose to use the hobby horse, surely, was the classic duck-rabbit rever-sal thrown up by the ragged end of the neck, with its notches for nose, mouth, and chin.) "To avoid likeness as you do is just *bravura*, the last kind that modern painting allows itself and as meretricious as all the rest." To which the oil and enamel return with equal force: "At least the test you propose is the right one. If the marks in this picture do not strike you as really aimless, then they have failed. If they come across as skillful—even in the art of avoiding skill, or dismantling it—then the game is up. This aimlessness intends to represent. It is meant to show what it is that stands in the way of likeness, and to what extremity of means art must resort if it aims for likeness all the same. For modern art is not somehow dogmatically resolved to avoid like-ness, but to come across it from a new direction. These thrown lines, this wretched meandering, the scratches of blue, red, and yellow which (almost) fill them out and give them body: they are ways of circling *around* likeness, ways of looking for likeness on the other side of resemblance. And not finding it. Here, if you like, is the cause of painting's obscurity; this is the process that strips it of its skills and pushes it back time and again to the infantile and disorganized. It is not that it occupies that territory with enthusiasm, necessarily (the very way it produces the infan-tile in a picture like this speaks to its impatience and disdain); but here, it believes, is where painting is obliged to operate. This is the only ground left on which representation might be reassembled."

No doubt there is an element of bizarrerie involved in staging *The Wooden Horse* as a kind of *agon* and giving its different idi-oms voices. But the picture is an argument, it seems to me. What marks it off from the previous history of collage is the sheer extremity—the shrillness—with which collage and painting are opposed: the absolute of blandness on the one side and the hec-toring of exasperation on the other. We may think the opposites end up all but pulling the picture apart, aesthetically; certainly the hobby-horse head is no sufficient fulcrum. There is likeness and

its opposite, the "found" and the "unfounded," what we know
too well already and what we know only "out of the unconscious." Whether the one kind of representation contradicts the
other (as Pollock believed it could) depends on the velocity at
which they collide.[82]

The Wooden Horse is an episode in Pollock's drip painting: it
does not represent what Pollock normally hoped and worked for
from his new technique. The pouring has stopped short too soon.
The point was for it to go further, to take over more fully from the
Unhappy Consciousness, and give rise to "states of order," "human needs and motives," "memories arrested in space."[83] Out
of that might eventually come some new kind of figuration, one
not "cut out," not negative, not introduced by fiat, not unformed
or unfounded but "One." Which brings us back to our starting
point, the photographs in *Vogue*.

Mentioning them in the same breath as *The Wooden Horse*
may seem like loading the dice. It is not done to glorify one moment of Pollock's painting at the expense of another, or even to
blacken the whole of abstract painting by associating it with Cecil
Beaton. The word "fashionable," as Michael Fried's use of it
demonstrates, is likely to recoil on all of us in time. What I mean
to suggest by the juxtaposition is simply that abstract art has
lived for much of its life in some kind of productive *anxiety* about
the uses which might be made of it in the culture. In particular it
has claimed that the forms and orders which art would discover
by doing away with resemblance would not be easy or merely
enticing; they would not be simply "decorative." This claim was
serious, and had real effects. But insofar as the claim is testable
by looking at the uses society actually made of abstract paintings,
then we could say that indeed they have been thought to be decorative and put through their paces in that spirit. They have
seemed the appropriate background to ball gown and bolero, to
the black-tie do at the local museum, to the serious business of
making money.

Of course someone might reasonably reply at this point that
any culture will use art in the ways it sees fit, and that the very
idea of art resisting such incorporation is pie in the sky. At a
certain level of low or high cynicism, there is no answer to that.
At other levels a few unsatisfactory answers are possible. Yes,
this idea about art's relation to its host culture *is* pie in the sky;
but so are most, perhaps all, other ideas about art's purposes

and responsibilities—art as the vehicle of some kind of transcendence or Truth, for instance, art as distilling the hard possibilities of *Geist*, art as opening onto a territory of free play or pleasure, art as bracketing the mere dross of worldly experience, art as Universal, art as the real form—the pure expression—of Individuality. The pie in these cases is so far in the sky as to be considerably less visible, to my way of thinking, than the pie we are looking at—the pie of resistance and refusal. And the test in *all* cases is not, it seems to me, the cogency or adequacy of the discursive claims, but whether the claims have led to production—whether the claims, for all their muddle and double think, have been associated with some real complexity and vehemence in the work of representation.

In this case it seems to me they have. There is a line of art stretching back to David and Shelley which makes no sense— which would not have existed—without its practitioners believing that what they did *was* resist or exceed the normal understandings of the culture, and that those understandings were their enemy. This is the line of art we call modernist. Pollock is part of it; perhaps at the end of it, perhaps not; it is hard to tell at present whether ideas of resistance and refusal have any sustaining force still left to them, or have been hopelessly incorporated into a general spectacle. The ideas have an old-fashioned ring to them, it is true; but then, so does the parent culture. This is the age of Reagan and Deng Xiaoping, not of Baudrillard and Peter Halley.

In any case the question is about the past, not the present; about the force these beliefs once had, in Pollock's case and before him. I shall put it dogmatically: in the visual arts since 1850, it seems as if no work of real concentration was possible without it being fired—superintended—by claims of this kind. The test of art was held to be some form of intransigence or difficulty in the object produced, some action against the codes and procedures by which the world was lent its usual likenesses.

This leads us back to *The Wooden Horse*. For if the test of art is intransigence, then surely it is clear—or at least understandable—why "abstract" and "figurative" go together in Pollock's practice and in others'. Because a work of art will only strike us as *difficult* if it succeeds in showing (or intimating) what its work against likeness is for, or about—on what other basis in our shared experience it might be seen to rest, how it could alter our attitudes to objects and processes we recognize as held in common, what the meaning of the abstract might be. There is a danger of misunderstanding here. The objects and processes we have in common include the objects and processes of art itself, so that part of our reaction to *The Wooden Horse* will be that it has its way so violently with our shared notions of unity in a picture, or of what counts as drawing and shading and "touch." Part of our difficulty has to do with having the category Art disrupted. ("Is this a painting?," as Pollock once asked about one of his own.[84] Whatever work against likeness Pollock was doing had to be done not just against likeness but also *against painting*, on the edge of the category Art, in the area where criteria for Art are lacking.) But *The Wooden Horse* has another aspect, it seems to me. The depth of our discomfort with it has to do with the fact that the work against likeness is still going on, and seemingly cannot be completed: that confident, self-evident simulacrum of horse is what the painting turns on and fails to negate. Likeness is the other side of abstractness: the "nonfigurative" happens because the world no longer falls into an order of images, or an order not overlaid with lies and banality (*Wooden Horse*, as a title, is full of undertones of deception and counterfeit). There may be ways in which abstract art can incorporate these conditions of its existence into itself and have them be signified. Perhaps no such ways exist. I believe that Pollock thought they did, or they might.

But even this much of affirmation, hedged in as it is by "mays" and "perhapses" and "mights," strikes me on second thought as too much. It says the wrong thing about Pollock's abstraction. It is still too conclusive. What I want to say, finally, is that Pollock's painting in its best period, in 1947–50, is contradictory; it lives on its contradictions, thrives on them, comes to nothing because of them. Its contradictions are the ones that any abstract painting will encounter, as long as it is done within bourgeois society, in a culture which cannot grasp—for all its wish to do so—the social reality of the Sign. That is to say, on the one hand, abstract painting must set itself the task of *canceling* nature, ending painting's relation to the world of things. It will make a new order to experience, it will put its faith in the sign, in the medium, it will have painting be a kind of writing at last, and therefore write a script none of us have read before. But on the other hand, painting discovers that none of this is achievable with the means it has. Nature simply will not go away: it reasserts its rights over the new handwriting, and writes its own familiar script with it—the script of *One*-ness, *Autumn Rhythm*, *Lavender Mist*. So that painting always reneges on its dream of anti-*phusis*, and returns to the Body—that thing of things, that figure of figures. It cuts the Body *out of the Sign, out of the field of Writing.*

There is a story about Mondrian in New York dancing to his beloved boogie woogie, when in midstream the band switches to another kind of jazz. "Let's sit down," Mondrian said to his partner, "I hear melody."[85] That is the dream and disappointment of abstraction in a nutshell. The idea of an art in outright opposition to the Natural—an art without melody, in other words—is a great notion, and a hopeless one. The band will always pick up the tune. "Let's sit down. I see a Figure." So let the Figure be in the picture on purpose—in the negative, taking the lordly, footling, infantile form that is the best (or worst) that painting can do with it. Let it be there *as* negation, as the sign of antinomy, not dialectic. For the grounds are lacking on which the contraries of bourgeois art—its claim to Nature and its wish for the free play of the signifier—could be dialectically reconciled.

I can see two or three ways this essay could end. One way would be concrete and limited. We could come back to the *Vogue* photographs again and make certain some basic—uncomfortable —points have not got lost in the flurry of argument. Nothing I have said in praise of Pollock's painting is meant to suggest that the bad dream of modern art—Tafuri's dream and Foucault's—is wrong. The photographs are nightmarish. They speak to the *hold* of capitalist culture, the way it outflanks any work against the figurative and makes it an aspect of its own figuration—a sign of that figuration's richness, the room it has made for more of the edges and underneath of everyday life. There is a danger in any discussion of modern art that the Other to modernism—the normal understandings it is supposed to be resisting or refusing— will come to seem a mere formula. That Other does exist. The *Vogue* photographs show it.[86] They show the sort of place reserved within capitalism for painting of Pollock's kind. These are the functions it is called on to perform, the public life it can reasonably anticipate. Nothing it can do, I think, will save it from being used in some such way as this. But that is a general verdict, a lofty one, a useless one. The fact is that some painting makes this public life its matter, and fights for room within it and in advance of it. Pollock's painting does so, it seems to me: which is to say, it turns back again and again to the root conditions of its own abstractness and tries to give them form. The form it chooses is a refusal of aesthetic closure: a cutting out, an interruption, a piece of infantile metonymy; dissonance meaning mimesis, meaning sensuousness *as well as* "Gothicness, paranoia and resentment"—the one in the form of the other.

Another way to end would be this. Here is a voice talking about abstract painting. It could be any Western speaker; any Westerner having his say about Soviet Russia and Socialist Realism and what we do in America. It comes from a book called *Where the Nights are Longest: Travels by Car through Western Russia*; but where it comes from does not matter. This is a piece of bourgeois wisdom. It is *Vogue* speaking:

> The fear of abstract painting, which may unlace the understanding to a world less simple than was apparent, is the fear that primacy may pass to the private, rather than the collective, vision. And there can be no return, once the journey has started, to tribal innocence.[87]

I do not think this needs much *explication de texte*. Here instead is another voice, one much closer to Pollock's time and world view, speaking to the First Closed Session of the American Artist's Congress in 1936. Abstract art is on the speaker's mind, and he does not much like it:

> As in the fantasy of a passive spectator, colors and shapes are disengaged from objects, and can no longer serve as a means in knowing them. The space within pictures becomes intraversable; its planes are shuffled and disarrayed, and the whole is re-ordered in a fantastically intricate manner. Where the human figure is preserved, it is a piece of picturesque still-life, a richly pigmented, lumpy mass, individual, irritable and sensitive; or an accidental plastic thing among others, subject to sunlight and the drastic distortions of design. . . .
>
> The individual is identified with the private (that is, the privation of other beings and the world), with the passive rather than the active, the fantastic rather than the intelligent. Such an art cannot really be called free, because it is so exclusive and private; there are too many things we value that it cannot embrace or even confront. An individual art in a society where human beings do not feel themselves to be most individual when they are inert, dreaming, passive, tormented or uncontrolled, would be very different from

modern art. And in a society where all men can be free individuals, individuality must lose its exclusiveness and its ruthless and perverse character.[88]

What I have quoted is the end of a speech by Meyer Schapiro, but once again whose voice it is is not important. It could be anyone, almost: any old Stalinist in full cry, exhorting us to wake from our separate, private dreams.[89] And these are the voices that call the tune of abstract art; it is as if the matter of abstraction has to be talked of in terms like these, as if our culture wants it as a little battlefield of basic cultural pieties—"individuals" versus "collectivities," freedom versus tribalism, anti-Soviet driveling versus Stalinist high moral tone. This seems to me a reason for studying abstract painting, not for avoiding the subject: something is at stake here, producing these false alternatives; but the fact that this is the general currency of debate does not make the job in hand exactly *easy*.

Abstract painting—this is my third attempt at an ending—could perhaps be compared to one of the forms of art it was supposed to replace, the series of strict classical and medieval revivalisms which made up such an important part of the nineteenth century in architecture and the other visual arts. We have given up feeling superior to that revivalism, and nothing we can say now is likely to derogate from Labrouste's achievement, say, or Burgess's, or Puvis de Chavannes's. Does that mean we should now learn to act as Labrouste's or Puvis's spokesmen and simply dismiss what the early twentieth century saw in them of desperation, dogmatism, pedantry, pomposity, dim fantasy, brittle didacticism, overbearing and empty Utopia? I do not think so. These things are written into revivalism, just as they are into the project of abstraction. Suppose that our object of study were the Bibliothèque Sainte-Geneviève or *Ave Picardia Nutrix* or the work of *Unovis* in Vitebsk. What we should need to see, in each of these cases, is the work's embattled resistance to the century it lived in—the fierceness of the acts by which it hoped to direct and compel our attention, the effort to make meaning unequivocal, to sign it and tie it down, to have it behave, to have it be reduced again to its bare elements. We should need to understand what it was these works were obliged to *exclude* from their worldmaking, what made for the distinctive thinness and brittleness of their formal language.

None of this would be done to belittle Labrouste, any more than Malevich and El Lissitsky. It would be done out of a sense that this was what the phenomena in question were like, and that pointing to their insufficiencies *is* pointing to their strength. Coming to understand a work of art, or a line of art—coming to see the way in which a certain idiom might make better sense in retrospect—is not the same thing as apologizing for it. A history of abstract painting is not the same thing as a public relations exercise on its behalf.

I know very well that nothing I can say will stop the public relations exercise from continuing. There is something about abstract painting that seems to elicit it: abstract art is hideously lively, but always seemingly on its last legs. And it has to be protected: something is at stake in it, something the culture is still trying to sort out, of which this art is an emblem.

Emblematic of what, precisely? Of the true form of individuality, or the false one? Of the free play of the signifier, or the impossibility of any such play—until the moment, that is, when the sign is discovered in its collective being? Of Victory over the Sun, or of Victory Boogie Woogie? Of some final giving-over of the self to meaninglessness, and even a kind of glorying in the fact—"the positive moment of practising what it does not understand"?

Looked at coolly, these claims and metaphors of abstraction are senseless. They put too much weight on the business of making a painting. And no doubt I have been infected by the general atmosphere of metaphorical overkill: this paper has spent too much time snooping round Pollock's studio, looking for culture heroes and signs of crisis. Not that I intend to draw back from that at the last moment. Ending with the two images I do—Pollock at work on *Autumn Rhythm,* and El Lissitsky's propaganda board, propped up on the pavement outside a factory gate in Vitebsk—is meant to raise the stakes, not lower them. These images are emblems, and they conjure up the purposes of abstract painting very well. Of course the purposes are contrary, but in each case what seems to me essential is their overweening, Utopian, slightly lunatic character. History is going to be *canceled* by painting. The human order is going to be remade. The picture will tell the Truth. Whether it did so, or could have done so, is another question. What the writing on El Lissitsky's painting says to the malingerer is "Get into the Workshop! Increase Production!" What kind of truth we take that to be depends on our view of War Communism and connected matters. But it is the *claim* to Truth that seems to me essential—the claim to totality. These claims are the substance of abstract painting; they are what give it its fierceness and sensuousness, and make it turn on its own disappointment.

Hans Namuth, Pollock
at work on Autumn
Rhythm with Number
32, 1950 on studio wall
and Number 6, 1950
visible, *photograph.*
Courtesy Hans Namuth.

El Lissitsky,
The Factory Workbenches
Await You,
media unknown.
Photograph taken in
Vitebsk, c. 1919.

Afterword

This essay comes out of teaching Pollock over twenty years. It takes a lot from lectures and seminars given along the way at Camberwell School of Art, UCLA, Leeds University, and especially a seminar at Harvard on the New York School. Four papers emerged from that seminar which altered my view of the issues: Whitney Davis's "Pollock's Wordlessness," Michael Leja's "Jackson Pollock, *Modern Man*," John O'Brian's "Greenberg on Matisse," and Jonathan Weinberg's "Picasso in Pollock." I have borrowed from all of them, probably more than I know. (A version of Weinberg's paper was published subsequently as "Pollock and Picasso: The Rivalry and the 'Escape'," *Arts Magazine* [June 1987], and one of John O'Brian's appears in this volume. The other two will also, I hope, be published before long.) Michael Leja has since completed a dissertation on the New York School, and a first indication of one aspect of his work has been published as "The Formation of an Avant-Garde in New York" in M. Auping, ed., *Abstract Expressionism: The Critical Developments* (Buffalo, 1987). With characteristic and extraordinary generosity Leja gave me access to the rich research materials from the later 1940s he has gathered. I am deeply grateful to him.

A version of the present essay was given as a lecture at the Symposium "Hot Paint for Cold War" at the University of British Columbia, Vancouver, in September 1986, and in several other places over the next few months. I gained a lot from criticisms received as a result, especially those of two people who suffered through the lecture twice, Benjamin Buchloh and Anne Wagner.

I should say straightaway that this essay makes no claim to completeness, even as regards the small part of Pollock's career it talks about. I have not attempted to deal with the drip paintings in the light of Pollock's encounters with psychoanalysis, not out of lack of interest in the subject, but because I cannot yet see how psychoanalytic categories or materials can be brought to bear with any closeness on Pollock's actual practice in 1947–50. It may be—to adapt a phrase of Stephen Greenblatt's that I use in my text—that the difficulty here has to do with the way these categories and materials are more successfully absorbed into the work during these years and are present there only "by implication and articulation." But I have to say that the confidence of much recent Pollock scholarship in a "psychoanalytic reading" even of Pollock's earlier figurative work seems to me most often foolhardy. It rests on a view of representation (and "reading") which in my view misses the point of Pollock's practice.

A more damaging omission is the matter of Pollock's gender. For the drip paintings are clearly implicated in a whole informing metaphorics of masculinity: the very concepts that seem immediately to apply to them—space, scale, action, trace, energy, "organic intensity," being *in* the painting," being "One"—are all, among other things, operators of sexual difference. It would be crass to deny that these operators served Pollock well. He was a master: that is to say, he wanted his viewers to see the (self-) risks he had taken and appreciate the physical powers he had at his command; he expected the public to empathize with his "Gothic-ness, . . . paranoia and resentment" and see them as part of his being a man. He got his wish.

These are necessary things to say, and in their way profoundly limiting; but they are not the be-all and end-all of the issue. I try in the body of my text to argue that the drip paintings are involved in a complex dismantling of metaphor; and one aspect of that dismantling, it seems to me, is a questioning or bracketing of the "masculine" theatrics of, say, *Number 1, 1948*. Of course such a questioning is partial, incomplete. All the same I should argue that *Lavender Mist* or *"One"* or *Autumn Rhythm* stand in a different relation to the myth of entry, action, and immediacy which fires the drip paintings of early or mid-1948; though not that they stand in any sense *outside* such a myth, nor that the terms of the myth do not continue to be strongly inflected by gender. There are, after all, still handprints visible in *Lavender Mist*, as there had been in *Number 1, 1948*, soldering the picture's edges and corners and proclaiming the artist's physical being-there; but they seem to me to be robbed by now of the self-assertive, heroizing tone that they had had in the earlier picture. (It may even be that part of the coming-to-an-end of the drip paintings in 1950, which again I try to discuss more fully in the text, was the disintegration of this previous *gendering* of technique—to the point where the practice no longer seemed rooted in some fictive project of self-risk and self-realization and therefore, for Pollock, no longer seemed sustainable.)

All of this, I realize, is still not worked out, much less integrated with the paper's main line of argument. I intend to return to it on another occasion.

Finally, I want to say that the present essay is not intended as some kind of refutation of previous work on the historical,

Cold War circumstances of New York School painting done by Serge Guilbaut, Eva Cockroft, John Tagg, Max Kozloff, and others. Clearly my analysis depends on theirs for its overall orientation; but equally clearly the specific character of Pollock's art has proved resistant to analysis in "conjunctural" terms. My essay tries to confront that resistance and to think through the relation of Pollock's art to late capitalism in a more general way—more general, that is, in its sense of the "history" Pollock's art addresses, though more particular, I hope, in its account of the forms of Pollock's address. My basic premise here is this: Pollock's art is characterized by its attempt to *generalize* its historical circumstance: that is the clue to its limitations as well as its strengths. And of course that tactic is itself historically caused: it is in the nature of the history Pollock encounters that it is experienced as a general (abstract) condition or fate: Pollock's art is accurate precisely in its representation of that "given"— slavishly accurate, one might say. This puts the interpreter in a bind: nothing very illuminating will be said unless we manage to enter into the abstract mode and lay hold of its particular ways of meaning, but each of those ways has to be understood at the same time as contingent and deceptive—garbling the history it tries to speak precisely, exalting the condition it suffers, repeating the lie of the culture at the same time as it rails against it. The interpreter is in a bind, as I say: I do not claim in my text to have escaped from it.

This afterword has gotten to be an essay in itself. But writing on Pollock is taking part in a conversation that has been going on for a long time, and I wanted to make clear how much I owe to those previous voices.

Notes

1.
Alfred Jeanroy, ed.,
Les Chansons de Guil-
laume IX, Duc d'Aqui-
taine 1071–1127 (Paris,
1927), p. 6. Translation
in Paul Blackburn and
George Economou,
Proensa: An Anthology
of Troubadour Poetry
(Berkeley and Los
Angeles, 1978), p. 7.

2.
To Louise Colet, Janu-
ary 16, 1852, in Francis
Steegmuller, ed., The
Letters of Gustave
Flaubert 1830–1857
(Cambridge, MA,
1979), p. 154.

3.
Clement Greenberg,
"The Present Prospects
of American Painting
and Sculpture," Hori-
zon (October 1947), in
Clement Greenberg, The
Collected Essays and
Criticism, ed. John
O'Brian (Chicago,
1986), 2, p. 168. Here-
after cited as CG. The
list represents Green-
berg's paraphrase of
Nietzsche on the Apol-
lonian—"the great and
absent art of our age."

4.
Letter from Rothko to
Annalee and Barnett
Newman, August 10,
1946, Newman papers,
Archives of American
Art. I owe this reference
to Michael Leja.

5.
Letter of late February
1951 to Alfonso Ossorio
and Ted Dragon, in
Francis O'Connor and
Eugene Thaw, eds.,
Jackson Pollock, a Cat-
alogue Raisonné of
Paintings, Drawings
and Other Works (New
Haven, 1978), 4, p. 258.
Hereafter cited as JP.

6.
In Mikhail Bakhtin,
The Dialogic Imagina-
tion (Austin, 1981),
p. 276.

7.
Ibid., p. 331.

8.
Ibid., p. 293.

9.
Ibid., p. 284.

10.
Ibid., p. 282.

11.
Statement in applica-
tion for a Guggenheim
Fellowship, in JP, 4,
p. 238.

12.
Last two quotations
from interview with
William Wright, 1950,
in JP, 4, p. 251.

13.
Greenberg, "Present
Prospects," in CG, 2,
p. 166.

14.
Ibid.

15.
Clement Greenberg,
"L'Art Americain au

XXe Siècle," Les
Temps Modernes
(August–September
1946), p. 350.

16.
Pollock's words in a
statement in Possibili-
ties I (1947–48), in JP,
4, p. 241.

17.
Herman Melville, Moby
Dick (London and New
York: Everyman's Li-
brary, 1963), p. 272.

18.
Stephen Greenblatt,
"Lear's Anxiety," Rari-
tan (Summer 1982),
p. 104. Greenblatt, like
me, invokes Bakhtin at
this point.

19.
G. W. F. Hegel,
Phenomenology of
Spirit, trans. Arnold
Miller (Oxford, 1977),
p. 455–456. Hegel is
comparing the Unhappy
Consciousness's an-
guished recognition of
meaninglessness—"the
statues are now only
stones from which the
living soul has flown"—
with modern scholar-
ship's complacent ac-
ceptance of the same
exteriority to the objects
it studies.

20.
Greenblatt, "Lear's
Anxiety," p. 103.

21.
We could leave unde-
cided for the time being
whether Pollock's sense

*of these negatives ruling
in the culture was accu-
rate or neurotic (not
that I accept the either-
or choice implied
here!). I have no doubt
they were accurate, in
fact. I do not believe
that Pollock's art would
possess the coherence
and force it has if it
were not somehow
rooted in an accurate
reading of its time—
however indirectly, in
however exacerbated a
form. But this is a mat-
ter of basic aesthetic
theory, and in any case
a lot of the description
and argument that fol-
lows would apply
whether Pollock's view
of the totality was para-
noid or not.*

22.
Bakhtin, The Dialogic
Imagination, *pp. 331,
294.*

23.
Ibid., p. 292.

24.
*Ibid., p. 282. This quo-
tation was singled out
for critical attention by
Paul de Man in "Dia-
logue and Dialogism,"*
Poetics Today *4:1
(1983), p. 105. It is
typical, he thinks, of
Bakhtin's falling back
at key moments into
"a precritical phenom-
enalism in which there
is no room for exotopy,
for otherness, in any
shape or degree," "a
gesture of dialectical*

*imperialism." The
choice Bakhtin is faced
with, de Man seems to
be arguing, is an all or
nothing one: either ab-
solute exotopy or none
at all, in any shape or
degree. This argument
depends in turn, as I
understand it, on a set
of metaphysical com-
mitments on de Man's
part, which we could
sum up by saying that
for him the Unhappy
Consciousness is en-
tirely correct in its view
of consciousness and its
objects, and that any
attempt to think the
question of otherness
and utterance further—
further than its anti-
nomies—will be ulti-
mately nothing but a
dialectical sleight of
hand.*

25.
Ibid., p. 277.

26.
*Letter of March 10,
1947, to Christos
Baziotes, in Baziotes
Papers N/70-24:77, Ar-
chives of American Art.
Again I owe this refer-
ence, and the next two,
to Michael Leja.*

27.
*Letter of December 2,
1947 from Capri, in
Greenberg Papers N/70-
7:472-3, Archives of
American Art.*

28.
*In "A Symposium: The
State of American
Art,"* Magazine of Art

*(March 1949), p. 95.
Greenberg was one of
the other fifteen con-
tributors to the
symposium.*

29.
*Greenberg, "Present
Prospects," in CG, 2,
p. 166; Clement Green-
berg, "Review of Exhi-
bitions of the American
Abstract Artists,
Jacques Lipchitz, and
Jackson Pollock,"* The
Nation *(April 13, 1946),
in CG, 2, p. 75; Cle-
ment Greenberg, "Re-
view of Exhibitions of
Marc Chagall, Lyonel
Feininger, and Jackson
Pollock," in* The Na-
tion *(November 27,
1943), in CG, 1, p. 165
("Pollock's titles are
pretentious," but the
adjective clearly ap-
plies, in Greenberg's
view, to too much of
American art in gen-
eral. "The task facing
culture in America is to
create a* milieu *that will
. . . free us (at last!)
from the obsession with
extreme situations and
states of mind. We have
had enough of the wild
artist . . . if art is wild
it must be irrelevant."
"Present Prospects," in
CG, 2, p. 168.)*

30.
*Greenberg, "Present
Prospects," in CG, 2,
p. 167.*

31.
*Clement Greenberg,
"Surrealist Painting,"*

The Nation *(August 12, 1944),* in *CG,* 1, p. 226.

32.
Clement Greenberg, *"Review of the Whitney Annual,"* The Nation *(December 28, 1946),* in *CG,* 2, p. 118.

33.
Clement Greenberg, *"Review of Exhibitions of Jean Dubuffet and Jackson Pollock,"* The Nation *(February 1, 1947),* in *CG,* 2, p. 124.

34.
Greenberg, *"L'Art Americain au XXe Siècle,"* p. 352. *"A moins que l'art américain ne se réconcilie avec ce minimum de positivisme sur lequel repose, à mon avis, la continuité et la force de l'art moderne en France, à moins que nous n'intégrions notre poésie dans les dimensions physiques immédiates de l'art . . . nous demeurerons incapables d'établir dans notre art une continuité qui nous permette de satisfaire nos ambitions actuelles. Nous ne devrions pas nous laisser abuser par le fait que le sentiment gothique a été dans le passé au principe de la plupart des meilleures oeuvres de la littérature et de la peinture américaines et qu'il anime encore nos talents les plus vigoureux."*

35.
See especially Bruce Glaser, *"Jackson Pollock: An Interview with Lee Krasner,"* Arts *(April 1967);* Bernard Friedman, *"Interview with Lee Krasner Pollock,"* in Jackson Pollock: Black and White *(New York: Marlborough-Greene Gallery, 1969), partially reprinted in JP, 4, pp. 151–152;* Barbara Rose, *"Pollock's Studio: Interview with Lee Krasner,"* in Hans Namuth and Barbara Rose, Pollock Painting *(New York, 1980);* Hans Namuth, *"Jackson Pollock,"* American Society of Magazine Photographers' Picture Annual *(New York, 1957), cited in Bernard Friedman,* Jackson Pollock, Energy Made Visible *(New York, 1972),* p. 161; Hans Namuth, *"Photographing Pollock—A Memoir,"* in Pollock Painting; *interview material in E. A. Carmean, Jr., "Jackson Pollock: Classic Paintings of 1950," in E. A. Carmean, Jr., Eliza Rathbone, and Thomas Hess,* American Art at Mid-Century, The Subjects of the Artist *(Washington D.C.: National Gallery of Art, 1978).*

36.
See, for example, Walter Darby Bannard,

"Cubism, abstract expressionism, David Smith," Artforum *(April 1968),* p. 28; or Robert Motherwell's remarks in *"Jackson Pollock: An Artists' Symposium, Part I,"* Artnews *(April 1967),* pp. 65–66.

37.
Ben Wolf, *"By the Shores of Virtuosity,"* The Art Digest *(April 15, 1946),* p. 16.

38.
Clement Greenberg, *"Review of an Exhibition of Willem de Kooning,"* The Nation *(April 24, 1948),* in *CG,* 2, p. 229.

39.
Greenberg, *"Present Prospects"* in *CG,* 2, p. 166.

40.
See the undated handwritten statement in the Pollock Archive, beginning *"Technic is the result of a need,"* in *JP,* 4, p. 253.

41.
Lee Krasner, conversation with E. A. Carmean, Jr., quoted in Carmean, *"Classic Paintings,"* pp. 133–135.

42.
Rosalind Krauss, *"Reading Photographs as Text,"* in Namuth and Rose, Pollock Painting, *n.p.*

43.
The two photos are plates 51 and 52 in JP, 4, p. 249.

44.
Hegel, Phenomenology of Spirit, p. 137: "Through these movements of surrender, first of its right to decide for itself, then of its property and enjoyment, and finally through the positive moment of practising what it does not understand, it truly and completely deprives itself of the unconsciousness of inner and outer freedom, of the actuality in which consciousness exists for itself. It has the certainty of having truly divested itself of its 'I,' and of having turned its immediate self-consciousness into a Thing, into an objective existence." The whole section on the Unhappy Consciousness, from Paragraph 206 onwards, remains for me the essential framework for an understanding of modernism and its permanently unresolved dialectic, and time and again the terms of Hegel's discussion seem to apply to Pollock's practice almost too directly. "This new form," writes Hegel (p. 126), "is, therefore, one which knows that it is the dual consciousness of itself, as self-liberating, unchangeable, and self-identical, and as self-bewildering and self-perverting, and it is the awareness of this self-contradictory nature of itself." I cannot imagine a better summing up of what I try to say later about the tension in Pollock between figures of totality and figures of dissonance—between "One" and Number 32, 1950—and the actual articulation of this self-contradictory nature in a picture like Cut Out.

I had been meaning to say nothing about the brief section (pp. 236–240) in Rosalind Krauss's "Reading Jackson Pollock, Abstractly" (see her collection The Originality of the Avant-Garde and Other Modernist Myths [Cambridge, MA, 1985]) where Hegel's logic is invoked in connection with Malevich and Mondrian, since it seemed to me to have little to do with what was valuable in the bulk of the essay, let alone with Krauss's other forceful writings on the subject of Pollock. But the fact that I recently came across the essay described as "a Hegelian reading of Pollock's poured paintings" makes me realize that saying nothing isn't enough. Krauss has a low opinion of "the art-historical literature, increasingly gripped by the picture theory of art," and invites us to "look down into an abyss of ignorance in which Hegel could be confused with 'formalism'." The onus is therefore on her to get Hegelian logic at least roughly right. She does not.

Maybe it is true, for instance, that Malevich and Mondrian "were fired by the dream of being able to paint Nothing, which is to say, all Being once it has been stripped of every quality that would materialize or limit it in any way." No doubt "so purified, this Being is identical with Nothing." This is standard fin- or commencement-de-siècle mysticism. I do not think we should blame Hegel for it. The statement which follows in Krauss's text, that "It is onto this experience of identity that Hegel's dialectic opens," seems to me the opposite of the truth. For is not the whole drift of Hegel's logic— its basic contra-Fichtean thrust—to deny just such an identity, and show instead that Being never can be "stripped of every quality that would materialize and limit it," any more than it can ever be identified with *those qualities? The logical doctrine that Krauss outlines, which may or may not have been Malevich's and Mondrian's, is exactly what Hegel calls the error of the Understanding, the positing of the mere "selfsame," "the supersensible world" which "has, in fact, the 'other' immediately present in it," though it fails to recognize that fact* (Phenomenology of Spirit, *para. 160); it is consciousness still locked inside "the nightlike void of the supersensible beyond"* (ibid., *para. 196). Of course I am leaning specifically on the* Phenomenology *in this, but at the level we are dealing with—the level of basic, formative philosophical commitments —Hegel's position does not change between 1805 and the* Logic *of 1812–16.*

A bit more is at stake here than Hegel scholarship. Under the philosophical trappings, I understand Rosalind Krauss to be stating the following about abstract art: that in it, or in some of it, experience(s) is (are) "de-specified" but nonetheless represented. Sure. But this is where the interesting questions start. What experience(s)? Difficult or easy ones, concentrated or vestigial; represented

with what degree of salience or vividness; interpreted by viewers how (with what kinds of criteria for correct or incorrect reading); contributing how, if at all, to some shared or shareable remapping of consciousness and its modes (everybody wants that: Hegel, Fichte, Mondrian, Malevich, Pollock, you name 'em)? These are the questions that still come up about abstract painting, and there may not be affirmative answers to all of them. In any case invocations of Hegel won't conjure them away.

45.
Among a mass of material I would single out Michael Fried, Three American Painters *(Cambridge, MA, 1965), especially pp. 10–19; William Rubin, "Jackson Pollock and the Modern Tradition,"* Artforum *(February– May 1967) (a lot of unconvincing stuff about Pollock and Impressionism, etc., and a general modernist anxiety to have Pollock sum up everything that is good about painting since 1870, but nonetheless some excellent description); Walter Darby Bannard, "Touch and Scale: Cubism, Pollock, Newman and Still,"* Artforum *(October 1971).*

46.
Fried, Three American Painters, *p. 14.*

47.
Jonathon Weinberg, "Pollock and Picasso: the Rivalry and the 'Escape'," Arts Magazine *(June 1987), p. 47. Weinberg counts three Ones: I think he should include* Number 1, 1950, *the first title of* Lavender Mist.

48.
Letter to James Johnson Sweeney, November 3, 1943, in JP, 4, p. 230.

49.
Handwritten draft of statement for Possibilities *(1947), in JP, 4, p. 241. The idea crops up in slightly different forms in the* Arts and Architecture *interview of 1944 and the William Wright interview of 1950.*

50.
See Michael Leja, "Jackson Pollock, Modern Man," unpublished paper (cf. Afterword). Leja makes a watertight case for specific echoes and borrowings from both sources. The drawing is in JP, 3, p. 384. Robinson's book was published in New York in 1921, Fergusson's in 1936.

51.
Selden Rodman, Conversations with Artists (New York, 1957), cited in JP, 4, p. 275.

52.
William Wright interview, 1950, in JP, 4, p. 250.

53.
Ibid., p. 251.

54.
Reported by Pollock's homeopath, Dr. Elizabeth Hubbard, in 1956, see JP, 4, p. 275.

55.
Selden Rodman conversation, cited in JP, 4, p. 275.

56.
Reported by Lee Krasner, Friedman interview, cited in JP, 4, p. 264.

57.
See JP, 1, pp. 172, 176, and 4, p. 242.

58.
Parker Tyler, "Jackson Pollock: The Infinite Labyrinth," Magazine of Art (March 1950), p. 93. Michael Leja tells me that Tyler wrote to Robert Goldwater in May 1950 claiming that Pollock was "delighted" with the piece. The word "delighted" is in quotation marks in Tyler's letter. See Jackson Pollock papers, 3046: 345, Archives of American Art.

59.
The Tempest, Act I, Scene 2: Ferdinand on Ariel's song. Compare the discussion in Weinberg, "Pollock and Picasso," p. 48. Anne Wagner has pointed out to me that Ariel's song was published in Tiger's Eye 2 (December 1947), p. 66.

60.
This is partly a matter of what the totality often is, in its overall configuration and expressive aspect; for instance in pictures like Number 34, 1949 or Number 15, 1949, two of Pollock's finest, neither of which fit at all well the terms of Fried's reading. And partly a matter of what the totality is made out of, when we consider it from a quite ordinary viewing distance—say, three feet or so. A lot of what Fried says about the materiality of pigment being "rendered sheerly visual" depends on the fiction of some ideal viewing distance at which the tactile surface volatilizes. It is surely not a fiction that Pollock himself would have sympathized with.

61.
Fried, Three American Painters, p. 13.

62.
Theodor Adorno, Aesthetic Theory, translated by C. Lenhardt (London and Boston, 1984), p. 21.

63.
Ibid., p. 161.

64.
Ibid.

65.
Don Judd, "Jackson Pollock," Arts (April 1967), p. 35.

66.
Tyler, "Jackson Pollock: The Infinite Labyrinth," p. 93.

67.
See, for the first photo mentioned, Namuth and Rose, Pollock Painting, the twenty-fourth photo in the section entitled "The Photographs."

68.
E. A. Carmean, Jr., has done some excellent work on the sequencing and technique of the 1950 pictures; see his "Classic Paintings," especially pp. 129–142. The interpretative conclusions he draws from the new information often seem dubious to me.

69.
On the titling, see JP, 2, p. 86.

70.
Hans Namuth, 1957 memoir, cited and discussed in Carmean, "Classic Paintings," p. 133.

71.
Guggenheim Fellowship statement, 1947, in JP, 4, p. 238.

72.
Visible in several of Namuth's and Burckhardt's photos, e.g. photo at bottom left, JP, 4, p. 249.

73.
For a discussion of these issues, particularly in relation to Pollock's attempt to reuse Picasso's formal language, see Weinberg, "Pollock and Picasso."

74.
Clement Greenberg, "Art Chronicle: Feeling is All," Partisan Review (January–February 1952), p. 102.

75.
Greenberg, "Review of Exhibitions," in CG, 2, p. 125.

76.
Clement Greenberg, "Review of Exhibitions of Adolph Gottlieb, Jackson Pollock, and Joseph Albers," The Nation (February 19, 1949), in CG, 2, p. 286.

77.
See JP, 4, pp. 106–107.

78.
See the tremendous account of Cut Out in Fried, Three American Painters, pp. 17–18, to which the present discussion is a kind of gloss.

79.
Cf. the Rudolph Burckhardt photo, plate 54 in JP, 4, p. 250, and the "Remarks" on Cut Out on p. 104.

80.
See JP, 2, p. 111.

81.
For example, JP, 2, p. 112 (catalogue no. 291—Silver Square); ibid., p. 28 (Number 18, 1948: Black, Red, Yellow); ibid., pp. 22–23 (Number 22A, 1948).

82.
This account of The Wooden Horse tries to respond to Benjamin Buchloh's criticism of its original form and to make clearer how I think the picture exceeds the normal terms of "collage aesthetic."

83.
Handwritten statement of 1950, in JP, 4, p. 253.

84.
Lee Krasner's memory, in the Friedman interview, in JP, 4, p. 263.

85.
Charmion Wiegand, "Mondrian: A Memoir of his New York Period," Arts Yearbook 4 (1961), pp. 59–60. My thanks to Johan Ahr for this reference.

86.
No doubt more could be said about the particular way Beaton's photographs make use of the drip paintings and what it is they use them for. I suppose the paintings stand, on one level, for Art and Modernity, and the obvious message is that Irene and Sophie's dresses, for all their formality, "go well" with both. But of course they also stand for Nature and Desire; for rawness and wildness, "intensity of feelings," as the captionwriter put it, already tamed by Artifice and hung upon a wall. Likewise the models and ball gowns: they are the body made over by Fashion into a form where Desire is stated only to be stayed and contained. The photographs, in other words, have a certain ideological density and play on real ambiguities in Pollock's work; they do not simply use it as wallpaper. (I am responding here to various comments on my lecture, especially those of Robert Baldwin and Howard Singerman.)

87.
Colin Thubron, Where the Nights are Longest: Travels by Car through Western Russia (New York, 1984), p. 90. I first came across this passage quoted with enthusiasm in the New York Times, and the book has lately come out in paperback.

88.
Meyer Schapiro, "The Social Bases of Art," Proceedings of the First Artists' Congress Against War and Fascism *(New York, 1936), pp. 36–37.*

89.
In saying this I do not mean to suggest that Schapiro's critique of modern art is worthless: on the contrary, in many ways I much prefer it to the inconsequential hedging-of-bets that comes a year later in "The Nature of Abstract Art" (where much of the same rhetoric survives, but hemmed in now by historical sketches proving the artists had meant well). What is wrong with the Stalinist account of modernism—the same could be said of Lukács, largely—is not so much the nature of its hostile descriptions as the implied alternatives to what it dislikes, and above all the implied way forward to such alternatives. And of course the descriptions are bad too: any account which flattens and evacuates modernism in this way, and refuses to see modernism's own struggle with the (social) conditions of its existence, is bound to end up bringing on the Party to save the Unhappy Consciousness from itself.

Audience

This may seem irreverent: however, it seemed to me that Pollock's paintings looked like wallpaper behind the models. The absence of figuration seems to be compensated for by the model posing in front of the painting.

T. J. Clark

Yes. Why is that irreverent, precisely? I'd say that the risk of the "decorative" was one that Pollock ran and knew he was running. It's one of the basic risks of abstraction, isn't it? An art that does without the figure lays itself open to being used as a ground on which—or maybe against which—*another* figuration can take place. That's partly what the paper was arguing.

Audience

But does it really make sense, when it's a photograph we are talking about, to say that the painting within the photo is being used? It seems to me that the experience of a *painting*—actually seeing it—is so transformed by photographs that, in a way, it's not really a Pollock at all that is accepted in this sense as a piece of decoration, just like it isn't really a particular fashion model that is portrayed. That is, I do not think that it is really Pollock that is being used because we are not talking about a painting, but about a photograph of a painting, and even the best of photographs completely alters that way a painting would look if we were to stand in front of it.

T. J. Clark

So the work is the work is the work, after all? And nothing Mr. Beaton's camera can do is going to rob it of its aura. Is that what you're saying? In other words, any mediated life that the painted image goes on to have in the culture is irrelevant, ultimately: it doesn't touch the object itself, the original act of production. You are right, of course, that the photograph does things with the painting. For instance, the photograph frames, cuts, and flattens the image. But that seems to me to open up an area for discussion, not close it. What is it that Beaton and *Vogue* think they can do with the work, or to the work, without it resisting much—maybe with it positively cooperating? Why is Pollock's work so immediately made part of another work altogether, whose purposes might seem inimical to it? Or are they? I don't think that these questions are about something else than—something neatly separable from—the paintings Pollock did in the first place. There is a relation between the original process of artistic production and the various (posterior) processes by which the work is (mis-)understood or (mis-)used by its audiences. That's a basic proposition of most of my writing. Which is not to say that the "meaning" of a work of art can be read unequivocally *out of* those posterior uses. I don't believe the *Vogue* photos somehow tell the truth about Pollock's abstraction. But they tell part of the truth, part of the truth that Pollock's work was designed to deal with.

Let's put it programmatically. Any artistic practice, however "pure," however seemingly hermetic, is always imagining the future life (the public life) its work may have. Bakhtin is excellent on this. The notion of *public* is built into signifying practice, into its very materials and syntax. The more complex the practice, the more vivid the imagining. Or that's my hypothesis.

Jeff Wall

When you mentioned Pollock working his way back to the realm of representation, you used philosophical terms that are very similar to the terms used by Heidegger and that lead back to metaphysics. That is, you seem to be developing a dialectic with something Hegelian and something Heideggarian about it all. For instance, you began discussing the process of defiguration that Pollock was involved in throughout the later 1940s and that climaxes at the time of the *Vogue* magazine photographs. After this, you begin to perceive an increasingly evident resurgence, recovery, of figuration in Pollock's work. Is this how you're feeling about it?

T. J. Clark

I'm not sure about the last bit, but in general I'd have to plead guilty. Yes, the reference to the Heideggerian notion was deliberate, though no doubt a bit cavalier. . . . I do think that there is a dream of priority in Pollock's painting, a dream of retrieval of that moment in which representing came into being. And it's one Pollock shares with abstract painting in general: back to the ground of being, back to the basic lexicon, back to the Black Square, and so on. *Let's start again* . . . if we start again, won't we be able somehow to *control* the terms on which painting is looked at, and avoid all the usual misunderstandings? . . .

Are you implicitly intending to apply a kind of Frankfurt school critique of the Heideggerian position?

T. J. Clark

Well, I wasn't explicitly meaning to because I don't feel on sure enough ground with Heidegger. However, I do think that the whole project of retrieval of origins is flawed—worse than flawed—in terms of what it really meant in twentieth-century culture. That links with what I said in the paper about primitivism. And yes, Pollock's work is partly a project of retrieval. But of course I mainly meant to say something else about it: that, in practice, it stands in a much more complex and mediated relation to the problem of representation: the dream of priority is in high, unresolvable tension with the ongoing *work* on the conditions of figuration—the possibility of referring.

Benjamin Buchloh

At one point in your discussion you say that you are doubting whether the indexical was really on its way out from this metaphorical relationship, and you were wondering what an end to metaphor could possibly look like anyway. Were you implying that there simply is no single incident in twentieth-century history where that condition has been achieved?

T. J. Clark

Yes.

Benjamin Buchloh

Okay.

T. J. Clark

Do you think that it is reasonable to think that?

Benjamin Buchloh

It is very tempting. But what about a text like Marcel Duchamp's *Standard Stoppages*; does it achieve that condition?

T. J. Clark

Well, the thing is, though, that that very work, and other connected works by Duchamp, have actually proved to be ideal free-fire zones for metaphorical reading-in. I'd certainly agree—at least, I think I'm agreeing—that Duchamp too has his dream of priority, one which seems to depend on an exit from metaphor, and putting in its place some form of "presentation" of being, or presence, or chance itself, instantiated. But I see the three *Standard Stoppages* as metaphors: metaphors of accident.

Benjamin Buchloh

I think that they *are* the accident, and that's the difference that we have to recognize between the condition that is produced within the work and the subsequent transformation that the work is subjected to in the reading process. It is necessary, at least for the moment, to maintain the difference and ask: Is he opening it up to metaphor? Or is he closing the door on metaphor? Perhaps it is only afterward that it is flooded again with a metaphorical relationship in the reading. For instance, his very decision to make the work closes the dimension of metaphor. That is, the work does not metaphorically represent gravity, randomness, arbitrary process; it incorporates—produces—the forms of gravity and randomness. I think that those are two very different phenomena. And, of course, they play in Pollock's work as well.

T. J. Clark

We're back again to the problem of "only afterward," aren't we? There is a disagreement here between us, but it would be silly to set up our two positions as polar opposites. Like you, I want to take Pollock's project of somehow or other blocking metaphor very seriously—that is, making a representation which stands in relation to the world in some way that cannot be appraised, framed, and totalized within one metaphorical schema. For me, that involves always accelerating, freeing, multiplying connotation, multiplying metaphor, and criss-crossing metaphor, rather than stepping out of metaphor into some other space of meaning: such as enacting rather than signifying. But in a way we could beg to differ on that and still say that the *impulse* to escape from the totalizing metaphor—the singular metaphor, the metaphor that confirms the categories of the world—is basic to modernism. It's one of its most potent myths.

Lary May

I just thought that I would add this to sum things up. This morning we had people questioning Serge Guilbaut on his assertion that much of Abstract Expressionist art could be understood as an effect of the Cold War and of the battle between New York and Paris. Also, we had people point out that, in fact, this development in art happened before the beginning of the Cold War. I wonder how your understanding—which seemed to be much more of an internalistic analysis of what Pollock was all about—fits into the debate that we had this morning? Where do you stand on that debate? How would you frame it? I mean, are we into two totally different and separate parallel streams or is there some kind of connection?

T. J. Clark

I think we come back to the kind of question I was trying to broach earlier, à propos of Cecil Beaton, etc. That is: how do we map the context of exploitation, misuse, rereading, misreading in the culture *onto* and *into* a certain practice, a certain set of intentions—intentions realized? Aren't we all still struggling with that?

"Struggling" really is the word. We still don't have even the beginnings of an adequate set of terms—set of coordinates—with which to *do* the mapping. The ones I've been using—all those metaphors of anticipation, figuring, internalizing, answering, etc. which the paper leans on at key points—are either too crude or too vague. I think Bakhtin helps, but only up to a point. At least he gives us a way of thinking beyond the metaphor of "internal"/ "external"—a work having an "inside" and an "outside," with different procedures of analysis appropriate in each case—which seemed to be haunting your question at times. Internal *versus* external is like "originally" *versus* "only afterward," or, come to that, "text" *versus* "context." Not that our work will ever magically escape from these metaphorical divisions, but the more pressure they're put under, in the actual process of historical inquiry, the better for all of us. That much, surely, we should have learned from Derrida, de Man, and company.

The Monochrome and the Blank Canvas

Thierry de Duve

Some Interpreted Facts

I wanted to get the paint out of the can and onto the canvas. . . . I tried to keep
the paint as good as it was in the can.

Frank Stella

In December 1959 a virtually unknown painter named Frank
Stella, aged twenty-three, was invited to participate in one of the
prestigious shows staged at MoMA by Dorothy Miller throughout
the fifties whose purpose was to promote the new American art.
Entitled *Sixteen Americans*, the show was a strange yet interesting mixed bag: it included second-generation Abstract Expressionists such as Alfred Leslie, James Jarvaise, and Richard
Lytle, as well as the "hard edge" abstract painters Ellsworth
Kelly and Jack Youngerman and the "proto-Pop" artists Robert
Rauschenberg and Jasper Johns. Among them was Stella, whose
work contrasted strongly with that of his colleagues. He presented four huge canvases painted mechanically with a regular,
repetitive pattern of black stripes executed with commercial
enamel on raw cotton duck with a flat, 2½-inch wide housepainter's brush. Their stretchers were thicker than usual, approximately as thick as the brush's width, and the sides of the painting
had been left unpainted so as to visually detach the painted surface from the wall and to project it into the room. The contrast to

the exuberant expressionism of most of the other participants could not have been more striking. By comparison, even Johns's *Flags* and *Targets* must have looked "painterly" and Kelly's Matissian compositions rather "arty."

Stella's self-presentation in the catalogue also stood in striking contrast to that of his fellow artists. Whereas the majority had been photographed in the studio, clad in the usual artist's attire and surrounded by the usual paraphernalia, Stella showed a deadpan image of himself wearing a tie and a dark gray suit, as if he were floating against an all-white, shadowless background reminiscent of Manet's *Fifre*. The photograph was taken by Hollis Frampton, then a close friend of Stella and a photographer, later to become one of the most interesting experimental filmmakers of the times. And whereas most other participants in the show either accompanied the reproductions of their work with an "artist's statement" or with the usual laudatory comment of a well-known art critic, Stella asked his friend Carl André, soon to become a leading Minimalist sculptor, to speak on his behalf. Here is André's laconic statement:

Preface to Stripe Painting
Art excludes the unnecessary. Frank Stella has found it necessary to paint stripes. There is nothing else in his painting. Frank Stella is not interested in expression or sensitivity. He is interested in the necessities of painting. Symbols are counters passed among people. Frank Stella's painting is not symbolic. His stripes are the paths of brush on canvas. These paths lead only into painting. Carl André.[1]

The show, followed a few months later by a show of all-aluminum shaped canvases at the Leo Castelli gallery, had an enormous impact on Stella's generation of artists. Though it may be an overstatement to say that Minimal art sprang from this show, it is clear that the show crystallized a new sensibility which had hitherto expressed itself only negatively, as a sheer lassitude with Abstract Expressionism. It also offered the possibility of rereading Abstract Expressionism, and Pollock's "all-overness" in particular, in formal rather than existential terms. Harold Rosenberg's concept of "Action Painting" became suddenly trite and hopelessly romantic, whereas Clement Greenberg's understanding of "American-type Painting" in terms of formal results, historical conventions and flatness of the medium gained momentum and credibility. Indeed, Greenberg's *Art and Culture* be-

came a bestseller among artists as soon as it came out in 1961.[2]
And his best-known essay, "Modernist Painting," also published
in 1961, instantly became a sort of aesthetic Organon for a whole
generation of artists, even for those who rejected it.[3] It offered a
bold yet simple reading of the history of modern painting, one
that gave painting renewed intellectual credibility and the avant-
garde a new sense of direction. In the forties and the fifties, there
was a revival of the late-romantic cliché of the artist as instinc-
tive resource of creativity, with no ties to history and no cultural
function besides his (never her) sacred vocation. The refreshing
and cleansing effect of Greenberg's text was to eliminate that
image and to provide instead a coherent aesthetic and historical
rationale for professionalism in painting. The romantic image of
the artist as the Bohemian or the social rebel was no longer plausible in the face of the academization of Abstract Expressionism
and its commercial success. The extended series of abandon-
ments, destructions or deconstructions, of pictorial conventions,
which Greenberg described as building up the history of Modernist painting were no longer presented as revolts or subversions,
but rather as the establishment of a secure area of competence.
This could only appeal to a generation of artists who needed to
shake the oedipal weight of their Abstract Expressionist elders
while also realizing that they had to compete with them, both
professionally and for the same market.

In that context, Carl André's "Preface to *Stripe Painting*"
appears utterly Greenbergian. It shares the same ontological assertion that painting is defined by its minimal, formal, and material "necessities" or conditions, which exclude any symbolic
subject matter. Stella's black paintings themselves bear witness
to this paragraph from "Modernist Painting":

> The essential norms or conventions of painting are also the
> limiting conditions with which a marked-up surface must
> comply in order to be experienced as a picture. Modernism
> has found that these limiting conditions can be pushed back
> indefinitely before a picture stops being a picture and turns
> into an arbitrary object; but it has also found that the further
> back these limits are pushed the more explicitly they have to
> be observed.[4]

Yet Stella's black paintings don't seem to have received Greenberg's stamp of approval. What Greenberg had in mind when
writing "Modernist Painting" was a view of the history of paint-

ing's reduction to flatness, a history in which the works of Manet
and Monet, Matisse and Picasso, Pollock and Newman were acknowledged landmarks, and in which the most recent examples
supporting his views were Morris Louis's *Veils* and Kenneth
Noland's "circle paintings," but not Stella's black paintings.
Why? "They were not good enough" is his most probable answer,
and there is no arguing with that.[5] But why are they "not good
enough," since "Modernist Painting" reads as if it had been
written in support of them? Greenberg has always insisted that
"Modernist Painting" was a neutral account of history, that it
was descriptive and did not in the least seek to establish criteria
for judgment. Still, it is informed throughout by its author's taste,
which seems to have evolved under the same pressure as Modernist painting itself. Thus, one would expect to see his taste surrendering in front of Stella's black paintings, since these observe
so explicitly the limiting conditions that "can be pushed back
indefinitely before a picture stops being a picture and turns into
an arbitrary object." Yet Greenberg's taste stopped short of including Stella's black paintings. Is it perhaps because they trans-
gressed this ultimate limit and became "arbitrary objects"? But
it would then mean that this limit could not "be pushed back
indefinitely" and that the history of Modernist painting might be
terminated. Or is it perhaps because the black paintings so con-
veniently illustrated "Modernist Painting," converting its historical account into a theory of sorts, and thus threatening free
aesthetic judgment? By compelling the viewer who finds them
"good enough" to see them as ultimate paradigms of Modernist
painting, the black paintings would make Greenberg's historical
description prescriptive, even normative; they would make the
minimal condition of flatness into a maximal one.

This is exactly what the young painters who were soon to
become the Minimalists must have felt. The impact of Stella's
black paintings on them was tremendous, as was the aura of
Greenbergian criticism. They must have felt that it was impossible to be a significant artist without being a painter and at the
same time that it was impossible to pursue Modernist painting
without going beyond the monochromatic literal flatness of
Stella's black and aluminum paintings. At that point they would
cease to be painters and would merely produce "arbitrary objects." At that point, they would also have to break with Greenberg, lest Greenberg break with them first. Both have happened,
of course, and it is quite ironic that the central debates concerning the art of the sixties and the seventies should have revolved

around a critical doctrine that sees itself as retrospective and descriptive, yet becomes prospective and prescriptive in the very works of those artists who took it for granted and who therefore had to reject it in order to create. In any case, most Minimal artists (among them Dan Flavin, Sol LeWitt, Donald Judd, Michael Steiner, Ronald Bladen, John McCracken) started out as painters around 1960. Their early work stems directly from Stella's black paintings, acknowledging their monochromatic flatness, mechanistic look and extra thickness. Consider, for example, Dan Flavin's *Icon V (Coran Broadway Flesh)* of 1962, a square masonite panel uniformly painted in a flesh color and framed by a series of lighted bulbs; or Donald Judd's *Light Cadmium Red Oil and Sand, Black and White Oil and Galvanized Iron on Wood* of 1961, a rectangular wooden panel painted in red to which a cornice of galvanized metal has been attached on both the top and the bottom sides; or Sol LeWitt's *Wall Structure, Black* and *Wall Structure, White*, of 1962, two monochrome canvases, one white, the other black, in the center of which a protruding wooden parallelepiped has been affixed. These works—and there are many others—depart from the two-dimensionality of painting by adding a three-dimensional element to it. They deliberately seem to transgress the limit where, according to Greenberg, *a picture stops being a picture and turns into an arbitrary object*. Moreover, they claim this arbitrariness as a quality in itself.

All this happened more than twenty years ago and seems far removed from current preoccupations. Meanwhile, the advent of Minimal art was followed by that of Conceptual art, Land art, performance art and, more recently, various "appropriation" practices. Varied as they are, all these movements have one thing in common: they put themselves against painting, and sometimes against sculpture as well. What they have retained from the sixties is the authorization to produce *generic* art, that is, art that has severed its ties with the *specific* crafts and traditions of either painting or sculpture. Meanwhile, the art world has also seen an overwhelming return of painting, but in the form of figurative and Neoexpressionist painting, whose specificity is defended with the most conservative arguments: a revival of craftsmanship, traditional authorship, the quality of oil or the smell of turpentine, and the like. What has been sacrificed in the process is Modernist painting in the Greenbergian sense, whose specificity was defined by its particular history, that very history which dispensed with, one by one, virtually every convention of painting and ended up in Stella's black paintings or in monochrome painting in general. The pendulum swings back and forth with predictable regularity, and it may be fascinating for those who like predictability to watch the current trend of Neo-Geo supplant that of Neoexpressionism in a parody of Greenbergian Modernism. For those who expect unpredictability from art, it is a saddening sight. The time has thus come to shift one's attention from the pendulum to the fulcrum where the pendulum is attached. And there lies a question in need of factual, then critical, interpretation. It is a question pertaining to the relation of painting in particular to art in general, in other words, between the specific and the generic. The question is art historical, critical, "theoretical," and, ultimately, ethical. Art historically, it is as old as modernity itself, but for the time being, there is one episode that deserves particular analysis, the one that overdetermines the present situation and draws us back to the issue of the monochrome in the early sixties in New York and to the case of "Modernist Painting" versus Minimalism.

Some Factual Interpretations

It remains that Modernism in art . . . has stood or fallen so far by its "formalism." Not that Modernist art is coterminous with "formalism." And not that "formalism" hasn't lent itself to a lot of empty, bad art. But so far every attack on the "formalist" aspect of Modernist painting and sculpture has worked out as an attack on Modernism itself because every such attack developed into an attack at the same time on superior artistic standards.

Clement Greenberg

In Greenberg's view of modern art, the relation of painting to art is equated with that of Modernist painting to Modernism at large. But "Modernism at large" is an elusive concept for which Greenberg never offered more than an elliptic definition:

> I identify Modernism with the intensification, almost the exacerbation, of this self-critical tendency that began with the philosopher Kant. . . . The essence of Modernism lies, as I see it, in the use of the characteristic methods of a discipline to criticize the discipline itself—not in order to subvert it, but to entrench it more firmly in its area of competence.[6]

Rigorously speaking, there is no "Modernism at large" since the self-critical tendency characterizing Modernism can apply only to a given discipline from within that discipline. Modernism doesn't allow for interdisciplinarity. Specificity is thus essential to Modernism, and Modernism in the arts proceeds from their strict separation:

> Each art, it turned out, had to effect this demonstration on its own account. What had to be exhibited and made explicit was that which was unique and irreducible not only in art in general but also in each particular art. . . . It quickly emerged that the unique and proper area of competence of each art coincided with all that was unique to the nature of its medium.[7]

What is this nature of the medium with regard to painting?

> Flatness alone was unique and exclusive to that art. . . . Flatness, two-dimensionality, was the only condition painting shared with no other art, and so Modernist painting oriented itself to flatness as it did to nothing else.[8]

This is the best-known aspect of Greenberg's doctrine of Modernist painting. It states its specificity in positive terms. Stated in negative terms, this specificity would be made of the residue of all the conventions which premodern painting shared with the other arts (above all, "literature") and which Modernist painting had to relinquish, one by one, so as to assert its own "area of competence."[9] But the more Modernist painting pushed back the limiting conventions of its medium, the closer it came to its immediate neighbor, sculpture, and the more explicitly it had to trace a borderline between sculpture and itself so that, defined negatively, the specificity of Modernist painting became equated with strong antisculptural qualities:

> Three-dimensionality is the province of sculpture, and for the sake of its own autonomy painting has had above all to divest itself of everything it might share with sculpture.[10]

Modernism is thus defined as specific and, in the case of painting, as a tendency toward flatness or "nonsculpture." In that sense, there is no Modernism at large.

But in another sense, there is. The retrospective historical account that Greenberg gives of Modernist painting privileges the Lessing-Wölfflin-Roger Fry lineage, that is, a *Formalist* tradition of criticism.[11] It is not devoid of value judgments, hierarchies, and exclusions. They may in part stem from intellectual preferences; they certainly correspond to a series of judgments of taste which also privileges a Modernist tradition of artists, precisely that which progressively uncovered painting's minimal and essential convention of flatness. Thus, the tendency toward flatness, of which Greenberg takes stock as an historian, shows itself to be inseparable from a tropism toward aesthetic value, which Greenberg judges as a critic:

> Modernism defines itself in the long run not as a "movement," much less a program, but rather as a kind of bias or tropism: towards esthetic value, esthetic value as such as an ultimate. The specificity of Modernism lies in its being so heightened a tropism in this regard.[12]

Aesthetic value is the outcome of a judgment of taste; it is neither an objective property of the works nor an a priori criterion or norm. The aesthetic value of a given work is what makes up its *content* for a given viewer, who can of course be the artist him- or herself:

> The quality of a work of art inheres in its "content," and vice versa. Quality is "content." You know that a work of art has content because of its effect. The more direct denotation of effect is "quality."[13]

Quality of content, also paraphrased as "gist, meaning, what works of art are ultimately about,"[14] must be carefully distinguished from "subject matter," which, in Modernist art, is the medium itself:

> In turning his attention away from subject matter of common experience, the poet or artist turns it upon the medium of his own craft. The nonrepresentational or "abstract," if it is to have aesthetic validity, cannot be arbitrary and accidental, but must stem from obedience to some worthy constraint or original. This constraint, once the world of common, extraverted experience has been renounced, can only be found in the very processes or disciplines by which art and litera-

ture have already imitated the former. These themselves become the subject matter of art and literature.[15]

The medium in its specificity is not simply a matter of physical constituents; it comprises technical know-how, cultural habits, working procedures and disciplines—all the conventions of a given art whose definition is throughout historical—even more so that the self-critical (or self-referential, but better called reflexive) tendency of Modernism is to take those conventions for subject matter and to test their aesthetic validity. This means that the conventions of a specific art such as painting are never a given. They are the momentary and fragile state of a consensus that is bound to be broken before it is reconstituted elsewhere. The individual work of art—more precisely, its *form*—embodies this call for a new consensus. Form is what translates into visual, describable appearance the state of the conventions of Modernist painting as they are incorporated in a work at a given moment in the history of painting. In other words, the *form* of a work is what makes its *subject matter* visible and offers access to its *content* or quality. It is a constraint that puts pressure on the artist's (and the viewer's) aesthetic judgment and that the work respects or transgresses, modifies or displaces and, in any case, remodels. In this sense, Greenberg can say, but only in retrospect, that Modernist painting's tendency toward flatness ran hand in hand with its tropism toward aesthetic quality, so that:

> Quality, aesthetic value originates in inspiration, vision, "content," not in "form. . . ." Yet "form" not only opens the way to inspiration; it can also act as means to it; and technical preoccupations, when searching enough and compelled enough, can generate or discover "content. . . ." That "content" cannot be separated from its "form."[16]

Readers of Greenberg have often confused "Formalism" with "Modernism." Greenberg himself is partly responsible for this, because he never explicitly distinguishes the two terms. They are indeed intimately intertwined because Modernism— contrary to both premodern art and non-Modernist tendencies within modern art—ascribes the aesthetic judgment not to imitation, expression, or imagination, but to the state in which artists leave the conventions they have inherited after having tested them. Whereas Modernism simply appears as a tendency, to which works belong or not, Formalism involves the way in which the aesthetic judgment, moved (or unmoved) by the *content* of a given Modernist work, is compelled to approve (or disapprove) of the *form* in which the work remodels its historical conventions:

> Reflection shows that anything in a work of art that can be talked about or pointed to automatically excludes itself from the "content" of the work. Anything . . . that does not belong to its "content" has to belong to its "form. . . ." The unspecifiability of its "content" is what constitutes art as art.[17]

Thus "art as art," that is, art as value, is not specifiable. If it were, it would mean that the conventions of a given art could restrict aesthetic judgment a priori and that one would have to judge according to those conventions, whereas it is clear to Greenberg that what Modernism compels us to do is judge those conventions themselves. Art as art cannot and may not be specific; it has to give the works of Modernism a generic content that is, so to speak, perpendicular to its specific form and subject matter. In other words, the sentence "this is art (as art)" is never trivial for Greenberg, but conveys an aesthetic judgment:

> It remains: that when no aesthetic value judgment, no verdict of taste, is there, then art isn't there either, the aesthetic experience of any kind isn't there. It's as simple as that.[18]

The word "art" evaluates quality, which is not to say that it is synonymous with quality. Greenberg has repeatedly said that the word "art" was not necessarily an honorific appellation. Indeed, the passage just quoted does not presume the direction in which the value judgment is to go. A negative aesthetic judgment is still an aesthetic judgment, and an unsatisfactory aesthetic experience is still an aesthetic experience. Thus bad art is art as much as good art. (Greenberg took issue with Croce on this.) As we shall see, it may turn out to be not "as simple as that." But the reasons things get problematic have everything to do with the events I shall recapitulate and interpret. In the meantime, what remains on the level of doctrine is that when it expresses an aesthetic judgment the sentence "this is art" is never trivial. It would be trivial if it meant, for example: "this is a painting—i.e., it obeys the conventions of painting—therefore it is art." The word "painting" would refer to a socially accepted set of norms and the word "art" to a category of human activity of which painting is a subcategory. The sentence "this is art" would merely take notice of a certain state of the social consensus; it would not judge it. But when there is an aesthetic judgment (and let us, for the sake of clarity, suppose that it is a positive one), it has to be the other way around: "this is art—i.e., my taste, sufficiently acquainted with and pressured by the historical state of the conventions of the medium, tells me this is good—thus it is a painting worthy of the name." This is what it means to say that "the unspecifiability of its 'content' is what constitutes art as art."

"This is good (or bad)," "this is beautiful (or ugly)," or "this is art (as art, good or bad)," expresses an aesthetic judgment. It is nonspecific and unspecifiable. Yet it has validity for Modernism only insofar as it refers to—and exerts itself on—the specific set of conventions making up the historical state in which a given medium finds itself. It can only mean something like "this is a good painting" or "this is beautiful within sculpture" or "this is bad poetry" or "as a piece of music this is art," etc. Between content and form, between the generic value judgment and the specific self-criticism of the particular medium, there has to be a mediation, but one that does not allow for a deduction. If it did, it would mean that content—aesthetic value—could be inferred from the state of the medium. Conversely, it would mean that the medium could be deliberately manipulated so as to produce content or quality, thus allowing for what Greenberg calls "concocted" art. The judgment of taste, in the first instance that of the artist, is obviously the mediation we are looking for. It expresses the quality of the work as it is felt; better still, it *is* this quality:

> Aesthetic value or quality is affect; it moves, touches, stirs you . . . it does that in being value and in compelling you to like it more or less, or not like it more or less. . . . Aesthetic value, aesthetic quality can be said to elicit satisfaction, or dissatisfaction. . . . Satisfaction or dissatisfaction is "verdict of taste."[19]

Satisfaction and dissatisfaction are affects or feelings, and a feeling cannot be feigned, or it ceases to be a feeling. Thus verdict of taste—or aesthetic judgment—is passive and involuntary:

Aesthetic judgment is not voluntary. . . . Your aesthetic judgment, being an intuition and nothing else, is received, not taken. You no more chose to like or not like a given item of art than you chose to see the sun as bright or the night as dark.[20]

As to the Modernist artist's aesthetic judgment, it has to be suggested, inspired, provoked by, or received from the medium itself, for the medium is the only subject matter of Modernism and the locus of the artist's aesthetic constraints:

The artist receives judgments-decisions—inspiration, if you like—from his medium as he works in it.[21]

As a result, it is also from the medium, indeed from the *form* it takes in a particular work, that the spectator receives his or her aesthetic judgment. Although there is a generic meaning to "Modernism," there can be no Modernism at large. Conversely, although the conventions defining a given medium historically are specific by definition, their specificity may not be taken for granted but ought to be judged "generically." The name of the necessary mediation between genericity and specificity is *Formalism*.

The sentence "this is beautiful" or "this is art (as art)" expresses, formulates, *formalizes* in language the affect or feeling of quality constituting the aesthetic judgment, as if quality were a property of the work in its visual appearance, in its *form*. As a methodology of art criticism, Formalism means that form and subject matter are the only things one can talk about. It certainly doesn't mean that it values form for the sake of form. To say that it values form for the sake of content would be closer to the truth. But, since "anything in a work of art that can be talked about or pointed to automatically excludes itself from the 'content' of the work," content is the one thing that never acquires discursive existence in Formalist criticism. Content is ineffable because it is a feeling and because feelings do not get communicated by talking about them. In a way, art critics cannot write about "art as art"; they can write about painting, sculpture, poetry, or music, that is, about the medium, and treat the medium as the only subject matter of art, even if the artist didn't. In this case they are Modernist, even if the work is not. They are Formalist if "art as art"—that is, their aesthetic judgment, their feeling of quality—is what makes them speak of a given work, whose form alone they can describe in language. This doesn't make their feeling of quality an objective or even linguistic property of the work's form, yet doesn't simply imply that beauty—or quality—is in the eye of the beholder. The paradox—actually built into sentences such as "this is beautiful" or "this is art"—is that the feeling of beauty, or of art, is formulated as if it were a noticeable fact ascribable to the form of the work. One recognizes in this paradox the antinomy of taste established once and for all by Kant.[22] It is not particular to Formalist criticism. What complicates the issue, tangles up Formalism and Modernism so closely and accounts not only for their confusion, but also for the false impression that Formalism values form for the sake of form, is the fact that the specific conventions of the medium are, in Modernism and in Modernism alone, the only subject matter that indeed matters for the verdict of taste. Though Formalism considers that its discourse cannot speak of content, it can speak of subject matter. But "once the world of common, extraverted experience has been renounced," there remains only one subject matter, to "be found in the very processes or disciplines" of a given, specific medium. And though the medium is specific, it is still a generality; only individual works can be appraised aesthetically. In other words, the self-critical tendency which Greenberg calls Modernism, and which is specific, yields individual *forms* whose generic art *content* is judged as if it were a function of their *subject matter*. The mediation between form and content hides in the necessary "as if" structure of the sentence "this is art" when it judges a work whose subject matter is the critique of its own medium.

For the sake of simplicity, from now on I shall reserve the name "Modernism" to designate Modernism as specific self-criticism and I shall use the name "Formalism" to designate Modernism as generic quality (art as art). As far as painting is concerned, "Modernism" thus refers to its specific tendency to assert the flatness of its medium, and "Formalism" refers to its tropism toward aesthetic value as such. Neither Modernism nor Formalism can be willed. That the two tendencies or tropisms converge in the properties of the medium and in the passivity of the aesthetic judgment is a result of the history of Modernist painting and, as such, can only be recognized retrospectively. It was never a deliberate intention or a program set forth by the painters. Yet it seems to have been, very early on, Greenberg's conviction that the two tendencies had to converge, as is confirmed by his use of the word "surrender" in his major early essay, "Towards a Newer Laocoon," to describe the history of

Modernist painting (or of avant-garde painting, as he was still calling it then):

> The history of avant-garde painting is that of a progressive surrender to the resistance of its medium; which resistance consists chiefly in the flat picture plane's denial of efforts to "hole through" it for realistic perspectival space.[23]

Some Reinterpreted Facts

I remember that when Stella was doing his black paintings, Motherwell told me: "It's very interesting, but it's not painting."

William Rubin

From Manet to Stella, Modernist painting has progressively surrendered to the resistance of its medium, to the point where very little was left beside its flatness itself. Accompanying a portion of this history, from Pollock to Morris Louis, the critic's taste has equally surrendered. Yet it stopped short of acknowledging Stella's black and aluminum paintings, judging, perhaps, that they had turned into *arbitrary objects*. Battling Greenberg on his own turf, the early Minimalists pushed their paintings into the third dimension, where they became objects indeed. It is of course not the first time that monochrome or quasi-monochrome painting appeared in the history of modern art. In each case, its advent has spelled out the zero degree of painting. For some (like Rodchenko) it meant its death, for others (like Malevich) it meant its birth or rebirth under a new name, for others still (like Tarabukin) it meant its birth and its death all at once. In each case one of the answers was a leap into the third dimension. As early as 1940 Greenberg had shown awareness of this:

> Sculpture hovers finally on the verge of "pure" architecture, and painting, having been pushed up from fictive depths, is forced through the surface of the canvas to emerge on the other side in the form of paper, cloth, cement and actual objects of wood and other materials pasted, glued or nailed to what was originally the transparent picture plane, which the painter no longer dares to puncture—or if he does, it is only to dare. Artists like Hans Arp, who begin as painters, escape eventually from the prison of the single plane by

painting on wood or plaster and using molds or carpentry to raise and lower planes. They go, in other words, from painting to colored bas-relief, and finally—so far must they fly in order to return to three-dimensionality without at the same time risking the illusion—they become sculptors and create objects in the round, through which they can free their feelings for movement and direction from the increasing ascetic geometry of pure painting.[24]

This paragraph from the "Newer Laocoon" might describe the advent of Minimal art, if it were not for a few crucial differences. Far from freeing themselves "from the increasing ascetic geometry of pure painting," the Minimalists claimed it and projected it into real space. Although some of them became sculptors or were sculptors already, indeed practicing a kind of sculpture that "hovers finally on the verge of 'pure' architecture" (think of Tony Smith, who began as an architect), others started out as painters, like Hans Arp. But unlike Arp, they would never be content to call their work "colored bas-relief." As we shall see, what to call it was very much an issue.[25] The Minimalists would have felt most uncomfortable to see their practice linked to the tradition of bas-relief, a tradition that is at least as old as easel painting and goes back to Ghiberti or even to Nicola Pisano, a tradition, also, that straddles painting and sculpture and that, therefore, cannot be Modernist in the Greenbergian sense because it is interspecific rather than specific. This shows to what extent Minimalism depends on Greenberg's doctrine, and all the more so since it rejected it. Its history is thus written three times: in the works themselves, of course, but also in the "theories" offered by the artists in justification of their works, and finally in Greenberg's resistance to both the works and the theories. I shall start with the latter. Its "theoretical" stumbling block is the issue of the monochrome repeating itself in particularly sensitive conditions of reception. The irony is that those conditions are set by the success of Greenberg's account of the progressive surrender of painting to its own specificity, and that the last chapter of the history so described appears to be, with the historical distance we have, that of the critic's progressive surrender to art's genericity.

This last chapter is written between the lines of Greenberg's writings throughout the decade that saw the advent of Minimal art. We will have to follow his surrender and his struggle to resist it step by step. In 1958, a year or so before Stella's show at

MoMA, Greenberg is still confident that Modernist painting has a bright future. In "American Type-Painting" he writes:

> Though it may have started toward modernism earlier than the other arts, painting has turned out to have a greater number of *expendable* conventions imbedded in it, or at least a greater number of conventions that are difficult to isolate in order to expend. It seems to be a law of modernism—thus one that applies to almost all art that remains truly alive in our time—that the conventions not essential to the viability of a medium be discarded as soon as they are recognized. . . . Painting continues, then, to work out its modernism with unchecked momentum because it still has a relatively long way to go before being reduced to its viable essence.[26]

In 1961, after Stella's two seminal shows, Greenberg feels compelled to keep his guard up. Although he still boasts in "Modernist Painting" that the limiting conditions or conventions of painting "can be pushed back indefinitely before a picture stops being a picture and turns into an arbitrary object," he feels the necessity of fencing off the excessive literalness of Stella's examples. A hesitation appears in the text that undermines his confidence, and a new line of defense is traced around what can be called residual illusionism, the very same illusionism for which he will praise Jules Olitski's spray paintings a few years later:

> The flatness toward which Modernist painting orients itself can never be an utter flatness. The heightened sensitivity of the picture plane may not permit sculptural illusion, or *trompe-l'oeil*, but it does and must permit optical illusion.[27]

Published in October 1962, "After Abstract Expressionism" stubtly articulates this new line of defense. With a rapid and tactical oscillation of "give and take" designed to dismiss the alleged dogmaticism of his doctrine, Greenberg grants Hoffman's "behind-the-frame" pictures, de Kooning's and even Johns's "homeless representation" or Fautrier's "furtive bas-relief" some positive qualities, which he nevertheless deems insufficient, the better to present his case in favor of Still, Rothko, and Newman, with concepts drawn from Wölfflin, such as painterliness and openness of form. It is thus, thanks to a nimbler historical narrative and a stronger theoretical apparatus, that he can regain confidence in Modernist painting and reassess aesthetically its limit or essence:

> By now it has been established, it would seem, that the irreducible essence of pictorial art consists in but two constitutive conventions or norms: flatness and the delimitation of flatness; and that the observance of merely these two norms is enough to create an object which can be experienced as a picture: thus a stretched or tacked-up canvas already exists as a picture—though not necessarily as a *successful* one.[28]

But only two months later, in December 1962, he publishes under the aggressive title "How Art Writing Earns its Bad Name" an angry defense of his Formalism, in which he is forced into a retreat of a new kind:

> Art turns out to be almost inescapable by now for anyone dealing with a flat surface, even if it is mostly bad art.[29]

What happened in between these two texts? The case under scrutiny is a hypothetical one, but one that the very history of Modernist painting has made plausible: the blank canvas, the empty flat surface. In October it was called a picture, "though not necessarily a successful one"; in December it was called art, "even if it is mostly bad art." The change in formulation may seem trivial: if something is a picture then it is art, and if it is an unsuccessful blank canvas, such as you would find at the artists' supply store, is a mere object, a worldly thing destined to be painted on; it is neither a painting nor a work of art as yet. The brash assertiveness of the October text hides an almost fatal surrender, and one that is not (or not exactly; more about that later) of the same nature as that of the critic's taste in front of a chronologically arranged series of paintings which, from Pollock to Stella, have observed the convention of flatness more and more explicitly. With the hypothetical case of the blank canvas, Greenberg did not simply surrender his taste to the resistance of the medium; he came very close to surrendering his aesthetic doctrine—which precisely articulates a doctrine of taste (Formalism) with one of specificity (Modernism)—to his Minimalist opponents. Once an unpainted canvas can be called a picture or a painting, then it is automatically called art. With the dismissal of

the very last "expendable convention" of Modernist painting—
that the canvas be painted at all—the specific surrenders to the
generic. The consequences branch out into two possibilities.
Either (this would be the left branch of the alternative) the making and the appreciation of art require nothing but a mere identification predicated on the conceptual "logic" of Modernism, and
aesthetic judgment is no longer necessary; Formalism would have
to be betrayed; or (this would be the right branch of the alternative) aesthetic judgment is still necessary. But the pressure that
the conventions of painting had put on its practice is now nil, and
one is forced to allow for an art that is no longer the outcome of
its specific history, a generic art. Modernism, this time, would
have to be abandoned. Although reluctantly and to a great extent
unconsciously, Greenberg chose the right branch of the alternative, which is why the line passing between a picture and a successful one had to be redrawn between art and good art. In the
process the aesthetic judgment has been saved, but specificity
had to be sacrificed. There is still room for quality, but purism or
reductivism is no longer tenable. Formalism is redeemed at the
expense of Modernism.

Some Factual Reinterpretations

The young artist of today need no longer say "I am a painter." He is simply an
artist.

Allan Kaprow

The door to generic art is now open, which is tantamount to a
blanket authorization for Minimal art. Yet Greenberg, who will
not surrender Formalism, is not ready to surrender Modernism
that easily. Minimal art may have been legitimized by the history
that led Modernist painting to the threshold of the blank canvas,
but in order to be judged convincing, it needs to pass the test of
aesthetic experience. Some works may pass it while others may
not. All works, however, need to be linked to their specific history
in order to be plausible candidates for aesthetic appreciation;
this is why a 1967 article entitled "Recentness of Sculpture," in
which Greenberg severely criticizes Minimal art, significantly
starts with a long recollection of his first reactions to monochromatic painting:

Advanced sculpture . . . worked out as badly as it did in the forties and fifties because it was too negatively motivated, because too much of it was done out of the fear of not looking enough like art. Painting in that period was much more confident, and in the early fifties one or two painters did directly confront the question of when painting stopped looking enough like art. I remember that my first reaction to the almost monochromatic pictures shown by Rollin Crampton in 1951 was derision mixed with exasperation. It took renewed acquaintance with these pictures to teach me better. The next monochromatic paintings I saw were completely so—the all-white and all-black paintings in Robert Rauschenberg's 1953 show. I was surprised by how easy they were to "get," how familiar-looking and even slick. It was no different afterwards when I first saw Reinhardt's, Sally Hazlett's, and Yves Klein's monochromatic or near-monochromatic pictures. These, too, looked familiar and slick. What was so challenging in Crampton's art had become almost overnight another taming convention. . . . A monochromatic flatness that could be seen as limited in extension and different from a wall henceforth automatically declared itself to be a picture, to be art.[30]

This paragraph reiterates the process which had led Greenberg in 1962 to accept that a blank canvas could be called a picture and thus art and that now conflates the two appellations: "to be a picture," "to be art" are now one and the same thing. But this perfect overlapping of the specific and the generic is not concluded from a hypothetical case; this time, it is arrived at through "renewed acquaintance" with concrete examples. Seeing the practice of monochromatic painting as an ultimate test of confidence and, in retrospect, relying on his negative aesthetic judgment of Rauschenberg, Reinhardt, and Klein, Greenberg once again concludes that painting (the specific) has ultimately surrendered to art (the generic). In the process, the word "art" has lost whatever honorific status it may have retained when applied to Crampton's quasi-monochromes. The sentence "this is art" is now automatically inferred from "this is a picture," itself an automatic deduction from the perceptual phenomenon of monochromatic flatness. At this point the aesthetic judgment is shunned and shunted. For if the word "art," or "art as art," had retained its evaluative meaning of aesthetic quality—or lack of quality—as such, never would a monochromatic flatness have automatically declared itself to be art. But is it not an ironic paradox that the short-circuit of the aesthetic judgment should be the outcome of one ultimate, negative aesthetic judgment, the one that declares all but Crampton's monochromes "familiar and even slick"? And is it not another, even more ironic paradox that these paintings could not have appeared familiar and slick to an eye untrained and unacquainted with Modernist painting's progressive "surrender to the resistance of its medium" down to Crampton? So that in fact the ultimate test of confidence to which the next monochromes—Rauschenberg's all-white and all-black paintings—have put Modernist painting had to be passed successfully before they could be called a failure. In other words, they had to be judged as bad paintings before they could automatically be called art. Around this paradox the whole case of "Modernist Painting" versus Minimalism revolves. There is no need to suspect that the account Greenberg gives of his aesthetic judgments in front of Crampton's residual illusionism is disingenuous[31] (although it is true that he has a tendency to pull virtually unknown names out of a hat so as to make them appear as the victims of everybody else's poor taste), in order to see that he is rescuing Crampton so as to retrieve a future for painting, while he is downplaying Rauschenberg, Reinhardt, and Klein so as to condemn the "recentness of sculpture," that is, Minimal art.

Greenberg's rejection of Minimal art is well known. There is no point in arguing on aesthetic grounds. Every art critic, after all, grows up with his own generation of artists, and I don't believe that the case "Modernist Painting" versus Minimalism can be settled by a forced choice between Crampton and Rauschenberg or between Olitski and LeWitt. But a critical reassessment of the "art theories"—rather, "art strategies"—implied on both sides is called for. Minimal art was a threat to Greenberg's aesthetics. Or rather, the success of Minimal art was sensed by Greenberg as a threat to high standards in art. It soon became pointless for him to try to fight back by declaring Minimal art illegitimate so that, from the mid-sixties on, he had to live with the fact that there is an art around which calls itself Minimal, which sometimes claims to be sculpture but never painting, and which relies on the perceptual experience of the "real" or the "literal," an experience, that is, unmediated by the conventions of a specific medium and hence not submitted to the strict constraints of Modernist history. If two-dimensionality is the last specific refuge of painting, three-dimensionality is the domain of this new generic art. Highly aware that most significant (and some insignificant) changes in Modernist art first appeared with the look of non-art—which simply means, as in the Rollin Crampton story, that it takes "renewed acquaintance" to judge otherwise—Greenberg seemingly grants Minimal art a major concession when, in "Recentness of Sculpture," he writes:

> Given that the initial look of non-art was no longer available to painting, since even an unpainted canvas now stated itself as a picture, the borderline between art and non-art had to be sought in the three-dimensional, where sculpture was, and where everything material that was not art, also was.[32]

The concession is apparently a huge one, since it means that art-making outside the specific conventions of either painting or sculpture is now recognized as valid. But validity or legitimation is nothing. Art status is not aesthetic quality. The former can be willed and contrived, the latter ought to be the involuntary outcome of an aesthetic judgment.

> In idea, mixing the mediums, straddling the line between painting and sculpture, seemed the far-out thing to do.[33]

Though the far-out might be valid in idea, in actual aesthetic experience it has to be convincing. Inasmuch as Modernism is tied up with specificity, it may be over, but the duties of Formalism cannot be shed. Taking Minimal art more seriously than he does "other forms of Novelty,"[34] Greenberg then makes his choice of convincing artists from the bulk of the Minimalists he more or less openly despises. Very few artists pass the test. Not surprisingly, Anthony Caro is among them. Less expected is the choice of Anne Truitt, who is the only artist whose work Greenberg discusses, in the following terms:

> It was hard to tell whether the success of Truitt's best works was primarily sculptural or pictorial, but part of their success consisted precisely in making that question irrelevant.[35]

Greenberg's endorsement of Anne Truitt is strategic but certainly no less sincere than was his endorsement of Rollin Crampton. It is actually crucial because it provided him with a passageway between the specific and the generic, between the conventions of either painting or sculpture and the wide-open domain of art at large. Whereas the works of most Minimalists, in straddling the line between painting and sculpture as "the far-out thing to do," "ideate" art status and shun aesthetic constraints, Truitt's works address the conventions of both painting and sculpture. What makes them relevant and successful is precisely that they compel the critic to deem their specific identification irrelevant. Greenberg's discussion of her work is not merely a strategic counter-move in his dealing with Minimalism. It also reveals how reluctant he was to abandon Modernism and to surrender specificity, forcing us to fine tune our interpretation of his struggle with generic art. Strictly speaking, a work that is stranded in the no man's land between painting and sculpture is freed from the constraints of both media and is thus unspecific. In that sense it cannot be Modernist, since Modernism does not allow for interspecificity. But this may be too rigid an interpretation of Greenberg's Modernism, and one that does not take into account his prejudice for the pictorial, even in sculpture. Had Greenberg been as consistent a proponent of purism in sculpture as he was in painting, he would have made a point of following a tendency in the history of modern sculpture toward the "essential conventions" of the medium equivalent but opposite to that which he deemed prevalent in painting. He would then have closely watched the reduction of the sculptural practice to questions of matter, tactility, mass, and weight, which are as "essential" to sculpture as flatness is to painting. Had he done so, even skeptical as he was with regard to the kind of Minimal art that had its origins in monochrome painting, it is probable that he would nonetheless enthusiastically have endorsed the art of Carl André or of Richard Serra. But he hasn't. Leaving singular aesthetic judgment aside, the reason is probably that Greenberg has always been convinced that sculpture never had to fear its proximity to painting in the way that painting had, for its own survival, "to divest itself of everything it might share with sculpture." If sculpture had anything to fear, it would more likely have been its excessive proximity to architecture; this is why, according to him, the tradition of the monolith was driven to its ultimate conclusion by Brancusi, after whom the best of Modernist sculpture (David Smith and Anthony Caro included), far from fencing off the pictorial, incorporated openness of form, textural effects, color, and, more generally, the opticality that also characterizes the best of Modernist painting.[36] With this bias of Greenberg in mind, it is easy to see why Truitt's work would be spared the

Minimalist limbo. Its redeeming quality is akin to the residual illusionism he advocates in Olitski and which he opposes to the utter flatness of the straight monochrome.[37] In another article on Truitt, the argument of interspecificity is repeated; it is also more focused:

> It was hard to tell, in Truitt's art, where the pictorial and where the sculptural began and ended. Had they been monochrome, the "objects" in Truitt's 1963 show would have qualified as first examples of orthodox Minimal Art.[38]

So, despite the doctrine of Modernist specificity, it seems that a hybrid of painting and sculpture is permissible, and that it can even be convincing, provided it is polychrome. Rather than an outright abandonment of Modernism, what we have is an expansion of Formalism taking advantage of a disparity in Greenberg's attitudes toward painting and sculpture. It may be that the monochrome, and certainly the blank canvas, set the limit beyond which "a picture stops being a picture and turns into an arbitrary object." But if this object can claim some acquaintance with a tradition of sculpture itself indebted to the opticality of painting, then it is not totally arbitrary. In other words, it is not free of constraints, and the judgment of taste can apply itself to it, significantly. Modernism, narrowly speaking, is jeopardized, but the essential thing is that Formalism is maintained. In order to be probatively called art (as art), an object, any object, needs to be (either) painting or sculpture. An overlapping of the two specificities is now allowed under certain conditions. If the object in question stems from the tradition of Modernist painting—as do Stella's black paintings, the monochrome in general and even the blank canvas—then no overlapping is allowed. The "either painting or sculpture" is the Latin *aut*; the disjunction is exclusive. If, on the other hand, the object in question stems from the tradition of Modernist sculpture, even if it steps out of it (Anne Truitt's objects certainly do so more than Carl André's), then hybridization is allowed and even welcome. The "or" is the Latin *vel*; the disjunction is inclusive. In this way (and although a major concession has been made to Minimalism), room is provided for a particular kind of unorthodox Minimal art—generic, yes, but multispecific rather than unspecific. It is both painting and sculpture.

What puzzles me is, why do we always find ourselves arguing painting, when we set out to talk about sculpture?

Carl André

The major "theoretical" manifesto of Minimal art is a text published in 1965 by Donald Judd entitled "Specific Objects." It starts with this sentence:

> Half or more of the best new work in the last few years has been neither painting nor sculpture.[39]

This statement applies to a great variety of works, among which Judd discusses those of Lee Bontecou, Claes Oldenburg, John Chamberlain, and Stella. He also cites Yayoi Kusama, H. C. Westermann, Richard Smith, even Yves Klein, and many others. The article is lavishly illustrated with works by Johns, Rauschenberg, Flavin, Artschwager, Morris, Stella, and with one of Judd's own works, which he modestly claims the editor has included, not he. Modesty notwithstanding, it is clear that the text is a manifesto in favor of his own conception of art. Some of the works Judd mentions definitely belong to painting, some to sculpture, most of them to an indeterminate realm straddling both. Many of his own works, for example, are colored and hang on the wall like paintings, but protrude into the third dimension like sculptures. The strange thing is that Judd claims for them a rather paradoxical status: although they combine qualities of both painting and sculpture, they are said to be neither. The paradox, however, becomes intelligible when one understands that Judd's justification for Minimal art is absolutely overdetermined, albeit *a contrario*, by the Greenbergian doctrine. Judd seeks to secure legitimation for generic art, more precisely (as we have seen from the example of his early work, as well as that of LeWitt and Flavin), for an art that deliberately oversteps the limit beyond which "a picture stops being a picture and turns into an arbitrary object," in other words, an art that stems from and steps out of painting rather than sculpture. On Greenberg's terms, it ought to obey and even defend its own specificity. This it precisely refuses to do; it leaps into the third dimension "where sculpture was and where everything material that was not art also was," and it proudly claims this arbitrariness.

As I have tried to show above, the influence of Greenberg's doctrine on Judd's generation of artists was so strong that the double bind they must have felt when confronted with Stella's black and aluminum canvases left them with no alternative other than to pursue the Modernist tradition even beyond the literal monochrome where it actually meets its end. The consequences are manifold and in direct opposition to Greenberg's views on Minimalism, to the judgment with which he saves Anne Truitt's work from the Minimalist doom, and to the arguments with which he backs it up. This is of course no surprise, since Judd's and Greenberg's rationales developed in dialectical opposition to each other. The arbitrariness Judd claims for his "specific objects" is precisely what makes them condemnable in Greenberg's eyes: they are neither painting nor sculpture, that is, they are not accountable to the tradition of either Modernist painting or Modernist sculpture. Hence, they can be "ideated" instead of judged aesthetically. The Formalist judgment which would call them art (as art) is lost in a limbo where confrontation with the constraints of a specific tradition can be avoided and where no aesthetic experience of significance can be had. The experience of such objects is merely phenomenal, says Greenberg, and Judd agrees. What we have is generic art with only logical, not aesthetic, ties to history.

Yet Judd's manifesto is not entitled "Generic Objects"; its title is "Specific Objects." This, more than anything else, shows the extent to which his thinking is indebted to that of Greenberg. But he takes the other branch of the alternative set by Greenberg, and quite systematically so. It is essential to Judd that Modernism should be allowed to progress beyond the limit set by the literal monochrome. Since the essence of Modernism lies "in the use of the characteristic methods of a discipline to criticize the discipline itself—not in order to subvert it, but to entrench it more firmly in its area of competence," Judd is bound to claim, for the area where painting overlaps with sculpture, a competence or specificity of its own, which would thus be severed from the traditions, or areas of competence, of both painting and sculpture. Within the generic domain of art and non-art alike—since by now virtually anything is readable as art[40]—the works of the Minimalists struggle to assert their unique specificity while having to acknowledge the genericity of their own conditions of production. Judd is aware of this double task:

> One of the important things in any art is its degree of generality and specificity and another is how each of these occurs. The extent and the occurrence have to be credible. I'd like my work to be somewhat more specific than art has been and also specific and general in a different way.[41]

A new "species" of art is born, for which the risk of confusion with non-art is greater than it has ever been. Hence the importance of its name. There is no end to the string of names which the critics and sometimes the artists coined for the new species: Minimal Art, Literal Art, ABC Art, Primary Structures, Art of the Real, Post-painterly Relief (this last one surely of Greenbergian ascent) and many others, the prize in barbarian neologism going to *Sculptecture*. The new hybrid discovered by the art world's natural scientists is a monster born out of the most improbable genetic manipulations. I am being ironic. What is crucial here is not to decide whether this or that name is better suited, but rather to figure out what this frantic naming activity reveals: in order to secure some legitimation for Minimal art, as it was cut from the traditions named (from the traditional names of) "painting" and "sculpture," it was vital to see that a specific name, preferably new, brought it under the generic name "art" as a brand new art devoid of tradition, but as an art in its own right.[42] Donald Judd chooses the appellation "Specific Objects," to which he ascribes the task of crossing the categories of Pop art, Minimal art and a few others, as his choice of artists in this text shows. If one absolutely had to choose a name, this one would be the most intelligent, no doubt, and the one that most clearly indicates what was at stake: to conquer, inside the generic name "art" now deprived of its aesthetic ambition, a nonetheless qualitative "area of competence." Stated in positive terms, the specificity of the works that Judd defends comprises a set of qualities which seek to affirm as strongly as possible the individuality of a given piece, so as to set it apart from all that is not art and, at the same time, establish a "family resemblance" among those works making up the new breed. Both Judd and Robert Morris have insisted on the nonrelational, noncompositional forms adopted by Minimalism, on the wholeness, compactness, and objectness of their Gestalt, on the reality of the time and space in which their presence is experienced, and on the obdurate literalness of their materials.[43] The word "specific" is meant to convey all these qualities:

> The characteristics of three dimensions . . . may persist, such as the work's being like an object or being specific. . . .[44]
> Materials . . . are specific. If they are used directly, they are more specific. . . . Also, they are usually aggressive. There is an objectivity to the obdurate identity of a material.[45]

Just as Greenberg had to define the specificity of Modernist painting in negative as well as positive terms and oppose its flatness to the three-dimensionality of sculpture, so Judd finds it easier to define the specificity of the new art by what it is not:

> Painting and sculpture have become set forms. A fair amount of their meaning isn't credible. The use of three dimensions isn't the use of a given form. There hasn't been enough time and work to see limits. . . . Since its range is so wide, three-dimensional work will probably divide into a number of forms. At any rate, it will be larger than painting and much larger than sculpture. . . . Because the nature of three dimensions isn't set, given beforehand, something credible can be made, almost anything.[46]

The tone of this paragraph is programmatic, if not prophetic. It probes the future and makes promises. But it also seeks to deny the past and it fails, quite symptomatically. The obsessiveness of Judd's disavowal of the painting tradition out of which his own art and many other "specific objects" emerged is indeed a symptom. Despite his claim that they have severed their ties with both sculpture and painting, the link with painting keeps creeping back into his text, sometimes as a plain admission:

> The new work obviously resembles sculpture more than it does painting, but it is nearer to painting.[47]

Or, sometimes as a rhetoric fighting back the shadow of painting which looms over the new work:

> Three dimensions are real space. That gets rid of the problem of illusionism and of literal space. . . . Actual space is

intrinsically more powerful and specific than painting on a flat surface.[48]

Or, sometimes as a denial of painting's future:

> The rectangular plan is given a life span. The sense of singleness also has a duration, but it is only beginning and has a better future outside of painting. . . . The plane is also emphasized and nearly single. It is clearly a plane one or two inches in front of another plane, the wall, and parallel to it. The relationship of the two planes is specific, it is a form.[49]

What is much harder to deny than painting's future is its past, especially the recent past of Modernist painting, which led to the monochrome and in particular to Stella's black canvases, the shock of which was so seminal for the advent of Minimal art. The way Judd eschews calling Stella's work painting in order to annex it to his "specific objects" is rather amazing, but there is no more need to see intellectual twisting in this than there was to see disingenuousness in Greenberg's judgments on Rollin Crampton or Anne Truitt. The surprise effect of Stella's canvases at the time was so strong that it was indeed difficult to see them as paintings. However, Judd knows that Stella himself wanted his work to be considered as painting. Yet he writes:

> Frank Stella says that he is doing paintings, and his work could be considered as painting. Most of the works, though, suggest slabs, since they project more than usual. . . . The projection, the absence of spatial effects and the close relation between the periphery and the stripes make the paintings seem like objects, and that does a lot to cause their amplified intensity.[50]

Again, apropos Stella's aluminum paintings:

> It is something of an object, it is a single thing, not a field with something in it, and it has almost no space.[51]

And again, apropos Stella and Flavin:

> Although they exclude painterly art, their work is decidedly art, and is visible art.[52]

More Factual Reinterpretations

"Non-art," "anti-art," "non-art art," and "anti-art art" are useless. If someone says his work is art, it's art.

Donald Judd

There is no doubt that in calling Stella's work "visible art," Judd is uttering a judgment. He is evaluating, even praising the work. The question is: is this judgment aesthetic? To be honest, I don't believe that today Judd would deny that it is, or that it was. But in the context of the times, he could not have acknowledged it. It is a matter of consistency: his Greenbergian anti-Greenbergianism left him no choice other than to opt for Modernism against Formalism. Indeed, the terms of the alternative are set by the Greenbergian doctrine. Generic art is permissible, either because it is in fact interspecific—it allows for the traditions of both Modernist painting and sculpture to put pressure on the artist's and the critic's taste, in which case a judgment of taste is called for, conveyed by the sentence "this is art"; such is the right branch of the alternative—or because anything is permitted and everything that is neither painting nor sculpture is encouraged. Once even a blank canvas can be called a picture, anything visible can be called art, in which case art has lost its aesthetic import and taste is not called for. The sentence "this is art" is a convention. Historical knowledge alone is required to make and judge art, some intellectual curiosity or interest for the "logic" of Modernism, some strategic desire or interest to see it further extrapolated and tested on mere institutional grounds. Art fades into "art theory." Such is the left branch of the alternative. It is all too easy to see that Minimal art and the movements that were to follow, Conceptual art especially, chose the left branch, expressed in a nutshell by Judd's most famous assertion from "Specific Objects": "A work needs only to be interesting."[53]

Donald Judd is too much of an artist to be really convinced of what he said there. And Greenberg is too intelligent not to have seen that the strategic extrapolation of the "logic" of taste pervades taste itself, and that it has played its provocative role with every significant leap in Modernism. I believe that Judd and Greenberg could still argue with each other. Things get more dogmatic with the eipgones, Michael Fried and Joseph Kosuth.

In view of their further development, it may be a little unfair to
pit them against each other as mere epigones of Greenberg and
Judd respectively, but it has the advantage of giving the debate
additional clarity. In the mid-sixties, Fried was not yet the fine
historian and phenomenologist of art he subsequently became.
Although he claimed to have departed from Greenberg's essen-
tialism, he was in a way more Greenbergian than Greenberg. His
much praised and much attacked 1967 article "Art and Objecthood" nevertheless still remains by far the best analysis done
on Minimal art at the time. Better than anyone else, Fried has
sensed what threat Minimalism posed to Formalism, and his
counter-attack is right on target.

Fried states the necessary link between Formalism and Modernism—that is, between the value judgment that puts a given
work to the test of being compared to the best work of tradition
and the very tendency of this tradition to identify itself with the
testing of the conventions of its medium—in terms that are stronger and more doctrinaire, even, than Greenberg's:

> The concepts of quality and value—and to the extent that
> these are central to art, the concept of art itself—are mean-
> ingful, or wholly meaningful, only within the individual arts.
> What lies between the arts is theatre.[54]

Although the generic value judgment expressed by the word
"art" (or "art as art" or "art as such" or "good art as such"[55]) is
of course still possible and indeed required, it simply cannot be
convincing outside the individual arts. The objectness (which
Fried calls "objecthood") of the Minimalist works (which he re-
dubs "literalist") is acknowledged for what Judd claims it to be,
neither painting nor sculpture; but for that very reason it is denied both its specificity and its aesthetic validity:

> It is as though objecthood alone can, in the present circum-
> stances, secure something's identity, if not as non-art, at
> least as neither painting nor sculpture. . . . Here the ques-
> tion arises: What is it about objecthood as projected and hy-
> postatized by the literalists that makes it, if only from the
> perspective of recent modernist painting, antithetical to art?
> The answer I want to propose is this: the literalist espousal
> of objecthood amounts to nothing other than a plea for a new
> genre of theatre; and theatre is now the negation of art.[56]

Fried's case against "literalism" is strong on the interpretive level, if not necessarily on the level of judgment. In calling the interspecificity of what falls in between painting and sculpture "theatre," he not only accounts for a number of phenomenological qualities of Minimalist works, such as their "presence," their involvement of the beholder and their existence in duration, but also hints at an explanation of the new practices which came about in the wake of Minimal art and, most significantly, of the new names such as "Performance art" and "Installation art" which they secured for themselves.[57] Interpretation aside, Fried's judgment, when he dumps Minimal art into the limbo of "theatre" or non-art, is in line with most non-art judgments uttered—mostly by academic critics—throughout the history of Modernism since Courbet: it is a refusal to judge aesthetically, and it means "literalism doesn't even deserve to be called art." But Fried is not an academic critic like those who a priori refuse to take into account anything that does not seem to fit the fixed rules of a genre. Like Greenberg, even more than Greenberg, he is far too aware that Modernism has ceaselessly put those "fixed" rules to the test of aesthetic experience and, in so doing, has abandoned or displaced them. And like Greenberg, he feels obliged to show that he is able to select a counter-example which, though situated in the same generic no man's land as the rest of literalism, would deserve to be called art. Among the happy few is Anthony Caro again. Anne Truitt is not mentioned, but a particular work by Jules Olitski receives a great deal of attention. Entitled *Bunga 45*, it is one of the first sculptures ever made by Olitski, in 1967, and consists of a cluster of ten-foot-high aluminum tubes spray painted in the same not quite monochrome manner as his canvases. It is highly probable that Olitski, if not induced, was at least encouraged by Greenberg to move into sculpture, especially this kind of sculpture, which seems really contrived to be Formalism's response to Minimalism. At any rate, *Bunga 45* is fairly unique in the production of Olitski, who shortly after went to work in Caro's studio in England and fell strongly under his influence. Here is Fried's comment on *Bunga*:

> It amounts to something far more than an attempt simply to make or "translate" his paintings into sculptures, namely, an attempt to establish surface—the surface, so to speak, of *painting*—as a medium for sculpture. The use of tubes, each of which one sees, incredibly, as *flat*—that is, flat but

rolled—makes *Bunga*'s surface more like that of a painting than like that of an object: like painting, and unlike both ordinary objects and other sculpture, *Bunga* is *all* surface. And of course what declares or establishes that surface is color, Olitski's sprayed color.[58]

The tone, emphasis, and argument of this paragraph betray this piece of writing as a paragon—or a cliché—of Formalist criticism. As with Greenberg's defense of Truitt, color and subtle polychromy (described at length a little earlier in the text), to which Fried has added the rather farfetched category of "rolled flatness," are invoked to ensure that *Bunga* is saved from the literalist limbo. Not that Fried's description of his aesthetic experience is wrong or unfaithful. But in electing Olitski, he is unfair to what he excludes. After all, Fried could have looked at Chamberlain in very much the same way he looked at Olitski (indeed he was tempted to), instead of resting his estimation of Chamberlain's work on a rationale which is neither his own nor the artist's but that of Judd. Fried never challenges the paradoxical claim that Judd had made for the works he advocated as "specific objects." He never underlines that Chamberlain's work, or Judd's for that matter, could be seen as both painting and sculpture rather than as neither. No, they are "theatre" or "non-art." Rather than using his own eyes as Formalism recommends, Fried is taking Judd at his own word. In a way, though, he is right, and his reasons have less to do with opting for the exclusive rather than the inclusive status given the indeterminate domain straddling painting and sculpture, than with the invitation, handed out by Judd, not to judge his (or Chamberlain's) work aesthetically. What is allegedly new in the sixties (in fact, it is as old as Dadaism) is a situation where the refusal to judge aesthetically— a tactic typical of academic critics since Courbet—is claimed by the artists themselves so that, as Fried says, "what non-art means today, and has meant for several years, is fairly specific."[59] There is thus a specificity of non-art (i.e., of nonpainting/nonsculpture) which Fried is forced to recognize yet rejects, not by way of a concrete aesthetic judgment, but in the name of aesthetic judgment at large—and thus in the name of art, generically speaking. Hence his mockery of Judd's assertion, "A work needs only to be interesting":

> Judd himself has as much as acknowledged the problematic character of the literalist enterprise by his claim "A work

needs only to be interesting." For Judd, as for the literalist sensibility generally, all that matters is whether or not a given work is able to elicit and sustain (his) interest. . . . Literalist work is often condemned—when it is condemned—for being boring. A tougher charge would be that it is merely interesting.[60]

To which, of course, Judd replied: "I was especially irked by Fried's ignorant misinterpretation of my use of the word 'interesting.' I obviously use it in a particular way but Fried reduces it to the cliché 'merely interesting.' "[61]

Although somewhat unfair to Judd, whose understanding of the works made by Stella, Flavin, or himself clings to "visible art," Fried's charge against the "merely interesting" is certainly valid when directed at the productions of Conceptual art, especially at those with an explicit theortical claim. But it is only valid, the Conceptualists argue, within the Formalist discourse which the theory of Conceptualism precisely claims to invalidate and which its practice seeks as much as possible to render without object. Under Judd's strong influence, Joseph Kosuth issued in 1969 a widely publicized manifesto entitled "Art after Philosophy," in which no effort was spared to prevent not only the aesthetic judgment in the Formalist sense, but also the judgment of "interest" or "interestedness" as sought by Donald Judd. Beyond taste and interest alike, there remains only a circular proposition to define art (as art):

A work of art is a tautology in that it is a presentation of the artist's intention, that is, he is saying that that particular work of art is art, which means, is a definition of art. Thus, that it is art is true a priori.[62]

Therefore, specific formal qualities such as the flatness of a painting or the holistic Gestalt and obdurate materials of a "specific object" are superfluous. Ideally, one would have to dispense with the object altogether in order to foreclose the possibility of any judgment other than logical or conceptual:

It comes as no surprise that the art with the least fixed morphology is the example from which we decipher the nature of the general term art.[63]

Consequently, Kosuth claims for art a condition beyond object-ness and linguistic in character:

> Works of art are analytic propositions. . . . One begins to realize that art's "art condition" is a conceptual state. . . . In other words, the propositions of art are not factual, but linguistic in character—that is, they do not describe the behavior of physical or even mental objects; they express definitions of art, or the formal consequences of definitions of art. Accordingly, we can say that art operates on a logic.[64]

Since art is a tautology, there is no specificity to this logic, nei-ther in terms of a medium nor in terms of a new, specific "area of competence" severed from, and added to, those of painting and sculpture. Kosuth's Conceptualism allows only for generic art:

> Being an artist now means to question the nature of art. If one is questioning the nature of painting, one cannot be questioning the nature of art. . . . That's because the word art is general and the word painting is specific. Painting is a kind of art.[65]

This is why the "kind of art" called painting ought to be ban-ished, made illegitimate and obsolete by the new generic Concep-tual art. But the more radically the generic is severed from the specific, the more insidiously the link with Modernist painting, especially with Stella's black and aluminum canvases, creeps back into the text, in the shape of a disavowal akin to that of Judd:

> Johns and Reinhardt are probably the last two painters that were legitimate *artists* as well.[66]

To which he adds, in an appending footnote that has the ring of a Freudian slip:

> And Stella too, of course. But Stella's work, which was greatly weakened by being painting, was made obsolete very quickly by Judd and others.

Even more than his "theory," Kosuth's disavowal makes it clear that Conceptual art was not a linear development from Minimal art but an even more radical reworking of the aporia, born out of the question of the monochrome, which forced a lot of artists who had been brought up on the Greenbergian doctrine and who, with or without reason, felt that they could not possibly go on painting after Stella, to separate Modernism and Formalism and to bank on the logic of the former the better to refute the latter. In "Art after Philosophy" Kosuth relentlessly attacks Greenberg, whom he accuses of being "the critic of taste," which is true, and rejects his Formalism, which he accuses of accepting "a definition of art resting solely on morpho-logical grounds," which is unfair, since Greenberg has no definition of art. Kosuth, in fact, took his own "definition" of art as tautology from yet another painter of quasi-monochromes, Ad Reinhardt, who, with Johns, was the last legitimate artist whom he was ready to recognize as being also a painter. But he took it from Reinhardt's writings and attitude more than from his paintings. And one imagines that Reinhardt's *"art as art as art"* so easily became Kosuth's *"art as idea as idea"* because drawing from a text allowed him to bypass the pictures. The denial of the specific is as obvious vis-à-vis Reinhardt as it is vis-à-vis Stella.

Conceptual art is thus another response to the same double bind that every would-be painter must have felt in New York in the early sixties, standing in front of Stella's black paintings with *Art and Culture* in his pocket. With the exception of the members of the English group *Art-Language*, in the early seventies Kosuth was the only proponent of hard-core Conceptual art, the kind he himself called TCA (Theoretical Conceptual Art), as opposed to the more poetic brand he disparagingly called SCA (Stylistic Conceptual Art). Yet even among the representatives of Conceptual art who did not share Kosuth's theoretical inclinations, the number of ex-painters is remarkable. Between 1966 and 1968, in New York and elsewhere, Robert Huot, John Baldessari, Robert Barry, Jan Dibbets, Mel Ramsden, Lawrence Weiner, and others produced their "ultimate" monochrome or acted out a variation on the blank canvas before they switched to Conceptual art. Their Conceptual works are intelligible and can be appraised only in reference to the abandoned craft and medium of painting, which, unfortunately for those artists, is precisely what they sought to escape, since they predicated their works on the "logic" of Modernist painting while refusing to let them be aesthetically evaluated with respect to painting. Sometimes, as in Weiner's distinction between his *Specific Statements*

and his *General Statements*, explicit reference was made to the
problem which overdetermined the art of the sixties: the passage
from the specific to the generic. This passage was always interpreted in terms of a shift from formal experimentation to conceptual inquiry. It was never undestood for what it actually was. Up
to the present, Generic art—an appellation mostly suited to the
latest trends exemplified by Allan McCollum, Haim Steinbach, or
Jeff Koons, all of whom produce "generic objects"—has dragged
in its wake an unresolved quarrel with Greenbergian Formalism.

Although Kosuth can hardly be taken as a spokesman for all
Conceptual artists, his 1969 manifesto "Art after Philosophy" is
exemplary of the state of this unresolved quarrel. Irksome and
self-serving as it is, his reasoning is in some way flawless, carrying Judd's escape from Formalism to its logical extreme. "The
intensification, almost the exacerbation, of this self-critical tendency that began with the philosopher Kant," which Greenberg
calls Modernism, has come full circle in Kosuth's tautology. Of
this absurd triumph of Modernism over Formalism, one might
think that Kosuth's ultimate conclusion would be to posit the end
of art. Not at all. Instead, it proclaims "the end of philosophy and
the beginning of art."[67] This can only mean two things—that
there is an absolute "separation between aesthetics and art,"[68]
art now being identified with "art theory" while aesthetics is relegated to the realm of taste; and that there is an absolute historical beginning to this separation:

> The function of art, as a question, was first raised by Marcel
> Duchamp. In fact it is Marcel Duchamp whom we can credit
> with giving art its own identity. . . . With the unassisted
> Ready-made, art changed its focus from the form of the lan-
> guage to what was being said. Which means that it changed
> the nature of art from a question of morphology to a question
> of function. . . . All art (after Duchamp) is conceptual (in na-
> ture) because art only exists conceptually.[69]

A Critical Reinterpretation

There is a superficial similarity between Modernist painting and Dada in one
important respect: namely, that just as Modernist painting has enabled one to see
a blank canvas . . . as a picture, Dada and Neo-Dada have equipped one to treat
virtually any object as a work of art—though it is far from clear exactly what this
means.

Michael Fried

Here, with the last of Kosuth's statements, we should pause, wonder, and meditate. Duchamp's first unassisted readymade is the *Bottlerack*, dated 1914. Out of what strange, fifty-five-year-long torpor has Kosuth's "discovery" awakened the art world? If it is true that all art after Duchamp is conceptual in nature, why did this revelation come to the surface only "in artistic endeavor since Abstract Expressionism, after which work began to appeal to the *logic of modernism* for art status rather than appealing to the tradition of Western painting for art status"?[70] Was it not precisely in an article entitled "After Abstract Expressionism" that Greenberg voiced his concern about work which could "appeal to the logic of modernism for art status rather than appealing to the tradition of Western painting for art" *quality*? And is it not the case that the thin line that separates logic and tradition, or status and quality, might be the one that Greenberg, confronted in October 1962 with the hypothetical case of the blank canvas, drew and refused to cross, the line between a picture and a successful one? Finally, is it not clear that this hypothetical case did not fall from the heaven of "art theory" but that its plausibility was prompted by the latest avatars of Modernist painting, Stella's black and aluminum canvases in particular? Well, the blank canvas is a readymade. Marcel Duchamp's first unassisted readymade had to wait fifty-five years before it gave Kosuth the "revelation" that all art is conceptual in nature, because it is only after Abstract Expressionism, and in the particular context that spawned the controversy between "Modernist Painting" and Minimalism, that it reappeared from within the history of Modernist painting under the guise of an unpainted canvas. Kosuth's contention that Duchamp's readymade "changed the nature of art from a question of morphology to a question of function" is ludicrous, as if a single artist could change the "nature of art." The readymade has, of course, demonstrated no such thing. But Kosuth's contention is a symptom, and one that is apt to give us a clue to the proper reinterpretation of the specific/generic problem which is overdetermining the art of the last thirty years.

Unlike Duchamp's bottlerack or urinal, the blank canvas is a *specific* readymade. It is a manufactured product, new and unused, as are all of Duchamp's unassisted readymades, but it is one that you can find at the artists' supply store, not at the Bazar de l'Hôtel de Ville where Duchamp bought the bottlerack. Even before it is touched by the painter's hand, it already belongs to the tradition of painting, or rather, to a particular tradition—that of Western painting since the Renaissance. While it is prepared to receive the traces of the painter's brush and is thus no more than a support, as part of the artist's materials, it has already incorporated, ready-made, the one convention established during the Renaissance—that one is to paint on a stretched canvas. To call it a picture, "though not necessarily a successful one," means to acknowledge the presence of that historical convention in an otherwise mundane commodity. But to call it a picture also means, of course, to recognize that this convention is the only one left from a five-hundred-year-old tradition. Greenberg, who knew this all too well, deemed this convention to be essential. As if in a mirror image to Kosuth's contention that Duchamp's readymades have changed the nature of art, there was already Greenberg's contention that the blank canvas had revealed the nature of painting. Since Duchamp did not actualize the blank canvas, Kosuth does not see its ready-made "nature," and Greenberg does not see the change in "nature" which the vantage point of the readymade imprints on it. The ready-made canvas is at once their common blind spot and the missing link between them.

But it needs to be reinterpreted. Greenberg sees flatness and its delimitation, as they are incorporated in the ready-made canvas, as an essential convention. While being recognized as a mere convention, it is also deemed irreducible, irremovable, something you could not abandon without altering the very nature of the medium. Now, that one should paint on a piece of cloth braced to a wooden stretcher is a prescription with no ontological privilege. A convention it is, but it is no more of an essential convention than the one it gradually replaced, which prescribed painting on a wooden board. Not until the Renaissance did easel painting substitute for the retable and open a new category of "specific objects," "limited in extension and different from a wall," as Greenberg said. Not until the Renaissance, when a painting began to be seen as an illusionistic window, did it detach itself from the wall, distinguish itself from the mural, gain mobility and autonomy from architecture, and become "a plane one or two inches in front of another plane, the wall, and parallel to it," as Judd said. There is nothing essential to this plane's flatness, nothing essential either to its whiteness. The easel painting may share its rigid flatness with the retable and with the wall; it does not share it with the baroque cupola, the Greek vase, or the Chinese scroll. And the painter's virgin canvas shares its whiteness with the writer's blank page more than it does with other artifacts belonging to its own tradition, linen fabric included. The Venetians did not gesso their canvases; they used a red undercoat. Not only are all conventions historical and not ontological, specific in the sense that they are embedded in a tradition rather than in the nature of the medium, but the one convention that Modernism has not relinquished, the one that has heightened its purist sensibility for the surface so much, owes more to Mallarmé and the Symbolist crossover of painting and poetry than it does to its own history since the Renaissance. After all, despite Lessing's Laocoon and Greenberg's "Newer Laocoon," Modernism did not succeed in doing away with the *ut pictura poesis*: kicked out of the illusionistic window, it crept back into the medium itself when painters began to take it for the subject matter of their practice.

Duchamp did not actualize the blank canvas. Nor did he actualize the tube of paint, which is, as I have argued elsewhere, the underground paradigm for all his readymades.[71] He abandoned painting in 1912 and switched to art. He abruptly jumped from the specific to the generic. Or so the story goes, both for all those—artists, critics, and art historians—who have applauded the invention of the readymade and seen in it new avenues and unprecedented freedom for art, and for those who have deplored it and read it as a symptom of a disastrous slackening in the standards of taste. Neither group has seriously asked what it meant to jump from the specific to the generic; neither has considered what had made it possible; neither has devoted careful attention to its timing in history and its various repetitions. But the switch from the specific to the generic is not at all self-evident. That one could be an artist without being a painter (or a sculptor or a musician or a poet . . .) is indeed unprecedented and should be startling to everyone, even today. How did Duchamp get away with it? is one question. Why? is another. Did he deserve it? is still another. The fact is that he succeeded, and the presumption is that the conditions were ripe. Another fact is that his success is rooted in a failure, partly personal, partly general, but on both counts extremely significant and made significant by the acute intelligence and irony of his work. It sheds light, for example, on this: the passage from the specific to the generic is never one for which sheer "art theory" can account; it takes an investigation that probes the existential and the historical at the same time. You may become an artist without being a painter, but hardly without having been one. As we have seen, this holds true for all Minimal and Conceptual artists. Fifty years after the readymade, they had to reenact a certain rite of passage, which Duchamp was the first to accomplish. Similarly, something Minimal or Conceptual beyond the blank canvas can be art without being a picture, but not without the blank canvas having been one—which is why, ironically, the Minimalists and the Conceptualists sought their authority to do generic art from Greenberg's 1962 article, where he set out to posit the blank canvas as the embodiment of painting's ultimate specificity, as if warning not to transgress it.

The blank canvas is not a picture; it was one. It was a picture, a viable would-be picture, a potential picture, in the days when Modernist painting had its tradition ahead of itself. For the Modernist sensibility striving for purism and attuned to the "elements" of painting, the blank canvas's potential to become a painting had an extraordinary aesthetic appeal. From Malevich to Mondrian, there is not one pioneer of abstract painting who did not respond to the appeal of the bare canvas. They were breaking with the past, relinquishing the strongest of all "expendable conventions," namely figuration; they also thought of themselves as laying down the basic alphabet of a future culture. Although none of them actualized the blank canvas, they sensed its promise. Kandinsky, for example, in 1913, praised "this pure canvas that is itself as beautiful as a picture."[72] This sensibility accompanied the history of Modernist painting all along. When, as early as 1940, Greenberg spoke of "the pristine flatness of the stretched canvas," he was still surrendering to its magnetic appeal.[73] In fact it is the Mallarmean seduction of the virgin canvas that is the secret center of convergence of Modernism as "self-critical tendency" with Formalism as "tropism towards esthetic value as such." And of course, it could keep this attractive power only as long as it was itself taboo. With each convention that proved "expendable," Modernist painting came closer to actualizing the blank canvas. But the closer its actualization, the thinner its capacity to promise a future. By 1962 this actualization seemed imminent, and so did the end of Modernist painting.[74] In calling the blank canvas a picture, "though not necessarily a successful one," Greenberg anticipated its imminent realization. He did not actualize it; he legitimized it instead and in so doing made its actualization futile. He would probably be very surprised to learn that he was joining hands with Duchamp on this issue.

In Greenberg's retrospective account, reinterpreted via Duchamp, the history of Modernist painting has, at the same time, both fulfilled and exhausted the promises of the blank canvas. In Kandinsky's eyes, it *was* a picture in 1914. It meant that on this tabula rasa a future abstract language called painting was going to be erected. In Greenberg's eyes, it *is* a picture in 1962. It means that Modernist painting has finally surrendered to its essence, to its *being*, in the present participle. But seen through Duchamp's eyes, the blank canvas *will have been* a picture, for in 1914 it was and in 1962 still is a *readymade*, in the past participle—a picture to be made and yet already made. It will have been the picture that Kandinsky saw, potential and promising, and the one that Greenberg sees, finished even before it gets started. For it was ready-made as early as 1914, the year of the first readymade, and would become a finished picture only in 1962, when Greenberg legitimized it. One can apply to the theme of the virgin canvas (between *Vierge* and *Mariée*, there has to be the *Passage de la vierge à la mariée*) the same, incredibly subtle treatment Duchamp has applied to the theme of the tube of paint. One would then see in it the same "avant-garde melancholy"[75] with which, in 1914, again, speaking as if in retrospective anticipation of the "possibility of several tubes of paint becoming a Seurat," he posited the "has-been" as a "would-be" painter.[76] Seurat had been dead for more than twenty years, and in that time span abstract painting had sprung out of his tubes, when Kupka and Delaunay "enlarged his pointilism in planes by color." In the same time span the abstract painters, and Duchamp himself in *Mariée* (his last canvas before the readymades), had raped the virgin canvas. Seurat's potential had been exploited and the blank canvas's promises were exhausted. How could you paint after that? While Modernist painting followed its course, inexorably attracted by the "pristine flatness of the stretched canvas" (which, however, was already a thing of its past), Duchamp quietly stopped painting, reserving the possibility of picking up his brushes again some day and of painting again, but *on glass*. And it is as though he told himself, in anticipated retrospection: "I shall have been a painter, therefore I am an artist." He did a few readymades and carefully refrained from doing any *specific* ones: neither tubes of paint nor blank canvases. Just as the tubes of paint had to remain sealed so as to retain their potential, just as the white canvas had to stay virgin so as to retain its promise, so the link between the specific and the generic had to be concealed in melancholy and humor, by way of a pun on *Peigne*, for example. Duchamp was simply waiting for 1962 to arrive, when a blank canvas not only could, but had to be called a picture, "though not necessarily a successful one."

Duchamp's extreme intelligence and acute sensitivity in not actualizing the blank canvas is echoed and, if properly interpreted, accounted for, in and by Greenberg's refusal to cross the thin line between a picture and a successful one. In order to call a blank canvas a picture, not an object or a piece of the artist's material, you need to "see" it as art. But only if your eye is trained and acquainted with the whole history of Modernist painting down to Stella and Reinhardt do you "see" it as art.[77] This then means that you judge it to be art, involuntarily, in accordance with the strictest requirements of Formalism. What you do is intuitively apprehend the blank canvas's generic *content*, the one that is, so to speak, perpendicular to its specific *form*. To call a ready-made canvas a picture thus requires, and indeed utters, an aesthetic judgment. It is only liminally a positive judgment, however, because it is virtually impossible to tell whether what you value is the thing you are supposedly beholding or the tradition that has made this thing a plausible candidate for aesthetic judgment. (The question is, of course, open as to whether this is not always the case with "advanced" Modernist art at the very moment when its "advance" verges on the far-out and challenges aesthetic judgment.) To go beyond this liminal judgment and to call the ready-made canvas a successful picture would entail an interpretation in terms that Kandinsky or avantgardistic art historians such as Herbert Read might have endorsed, but not Greenberg. You would have to sense either its liberating potential or its provocative "anti-art" value, or both. Yet to call it unsuccessful would entail a disavowal of the aesthetic pressure that the series of surrenders constituting the history of Modernist painting had built up. It would have a retroactive effect on what appears, but only in retrospect, as the "logic" of Modernism. (The confusion between retroactive and retrospective accounts for much of the hasty revisionism going on under the name of Postmodernism.) It is thus essential to Greenberg's Modernism and Formalism that he should walk the thin line between a picture and a successful (or unsuccessful) one, and that he should suspend his judgment on the hypothetical case of the blank canvas, leaving it in its liminal, nominal state. Had the verdict fallen, whether positive or negative, it would have been final, if due only to the fact that when it is possible to aesthetically judge a hypothetical case—and it is perfectly feasible with the blank canvas; you don't need to see it (although, again, you would need to have seen one)—then a norm is set which is inescapable. The critic judging the blank canvas as successful would have been equivalent to an artist actualizing it.

I find it extremely striking that, to my knowledge at least, there is not one Minimal or Conceptual artist who actualized the blank canvas per se. Robert Barry surrounded an area on the wall with a "frame" made of several tiny stretched and unpainted canvases; Jan Dibbets stacked a series of empty canvases and called the resulting assemblage *My Last Painting*; John Baldessari, in a very Duchampian move, had a sign painter inscribe sentences such as "Everything is purged from this painting but art" on otherwise unpainted canvases; but as far as I know, nobody did the ready-made canvas, and just that. Many of these artists wanted to be anti-painters and show their scorn for Formalism, yet it is as if they dared not transgress this ultimate taboo. They went beyond the blank canvas, into real space or the linguistic realm; they acted out a variation on the theme of the ready-made canvas; but they avoided tackling the theme head on. Perhaps they were aware that it would have been nothing but a bland repetition of Duchamp's gesture. Perhaps they even feared that such a move would have appeared less radical than Duchamp's. I suspect that the real reason was that they would have proffered an object which would have been vulnerable to a Formalist judgment. Whether they wanted to or not, they would have claimed that an unpainted canvas is a successful picture, in other words a viable painting. They would have fulfilled their wish, no doubt, to make the blank canvas into an idea, a strategic move toward generic art status (or toward specific art status in Judd's sense, that is, art qualified as "Minimal" or "Conceptual"). Yet because the blank canvas remains specific in Greenberg's sense, they would also have invited the quality judgment that would call it art as a successful—or unsuccessful—painting. (In more psychological terms: they would have exposed their impotence as painters.) This is why the blank canvas had to remain hypothetical. These artists sought to pursue Modernism—Modernist art, not Modernist painting—beyond the threshold of the blank canvas, while seeking to halt Formalism—the necessity of aesthetic judgment—on that very threshold. They chose the left branch of the alternative set by Greenberg. Of course, there was a lot of wishful thinking in this. It did not succeed in intimidating Greenberg and other Formalist critics (and all good critics are Formalist in the sense that they judge aesthetically) or in preventing them from saying out loud that a lot of Minimal and Conceptual art is simply bad art. But in so doing, the Formalist critics, like the artists, in the course of their everyday practice, have jumped the threshold of the blank canvas. Despite Greenberg's conviction that "when no aesthetic value judgment, no verdict of taste, is there, then art isn't there either, it's as simple as that," he was forced by the social context into accepting that these things, which claim to forbid judgment of taste, be viewed as art. Thus, the consequences of the right branch of the alternative, the one Greenberg chooses in practice when he allows for a non-Modernist hybrid of painting and sculpture in order to save Formalism, are worth considering, on a doctrinal level, when applied to the case of the blank canvas. These consequences are hypothetical, as is the blank canvas itself: what if Formalism were allowed to pass the threshold of the ready-made canvas by calling it successful, while Modernism would halt there? In a very interesting remark on Greenberg's paragraph on the bare canvas, Michael Fried has envisaged precisely these consequences, heretical as they may be for Formalism:

> It is not quite enough to say that a bare canvas tacked to a wall is not "necessarily" a successful picture; it would, I think, be more accurate to say that it is not *conceivably* one. It may be countered that future circumstances might be such as to *make* it a successful painting; but I would argue that, for that to happen, the enterprise of painting would have to change so drastically that nothing more than the name would remain.[78]

Must we be grateful that, until now, no "future circumstance" has occurred that would make a bare canvas a successful painting? Are we so sure that such a circumstance cannot be anticipated at this point? Is it not what the likes of Peter Halley and Ross Bleckner and Philip Taaffe would like to see established, perhaps in spite of themselves? With an eye on her previous work, can we not extrapolate the "logic" of Sherrie Levine to the point where the unpainted painting is the predictable end of the line? The blank canvas is once again in sight and, inasmuch as blind predictions are not foolish, there is nothing, this time, that upholds an a priori rejection of its putative success. Yes, a successful, even a convincing blank canvas is plausible, as a would-be painting that has come full circle, having recycled Modernism, from Kandinsky to Greenberg and back, through Duchamp. Indeed, Fried's "future circumstance" has already happened: it was the invention of the readymade. Toward the end of 1912 Duchamp abandoned painting and, in 1914, he put this abandonment on the record and gave it the shape of a ready-made bottlerack. That very same year, he scribbled on a piece of paper: *A kind of pictorial Nominalism (Control)*. In 1916 he chose a small iron comb as a readymade. Its name (in French: *un peigne*) put the name of painting, in turn, on the record, by way of a pun on the subjunctive of the verb *peindre* (to paint), a verbal mode which, in French, also acts as a weak, hypothetical, and melancholic imperative: *que je peigne!* (best translated: "I ought to paint" or "If only I could paint").

Has pictorial Nominalism seen to it that the "enterprise of painting" changed "so drastically that nothing more than the name" remains? Apparently, yes: there is nothing pictorial in a comb but the pun in its name. In fact, no: Duchamp did not actualize the blank canvas. It is still poised on the *infra-thin* line between a picture and a successful one, as Greenberg wanted it to be. But there is nothing inconceivable about its being success-ful, even convincing: not in the sense that it would have poten-tial, much less in that it would incarnate the "last painting," but inasmuch as a successful blank canvas would simulate. It would be a *replica* of a blank canvas, like most readymades, by the way, which have come down to us as replicas. There is much talk about simulation these days, and Baudrillard's writings have been put to frantic ideological use by more than one Neo-Geo painter.[79] Whether their work is hailed or dismissed, it is for the same reasons: they are insincere and rhetorical, they deny origi-nality, they strip Newman of the sublime, Mondrian of his strug-gle against the tragic, Malevich of Ouspensky. They appropriate Modernist painting and regurgitate it ready-made. I have seen too little of this painting to judge it with assurance, and I have yet to see the "ultimate" blank canvas. While I am not enthralled at the prospect, I am not ready, as is Michael Fried, to rule out a priori the eventuality of its being a successful painting, but on terms that are, of course, no longer Modernist, that is to say, utopian or apocalyptic.[80] Fried and Greenberg have taught me not to trust the "logic" of extrapolation but to let my eye decide. So I shall let my eye, not Fried, be the judge. In the meantime, and since the blank canvas is not yet a fact, I shall consider what simula-tion, when it does not foreclose emulation, teaches the retro-spective eye of the historian. Was it not there all along in Modernist painting? Have I not heard many times, even from Claude Lévi-Strauss, that the abstract painter paints what he would paint if, by any chance, he set out to paint a picture? Was it not Greenberg who said, in 1939, that avant-garde painting was "the imitation of imitating"?[81] Was it not Manet who let the simulation of the photographic simulacrum infect painting from within? Was it not Baudelaire who first understood that authentic aesthetic experience had to be sought in and regained from vicarious experience? Why would simulation, which is definitely not Modernist in the Greenbergian sense (but then, was modern painting?) be more threatening for the future of painting now than it was throughout modernity? A successful ready-made canvas is no more—and no less—inconceivable now than Impressionism was in David's time, Cubism in Manet's time, or abstraction in Cézanne's time. Not only has successful painting always been inconceivable beforehand, but with each successive passage in Modernism, the same anxiety about "future circumstances"— the one Fried expresses regarding the bare canvas—was felt, and the same risk was run regarding painting: "that nothing more than the name would remain."

A Reinterpreted Critique

Something of the harmony of the original white square of canvas should be restored in the finished painting.

Clement Greenberg

Since Fried's "future circumstance" is past, here is a string of past circumstances showing that the name of painting was at stake in its practice. In 1874 Manet submitted four canvases to the Salon; two of them were rejected (*Masquerade at the Opera* and *Swallows*) on the grounds that they were not finished enough. Mallarmé wrote an article in defense of Manet in which he asked:

> What is an "unfinished work," if all its elements are in accord, and if it possesses a charm which could easily be broken by an additional touch?[82]

The times were far from ripe for a particularly unfinished painting—that is, the blank canvas—to be conceivable, but the "logic" (which is only retrospectively a logic, I insist) is the same. Mallarmé then went on to say:

Entrusted with the nebulous vote of the painters with the responsibility of choosing, from among the framed pictures offered, those that are really paintings in order to show them to us, the jury has nothing else to say but: this is a painting, or that is not a painting.[83]

There the jury's task ought to stop, contends Mallarmé. Enter the spectators, the public at large. Let them judge which paintings are good and which are bad. Now, what we have here, *mutatis mutandis*, is a situation identical to the one Greenberg found himself in when confronted with the hypothetical case of the blank canvas. The jury ought to judge aesthetically, otherwise it is not a jury. Its task is not to recognize a certain family of objects that are called pictures in the way tables are called tables, but to choose, "from among the framed pictures offered, those that are really paintings." Really paintings, but not, for all that, successfully. Mallarmé wanted the jury to refrain from going beyond this nominal verdict, in order to let the public judge freely. Greenberg performed exactly this task. He gave the blank canvas the name "picture" and stopped short of calling it successful, leaving it instead in a nominal state and handing over the decision as to its quality to us, hypothetical or future spectators. This, Fried confirmed in his remark, when evoking "future circumstances" which "might be such as to make it a successful painting," without, however, seeing that an aesthetic judgment had already been expressed, albeit a liminal one:

Moreover, seeing something as a painting in the sense that one sees the tacked-up canvas as a painting, and being convinced that a particular work can stand comparison with the painting of the past whose quality is not in doubt, are altogether different experiences: it is, I want to say, as though unless something compels conviction as to its quality it is no more than trivially or nominally a painting.[84]

There was certainly nothing trivial about the attribution of the name "painting" to Manet's *Masquerade at the Opera* in 1874; otherwise, it would not have been rejected. It is trivial now, but the fact that *Masquerade* has "compelled conviction as to its quality" has everything to do with this. I strongly doubt that to call the work a painting and to call it a convincing painting were "altogether different experiences." I say this in retrospect, of

course, but that is precisely the point in avant-garde or Modernist
art. What was the nature of Manet's experience and judgment—
the one Mallarmé calls "the nebulous vote of the painters"—
when he declared the painting finished, although he knew that
the jury would most probably find it too unfinished to even call it
a painting? He had already gone through the Salon des Refusés,
and we know of his anxieties and striving for public recognition.
Was that experience, that aesthetic judgment, not in the nature
of anticipated retrospection? Was it not a call for a consensus yet
to come and retrospective by necessity, since the spectators always approach the work after the artist? Lee Krasner recalls this
about Pollock: "He asked me: 'Is this a painting?' Not is this a
good painting, or a bad one, but a painting! The degree of doubt
was unbelievable at times."[85] Manet had more confidence in his
own talent than Pollock and perhaps had only contempt for the
jury, but even he could not guarantee posterity's verdict without
a leap of faith. Was it not Fried who said:

> Manet's problem, one might say, was not so much to know
> when a given picture was finished as to discover in himself
> the conviction that it was now a painting.[86]

Or, to put Fried's remark in its context, which is a discussion
of Manet's relation to Courbet: that it was *un tableau*, and not
merely *un morceau*.[87] I see no reason not to accept that the minimal, nominal judgment that was required of the jury in order
to call *Masquerade* a painting is of the same nature as the one
Manet asked of himself in order to call it *un tableau*. Both judgments are nominal and neither is trivial. And I see no more reason to suppose that seeing "the tacked-up canvas as a painting,
and being convinced that it can stand comparison with the painting of the past whose quality is not in doubt, are altogether different experiences." Manet's work is now among the painting of the
past whose quality is not in doubt, and it is the history of Modernist painting from Manet on, as told by Greenberg and Fried,
which has allowed even a blank canvas to be compared with it. It
takes far less conviction, I agree, for Greenberg to have called a
blank canvas a picture in 1962 than it took for Manet to call *Masquerade at the Opera* a painting in 1874, but I am not accountable
for the Modernist narrative; Fried and Greenberg are. It may be
that the bare canvas is nominally a picture only in comparison to
a Stella, a Noland, or other immediate precedents, but Stella and
Noland themselves (according to the Modernist narrative) are

painters only in comparison to their immediate predecessors, and so on. Fried, who reportedly once said that Stella painted stripes because he wanted above all to paint like Velásquez,[88] knows all too well that he could afford such bold ellipses only because the range of comparisons, although organized by the Modernist narrative into a long chain extending far into the past, is explored by an eye that is shortsighted at each link.

Along with the Salon des Refusés and Mallarmé's protest against Manet's partial rejection from the 1874 Salon, the Impressionist show at Nadar's that same year and other "alternative" events were among the responses which led those artists ostracized from the 1884 Salon to unite against the Société des Artistes Français, to set up their own Salon des Indépendants in April, and, finally, to found the Société des Artistes Indépendants in June. The Société's motto for its annual "anti-salon" was *"Ni récompense ni jury."* Thus, it went a significant step further than what Mallarmé had advocated for the jury ten years before: it granted the public at large—the crowd, the Baudelairian *foule*—not just the right to estimate the good and the bad in painting, but also the responsibility of tracing the nominal boundary between painting and nonpainting. This means that from then on, in France (and why was the avant-garde launched in France?), all the moves by which the Modernist painters tested the aesthetic validity of their conventions were at the mercy of public approval. What Greenberg calls a convention of the medium is an agreement, a pact, of which he never tells us between whom it is signed. It is as though only artists were involved. In a way this is true: artists are accountable only to their tradition and, of course, not to the average taste of the public. This is what "avant-garde" means. But there would be no avant-garde—we would simply call it the continuation of tradition—if the most intimate aesthetic decision made in the studio did not have to take into account, in advance, the probable verdict of the crowd. So-called provocation and so-called non-art are only the inevitable by-products of the relentless testing, deconstruction, or dismissal of painting's "expendable conventions." Conventions prove expendable in the eyes of the avant-garde painters because, once too easy a consensus is reached satisfying the middlebrow taste of the public, this can only mean that tradition has been betrayed. Greenberg, who, in "Avant-Garde and Kitsch," has described this situation better than anyone, saw the momentary state of the social consensus as technical constraints immanent to the medium. Painters may indeed experience them that way. Fried saw them as more explicitly historical. Avant-garde artists indeed have that awareness. But neither Greenberg nor Fried considered critically that to call these technical and historical constraints "conventions" was misleading, since they are conventions only in retrospect, when they are abandoned and thus revealed as mere conventions, when the painter parts with the crowd and leaves a given state of the social consensus behind. It is not when the crowd says *"this is a painting"* that we have a true Modernist or avant-garde painting, but rather when it says *"that is not a painting."*

The Society of Independent Artists was founded in New York at the end of 1916 by a group of artists who had belonged to or were closely associated with the only avant-garde movement in America at the time, the Ash Can School. Marcel Duchamp, whose reputation as a provocative Cubist painter had been established in New York by the presence of his *Nude Descending a Staircase No 2* at the Armory Show in 1913, was a founding member. It is he who suggested that the Society be modeled after the Parisian Société des Artistes Indépendants and that it adopt the same motto for its exhibitions: "No jury, no prizes." He also suggested, and this was an innovation, that a letter be drawn at random and that the works be hung in alphabetical order, starting with that letter.[89] He had been nominated chairman of the hanging committee when, under the pesudonym of R. Mutt, he submitted a ready-made urinal rebaptized *Fountain*. It was a shrewd strategic move that put the members of the hanging committee in a nice quandary. If they abided by their democratic principles, they would make fools of themselves in the eyes of the crowd (and the press), and if they censored Mr. Mutt's entry, they would become a jury again, in the traditional sense, making Mr. Mutt the victim of a new *Salon des Refusés*. There are too many conflicting stories of what subsequently happened, but it is certain that the urinal was not shown at the Independents, that *Fountain* was not mentioned in the catalogue, and that Duchamp, who had made a point of concealing Mr. Mutt's true identity, resigned from the hanging committee. He also made sure, but later, when the show closed, that word got around by publishing, in his little magazine *The Blind Man*, an unsigned editorial entitled "The Richard Mutt Case."[90] What interests me here is that the outcome of his strategic move is that, whether they wanted it or not, the members of the hanging committee were turned into a jury again, but a jury in Mallarmé's sense: they were forced to say *"this is art,"* or *"that is not art."* What-

ever the true story may be, all versions show what their predica-
ment was: they could not decide. It seems that history has
decided instead. Unless one is ready to erase from art history the
innumerable works that have been authorized by Duchamp's
readymades, it is impossible to deny that, whether good or bad,
these are art.

The readymades are art, not painting, not sculpture, and
not something interspecific straddling both. They are not even
specific in Donald Judd's sense, since they do not defend their
identity through "holistic Gestalt" or "obdurate materials"
against confusion with non-art. Quite the contrary: they are generic and nothing but generic. Thus, they are not even eligible
for a Formalist judgment, which is why they have been hailed by
the anti-Formalist proponents of Conceptual art. It is their context, not aesthetic judgment, which supposedly determined their
"art status." Greenberg and Kosuth agree on this. Kosuth says:

> A work of art is a kind of proposition presented within the
> context of art as a comment on art. . . . The "art idea" (or
> "work") and art are the same and can be appreciated as art
> without going outside the context of art for verification.[91]

Greenberg says:

> All art depends in one way or another on context, but there's
> a great difference between an aesthetic and a non-aesthetic
> context. The latter can range from the generally cultural
> through the social and the political to the merely sexual.
> From the start avant-gardist art resorted extensively to ef-
> fects depending on an extra-aesthetic context. Duchamp's
> first Readymades, his bicycle wheel, his bottlerack, and
> later on his urinal, were not new at all in configuration; they
> startled when first seen only because they were presented in
> a fine art context, which is a purely cultural and social, not
> an aesthetic or artistic context.[92]

The issue of context is far too complex to be more than touched
on here. But what Kosuth means by "context" is fairly clear: he
means the *art world*. Kosuth the artist identifies art with art theory, and his art theory is institutional; in fact, it is the same as
that of the aesthetician George Dickie, developed around the
same time.[93] Institutional theories always claim to be circular and
beg the question of the institution's empowerment. A political

critique of the patronage system could break that circle but would yield another danger, that of explaining away the aesthetic "power" to call something art by other power privileges such as money or social status. Unless very carefully handled, that kind of critique often leads to a blanket suspicion that the artists are compromised in advance by their patrons' aesthetic ideology (and sometimes leads to the conclusion that aesthetics is nothing but an ideology). As a result of combining such suspicion with a circular institutional theory, much of Conceptual art—Kosuth's in the first place—was never able to get out of the entrapment in petty art-world politics which it designed for itself. Rather than taking Kosuth's and Greenberg's agreement on the issue of context at face value, we should examine a little more closely the kind of aesthetic context that Greenberg deems relevant to art, not merely as status but as quality, and in which, according to him, Duchamp's urinal would not have been startling:

> Taste develops *as* a context of expectations based on experience of previously surprised expectations. The fuller the experience of this kind, the higher, the more truly sophisticated the taste. . . . Surprise demands a context. According to the record, new and surprising ways of satisfying in art have always been connected closely with immediately previous ways, no matter how much in opposition to these ways they may look or actually have been.[94]

I want to suggest that the "Richard Mutt case" belongs in such "a context of expectations based on experience of previously surprised expectations." For a number of reasons I would hesitate to call it taste, though, but I definitely call it aesthetic, in due faithfulness to Formalism: it is a context made solely of aesthetic judgments (and when not, it is irrelevant). All appearances work against Duchamp, for it is true that the urinal was a strategic coup with regard to the institutional context (but here the question is: how are we to understand the nature of this very particular institution called Society of Independent Artists?), and that the institutional context does not seem aesthetic at all (and here the question is to see how the coup, in fact, forced the institutional context to be aesthetic).[95] Appearances are misleading: the coup involving the urinal is not "political," it is aesthetic. Duchamp had gained his institutional position as chairman of the hanging committee thanks to his reputation as a painter, and he had gained the latter (as far as New York is concerned) in the context of the Armory Show, where, to say the least, the *Nude Descending a Staircase* was striking in its newness, but a newness "connected closely with immediately previous ways" of generating aesthetic surprise, Cubism. There is no doubt that the other founding members of the Society had expectations vis-à-vis Duchamp: they wanted him to honor them with his presence in the show, and what they expected from him was a painting, maybe a painting as surprising and scandalous as the *Nude* had been four years before, but a painting nonetheless, something they could call *un tableau* in the same liminal and nominal way that Mallarmé requested of the 1874 jury with regard to Manet's *Masquerade at the Opera*. Instead, they got a urinal, which a perfect unknown by the name of Richard Mutt requested them to call a *work of art*.

In comparison with the Paris Indépendants in 1884, the New York Independents in 1917 went another significant step beyond Mallarmé's admonishing of the jury in 1874: the members of the public at large—already entrusted by the Independents' motto "Ni récompense ni jury" (or "No jury, no prizes") with the responsibility of tracing the nominal borderline between a *framed picture* and *un tableau*, successful or not—also received the duty of tracing the line between a mere thing, vulgar and tasteless and thus without any aesthetic context, and art in general. They were handed this duty by Richard Mutt. Why present them with a *specific object*, some flat thing hung on a wall and covered with colors assembled in a certain order, for example, since for such things, called paintings, they have no more specific competence than the layman? They are not professionals, after all. They know the conventions of painting, but have they experienced them aesthetically, have they judged them? Why then be more complacent than Manet when he refused to "finish" *Masquerade at the Opera* in order to please the jury? The New York public had already rushed to the Armory Show three years before. It had liked the *Nude Descending a Staircase* for the quantity of surprise it offered. Thanks to the publicity around the first Independents' show, the public was prepared—socially—for any surprise, but not for this one, not for the one that would compel the leap from the specific to the generic. Since the painters' tradition was no longer transmitted through the mediation of a jury of peers but through the crowd at large, there was the need to give the crowd something it could judge on its own scale: art at large. *Fountain* was conjured away before the crowd got a chance to judge. And the hanging committee had to betray its principles, in

the name of specificity. It played the ostrich. In order not to become a jury again, in order not to judge aesthetically, it got away
with saying, like Fried and Greenberg would say fifty years later,
that what falls in between the arts is not art, rather some kind of
theater, if not of circus. And so *Fountain* became non-art. And
so *Fountain* became, like the blank canvas fifty years later, a
candidate for aesthetic judgment of which it is impossible to
know whether what you judge is the thing you don't even need to
see (though you would need to have seen one of its kind), or the
tradition that has made this thing plausible. And so *Fountain*
became, *"with all kinds of delays,"* Duchamp would have said,
the outcome of an aesthetic judgment as well.

Duchamp's urinal is the outcome of an aesthetic judgment as
surely as non-art is a "category" of art. There is no other way to
account for its existence as art, unless you are ready to erase
from art history the tradition it founded, which is, I am afraid,
what Greenberg and Fried more often than not seem to wish to
do. Or unless you are ready to erase from art history the whole
of tradition before Duchamp, which is obviously what Kosuth
wished to do. The Formalist doctrine, which is, on the whole,
just, maintains that anything that is judged aesthetically—and
thus deserves to be called art (as art)—needs to stand up to a
comparision with the art of the past, at least of its immediate
past. Before something can withstand comparison to something
else, a comparison must be made. The Modernist doctrine, which
is incorrect or only partially correct, maintains that two things
cannot be compared unless they share the conventions of a given
medium. How could one compare a urinal to a painting! There
were two ways of demonstrating that this was feasible, and I explored them both. The first was to cling as faithfully as possible
(too faithfully, as I did) to the Modernist narrative of the history
of modern art and to seek the missing link between the urinal and
painting, between the generic and the specific. The second was
(or would be, since I hardly scratched its surface) to replace the
Modernist narrative with another way of writing the history of
modern art, a way that would reintegrate its political and institutional context into its aesthetic context.[96] The first way quite
naturally led me to investigate an episode in history to whose
shaping the Modernist narrative literally contributed, and to notice—quite naturally—that it provided the missing link between
the urinal and painting. Indeed, the blank canvas can be compared to both: it is a picture, "though not necessarily a successful one," and it is a readymade, though, if I may add, not as

successful a readymade as Duchamp's. As to the second way, and just as naturally, it led me to investigate the chain of "contexts." Kosuth had brought me back to Duchamp's first unassisted readymade by claiming that it had "given art its own identity," its generic identity. The readymades' public career begins with the Richard Mutt case. Thus I sketched a narrative which, run backwards, goes from the Independents' Show in 1917 to the Salon des Indépendants in 1884 to Mallarmé's admonition to the jury and Manet's partial exclusion from the Salon in 1874. It extends further back to the Salon des Refusés in 1863, to Courbet's strategies vis-à-vis the Exposition Universelle of 1855, and to his quarrels with the Salon of 1851, when, I would venture to say, something called the avant-garde began. This narrative is institutional but it is also aesthetic throughout. If worked out in details it would show itself not just as art-world politics, although it is that too, but also as the history of institutionalized aesthetic judgment.[97] Such a narrative presumes that conventions in art—and there are no conventions without a certain degree of institutionalization—do not mean properties of the medium (as if the medium could, of itself, stake such ontological claims) but rather a given momentary state of the social consensus, which is the context of aesthetic expectations that the amateur with a "truly sophisticated taste" precisely expects to see breached or surprised by the avant-garde artist.[98] Now, did Duchamp not fulfill these expectations admirably? He invited the jury or non-jury of the Independents to compare a urinal to the remake of the *Nude Descending a Staircase* they expected, and then to call it art. The jury proved that it was indeed a non-jury by not deciding: it had no grounds for comparison. And the non-jury proved that it was a jury by deciding in spite of itself: what had no grounds for comparison fell into non-art. There the urinal stayed for quite a while. Meanwhile, the non-art limbo became a category in itself, generic through negation, a strange "multimedia" medium progressively filled in with myriads of things, not always mediocre, to which Duchamp's urinal can be compared and, if I may add, to its advantage. We are the jury that the 1917 hanging committee did not want to be. We have a whole tradition of things behind us that are neither painting nor sculpture, from Dadaism and Constructivism to Minimal and Conceptual art and beyond, in which to inscribe the readymade and verify its historical resonance. And we have the missing link—the blank canvas. Thus, we also have the tradition of Modernist painting and the whole tradition of pre-modern painting as well, to which we can and must refer the readymade, so as to judge whether or not it withstands comparison.

It does. Who am I to say this? Nobody in particular. I judge like any member of the Baudelairian *foule* having access to today's generic art salons. Or maybe not. I judge like someone who has enough aesthetic acquaintance with modern art, especially with the sequence of works Greenberg called Modernist painting. I agree with Greenberg that painting has a privileged position in the history of modern art, but not for the same reasons: the passage from the specific to the generic was acted out in painting and nowhere else. Modern music remained music, literature sought generalization under the name "text" of "textuality," but the "spatial arts," as they have been called since Lessing, became art *tout court* with the passage from painting—not sculpture or architecture—to art.[99] It was a switch of names, but it did not erase history. I do not share Fried's fear that if a blank canvas deserved to be judged a successful painting, nothing more than the name would remain. I believe that in Modernist painting, the essential thing was that the name remain and be transmitted. It has been, until now, and with Duchamp providing us with the link with the past of painting, I can be more optimistic as to its future: two of the greatest living painters, Robert Ryman and Gehrard Richter, are great precisely because they have acknowledged the readymade in their work while withstanding comparison with Manet. At the same time, I share Greenberg's conviction (not only for American art but for art in general) that "to define the exact status of contemporary American art in relation to the history of art past and present demands a certain amount of mercilessness and pessimism."[100] Duchamp's urinal requires and deserves an aesthetic judgment. Perhaps it is only liminally and nominally positive; perhaps it is even undecidable, for us now as it was for the hanging committee in 1917. But then it would be with the same kind of undecidability that still puzzles me when I read Baudelaire's famous address to Manet: "You are only the first in the decrepitude of your art." Perhaps Duchamp was only the first in the decrepitude of art at large. In the light of Manet's achievement, it is not that trivial a compliment. Yet I am not ready to call the urinal great art. It is significant art, highly significant of the plight of our culture. We live in a century in which great art is simply not possible, and all the great artists of modernity have woven the stuff of their art out of that recognition. When Greenberg settles for Olitski after having understood Pollock so well, I find it sad. The fate of Kosuth and his colleagues in Conceptual art is rather distressing too, and certainly I shall not vouch for them. But the saddest thing is to see Greenberg and Kosuth agree on Duchamp. If it were a matter of taste, I would leave it at that. No one can prove his or her aesthetic judgment. But they both claim that no aesthetic judgment is required in order to call a urinal by the name "art," and that Duchamp wanted it that way. In this case, the burden of proof is on them. It is not quite enough to say that I feel free to judge the urinal aesthetically; it would, I think, be more accurate to say that I feel obliged to, and all the more so because, in fact, Greenberg's surrender did not end with the blank canvas:

> If anything and everything can be intuited aesthetically, then anything and everything can be intuited and experienced artistically. What we agree to call art cannot be definitively or decisively separated from aesthetic experience at large. (That this began to be seen only lately—thanks to Marcel Duchamp for the most part—doesn't make it any the less so.) . . . If this is so, then there turns out to be such a thing as art at large: art that is, or can be, realized anywhere and at any time and by anybody.[101]

Notes

1.
Carl André, "Preface to Stripe Painting," in Dorothy C. Miller, ed., Sixteen Americans (New York: The Museum of Modern Art, 1959), p. 76.

2.
Clement Greenberg, Art and Culture (Boston: Beacon Press, 1961).

3.
Greenberg, "Modernist Painting," Arts Yearbook IV (1961), repr. in Gregory Battcock, ed., The New Art: A Critical Anthology (New York: Dutton, 1973), pp. 66–77.

4.
Ibid., pp. 72–73. I shall, throughout this essay, assume that Greenberg's definition and descriptions of Modernism, of Modernist painting, and of its history are correct, granted that Modernism is not congruent with modernity and that Modernist painting is not the whole of modern painting. My concern is to somewhat disentangle the intricacies of a particular episode—indeed, the beginning of a pivotal crisis—in Modernist art and Formalist criticism alike. It is an episode in which, whether correct or not, Greenberg's views literally shaped the work of so many artists—especially of those, ironically, who rejected them—that they made history, although they may not have described it adequately or judged it fairly. With some inevitable simplifications, the Greenbergian doctrine and its success, the controversies it raised and the counter-theories it gave rise to in the work of some artists, are here all taken as facts, to be interpreted from the viewpoint of a historian or an "archaeologist," not to be criticized from the viewpoint of a critic, an aesthetician, or an art "theorist." However, the critical reinterpretation I shall offer in the last part of this essay will, I hope, "reformat" the episode under scrutiny, and even some of its antecedents and consequences, in such a way that it will show on which crucial works and issues my judgment and my interpretation differ from those of both Greenberg and his opponents. The implications of this, for aesthetics and art "theory," I shall merely suggest and leave for another essay.

5.
Since I wrote this, I have had a chance to ask Greenberg the question. This was his reply: "As for Stella's black paintings: they're plausible, but not good enough; his aluminum ones are better, but still not good enough." (Letter to me, January 23, 1987.)

6.
Greenberg, "Modernist Painting," p. 67.

7.
Ibid., p. 68.

8.
Ibid., p. 69.

9.
In Greenberg's early writings, where he was defending the superiority of abstract art, the word "literature," which meant not only narrative content but also "ideas," every sort of psychological subject matter, and even "the ideological struggles of society," encompassed everything that painting had to dispense with so as to be "pure." See C. Greenberg, "Towards a Newer Laocoon," Partisan Review 7:4, repr. in John O'Brian, ed., Clement Greenberg, The Collected Essays and Criticism, Volume I, Perceptions and Judgments, 1939–1944 (Chicago: University of Chicago Press, 1986), pp. 23–38 (p. 28 in particular).

10.
Greenberg, "Modernist
Painting," p. 70.

11.
See my essay, "Clement
Lessing," in Thierry de
Duve, Essais datés I
(Paris: Editions de la
Différence), 1987, pp.
65–117.

12.
Greenberg, "Necessity
of Formalism," New
Literary History 3:1
(1971), repr. in Richard
Kostelanetz, ed., Es-
thetics Contemporary
(Buffalo: Prometheus
Books, 1978), p. 207.

13.
Greenberg, "Complaints
of an Art Critic," Art-
forum (October 1967),
p. 38.

14.
Ibid.

15.
Greenberg, "Avant-
Garde and Kitsch," in
Art and Culture, p. 6.

16.
Greenberg, "Necessity
of Formalism," p. 174.

17.
Greenberg, "Complaints
of an Art Critic," p. 39.

18.
Greenberg, "Seminar
Seven," Arts Magazine
52 (June 1978), p. 97.

19.
Greenberg, "Seminar
One," Arts Magazine
48 (November 1973),
p. 45.

20.
Ibid., p. 45.

21.
Greenberg, "Seminar
Five," Studio Interna-
tional 189–190 (May–
June 1975), p. 191.

22.
The aesthetic judgment
according to Greenberg
is the judgment of taste
according to Kant, not
the judgment about the
sublime. The parts that
I left out in the above
quotation distinguished
"affect" from "emo-
tion," and elsewhere
Greenberg has linked
emotion to the sublime
and the sublime to
"concocted art." See
Avant-Garde Attitudes
(Sydney: The Power In-
stitute of Fine Arts,
University of Sydney,
1969), p. 12.

23.
Greenberg, "Towards a
Newer Laocoon," p. 34.

24.
Ibid., p. 36.

25.
It is this issue which is
new and particular to
the Minimalist episode.
Arp had no objection to
calling his works "re-
liefs"; quite the con-
trary. And to shift
contexts, one remembers
that in England, in the
early fifties, relief had
become a category in it-
self for the "construc-
tionists" gathered
around Victor Pasmore,

especially for Mary
Martin, who quit paint-
ing in favor of relief in
1951. Like the Min-
imalist one, this epi-
sode was governed by
the feeling, spread by
Charles Biederman,
that abstract painting
could not "go any fur-
ther." When you think
that it is in 1951 that
Fontana did his first
pierced monochromes,
Rauschenberg his seven
white panels, and Kelly
his white reliefs, you
come to think that there
is another crucial epi-
sode, here, on an inter-
national scale, in the
recursive history of the
monochrome. As al-
ways, it was an attempt
at finding a way out
of a crisis in abstract
painting by jumping
into the third dimen-
sion. But unlike what
happened in New York
in the sixties, this epi-
sode was not overdeter-
mined by a doctrine of
specificity which ex-
cluded from Modernism
the hybrid tradition of
relief or bas-relief.

26.
Greenberg, "American
Type-Painting," in Art
and Culture, p. 208.

27.
Greenberg, "Modernist
Painting," p. 73.

28.
Greenberg, "After Ab-
stract Expressionism,"
Art International 6:8
(October 1962), p. 30.

29.
Greenberg, "How Art Writing Earns its Bad Name," Encounter 19 (December 1962), p. 69.

30.
Greenberg, "Recentness of Sculpture," in American Sculpture of the Sixties (Los Angeles County Museum of Art, 1967), repr. in Gregory Battcock, ed., Minimal Art: A Critical Anthology (New York: Dutton), 1968, pp. 180–181.

31.
Especially since he has warned us against this: "But it is one thing to have an aesthetic judgment or reaction, another thing to report it. The dishonest reporting of esthetic experience is what does most to accustom us to the notion that esthetic judgments are voluntary." Greenberg, "Complaints of an Art Critic," p. 38.

32.
Greenberg, "Recentness of Sculpture," p. 182.

33.
Ibid., pp. 182–183.

34.
Ibid., p. 186. Greenberg often opposes "novelty" to "newness."

35.
Ibid., p. 185.

36.
Greenberg's preference for the optical over the "haptical" in sculpture is rooted in his interpretation of Cubist collage. See "Collage," in Art and Culture, pp. 70–83. In this article dated 1959—the year of Stella's black paintings —he understands the Cubist collage works as an episode of the history of painting where the flatness of the pictorial plane was momentarily made to identify literally with that of the support. The parallel with what is happening all around him in 1959 is striking. But the emphasis is on "momentarily." The outcome of collage is, according to him, an increased awareness that illusionism had to be turned against itself in order to be maintained. So he sees Synthetic Cubism and abstract painting as consequences of collage (hence opticality and residual illusionism), whereas, with some exceptions (Arp and Schwitters, e.g.), he ignores its Dadaist and Constructivist consequences (which some Minimalists will, on the contrary, claim as a source of influence). Moreover, he relies on collage in order to make "construction-sculpture" or "drawing-in-space-sculpture," notably that of González, depend on pictorial opticality. From there, the road leading to David Smith and Anthony Caro is straight. It can be walked by reading "The New Sculpture," "Modernist Sculpture, Its Pictorial Past," and "David Smith," all three in Art and Culture.

37.
One gets an idea of the complex subtlety of Greenberg's debates with himself when it comes to painting/ sculpture relationships if one notices that he grants Olitski's spray paintings, precisely, a "grainy surface" offering "tactile associations hitherto foreign, more or less, to picture-making," only to add that "together with color, it contrives an illusion of depth back to the picture's surface; it is as if that surface, in all its literalness, were enlarged to contain a world of color and light differentiations impossible to flatness but which yet manages not to violate flatness." (Greenberg, "Jules Olitski," in XXXIII International Biennial Exhibition of Art [Venice, 1966], p. 38.) Here we would have a belated version of the benefit that Greenberg grants the Cubist collage works (Pollock's drips offering the link), namely, anti-illusionistic tactility turned against itself, this time more highly

abstract and "micro-logical" since it is in-scribed at the level of the "grainy surface" that the technique of spray painting achieves. Rosalind Krauss ("On Frontal-ity," Artforum [May 1968]) has pushed this micrological analysis of the grain as tactical opticality into almost absurd refinements. Generally speaking, the fact that Olitski, who nowadays appears as a sumptuously decorative painter but not much more, was a "test case" for all the critics whom Judd nastily called the "Greenbergers," has to do, it seems to me, with the extreme doctrinal importance that the sort of oxymoron repre-sented by "tactical op-ticality" had for the Formalist/Modernist approach. It has left its imprint on the writ-ings, beside those of Greenberg himself and Rosalind Krauss, of Michael Fried (Three American Painters [Cambridge: Fogg Art Museum, 1965]), Darby Bannard ("Quality, Style and Olitski," Art-forum [October 1972]), and Kenneth Moffet, throughout his mono-graph Jules Olitski (New York: Abrams, 1981).

38.
Greenberg, "Anne Truitt, An American

Artist whose Painted Structures Helped to Change the Course of American Sculpture," Vogue Magazine (May 1968), p. 284.

39.
Donald Judd, "Specific Objects," Arts Year-book VIII (1965), repr. in D. Judd, Complete Writings 1959–1975 (Halifax: The Press of the Nova Scotia College of Art and Design, 1975), p. 181.

40.
"Minimal works are readable as art, as al-most anything is to-day—including a door, a table, or a blank sheet of paper." Greenberg, "Recentness of Sculp-ture," p. 183.

41.
Judd, Statement that appeared in Barbara Rose, "ABC Art," Art in America (October–November 1965), repr. in Complete Writings, p. 181.

42.
Do I need to underline the extent to which this phenomenon accom-panied the whole of modernity? From Cour-bet's Realism to Bre-ton's Surrealism, through Impressionism, Expressionism, Divi-sionism, Cubism, Fauvism, Futurism, Constructivism, Neo-plasticism, not counting all the other

"Neos" and all the "Posts" since Signac or Roger Fry, and leaving aside bizarre things such as Rayonism, Syn-chromism, Orphism, Amorphism, Vorticism, and others, never in the whole of art history did an epoch coin more "ism-names"—which, even when coined by their detractors, always carry a desire for legiti-mation and periodiza-tion—than modernity. But most "isms," unless they express a sensibil-ity running through all the arts (like Symbol-ism), qualify one art in particular. Not by chance, it is painting that was granted the greatest amount of "isms." A new phenom-enon appeared after World War II—with Pop art actually—which I believe to be a major symptom of the fact that what over-determines the art of the postwar era is the passage from the spe-cific to the generic: the invention of "isms" gets stifled (whereas that of "Neos" and "Posts" appears at the horizon) and a new naming activity begins, which gets hold of the generic name "art" and adds to it an adjective meant to respecify it. So we have had Pop art and Op art, Kinetic art, Body art, Minimal art, Conceptual art, Narrative art, and many others. The fact that this phenomenon begins with Pop art—i.e., with Neo-Dada, as it was sometimes called— seems to me highly significant. Equally significant is the fact that it is only in the work of the postwar artists and art historians who legitimized Dada (Motherwell's book was published in 1951) that this name "Dada," which the artists had chosen because it was a perfectly absurd anti-name, was turned into "Dadaism."

43.
See Robert Morris, "Notes on Sculpture, Part I," Artforum (February 1966), and "Part II," Artforum (October 1966), repr. in Battcock, ed., Minimal Art, pp. 222–235.

44.
Judd, "Specific Objects," p. 184.

45.
Ibid., p. 187.

46.
Ibid., p. 184.

47.
Ibid., p. 183.

48.
Ibid., p. 184.

49.
Ibid., p. 182.

50.
Judd, "Local History," Arts Yearbook VII (1964), repr. in Complete Writings, p. 153. Between the lines of Judd's interpretation is the fact, often remarked upon, that the black canvases, the aluminum canvases, the Copper paintings, and the purple canvases with a hole in their middle, from 1963–64, have an unusually thick stretcher, of the same thickness, apparently, as the stripes' width. Extending the picture on its side, this gives the painted surface the look of a three-dimensional object. Stella always rejected this interpretation, saying that he does not consider the stretcher's thickness as a function of the painting's module and that, for him, the shadow cast by the stretcher on the wall (another argument, particularly strong in the case of the hollowed out canvases), far from turning the painting into an object, was meant to emphasize its two-dimensionality. See Bruce Glaser, "Questions to Stella and Judd," Art News (September 1966), repr. in Battcock, ed., Minimal Art, p. 162; see also William Rubin, Frank Stella (New York: The Museum of Modern Art), 1970, p. 15 and p. 151, note 16.

51.
Judd, "In the Galleries," Arts Magazine (September 1963), repr. in Complete Writings, p. 91.

52.
Judd, "Nationwide Reports: Hartford," Arts Magazine (March 1964), repr. in Complete Writings, p. 119. Who would say today that Flavin "excludes painterly art," when the most striking effect of his fluorescent tubes is to reestablish—literally, indeed—the identification of color and light that the ancient painters, at least since Bellini, perhaps Van Eyck, took for granted, an identification that had been split in two—either color or light—by the beginning of abstract art with, as an (almost immediate) consequence, of course, flatness and monochromy? (I would see the disjunction take place in Delaunay especially, between the Windows and The First Disk, but the seeds had been planted by Seurat.)

53.
Judd, "Specific Objects," p. 184.

54.
Michael Fried, "Art and Objecthood," Artforum (June 1967), repr. in Battcock, ed.,

Minimal Art, *p. 142.
The same argument can
be found in "Shape as
Form: Frank Stella's
New Paintings,"* Art-
forum *(November 1966).*

55.
*Let us remember that
"art as such" and
"good art as such" are
not synonymous for
Greenberg: Formalism
requires that the word
"art" convey an aes-
thetic judgment, not
that the judgment be
positive, which is why,
in his views, once the
irreducible essence of
painting has been re-
vealed with the blank
canvas, a shift of ques-
tion occurs. A few lines
after having said, in
"After Abstract Expres-
sionism," that "a
stretched or tacked up
canvas already exists as
a picture—though not
necessarily as a success-
ful one," Greenberg
goes on to say, apropos
Newman, Rothko, and
Still: "The question
now asked through their
art is no longer what
constitutes art, or the
art of painting, as such,
but what irreducibly
constitutes good art as
such." In a footnote
from "Art and Object-
hood," Fried takes is-
sue with this: "But I
would argue that what
modernism has meant is
that the two questions—
What constitutes the art
of painting? And what*

*constitutes good paint-
ing?—are no longer
separable; the first
disappears, or increas-
ingly tends to disap-
pear, into the second"
(p. 124). So that for
Fried, "art as such"
and "good art as such"
are synonymous, though
of course valid only for
painting (or for sculp-
ture), i.e., "within the
individual arts." My
own views on the ques-
tion of "art" and "good
art" are different from
both Greenberg's and
Fried's. Paraphrasing
Fried, I would argue
that what Modernism
has meant (notice the
past tense in Fried's
text as in mine) is that
the two questions "what
is painting?" and
"what is good paint-
ing?" were not separa-
ble (the past tense is not
in Fried).*

56.
*Fried, "Art and Object-
hood," p. 125.*

57.
*See my essay, "Per-
formance Here and
Now: Minimal Art, a
Plea for a New Genre of
Theatre,"* Open Letter
*(Toronto) 5–6 (Sum-
mer–Fall 1983), pp.
234–260.*

58.
*Fried, "Art and Object-
hood," p. 139.*

59.
Ibid., p. 123.

60.
Ibid., p. 142.

61.
*Judd, "Complaints:
Part I,"* Studio Inter-
national *(April 1969),
repr. in* Complete Writ-
ings, *p. 198.*

62.
*Joseph Kosuth, "Art af-
ter Philosophy," I and
II,* Studio International
*(October and November
1969), repr. in Gregory
Battcock, ed.,* Idea Art,
A Critical Anthology
*(New York: Dutton),
1973, p. 83.*

63.
Ibid., p. 89.

64.
Ibid., pp. 83, 84.

65.
Ibid., p. 79.

66.
Ibid., p. 100.

67.
Ibid., p. 73.

68.
Ibid., p. 75.

69.
Ibid., p. 80.

70.
Kosuth, "1975," The
Fox *2 (1975), p. 90.*

71.
See Thierry de Duve,
Pictorial Nominalism,
Marcel Duchamp,
Painting and Modernity
*(Minneapolis: Univer-
sity of Minnesota Press,
forthcoming), the last*

three chapters, and "The Readymade and the Tube of Paint," Artforum *(May 1986)*, pp. 110–121.

72.
Wassily Kandinsky, Reminiscences, *in* Kenneth C. Lindsay and Peter Vergo, eds., Kandinsky: Complete Writings on Art *(Boston, G. K. Hall & Co., 1982)*, 1, p. 372.

73.
Greenberg, "Towards a Newer Laocoon," p. 36.

74.
One wonders in retrospect whether, when writing "American-Type Painting" (1955–58), Greenberg was not displaying an artificial overconfidence in the supply of "expendable conventions" that Modernist painting had at its disposal. Perhaps it is the rather propagandistic overtone of this text, obviously written to sum up the achievements of American Abstract Expressionism in the face of the then still dominant French art, that led him to silence the pessimism which is after all at the root of his conception of Modernist painting. The "end of Modernist painting" which he must have feared in 1962, when facing the imminent actualization of the blank canvas, seems to me to have more to do with a return of this repressed pessimism than with a linear escalation in the actual history of Modernist painting. To remind the reader that the appeal of the blank canvas was from the very outset haunted by the apocalyptic prospect of the end of painting, let me quote Barnett Newman twice: "The artist must start, like God, with chaos, the void: with blank color, no forms, textures or details" (quoted in Thomas Hess, Barnett Newman *[New York: The Museum of Modern Art, 1971]*, p. 56); and "Painting was dead a quarter of a century before God even realized it existed" (quoted in French by Barbara Rose, "Jackson Pollock et l'art américain," in Jackson Pollock *[Paris: Centre Georges Pompidou, 1982]*, p. 18). As Yve-Alain Bois said in a very thorough article entitled "Painting: the Task of Mourning": "The pure beginning, the liberation of tradition, the 'zero degree' which was searched for by the first generation of abstract painters could not but function as an omen of the end" *(in* Endgame, Reference and Simulation in Recent Painting and Sculpture *[Boston: The Institute of Contemporary Art, 1986]*, p. 30).

75.
I used this expression in an unpublished paper on Manet delivered at the 1984 CAA convention in Toronto in order to describe the dialectic of retrospective anticipation and anticipated retrospection in avant-garde art. I was speaking of the veil of melancholy in the eyes of Victorine—or Olympia: "It says: when you'll see me from where you are, there in 1984, I'll be dead for a long time. What you'll see in my eyes is the anticipation of my own death and the awareness that I have to look ahead into a future that I'll never inhabit, so that you'll be able to see me stare at you. And it also says: I still see in your eyes, your gaze only has meaning insofar as it is locked in mine and accepts the burden of looking back upon the time span that separates us, so that what you'll see in my eyes is my own future, still promising, yet accomplished. History undefeated, but disillusioned."

76.
See my article, "The Readymade and the Tube of Paint."

77.
Of course there is another possibility. You can be a total philistine

and still see the blank canvas as art provided you are informed of the latest trends. This is of course what Greenberg dreaded, and rightly so. But it can hardly apply to his own acknowledgement of the blank canvas.

78.
Fried, "Art and Objecthood," p. 123, note 4. I have actually quoted a slightly modified version of this note, as it is taken up again in M. Fried, "How Modernism Works: A Response to T.J. Clark," Critical Inquiry 9 (September 1982), p. 223. I believe that the unstated and underlying reason why a successful blank canvas is inconceivable for Fried is that it is not meant to be beheld. It would be the ultimate in "absorption" and "theatricality" at once. If my surmise is correct, then I can anticipate a few strong objections on Fried's part to the last part of my essay, and I agree with him in advance that they would be tough. For Duchamp's readymades are not meant to be beheld either, especially in Fried's sense of "to behold." I confess that I am not ready yet to engage in a discussion on this, but it may be unavoidable some day.

79.
See Jean Baudrillard, Simulations, trans. P. Foss, P. Patton, P. Beitchman (New York, 1983); Peter Halley, "The Crisis in Geometry," Arts Magazine (Summer 1984); Ross Bleckner, "Transcendent Anti-Fetishism," Artforum (March 1979).

80.
Going over my text again, I realize that I have done exactly the same thing that Greenberg did in 1962, but in relation to today's dominant ideology. I just legitimized in writing a blank canvas that no one has actualized yet. I would be lying if I tried to hide that it is in the hope that it will never be.

81.
Greenberg, "Avant-Garde and Kitsch," p. 7. And this, apropos of Picasso, trapped between painting and object and "committed to a notion of painting that leaves nothing further to explore": "The picture gets itself finished, in principle, before it gets started; and in its actual finishing, it becomes a replica of itself" ("Picasso at Seventy-five," in Art and Culture, p. 67).

82.
Quoted in George Heard Hamilton, Manet and His Critics (New York: Norton, 1969), p. 184.

83.
Ibid., p. 185. I modified the translation slightly in order to be closer to the French.

84.
Fried, "Art and Objecthood," p. 123, note 4.

85.
Lee Krasner Pollock, Interview with B. H. Friedman, Jackson Pollock (New York: Marlborough-Gerson Gallery), 1964.

86.
Fried, "Manet's Sources, Aspects of his Art, 1859–1865," Artforum (March 1969), p. 73, note 99.

87.
"The ability to paint wonderfully—to paint wonderful morceaux— was something which even Courbet's detractors granted him without stint. What they refused to grant was that the final result amounted to a painting, un tableau" (ibid.).

88.
See Rosalind Krauss, "A View of Modernism," Artforum (September 1972).

89.
See Clark S. Marlor, The Society of Inde-

pendent Artists, The Exhibition Record 1917–1944 *(Park Ridge, N.J.: Noyes Press, 1984), pp. 1–6.*

90.
For a detailed analysis of the facts, see William Camfield, "Marcel Duchamp's Fountain: *Its History and Aesthetics in the Context of 1917,"* Dada/Surrealism *16 (1987), pp. 64–94. For an analysis of the stratagem and of the legitimation "mechanism" of* Fountain, *see my forthcoming essay, "Given the Richard Mutt Case."*

91.
Kosuth, "Art after Philosophy," pp. 82–83, 85.

92.
Greenberg, "Counter-Avant-Garde," Art International *(May 1971), repr. in Joseph Masheck, ed.,* Marcel Duchamp in Perspective *(Englewood Cliffs, NJ: Prentice-Hall, 1975), p. 128. Notice the adjective "avant-gardist." In this text as elsewhere, "avant-garde" is opposed to "avant-gardism" in the same way "Modernist art" is opposed to "concocted art."*

93.
George Dickie, Art and the Aesthetic: An Institutional Analysis *(Ithaca: Cornell University Press, 1974).*

94.
Greenberg, "Counter-Avant-Garde," p. 131.

95.
These questions require long developments which I cannot make here. I have tried my hand at them in the essay "Given the Richard Mutt Case."

96.
One should remember, here, that Greenberg's early Modernism, toward the end of the thirties, is the thinking of a Marxist, more exactly, of a Trotskyite. The fact that in time his Formalism took a more and more fiercely apolitical stance has much less to do, as is often thought, with the fact that the man became conservative as he grew older, than with his early interpretation—in fact typical of a leftist intellectual who keeps in mind the recent encounter between Breton and Trotsky in Mexico—of the phenomenon of the avant-garde as a pocket of resistance where the progressive cultural forces came to nest in order to maintain aesthetic standards at their highest level of expectation and defend them against the philistinism of the industrial bour-geoisie. According to this interpretation, the avant-garde signed a sort of tacit and probably unconscious contract with the enlightened faction of the bourgeoisie, the only one that didn't seem to renounce cultural ambition, in order to autonomize the artistic sphere and eliminate all political and institutional considerations from aesthetic experience and judgment. With this rationale the young Greenberg believed he could clearly separate the aesthetic and the social context: the former's autonomy is the effect of the latter. Growing older, Greenberg has indeed abandoned his Marxism, but he has never relinquished this conviction that the avant-garde's apolitical stance was the necessary and paradoxical fruit of the political contradictions of modernity. The critics who reproach Greenberg for having abandoned Marxism, in order to condemn the way Formalism silences the political and institutional dimensions of aesthetic experience (and who sometimes deduce from this that all aesthetics is but ideology), have chosen the wrong target. To the contrary, and paradoxi-

cally, it is the traces of Marxism in Greenberg's conception of the avant-garde which are in need of a critique, if one wants to reintroduce those dimensions into aesthetics.

97.
The Salon des Refusés is of course paradigmatic because it is there that the aesthetic judgment was structurally cast into the binary form "either/or," substituting for the continuous scale of "taste." I believe the ubiquity of the paradigm of refusal (together with the very existence of public salons) to be largely responsible for the fact that the phenomenon of the avant-garde was born in France. There is however another modern paradigm that appeared later and is relevant for Central Europe, that of Secession. I tried to posit Duchamp in relation to both refusal and secession in my book Pictorial Nominalism. See the chapter "Resonances of Duchamp's Visit to Munich," also published in Dada/Surrealism 16 (1987).

98.
How to disentangle the social and the aesthetic contexts is ultimately a matter of ethics. We would have to discuss

them case by case. Here is an instance in which an artist, in a facsimile of Duchamp's "strategic" gesture, anticipated the advent of the blank canvas long before 1962. In 1949 Clyfford Still, who was teaching at the California School of Fine Arts in San Francisco, was invited to take part in a drawing show at the California Palace of the Legion of Honor, which was going to be a big social event for most faculty members. He declined, and when insistently begged, he replied in exasperation: "O.K. I'll give you a picture. After all, this show to an artist of integrity can only be a gesture. Since it is made for a museum program, I will give you my gesture, my respect for the public and gallery working in these terms. I will give you my contempt for the whole business: a six-by-ten-foot canvas blank as the fabric comes from the factory." The matter was not mentioned again, but there is a coda to the story: "I told the story years later to Ed [Holger] Cahill in New York. He said, 'I would have taken you up on that and hung your canvas.' I replied, 'I know you would have, Ed. That is why I

wouldn't have made even that offer to you' " (John P. O'Neill, Clyfford Still [New York: Abrams, 1979], pp. 27–29).

99.
Greenberg saw this in his own way when he said, "Back in the middle of last century a few poets, novelists and painters (not sculptors or architects) saw, in a surprisingly decided way, the need to maintain high expectations in and of art as they were no longer being maintained by cultivated art-lovers at large" ("Seminar Four," Art International 19 [January 1975], p. 17).

100.
Greenberg, "The Situation at the Moment," Partisan Review (January 1948), repr. in The Collected Essays and Criticism, Volume II, Arrogant Purpose, p. 192.

101.
Greenberg, "Seminar One," p. 44.

Saturday Disasters: Trace and Reference in Early Warhol

Thomas Crow

The public Warhol was not one but, at a minimum, three persons. The first, and by far the most prominent, was the self-created one: the product of his famous pronouncements and of the allowed representations of his life and milieu. The second was the complex of interests, sentiments, skills, ambitions, and passions actually figured in paint on canvas. The third was his persona as it sanctioned experiments in nonelite culture far beyond the world of art.[1] Of these three, the latter two are of far greater importance than the first, though they were normally overshadowed by the man who said he wanted to be like a machine, that everyone would be famous for fifteen minutes, that he and his art were all surface: don't look any further. The second Warhol is normally equated with the first; and the third, at least by historians and critics of art, is largely ignored.

This essay is primarily concerned with the second Warhol, though this will necessarily entail attention to the first. The conventional reading of his work turns around a few circumscribed themes: the impersonality of the images he chose and their presentation, his passivity in the face of a media-saturated reality, the suspension in his work of any clear authorial voice. His choice of subject matter is regarded as essentially indiscriminate. Little interest is displayed in his subjects beyond the observation that, in their totality, they represent the random play of a consciousness at the mercy of the commonly available commercial culture. The debate over Warhol centers on whether or not his art fosters critical or subversive apprehension of mass culture and the power of the image as commodity,[2] succumbs in an innocent but telling way to that numbing power,[3] or exploits it cynically and meretriciously.[4]

A relative lack of concentration on the evidence of the early pictures has made a notoriously elusive figure more elusive than he needs to be—or better, only as elusive as he intended to be. This discussion could, I think, be recast by addressing a contradiction at its core. The authority normally cited for this observed effacement of the author's voice in Warhol's pictures is none other than that voice itself. It was Warhol who told us that he had no real point to make, that he intended no larger meaning in the choice of this or that subject, that his assistants did most of the physical work of producing his art. Indeed, it would be difficult to name an artist who has been as successful as Warhol was in controlling the interpretation of his own work.

In the end, any critical account of Warhol's achievement as a painter will necessarily stand or fall on the visual evidence. But even within the public "text" provided by Warhol, there are some less calculated remarks that qualify the general understanding of his early art. One such moment occurs in direct proximity to two of his most frequently quoted pronouncements: "I want everybody to think alike" and "I think everybody should be a machine." In this section of his 1963 interview with G. R. Swenson, he is responding to more than the leveling effects of American consumer culture. His more specific concern is rather the meanings normally given to the *difference* between the abundant material satisfactions of the capitalist West and the relative deprivation and limited pesonal choices of the Communist East. The sentiment, though characterized by the prevailing American image of Soviet Communism, lies plainly outside the Cold War consensus: "Russia is doing it under strict government. It's happening here all by itself. . . . Everybody looks alike and acts alike, and we're getting more and more the same way."[5] These words were uttered only a year or so after the Cuban Missile Crisis and within months of Kennedy's dramatic, confrontational appearance at the Berlin Wall. It was a period maked by heightened ideological tension, in which the contrast of consumer cultures observable in Berlin was generalized into a primary moral distinction between the two economic and political orders. The bright lights and beckoning pleasures of the Kurfürstendam were cited over and over as an unmistakable sign of Western superiority over a benighted Eastern bloc. One only had to look over the

Wall to see the evidence for oneself in the dim and shabby thoroughfare that the once-glittering Unter den Linden had become.

In his own offhand way, Warhol was refusing that symbolism, a contrast of radiance and darkness that was no longer, as it had been in the 1950s, primarily theological, but had become consumerist in character. The spectacle of overwhelming Western affluence was the ideological weapon in which the Kennedy administration had made its greatest investment, and it is striking to find Warhol seizing on that image and negating its received political meaning (affluence equals freedom and individualism) in an effort to explain his work. Reading that interview now, one is further struck by the barely suppressed anger present throughout his responses, as well as by the irony in the phrases that would later congeal into the clichés. Of course, to generalize from this in order to impute some specifically politicized intentions to the artist would be to repeat the error in interpretation referred to above, to use a convenient textual crutch to avoid the harder work of confronting the paintings directly. A closer look at such statements as these, however, can at least prepare us for unexpected meanings in the images, meanings possibly more complex or critical than the received reading of Warhol's work would lead us to believe.

The principal thesis of this essay is that Warhol, though he grounded his art in the ubiquity of the packaged commodity, produced his most powerful work by dramatizing the breakdown of commodity exchange. These were instances in which the mass-produced image as the bearer of desires was exposed in its inadequacy by the reality of suffering and death. Into this category, for example, falls his most famous portrait series, that of Marilyn Monroe. He began the pictures within weeks of her suicide in August 1962, and it is remarkable how consistently this simple fact goes unremarked in the literature.[6] Her death was something with which Warhol clearly had to deal, and the pictures represent a lengthy act of mourning, much of the motivation for which lies beyond our understanding. (Some of the artist's formal choices refer to this memorial or funeral function directly, especially the single impression of her face against the gold background of an icon (*Gold Marilyn Monroe*, Museum of Modern Art), the traditional sign of an eternal other world.) Once undertaken, however, the series raised issues that continue to involve us all. How does one handle the fact of celebrity death? Where does one put the curiously intimate knowledge one possesses of an unknown figure, and how does one come to terms with the sense of loss,

Andy Warhol, Marilyn
Monroe, *1952, acrylic
on canvas, 81 x 63¾ in.
Collection René Mon-
tagu, Paris. (Photo-
graph courtesy Leo
Castelli)*

the absense of a richly imagined presence that was never really there? For some it might be Monroe, for others Buddy Holly or a Kennedy: the problem is the same.

Any complexity of thought or feeling in Warhol's *Marilyns* may be difficult to discern from our present vantage point. Not only does his myth stand in the way, but the portraits' seeming acceptance of the reduction of a woman's identity to a mass-commodity fetish can make the entire series seem a monument to the benighted past or unrepentant present. Though Warhol obviously had little stake in the erotic fascination felt for her by the male intellectuals of the fifties generation, de Kooning and Mailer for example,[7] he may indeed have failed to resist it sufficiently in his art. It is far from the intent of this essay to redeem whatever contribution Warhol's pictures have made to perpetuating that mystique. But there are ways in which the majority of the Monroe paintings, when viewed apart from the Marilyn/Goddess cult, exhibit a degree of tact, even reverence, that withholds outright complicity with it.

That effect of ironic remove began in the process of creating the silk-screen transfer. Its source is a bust-length publicity still in black and white taken in 1953 for the film *Niagara*.[8] The print that Warhol used, marked for cropping with a grease pencil, survives in the archives of his estate. A face shot in color from the same session was one of the best-known images of the young actress, but Warhol instead opted for a physically-smaller segment of one taken at a greater distance from its subject. In its alignment with the four-square rectangle of Warhol's ruled grid, the face takes on a solid, self-contained quality that both answers to the formal order of Warhol's compositional grids and undercuts Monroe's practiced and expected way of courting the male eye behind the camera. An instructive comparison can be made between the effect of Warhol's alteration of his source and James Rosenquist's *Marilyn Monroe I* of 1962 (Museum of Modern Art); for all of the fragmentation and interference that the latter artist imposes on the star portrait, its mannered coquettishness is precisely what he lingers over and preserves.

The beginning of the *Marilyn* series coincides with the moment of Warhol's commitment to the silk-screen technique,[9] and there is a close link between technique and meaning. Compared to the Rosenquist or to the vivid, fine-grained color of the studio face portrait, his manipulation and enlargement of a monochrome fragment drain away much of the imaginary living presence of the star. The inherently flattering and simplifying effects of the transformation from photograph to fabric stencil to inked canvas are magnified rather than concealed. The screened image, reproduced whole, has the character of an involuntary imprint. It is a memorial in the sense of resembling memory: powerfully selective, sometimes elusive, sometimes vividly present, always open to embellishment as well as loss.

In the *Marilyn Diptych* (Tate Gallery), also painted in 1962, Warhol lays out a stark and unresolved dialectic of presence and absence, of life and death. The left side is a monument; color and life are restored, but as a secondary and invariant mask added to something far more fugitive. Against the quasi-official regularity and uniformity of the left panel, the right concedes the absence of its subject, displaying openly the elusive and uninformative trace underneath. The right panel nevertheless manages subtle shadings of meaning within its limited technical scope. There is a reference to the material of film that goes beyond the repetition of frames. On a simple level, it reminds us that the best and most enduring film memories one has of Monroe—in *The Seven-Year Itch, Some Like It Hot, The Misfits*—are in black and white. The color we add to her memory is supplementary. In a more general sense, she is most real and best remembered in the flickering passage of film exposures, no one of which is ever wholly present to perception. The heavy inking in one vertical register underscores this. The passage from life to death reverses itself; she is most present where her image is least permanent. In this way, the *Diptych* stands as a comment on and complication of the embalmed quality, the slightly repellent stasis, of the *Gold Marilyn*.

Having taken up the condition of the celebrity as trace and sign, it is not surprising that Warhol would soon move to the image of Elizabeth Taylor. She and Monroe were nearly equal and unchallenged as Hollywood divas with larger-than-life personal myths. Each was maintained in her respective position by a kind of negative symmetry with the other, by representing what the other was not.

He then completed his triangle of female celebrity for the early sixties with a picture of Jacqueline Kennedy in the same basic format as the full-face portraits of Monroe and Taylor. The President's wife did not share film stardom with Monroe, but she did share the Kennedys. She also possessed the distinction of having established for the period a changed feminine ideal. Her slim, dark, aristocratic standard of beauty had made Monroe's style, and thus her power as a symbol, seem out of date even

before her death. (That new standard was mimicked within the
Warhol circle by Edie Sedgewick, for a time his constant companion and seeming alter ego during the period.) Warhol reinforced that passé quality by choosing for his series a photograph
of Monroe from the early fifties; by that simple choice he measured a historical distance between her life and her symbolic
function, while avoiding the signs of aging and mental collapse.

The semiotics of style that locked together Warhol's images
of the three women represents, however, only one of the bonds
between them. The other derived from the threat or actuality of
death. The full-face portraits of the *Liz* series, though generated
by a transformation of the *Marilyns*, in fact had an earlier origin.
Taylor's famous catastrophic illness in 1961—the collapse that
interrupted the filming of *Cleopatra*—had entered into one of
Warhol's early tabloid paintings (*Daily News*, 1962). The contemporaneous rhythm of crises in the health of both women had
joined them in the public mind (and doubtless Warhol's as well)
in that year; it was a bond that the third would come to share in
November 1963. The Kennedy assassination pictures are often
seen as an exception in the artist's output, exceptional in their
open emotion and sincerity,[10] but their continuity with the best
of his previous work seems just as compelling. As with the *Marilyns*, the loss of the real Kennedy referent galvanizes Warhol into
a sustained act of remembrance. Here, however, he has a stand-
in, the widow who had first attracted him as an instance of celebrity typology. Again, he limits himself to fragmentary materials,
eight grainy news photographs out of the myriad representations
available to him. These he shuffles and rearranges to organize his
straightforward expressions of feeling: in *Nine Jackies* of 1964
(Sonnabend Collection), one sees the irrevocable transformation
of the life of the survivor, Jackie happy and Jackie sad, differentiated by the color of the panel; the print *Jackie II* of 1966 uses
a simple doubling within one undivided field both to multiply the
marks of stoicism and grief and to make the widow less solitary
in her mourning. The emotional calculus is simple, the sentiment
direct and uncomplicated. The pictures nevertheless recognize,
by their impoverished vocabulary, the distance between public
mourning and that of the principals in the drama. Out of his deliberately limited resources, the artist creates a nuance and subtlety of response that is his alone, precisely because he has not
sought technically to surpass his raw material. It is difficult not to
share in this, however cynical one may have become about the

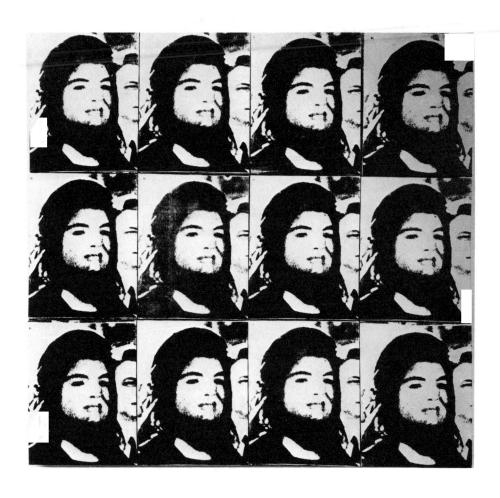

Andy Warhol, Jackie,
1964, silkscreen on can-
vas, 12 panels, each 20
x 16 in. Collection Per-
luigi Pero. (Photo-
graph: Rudolph
Burchhardt)

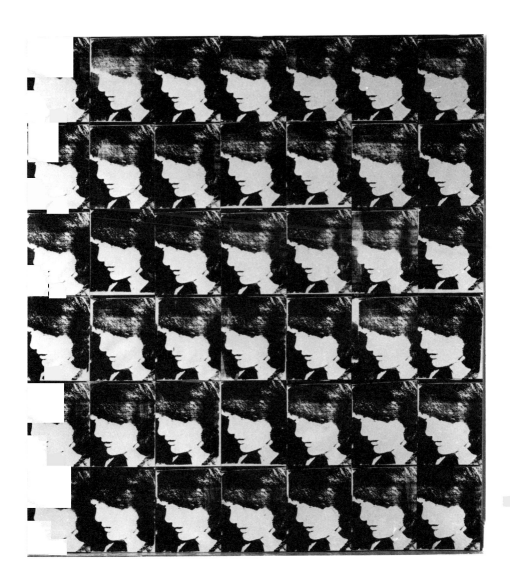

Andy Warhol, Jackie,
1964, silkscreen, 35
panels, each 20 x 16 in.
Collection, Hessisches
Landesmuseum, Darm-
stadt, Germany, Karl
Stroler Collection.

Kennedy presidency or the Kennedy marriage. In his particular dramatization of medium, Warhol found room for a dramatization of feeling and even a kind of history painting.

My reading of Warhol has thus far proceeded by establishing relationships among his early portraits. It can be expanded to include the apparently anodyne icons of consumer products for which the artist is equally renowned. Even those familiar images take on unexpected meanings in the context of his other work of the period. For example, in 1963, the year after the Campbell's soup-can imagery had established his name, Warhol did a series of pictures under the title *Tunafish Disaster*. These are, understandably enough, lesser-known works, but they feature the repeated images of an analogous object, a can of A&P-brand tuna. In this instance, however, the contents of the can were suspected of having killed people, and newspaper photographs of the victims are repeated below those of the deadly containers. The wary smile of Mrs. McCarthy, the broad grin of Mrs. Brown, as each posed with self-conscious sincerity for their snapshots, and the look of the clothes, glasses, and hairstyles speak the language of class in America. The women's workaday faces and the black codings penned on the cans transform the mass-produced commodity into anything but a neutral abstraction.

More than this, of course, the pictures commemorate a moment when the supermarket promise of safe and abundant packaged food was disastrously broken. Does Warhol's rendition of the disaster render it safely neutral? I think not, no more than it would be possible for an artist to address the recent panics over tampering with nonprescription medicines without confronting the kinds of anxiety they express. In this case, the repetition of the crude images does force attention to the awful banality of the accident and the tawdry exploitation by which we come to know the misfortunes of strangers, but it does not mock attempts at empathy, however feeble. Nor do the images direct our attention to some peculiarly twentieth-century estrangement between the event and its representation: the misfortunes of strangers have made up the primary content of the press since there has been a press. The *Tunafish Disaster* pictures take an established feature of Pop imagery, established by others as well as by Warhol, and push it into a context decidedly other than that of consumption. We do not consume the news of these deaths in the same way that we consume the safe (one hopes) contents of a can.

Along similar lines, a link can be made to the several series that use photographs of automobile accidents. These commem-

Andy Warhol, Tunafish
Disaster, *silkscreen on
canvas, 123 x 82 in.
Courtesy Andy Warhol
Studio.*

orate events in which the supreme symbol of consumer affluence, the American car of the fifties, has ceased to be an image of pleasure and freedom and has become a concrete instrument of sudden and irreparable injury. (In only one picture of the period, *Cars*, does an automobile appear intact.) Does the repetition of *Five Deaths* or *Saturday Disaster* cancel attention to the visible anguish in the faces of the living or the horror of the limp bodies of the unconscious and dead? We cannot penetrate beneath the image to touch the true pain and grief, but their reality is sufficiently indicated in the photographs to force attention to one's limited ability to find an appropriate response. As for the repetition, might we just as well understand it to mean the grim predictability, day after day, of more events with an identical outcome, the leveling sameness with which real, not symbolic, death erupts in our experience?

In his selection of these photographs, Warhol was as little as ever the passive receptor of commonly-available imagery. Rather than relying upon newspaper reproductions that might have come to hand randomly, he sought out glossy press-agency prints normally seen only by professional journalists.[11] (Some of these were apparently regarded as too bizarre or gruesome ever to see print; that is, they were barred from public reproduction precisely because of their capacity to disturb.) They have in common with the celebrity portraits and product labels discussed above a fascination with moments where the brutal fact of death and suffering cancels the possibility of passive and complacent consumption. And he would take this further. Simultaneously with his first meditations on the Monroe death, Warhol took up the theme of anonymous suicide in several well-known and harrowing paintings. *Bellevue I* (1963) places the death within a context of institutional confinement. And again the argument could be offered that the repetition of the photographic image within the pictorial field can increase rather than numb sensitivity to it, as the viewer works to draw the separate elements into a whole. The compositional choices are artful enough to invite that kind of attention. Take, for example, the way the heavily inked units in the upper left precisely balance and play off the void at the bottom. That ending to the chain of images has a metaphoric function akin to the play of presence and absence in the *Marilyn Diptych*—it stands in a plain and simple way for death and also for what lies beyond the possibility of figuration.[12] In the 1962 print on paper *Suicide*, the implacable facade of the building from which the victim has jumped (we can see neither its top nor its bottom)

Andy Warhol, Bellevue
1, 1963, 82 x 82 in.
Courtesy Andy Warhol
Studio.

becomes an area of obscure abstraction marked only by dim ranks of unseeing windows; it is the dark complement to the bright wedge that surrounds the leaper's horrific silhouette.

The electric-chair pictures, as a group, present a similarly stark dialectic of fullness and void. But the dramatic shifts between presence and absence are far from being the manifestation of a pure play of the signifier liberated from reference beyond the sign. They mark the point where the brutal fact of violent death entered the realm of contemporary politics. The early 1960s, following the execution of Caryl Chessman in California, has seen agitation against the death penalty grow to an unprecedented level of intensity.[13] The partisan character of Warhol's images is literal and straightforward, as he is wont to be, and that is what saves them from mere morbidity. He gave them the collective title *Disaster* and thus tied a political subject to the slaughter of innocents in the highway, airplane, and supermarket accidents he memorialized elsewhere. He was attracted to the open sores in American political life, the issues that were most problematic for liberal Democratic politicians such as Kennedy and Edmund Brown. At this time he also did a series on the most violent phase of civil-rights demonstrations in the South; in the *Race Riots* of 1963, political life takes on the same nightmare coloring that saturates so much of his other work.

We might take seriously, if only for a moment, Warhol's dictum that in the future everyone will be famous for fifteen minutes, but conclude that in his eyes it was likely to be under fairly horrifying circumstances. What this body of paintings adds up to is a kind of *peinture noire* in the sense that we apply the term to the *film noir* genre of the forties and early fifties—a stark, disabused, pessimistic vision of American life, produced from the knowing rearrangement of pulp materials by an artist who did not opt for the easier paths of irony or condescension.

By 1965, of course, this episode in his work was largely over; the *Flowers, Cow Wallpaper*, silver pillows, and the like have little to do with the imagery under discussion here. Then the clichés began to ring true. But there was for a time, in the work of 1961–64, a threat to create a true "pop" art in the most positive sense of that term—a pulp-derived, bleakly monochrome vision that held, however tenuous the grip, to an all-but-buried tradition of truth-telling in American commercial culture. Very little of what is normally called Pop art could make a similar claim. It remained, one could argue, a latency subsequently taken up by others, an international underground soon to be overground, who created the third Warhol and the best one.

Notes

1.
There are as yet only fragmentary accounts of this phenomenon. For some preliminary comment, see Iain Chambers, Urban Rhythms: Pop Music and Popular Culture *(London, 1985), pp. 130ff.*

2.
See, for example, Rainer Crone, Andy Warhol, *trans. J. W. Gabriel (London, 1970), passim.*

3.
See, for example, Carter Ratcliff, Andy Warhol *(New York, 1983), passim. For an illuminating discussion of the power and effects of this view in West Germany, see Andreas Huyssen, "The Cultural Politics of Pop,"* New German Critiques 4 *(Winter 1975), pp. 77–98.*

4.
See, for example, Robert Hughes, "The Rise of Andy Warhol," in B. Wallis, ed., Art after Modernism *(New York, 1984), pp. 45–57.*

5.
In an interview with G. R. Swenson, "What Is Pop Art," Art News 62 *(November 1963), p. 26. Warhol's assistant during the sixties, Gerard Malanga, offered this interpretation of*

the passage in a recent interview (Patrick S. Smith, Warhol: Conversations about the Artist *[Ann Arbor, 1988], p. 163): "Well, Andy's always said . . . . He said somewhere that he thought of himself as apolitical. And if you remember reading that really good interview with Andy by Gene Swenson in '63, in* Art News, *when Andy talks about capitalism and communism as really being the same thing and someday everybody will think alike—well, that's a very political statement to make even though it sounds very apolitical. So, I think, there was always a political undercurrent to Andy's unconscious concern for politics, or of [sic] society for that matter."*

6.
Crone, p. 24, dates the beginning of the Monroe portraits in a discussion of silk-screen technique without mentioning the death. Ratcliff, p. 117, dates the first portraits to August in a brief chronology appended to his text, also without mentioning her death in the same month.

7.
De Kooning titled one of his Woman *series after her in 1954. Norman Mailer's fascination*

with the actress is rehearsed at length in Marilyn, A Biography *(New York, 1973). Warhol was himself fascinated by the aura that surrounded the artists of the first generation of the New York school and was calculatedly looking for ways to move into their orbit. His interest in de Kooning, though no doubt real, has taken on a spurious specificity based on remarks mistakenly appended to the 1963 Swenson interview when it was reprinted in John Russell and Suzi Gablik,* Pop Art Redefined *(New York, 1969). The statement (p. 118) "de Kooning gave me my content and my motivation" actually comes from Swenson's interview with Tom Wesselmann (see* Art News 62 *[February 1964], p. 64). I and others had given credence to this scholarly virus in the past. The record was publicly corrected by Barry Blinderman (letter to the editor,* Art in America 75 *[October 1987], p. 21). The misattribution has, however, reappeared in the catalogue of the Museum of Modern Art exhibition,* Warhol: A Retrospective *(New York, 1989), pp. 18, 23n.*

8.
The print, from a photograph by Gene Kornman, was uncovered in the archives of the Warhol estate by the organizers of Andy Warhol: A Retrospective (an illustration of the print with Warhol's markings appears on p. 72). Before it had come to light, I had surmised that he had used a portion of the color face portrait in a composite image, basing that conjecture on the seemingly identical aspect of the hair in that photograph and in the Warhol screen (see my comments and an illustration of the other portrait in Art in America 75 [May 1987], p. 130). I am grateful to Jennifer Wells of the department of painting at the Museum of Modern Art for her knowledge and assistance on this and other points.

9.
See Crone, p. 24, who dates Warhol's commitment to the technique to August 1962. The first screened portraits, he states, were of Troy Donahue. Marco Livingston ("Do It Yourself: Notes on Warhol's Techniques," Andy Warhol: A Retrospective, p. 69) states that Baseball (Nelson-Atkins Museum, Kansas City) was among the very earliest, along with "Disasters" on both paper and canvas, such as Suicide (Adelaide de Menil collection).

10.
See, for example, Coplans, p. 52. The source of most of the photographs was Life 55 (29 November 1963), pp. 22, 31 (6 December 1963), pp. 43, 48.

11.
See interview with Gerard Malanga in Smith, Warhol: Conversations about the Artist, p. 163.

12.
This control, of course, could take the form of understanding and anticipating the characteristic imperfections and distortions of the process; that is, of knowing just how little one had to intervene once the basic arrangement, screen pattern, and color choices had been decided. For a first-hand account, see the illuminating if somewhat self-contradictory comments of Gerard Malanga in Patrick Smith, Andy Warhol's Art and Films (Ann Arbor, 1986), pp. 391–392, 398–400. See also Livingston's remarks ("Do It Yourself," p. 72) on the ways in which the rephotographed full-sized acetate would be altered by the artist ("for example, to increase the tonal contrast by removing areas of half-tone, thereby further flattening the image") before its transfer to silk screen, as well as on the subsequent use of the same acetate to plot and mark the intended placement of the screen impressions before the process of printing began. Warhol's remarks in a conversation with Malanga (Print Collector's Newsletter 1 [January–February 1971], p. 126) indicate a habit of careful premeditation; he explains how the location of an impression was established if color was to be applied under it: "Silhouette shapes of the actual image were painted in by isolating the rest of an area on the canvas by means of masking tape. Afterwards, when the paint dried, the masking tape would be removed and the silk screen would be placed on top of the painted silhouette shape, sometimes slightly off register."

13.
For a summary of press accounts of the affair, see Roger E. Schwed, Abolition and Capital Punishment (New York, 1983), pp. 68–104.

Discussion

Audience

I'm very impressed with your presentation of the early Warhol
and I think that your talk was not only interesting, but in fact
very close to what Warhol was actually doing during the period in
question. It is hard to reconcile what he has done afterward with
his early stuff. I wonder if you could speculate on why that tremendous shift happened?

Thomas Crow

Well, the simple answer would be no. I haven't a clue why he
changed; why he became this bizarre, right-wing media creature
(and a very wealthy man, with his publishing enterprise and
steady line in celebrity portraits and so on). It's hard to say. I
think that the pictures that I've been talking about have everything to do with where Warhol came from: a working-class, disorganized early life in Pennsylvania, many details of which are
unknown. He was a man with a kind of loyalty to his origins that
lasted a little while and then was shed.

Audience

Would it be possible, since Warhol was focusing in on celebrities, that his own growing celebrity status disillusioned him a
great deal? I ask this because a lot of the criticism of his work
at the time these pictures were introduced was not about what
you've been talking about. You've been talking about the sincerity and the horror and the *film noir* aspects of his work, whereas
a lot of the criticism of Warhol at the time that you're referring to
was about Warhol as a full person.

Thomas Crow

Yes, the game may have just worked so well . . . though I do see
a lot of the things that he verbally claimed about his art to be a
kind of defense mechanism about their rather embarrassing ele-
mental and sincere qualities. Of course, you can't underestimate
the assassination attempt either, in which all of this came true in
his life, and the kind of fear, disillusionment, and pain—terrible
lengthy pain—that caused him. That would change anybody.

Audience

I'd like to ask you something to do with what you said about
Warhol's treatment of the subject of Marilyn, where the words

that stuck in my mind were "reverence" and "tact." Can you clarify what you mean by that? My reaction is to say that they are irreverent and tactless.

Thomas Crow

This may just come down to an irreducible difference in our senses of the way that Monroe is being presented. I think that one way to begin an answer to the question is to start comparing the way that she appears in Warhol's work to the way that she gets taken up in the hands of other artists, or to the way that she has been turned into a kind of publishing industry of reproductions of her image ever since. There's that picture by Rosenquist in which she appears in one of those pin-up poses, tossing her head back and smiling, obviously trying to please the camera, please the viewer. Warhol took a lot of what we take to be the normal signs of glamor and of seductiveness out of the picture. I think that the qualities of a certain kind of respect for Monroe, and for what she symbolized, are much more apparent where she's not covered by color than where she is. And I think that there is a layering there in which one is asked to attend to the fact that there is a deeper layer underneath the color, one that can change and shift and that occasionally gets exposed, as it does in the Monroe diptych.

Audience

Do you really think that was a difference for Warhol between Marilyn and what she symbolized?

Thomas Crow

Oh yes, absolutely. I think that Warhol sensed it. Biographical data is going to be no confirmation for this argument, but the man had spent ten years in the fashion industry, in which keeping your finger on the slightest seismic tremors having to do with stylistic signs and distinctions is what you do to survive. And to think that he would be producing Monroe as some univalent symbol of sexuality or of Hollywood seems to be at odds with everything one would expect from the man. So I think that one starts to look for complications, and these are the ones that I see in the image. I don't think that the *Gold Marilyn* is a mockery. The image does have something of the overpretty and of the slightly repellent character of an embalming, but that is our funerary ritual, isn't it? I mean, in most of American life, that embalming, though it repels everyone, is still adhered to. That would be a way of constructing irreverence too, in a way that would allow for its slightly perverse qualities. But they're not images which are about pandering, except maybe the *Lips*. And, although it's not an iron-clad connection, I'm struck by the de Kooning parallel there.

Thierry de Duve

This is a very interesting debate. It makes me a little bit uncomfortable with the subject strategy that you have developed, presenting a humanistic view of early Warhol, and that is why I am hungry for more information about how you explain the shift that is supposedly occurring in 1965. I myself don't see so much difference between a pure, working-class boy making his way through advertising to become a high-art figure and then the cynical superstar that he has become since then. Maybe symmetrical to this historical problem, or going hand-in-hand with it, there is the problem that the discussion is now framed between respect and irrespect, appropriation and mourning, and things like that. I feel a little bit uncomfortable with that.

I would, for example, suggest another track to thinking about Marilyn. As you know, for the year or so before her death Marilyn spoke of her own image in absolutely schizophrenic terms. She could not deal with her own image and referred to her own photographs of herself as "this woman." Warhol may be the one person who has understood, consciously or not I don't know, that to be a star is to be a blank screen. He has lived by that. A blank screen for the projection of spectators' phantasmas, dreams, and desires. The connection between Eros and Thanatos in his work is indeed an extremely poignant thing, which I am afraid cannot be dissociated. You seem to think that his saying that he's "just surface," "I want to be a machine," and all that, is a foil, or is a defense system. Well, why do his private image and his public image coincide so well then? And why has he been able to sustain a life for more than twenty years like that, and an art practice which, even if it is recuperated, is still of relatively good quality?

Thomas Crow

Well, I should try to just craft a kind of simple response to the complex of things that you raised. In one sense, I beg off dealing with the problem of Warhol's biography even by the standard I tried to set in the talk itself. Which is to say that trying to think of Warhol as a character, as a media personality, has been a trap for interpretation. As long as this kind of thinking has gone on, the actual character of the work has been relatively neglected. One thing that one has to say to all of this business of Monroe understanding that she was an image, and Warhol being sensitive to this, and so on, is that he didn't have to be all that sensitive to be able to use those ideas: it was in *Life* magazine. There was a long interview, in fact, which happened by coincidence to be published the very week that she died, in which she used her education of the last ten years or so to reflect on all of these issues. It was part of the culture; it wasn't something that the artistic sophisticate had to supply to mass culture. It was there, and Warhol was just interested in it and able to make some painting out of it.

Thierry de Duve

"Interested" is too weak a word; I think that it's a matter of an extraordinarily strong desire on the side of the death drive. He is touching on the pleasure that people derive from what makes other people suffer. Marilyn kills herself, and Warhol derives that strange pleasure out of it.

Thomas Crow

Well, we're getting into a level of psychoanalytic exploration that I just fear to follow.

Thierry de Duve

Not really, it also has to do with surfaces, images, make-up, to be a strip of film, to have one's body employed by the movie industry. The body doesn't count because the body is mortal, but the image is immortal. So how can one convert that psychic and desire economy into magnificent paintings which transform these things into a pleasure?

Audience

I do have a problem with the presentation. This is because it does not really deal with the whole convention of disorder, the whole notion of the "aura" or of the authenticity of the work of art. How does Warhol's work relate to that? And how does Warhol's work relate to the image of the star? . . . To real subjectivity? . . . To real humanity? . . . To what a real woman is as opposed to what her image is? . . . None of that stuff was really addressed, and I think that all of that was really an issue on the screen, working and presenting the images.

Another thing is that in my reading of the sixties, there is talk of how there was this tremendous barrage of imagery which people were confronted with every day, such as the war, race riots, car crashes, and so on. The result was a highly intellectual combat with television. So there was this resulting desensitization, and that's why you get "hot" imagery that takes the form of images like Marilyn. I just think that all of that is perhaps more of a sociological phenomenon.

Thomas Crow

To me that just sounds like journalism that needs to be interrogated. To elide things like racial clashes with car crashes, say, would be just to talk about them on one plane as being part of some image saturation. This seems to be very incurious about where such images come from, and where they're most likely to be taken seriously.

The images of car crashes are the staple of small-town journalism. They are about local people you might know, they are about very intimate forms of disaster that can erupt in a town. I remember them from my own childhood as being something to which you were exposed all the time. Maybe you could try a macro-sociological explanation that with the great increase in car ownership in the fifties—cars that were just rolling death traps, no safety devices at all—people were really being killed, and it was an intimate form of confrontation with terrible danger that was a part of everyday life. It didn't have anything to do with the sixties and some kind of image saturation; it was a localized and very modest kind of media phenomenon.

I don't know, do you all feel overwhelmed now? I mean, it's bound to have gotten worse in the meantime. Do you carry around this feeling that your consciousness has been completely leveled by news of Lebanon, and Nicaragua, and hijackings so that you can't think anymore? . . . so that discriminations are impossible? Granted that it's a complicated thing, but you can still think.

The Politics of Consumption: The Screen Actor's Guild, Ronald Reagan, and the Hollywood Red Scare

Lary May

Coming out of the cage of the Army . . . a series of hard-nosed happenings began to change my whole view of American dangers. Most of them tied in directly with my own bailiwick of acting. . . . From being an active (though unconscious) partisan in what now and then turned out to be Communist causes, I little by little became disillusioned or perhaps, in my case, I should say reawakened.

Ronald Reagan, former President of the Screen Actor's Guild, 1960

Really and truly, the triumph of McCarthyism was, in effect, the cutting off of a generalized social movement that began before the war. . . . The picking on the Hollywood people . . . received a lot of attention because everybody knew who the stars were. What I'm trying to say is that you're not dealing with an isolated event, but the focus of such a national event as it happened in Hollywood.

Abraham Polansky, blacklisted film director, 1970

And we must strive constantly to use all the tools of modern communication to tell the democratic story. Because motion pictures are my business I think of them in this connection, too. Our films are being shown in every country in the world except in Russia and Yugoslavia. In some areas they are about the last link which the people have with America.

Eric Johnston, President of the Motion Picture Producers Association, 1948[1]

Shortly after World War II a remarkable article appeared on the front page of the Screen Actor's Guild magazine, suggesting that the rise of anti-Communism in Hollywood was indeed connected to a struggle over national values and politics. Written by Eric

Johnston, the former head of the U.S. Chamber of Commerce and recently appointed president of the Motion Picture Producers Association, it brought together under the auspicious title "Utopia is Production" Johnston's repeated arguments that Americans had found a way to overcome the crisis of identity that bedeviled them in the twentieth century. Like a Puritan minister, Johnston preached that in the new world, the people had created a democratic culture, free of European exploitation and conflicts. The rise of the corporations at the turn of the century, however, aroused fears that the frontier was gone, and the depression generated the "nightmare" of class conflict and anti-monopoly "rhetoric." In this weakened condition, the nation was attacked by foreign enemies. Yet Johnston argued that the wartime cooperation showed that the citizens could end battles over scarce resources, while free trade and defense against the Soviet Union would end the fear of depressions and war. At a time when a vision of a new America had to be spread to the world, the miracle of mass communications provided a great advantage. As he explained:

> It is no exaggeration to say that the modern picture industry sets the styles for half the world. There is not one of us who isn't aware that the motion picture is the most powerful medium for the influencing of people that man has ever built. . . . We can set new styles of living and the doctrine of production must be made completely popular.[2]

Johnston's desire to transform American politics and culture was no mere platitude, for he wrote at a time when the most militant strike wave in history erupted across the country and in the film capital.[3] As celebrities walked on picket lines and violence erupted, it was not surprising that Johnston would try to convince the most important group in the labor conflict, the film stars, to support the producers. Yet given our knowledge of the era, it is surprising that Johnston should seek the support of the Screen Actor's Guild as part of a contest to determine political ideology and national values. Generally we have been taught that the period from the Great Depression to the Cold War generated a series of major developments, from the creation of a welfare state to the nation's rise as a world power.[4] Yet scholars examining the mass media over the same era have stressed that movies, radio, and magazines reinforced conservative myths and escapist dreams, presumably diverting attention away from injustice and political reform.[5] Investigators of the Hollywood "red scare" have endorsed this division by ignoring the relation of anti-Communism to larger social issues and by slighting the charge that politics and cinematic images were intimately intertwined.[6]

Yet the example of Johnston's article points toward a major corrective of these views. First, it suggests that what happened in the film capital was not unique, but a process that had deep affinities with political transformations occurring across the country. Second, it suggests not only that popular culture and politics were intertwined, but also that the distinctiveness of Hollywood was that it used the mass media to spread a new vision of American identity from 1932 to 1948. To this writer, this provides a framework for answering some of the major questions about postwar America. Why did anti-Communism take on such power after 1945? Why did that crusade come to focus on the film capital? Why did elites like Eric Johnston see the Hollywood labor disputes as part of a contest to determine national values and popular culture in the Cold War era?

Hollywood and the New Life

To answer these questions, we must place Hollywood squarely within the major social and economic transformations of the twentieth century. Within that context, we need to see how the film capital became identified with attempts to revitalize modern middle-class life. Ever since the turn of the century, dominant Anglo-Saxon opinion-makers like Eric Johnston feared that with the end of the frontier, the promise of individualism and democracy might be lost within a rising corporate order and cities populated by the "new" immigrants from Eastern Europe. Yet in those same big cities, the employees of large firms turned to new amusements that broke down the divisions between the prosperous and workers, men and women, immigrants and old-stock Americans. By 1914 nightclub and film stars became the models of this new life and the "American film star," commented a noted producer, became the means by which the movies "reached the masses." Stars gave form to "intimate experiences," exerting "a tremendous chemical effect on audiences." And unlike in the past, fans wanted the actor to "invest their real lives with the attributes of the screen" and "stay in character" off the screen as well.[7]

By the twenties, the stars were thus the living embodiment of a rising urban culture. And Hollywood became a highly pub-

licized utopia where the stars pioneered a democratic experience
rooted in leisure consumption. A star like Douglas Fairbanks or
Mary Pickford would portray on the screen men and women dissatisfied with modern work and finding rejuvenation in sports,
dancing, and a modern sexual style. Off the screen they would
live that happy ending on the West Coast, finding a new democratic arena in leisure and affluence. Yet as this merger of life
and art unfolded, men like Eric Johnston saw that this new culture encouraged decadence and even cynicism. Part of the reason was that moralists passed censorship codes that channeled
the moral revolution into private life, and film entrepreneurs
responded by identifying mass culture with foreign mores and
styles. Indicative of that split, film entrepreneurs built movie
theaters that emulated the lavish styles of the theaters and opera
houses for European artistocrats and the rich, while major film
formulas associated stars with the foreign eroticism of a Rudoph
Valentino or the exotic family ideal portrayed by Cecil B. De
Mille. A film producer's son thus recalled that "jazz age" Hollywood had a "terrible case of the Valentino vapors, as even the
most Anglo-Saxon profiles in town were being pressed into service as irresistible Arabs . . . and 'sheik' went into the language
as the generic term for the playboys of . . . the generation."[8]

Much of this began to change after the crash of 1929. At a
time when the fans distrusted faltering political and economic
institutions, popular culture began to fuse with the American
values and civic life. Symbolizing that reorientation was the replacement of the foreign-styled movie houses with moderne theaters. Soon the smooth, slick, glimmering lines of the moderne
spread to hundreds of small towns and urban neighborhoods,
spearheading an expansion of the audience that far surpassed
the previous era of prosperity. In the midst of hard times, these
"American" arenas also began to house rotary clubs, high
school graduations, and local events, while producers as well as
politicians held film openings that celebrated local holidays and
state heroes. "Unlike in the past," pointed out one trade journalist, "virtually every studio in Hollywood has some of its important
players making public appearances in theatres around the country, also at festivals, fairs, dinners, dances and other events."[9]

Within this context, films as well as stars began to be more
socially engaged. Escapist and foreign-styled productions still
remained popular, and portrayals of common myths validated
traditional values. But a new tone also arose. Now Hollywood
innovators condemned the older silent productions for their for-

eign luxury, selfish individualism, and escapist romance. In contrast to the "jazz age," critics praised new figures like Will Rogers, Edward G. Robinson, James Cagney, and George Murphy. These heroes embodied vernacular and ethnic styles, and films like *Little Caesar* revealed how "gangsters were not too different from established businessmen" and politicians, while *Wild Boys of the Road* showed a society unable to deal with youthful rebels, *Gentlemen Are Born* told the story of a college man unable to get a job, and *I Am a Fugitive from the Chain Gang* dramatized the need for prison reform. To counter this chaotic world, films such as the *Grapes of Wrath* and *Mr. Deeds Goes to Town* and the Busby Berkeley musicals featured American heroes inspiring the people to create a better future.[10]

Popular Culture and Labor Insurgency

An equally dramatic quest for a new society occurred off the screen. In an industry where the stars were expected to carry their movie appeal into real life, a significant number began to identify with the rise of Franklin Roosevelt to the presidency and organized labor as the major mass movement of the era. As a business indentified with cultural renewal, and dominated by immigrants and city people, Hollywood in 1936 voted more than 6 to 1 for Roosevelt. Initially industry leaders supported reformist efforts to create cooperation between business and government. But when Roosevelt started a second New Deal in 1935, politics within the film capital came to be highly contested. In an industry that was virtually devoid of unions in 1929, the administration helped make Hollywood 100 percent organized by 1945, a percentage far ahead of national trends. At the forefront of that drive were not just workers, but the writers, directors, and performers.

Perhaps the most important group, however, was the stars. Mobilized in the Screen Actor's Guild (SAG), the actors and actresses controlled the product without which no film could be successful—the celebrity—and became, unlike the other unaffiliated guilds, active members of the national American Federation of Labor (AFL). In their first efforts to organize in 1932, the actors also had a great advantage because the top leadership stratum was consistently composed of major figures like Eddie Cantor, James Cagney, and Robert Montgomery, the top box office of the day. After the Guild received a contract in 1937, it would control about 50 percent of all the artists and 25 percent of all the workers in the industry. Further, throughout the period the SAG helped other talent guilds and unions organize.[11]

At the same time, the Guild's efforts yielded a series of major innovations in middle-class life. In terms of economic interests alone, it would seem that this development should not have happened. In 1939, for example, a sociological study funded by the Carnegie Foundation tabulated the background of Guild actors and actresses. Excluding the unskilled extras (who had no speaking lines in films), they found that over fifty-four members made more than $100,000 a year, higher than any other trade in the film capital. When the investigators tabulated the occupations of the performers' parents, they found that over 80 percent came from families with professional or proprietary backgrounds (they were small merchants and tradespeople). Less than 10 percent came from worker or farmer backgrounds. Nearly half had gone to college, and the overwhelming majority had finished high school. Over 60 percent entered the industry in the thirties, and almost 50 percent were under the age of thirty-five. As one writer observed, the Guild was "something new in America, a pioneer organization of professional people. Its birth and steady growth," he continued, "make one of the most significant labor developments of the last ten years."[12]

Naturally, contemporary observers often expressed perplexity as to why the sons and daughters of the solid middle class should join the labor movement. A common answer was that the stars organized in 1932 to protect their high salaries. While that is true, it cannot explain why after prosperity returned they continued their active involvement in local and national unions. No, something more was going on than high wages, and that something more was repeatedly commented on in the Guild press. A typical writer framed the issue by asking a mythical actor, "Are We Labor?" If the answer was no, then the reader did not understand the realities of the twentieth century. In the past, the citizenry defined their country in terms of an exodus from Europe into a country of free land and small property. Whereas individuals might earlier have found autonomy on the frontier, that "safety valve" was no longer available. Big businessmen like the Hollywood producers, "corresponding in a sense to the hereditary feudal lords, grew steadily in number and more concentrated," and their employees served as wage earners. When the crash came, monopolists fired their old stars and subjected all to the "tyranny" of producers who worked them long hours and lowered wages. "An artist is an artist," explained the writer, "only as long as he preserves his artistic integrity, and he can preserve his artistic integrity only as long as he can exercise, to a reasonable degree, some control over his artistic destiny."[13]

Unfolding within the Guild, then, was perhaps the country's most advanced play of the "new" middle class coming to political consciousness. Though they were performers and artists in Hollywood, they were still professionals receiving a salary from someone else. As the offspring of a bourgeoisie deeply committed to individualism, they also experienced the changes occurring in a national middle class increasingly working for large organizations. At a time when much of this salaried work rested on selling personality, the actors' sense of being a manipulative commodity was heightened by their participation in a film industry that duplicated their images as models of freedom. Yet in reality their artistic expressions were bought and sold by monopolists, while they had little control over their roles and profits. So Guild writers realized that to reassert democracy in the world of work, they had to shed their "class superiority" and form alliances with workers.

Yet this did not mean they turned to Marxist or socialist ideas as a guide. On the contrary, right from their first public pronouncements in 1932, they consistently drew on a progressive, republican tradition. Reworking a democratic faith that saw capitalism as an alien influence within America, Guild leaders contrasted their efforts with the "economic-royalists" whose "oppressive corporate practices" demanded a new "Declaration of Independence" to free the modern "slave class." The SAG president, Eddie Cantor, drew on that tradition when he wrote to Franklin Roosevelt in 1932 that the actors were "patriotic Americans," aligned against "monopolistic tyrants" and financial "buccaneers." No longer could the actors remain powerless before those who took "oppressive measures in their race for power." Rather, to recover their "American birthright," the performers had to form their own organization, for as Cantor wrote, "When the millenium comes the lion may lie down with the lamb, but in the present the Guild thinks it indiscreet of the lamb to lie down with the lion."[14]

Along with juxtaposing American democracy and monopoly capital, the Guild leaders also modernized the republican tradition. Formerly the dominant middle classes rejected urban ethnics, and actors were considered outsiders and were even excluded from respectable graveyards. Yet in an industry of young people that dramatized cultural mixing and moral experimentation, over 25 percent of the Guild members were foreign born, and at least that many probably came from immigrant backgrounds. In advancing a new middle-class identity rooted in upwardly mobile immigrants and minorities, Guild writers would condemn racial and ethnic exclusionism, equating it with European fascism. "Scratch an anti-Semite, anti-Catholic or anti-Negro," commented one cartoon, "and you will find an enemy of labor." Similarly, female board members like Gale Sondergaard argued for women's emancipation; and leaders from racial minorities or ethnic backgrounds, like Lena Horne, Eddie Cantor, George Murphy, Ronald Reagan, and James Cagney, looked to the Guild to legitimize the new peoples as the source of a more vibrant and productive industry. When, for example, a producer was assured that if he signed a contract with the Guild, the "Rich" brothers, a comedy team noted for its zaniness and tardiness, would be required to "show up on time," he immediately said "I'll sign."[15]

Guild members also sought to legitimize another worrisome aspect of middle-class life: consumerism. Instead of seeing affluence as the province of the rich or as a threat to the work ethic, Guild leaders identified unionization with the attainment of affluence and national prosperity. The Guild press was thus filled with ads for slick cars endorsed by stars like Bing Crosby, along with promotions for recruitment picnics, rodeos, fairs, and "gambols of the stars" at local cabarets, where on one occasion members auctioned off Franklin Roosevelt's hat to support the Guild's retirement home. At these festivities, the members would support unionizing drives in the California fields, and the actors' magazine ran endorsements of local and national firms that employed union workers. At the same time, famous members had their own radio shows and appeared in specials sponsored by unions to "make the needs of labor articulate." Others attended parties at the White House for the president's birthday, and sponsored exhibits at world's fairs to "sell" unionization. In 1936, the SAG president, Robert Montgomery, captured the playful quality of these activities when, on the birth of his son, he wrote under the infant's byline:

Since my advent into this world at the Cedars of Lebanon Hospital, I have in my small way done a certain amount of work which may be of interest to you. I have organized the children in the nursery into the Junior Guild and we have now pickets outside the door bearing placards "Cedar of

*The Guild's affirmation
of ethnic and racial
pluralism as the new
code of labor and the
nation. Screen Actor.
September 1944. Cour-
tesy Screen Actor's
Guild.*

An ad for union mobilizing and fun merges the appeal of Hollywood, the stars, and labor. Screen Guild Magazine, *May 1933. Courtesy Screen Actor's Guild.*

A typical ad in the Guild press identifies the star with consumerism. Next to these would often be articles on Guild boycotts and activities: the desire for consumerism thus was a spur rather than a hindrance to labor organizing. Screen Guild Magazine, *November 1937. Courtesy Screen Actor's Guild.*

Lebanon nurses are unfair to union babies." You may be interested to learn that we discovered a child who claimed to be related to a producer in the motion picture business. We took care of him![16]

Such a merger of play and the serious business of politics had wider implications. Not only did these activities elevate class conflict above ethnic or racial divisions, but they also generated public rituals that united diverse groups behind that common cause. Nowhere was that better dramatized than in the Los Angeles Labor Day Parade of 1937. After a moribund period, the event was revived by New Dealers as a major civic activity. Preparations saw the union press running photos of Franklin Roosevelt, with captions explaining that the president was "loved by labor for the enemies he has made." Next came a cartoon proclaiming that high wages provided the purchasing power to realize mass consumption and an article explaining that the Screen Actor's Guild was "going to the limit to contribute all the fanfare of show business at its command." On the big day, it "stole the show" with cars carrying Robert Montgomery, Edward Arnold, and "Brother" Eddie Cantor; with floats carrying "bathing beauties" serenaded by a swing band; with "cowboys and Indians" rider groups; with marchers dressed in native garb from Eastern Europe, the South Seas, Africa, the East Indies, and China. Along the way, an actor dressed as Abraham Lincoln proclaimed that workers deserved the fruits of their labor, and others dressed as Popeye and the Keystone Cops chased away "scabs." At the end of the march, the local mayor led a crowd estimated at "300,000 strong" in singing the *Star Spangled Banner*, and newspaper reporters observed that the marchers were "irresistibly headed for victory over the forces that have so long blocked the way."[17]

As this march to victory suggests, the Guild was also aligned with a diverse coalition of political groups in Hollywood and the nation. Within the film capital, the performers had to organize not only against the producers, but also against a gangster-dominated craft, the International Association of Studio and Stage Employees (IA). Given the outsider status of labor before the New Deal era, the IA emerged within the AFL, where it was the policy to organize the skilled workers in bureaucratic unions far removed from the unskilled and the middle classes. The Hollywood union was also dominated by gangsters who received payoffs from producers to keep wages low and the majority of workers unorganized and divided by race or national origin. In response, Guild leaders worked to put the gangster leadership in jail and supported the efforts of an ex-boxer and painter, Herbert Sorrell, to organize the craftsmen, office workers, and female secretaries into the Conference of Studio Unions (CSU).[18] The Guild and CSU press drew on common interest as well as the politics of popular culture. The CSU held beauty contests to choose the "Sweetheart of the Picket Line," complete with secretaries in short-shorts posing for glamour photos, like the chorus girls at Earl Carroll's local cabaret. Strikers, in turn, maintained morale though jitterbugging to swing music. When asked why he was so militant, Sorrell answered, so his "happy bunch of kids" could dress like the stars.[19]

Yet no matter how distinct these innovations were to the local atmosphere, they also brought the Hollywood insurgents squarely into alliances with radical unions and left-wing organizations all across the country. No doubt the most important was the Congress of Industrial Organizations (CIO), dedicated to forming all mass-production workers into an alliance against capital, and the American Communist Party. Despite the fact that the Guild and the CSU drew on a republican tradition hostile to Marxism, and remained within the AFL, they were often allied with the CIO, and party members were a minority in the unions and guilds. A host of issues might divide the CSU and Guild from local party members, ranging from a disdain for secrecy, strike tactics, proper democratic procedures, and respect for religion. But in their common commitment to an antimonopoly tradition and insurgent labor, the Guild would often condemn the producer's and the IA's "red baiting" by arguing that it was "un-American" and "fascist." And when these two enemies attacked the Longshoremen's Union for keeping "scab" actors off location sets, the Guild typically praised that Communist-influenced union because they believed in "solidarity . . . regardless of apparent immediate advantages":

In the long run the slogan "one for all, all for one" is the proper guide for union action. Following this line of action they have built one of the strongest labor organizations in America. They have eradicated gangster control, raised wages, shortened hours and elevated the spirit of their men not only educating them into the important role they are playing in their locality but making them conscious of their duty to aid American labor in its progressive march.[20]

The Los Angeles union press wrote of the Guild's participation in Labor Day parades and ran this cartoon dramatizing the new way to prosperity. The Los Angeles Citizen, *July 1937. Courtesy Special Collections, University of California at Los Angeles.*

The officers of the Guild, Robert Montgomery and Chester Morris, participate in the 1937 Los Angeles Labor Day parade. The event symbolized the convergence of the star, the middle class, and labor insurgency in the Great Depression. Screen Guild Magazine, September 1937. Courtesy Screen Actor's Guild.

The veterans division of SAG in the 1937 Los Angeles Labor Day parade, followed by the Chinese and Slovakian floats and band of the Guild. Screen Guild Magazine, September 1937. Courtesy Screen Actor's Guild.

Finally and most strikingly, the coming of the war was not the
end but the realization of the culture and politics pioneered in
the thirties. With the United States and the Soviet Union allied
against the Axis powers, the new unions, the Communist Party,
and Hollywood were united in a progressive march against the
fascists abroad. Yet, in contrast to its stance in World War I,
Hollywood did not dramatize that unity by portraying an Anglo-
Saxon people hostile to the immigrants and modern morals.
Rather, the most popular production of the war, *This is the
Army*, starring the current and future presidents of the Guild,
George Murphy and Ronald Reagan, celebrated a rejuvenated
America grounded in consumption, ethnicity, and racial harmony. Consistent with the merger of the star's image to real life,
Guild members enlisted in the armed services and toured on
bond drives; and their magazine pictured the world's seven conti-
nents with a caption explaining that a "public once limited to the
physical capacity of a single theatre has expanded through film
and radio to global proportions."[21]

What is more, many saw the lessons of wartime Hollywood
providing the basis for the postwar era as well. The significance
of these lessons, however, was a matter of some dispute. To business leaders like Eric Johnston, the new leader of the Motion
Picture Producers Association, the war seemed to offer the possibilities of abundance through class collaboration rather than
class confrontation. And as part of a group of liberal businessmen and politicians endorsing Henry Luce's vision of an "American Century," Johnston argued in books like *America Unlimited*
(1943) that the war had accomplished what the unpatriotic and
"class rhetoric" of CIO and New Deal leaders had not: transformed businessmen from incompetent, selfish buccaneers and
unleashed the prosperity and military strength to ward off aggression. In the future, he called on businessmen and unions
to affirm the welfare state and construct an international order
grounded in free trade and hostility to Communist Russia. The
result would restore economic growth and the American mission.
As he explained:

> The real breeding ground of Communism is in the slums. It is
> everywhere where people have not enough to eat or enough
> to wear through no fault of their own. Communism hunts
> misery, feeds on misery and profits by it. Freedoms walk

hand in hand with abundance. That has been the history of America. It has been the American story. It turned the eyes of the world to America, because America gave reality to freedom, plus abundance when it was an idle daydream in the rest of the world.[22]

To many inheritors of the radical New Deal tradition in Hollywood and the country, however, the call for national consensus rooted in corporate power was anathema. Indeed the eruption after the war of a massive strike wave sparked by the CIO and other unions testified that Johnston's ideas were being deeply contested. Particularly in the film capital the insurgents were led by Herb Sorrell and CSU members, who gained inspiration from the "Century of the Common Man" speech given by Franklin Roosevelt's former vice president Henry Wallace. Unlike Johnston, Wallace saw national identity rooted in antimonopoly traditions, and he called for cooperation with the Soviet Union. And when Sorrell demanded more control of the shop floor, a guaranteed annual wage, and more participation by workers in management decisions, the producers locked the CSU out of the studios in a jurisdictional dispute. Predictably, Johnston saw Sorrell's desire to realize democracy in the world of work and production as un-American, leading him to lament that "you cannot have a healthy body with a sick heart . . . and certainly the heart of this industry in Hollywood is not functioning today."[23]

Undoubtedly, the balance of power lay with the Guild. As *Fortune* magazine observed, the "actors are the only workers in Hollywood who can shut the studios down tight by simply rolling over in bed and refusing to get up for work."[24] Yet as Johnston saw it, the stars were at the center of more than a labor dispute. As he posed the issue in speech after speech, at stake was nothing less than a struggle to reorient national politics and symbols. Would the exemplars of a rising "new middle class" country continue to identify with a militant New Deal tradition of antimonopoly that juxtaposed democracy and capitalism? Or would the stars in the most well-publicized industry in the country support the reformed IA and the producers, helping to make Hollywood a model of the new political consensus, with all its implications for postwar politics and the popular culture?

By no means was the answer clear in 1946. In choosing which side to support the Guild members knew that their most formidable political and cultural ally had been Herbert Sorrell. Yet Johnston was also aware that the class conflicts erupting within the Guild had made the leaders more receptive to an alliance with business. That began when the Guild and other union leaders joined war industry boards enforcing wage and price controls. Yet the same leaders also experienced wildcat strikes from members whose wages did not keep up with inflation. In Hollywood this surfaced within the Guild when the extras demanded a renegotiation of their contract.[25] When the leaders refused, the extras successfully petitioned the government to secede and received a charter from none other than Sorrell, who was organizing other workers who felt "left out" of the wartime prosperity. In response, the board dismissed hundreds of "incorrigibles" and organized their own loyal extras' group. Meanwhile, the Guild's chief consul, Kenneth Thomson, came close to getting into a fistfight with the dissidents' leader in court and wrote a report that the new extras' union was a "Frankenstein monster" that could "destroy" us.[26]

The monster, of course, did not destroy the Guild. Yet the eruption of class conflict within the Guild did force the leadership into an unprecedented alliance with corporate elites represented by Johnston and conservative union leaders. As late as 1945 the leadership helped Sorrell win a Hollywood strike. But by 1946 the board formed an extras' union loyal to SAG. Then the Guild leaders secured a charter for that group from the reform leader of the IA, Roy Brewer.[27] Shortly thereafter, Brewer and Johnston asked the Guild to support a lock-out of the militants. The minutes of that secret meeting show that despite the unwillingness of a vocal minority to back the proposal, the executives found that it would be "hard to refuse" in light of the former enemies' "unsolicited support in the extras dispute." Collusion among the three was vehemently denied in subsequent congressional investigations, but the result was that Sorrell's members were locked out of the studios, Brewer's men took their jobs, and the actors and actresses crossed the picket lines.[28] Within days, the strikers initiated a national boycott of the stars' films, symbolizing the unraveling of a cultural and political alliance that had lasted for over a decade.[29]

Domestic Anti-Communism and Cultural Conversion

Little of this makes sense unless we explore the meaning behind these events within the long-term aims of the Guild. Ever since the thirties, the SAG had two overlapping goals. It was, on the one hand, a union that revived traditional, antimonopoly traditions to justify its class struggles and alliance with labor unions

across the country. As that movement merged with the larger
politics of the New Deal, it also had an equally powerful cultural
goal; namely, to make unions, ethnics, and the new morality
spread by mass culture a legitimate part of American life. The
great expansion of the economy in the war effort, and the emphasis on consumption and the new culture as the heart of the American way, served to accomplish the cultural side of these efforts.
At the same time, however, the mobilization of the Guild and
other unions into the defense effort, coupled to the rise of wildcat
strikes, served to undercut the leaders' commitment to the politics of antimonopoly and class conflict. Aware that it still had to
show that Hollywood, despite its identification with outsiders,
was loyal, the Guild was desperate to find some understandable
way of sanctioning the new state of affairs and converting its
members from their old hostility to capitalism.

What allowed the new allies to transform the ideology that
bound rank-and-file Guild members to the CSU was the rise of
anti-Communism as the most important issue in domestic politics. The politics of subversion, of course, were not new. A short-
lived "red scare" arose after World War I, expressing the dislike
of the small-propertied, Anglo-Saxon middle class, as well as the
AFL leaders, for radical unions, minority groups, and city life.
During the thirties, conservatives helped form the House Un-
American Activities Committee (HUAC), which investigated
Communism in labor unions, especially the radical CIO. When
the congressmen came to Hollywood, they found support among
some producers and the IA, but generally the industry leaders
and the Guilds roundly condemned the committee. In the name
of a democratic tradition hostile to monopoly and political corruption, satires of "red baiting" and support for the Soviet Union
occurred in several major films, all the way from *Front Page* to
Mission to Moscow.[30]

Yet as the Cold War began abroad, domestic anti-Communism took on unprecedented power. What intervened, of course,
was not just hostility with the Soviet Union, but the legacy of
World War II at home. The vast mobilization of the population
between 1941 and 1945 led to the internment of Japanese-Ameri-
cans and the expansion of a national security state which initiated loyalty questionnaires in the Guilds. And now that the
foreign enemy was a country hostile to capitalism, conservatives
as well as IA leaders gained new support for their argument that
the CSU was part of a "foreign plot" to take over the movies and
Hollywood unions for Soviet ends. Compromise was equivalent to

A cartoon from the CSU News, December 1946, dramatizes the republican antimonopoly tradition that formerly held the Guild and its allies together. Note the Motion Picture Producers' Association as a mudslinger manipulated by a fat capitalist banker and assisted by "Greed," the "Paid Press," and "Goonism." Herbert Sorrell Collection, Special Collections, University of California at Los Angeles.

The CSU dramatizes its national boycott of the stars in the 1946 strike, an act which symbolized the split between the insurgents and the Guild that had lasted since the late thirties.

Herbert Sorrell Collection, Special Collections. University of California, Los Angeles.

appeasement at "Munich" and unpreparedness at "Pearl Harbor." And when asked what to do with the CSU, the attorney for the IA, Mathew Levy, drew on the precedent of Japanese internment as an apt model. Though his own immigrant, Socialist, and Jewish background might have cautioned his advocacy of concentration camps, he told members of the Congress:

> If I were the producers, I would isolate them . . . for my own protection, just as America isolated the Japanese when the war started. Just as I hope the FBI will isolate the Communists if we ever get into trouble again.[31]

What made postwar anti-Communism so effective in the film capital, however, was that it was not just a paranoid, negative doctrine. Unlike in the past, the doctrine preached by Eric Johnston was part of a reform effort promising an escape from the crisis of twentieth-century life. As part of a liberal coalition of businessmen and politicians supporting Henry Luce's call for a "New American Century," Johnston made it clear that he was not hostile to unions or to the new ethnic Americans. Instead he was a corporate reformer who saw that the innovations of the war years—the break from Anglo-Saxon exclusiveness, the rise of the welfare state and unions—provided the foundation for a new world order grounded in capitalist expansion. If Americans and radical unions nationwide shed antimonopoly attacks, the ensuing policies would make real the abundant American dream pioneered by Hollywood in the Depression and war years. In converting the country to that ideal, Johnston also saw that Hollywood had a major role. As he explained, the greatest means of communication today is the motion "picture . . . the only thing to stop Russia from expanding is force, not necessarily physical force, but the force of an ideal. America," he added, "has that ideal in democratic capitalism and the motion picture industry with its huge audience around the world can be a potent factor in explaining America."[32]

Nowhere were the implications of that promise better illustrated than in the rise of Ronald Reagan to undisputed leadership of the Guild in 1947. As the president of the IA, Roy Brewer, phrased it in reference to purging Hollywood of Communism, "there has been no one more effective in the effort to rid the industry of this menace that Ronald Reagan." Like most of the Guild membership making the transition from the depression to the war years, Reagan was a New Dealer, a loyalty he also inherited from his father, who was a small businessman and Midwestern Irish Catholic. Coming to the film capital, Ronald performed in the most pro-Roosevelt of all the studios, Warner Brothers, and worked to advance the dream of a revitalized middle-class culture advanced by the Guild. Since that American ethos ran counter to monopoly, as late as 1945 Reagan could be found in organizations supporting an insurgent New Deal tradition, militant labor, and the CSU.

Yet Reagan was also different from those of the founding generation. His arrival in Hollywood in 1937 meant that he missed the great organizing drives of the thirties; indeed, he joined only after the Guild's closed-shop agreements made it virtually mandatory. Nor did he rise to leadership by mobilizing mass support of the membership. Rather, he was appointed to the board and later the presidency, where he ran unopposed through the early fifties. Even more important, like Johnston and the newer members, he saw the vision of a rejuvenated, affluent America realized less in the union struggles of the thirties than in the business-labor cooperation of the war years. The advent of the conflict saw him dramatizing the dream of a more secure and powerful nation in *This is the Army*, volunteering as an army officer, advocating loyalty questionnaires with the Guild, and serving as the board's representative to the American Veteran's Committee. Then, as the extras conflict erupted, as the Cold War started, as Johnston preached a new American Century, Reagan became an undercover agent for the FBI and dropped his involvements in progressive groups or "Communist fronts," seeing them as tools of the enemy. "I learned my lesson, the bulk of Communist work is done by people who are sucked into carrying out red policy without knowing what they are doing."[33]

As Reagan converted, anti-Communism became part of a struggle to "bring about the regeneration of the world I believed should have automatically appeared following the war." In seeking to realize the new America promised by Johnston and other postwar liberals, Reagan first served on a commission to arbitrate the CSU conflict, and ended up giving a major speech persuading Guild members to cross the picket lines of the CSU. Shortly thereafter, when the extras legitimately complained that the board was dominated by actors who had become producers, the top leadership resigned and Reagan was appointed to the presidency. In this vacuum, the executive secretary, Jack Dales, recalled that Reagan not only "disliked the extras tremendously," but he fought "his own people . . . the pro-Russian Americans."[34]

He condemned the supporters of the CSU in the Guild as "foreign dictators" who would "enslave people" and helped streamline its democratic procedures so that power over meetings and petitions was much more centralized in the hands of the leaders.[35]

At the same time, the elimination of class conflict within the Guild overlapped with efforts to build a national consensus. By 1947 the New Deal loyalists Reagan and Roy Brewer of the IA helped Johnston create the Motion Picture Industry Council (MPIC), which they publicized as a model of the cooperative spirit possible between management and labor.[36] Then as the Democratic Party split in 1948 and Henry Wallace ran on the Progressive ticket, Reagan and Brewer formed a local chapter of Americans for Democratic Action and an AFL film council. Together with Johnston they attacked Wallace and his Progressive Party as a "fifth column" that like Chamberlain at Munich would encourage appeasement with the Soviet Union.[37] Sorrell and the remnants of the Communist Party responded by mobilizing in support of Wallace and his "Century of the Common Man" notables like Orson Welles, Charles Chaplin, Katharine Hepburn, and Paul Robeson. But as political and labor radicals were defeated, the film director Abraham Polansky caught the essence of these events when he recalled that the main battle in the "country was a struggle within the trade unions. . . . That struggle," he noted,

> was enormous and its consequences were fatal because it
> made it possible for McCarthy to operate against people who
> had lost their allies. Because the main political allies for the
> artistic and intellectual movement had been, of course,
> the organized trade unions, with all the alliances around the
> bourgeoisie so to speak.[38]

Yet as Polansky pointed out, this was not politics as usual. Rather, the efforts to transform the radical legacy of the New Deal in Hollywood merged directly with the most well-publicized event of the era, the arrival in 1947 of HUAC in the film capital. In fact, so well have investigators covered the subsequent blacklisting of writers and artists like Polansky that it is possible to miss the way hearings provided a stage for building a new American Way. True, Communist writers known as the Hollywood Ten were discovered and sent to jail. Yet their subversion was endlessly associated with the ideologies of class conflict that were presumably disloyal to the United States, namely the radicalism of the CSU and the CIO. In a period of Cold War, such ideas, as Johnston pointed out, were "foreign" to "American Civilization," and its adherents were irrational "crackpots" under the influence of a delusion. Characteristically, a congressman questioning Sorrell remarked, "I was beginning to wonder, whether the Communists would find a better champion of their cause, and if you were not doing a pretty good job outside the party." Sorrell, an ardent and outspoken patriot, replied, "Well, I'll be damned."[39]

Given that the crusaders sought to discredit an antimonopoly tradition that had sustained many Americans' democratic identity for over a century, Sorrell and the CSU were truly damned. Yet to dramatize the conversion to a new consensus, Reagan, Brewer, and the MPIC demanded of those who wanted to work again highly publicized confessions. A prime example was the noted director Edward Dmytryck's interview for the *Saturday Evening Post*. On the first page was a photo of Dmytryck holding a newspaper with the headline, "Trial Board Convicts Sorrell." As the story unfolds, the author tells of being discriminated against because of his immigrant roots. In response he joined progressive causes, which because they were hostile to capitalism provided the breeding ground for Communist subversion. From there he joined the Communist Party in World War II, but afterward realized that abundance and racial acceptance would come only through the American Way of class cooperation and economic growth.[40]

Once this process began, there could be no end to it. After all, the industry was being investigated not just from within, but from without by traditional groups who saw much of Hollywood as suspect. As a result the reformed guilds asked for voluntary confessions to the MPIC to ward off mistaken identity, a process exemplified in a letter that arrived at the Guild in January of 1953.[41] Written in response to a complaint by Nancy Davis, an executive at Columbia Studios apologized to the new Mrs. Ronald Reagan for unfortunately being denied work because she had the same maiden name as a woman who had signed a petition supporting free speech for the Hollywood Ten. The executive explained: "As you are aware we make a check on all actors, writers, directors being considered for employment. This is a regular routine. This investigation is made by a reputable organization in New York City." Despite the fact that a mistake had been made, "I question whether your criticism of the organization that checks for us is justified. Of course we could have taken it for granted that the wife of Ronald Reagan could not be of questionable loyalty, and we could have disregarded the report." Yet he went on to say that since many in Hollywood were known for their former radicalism, they could not trust appearances. Although Nancy Reagan drew on her husband's support to prove her innocence, others were not so lucky. As the executive secretary of the Guild, Jack Dales recalled years later:

> What I have debated about since is that so many people were tarred by that brush who I don't think should have been now. . . . Even at the time, I'm saying my doubts came to the fore. I was not Ronnie Reagan or Roy Brewer. . . . I would argue about how far we were going, particularly when it got to be this clearing depot, you know, for work. I think people who were terribly, unfairly treated, like Larry Parks, Marsha Hunt, who had viewpoints that were different from the majority of the Board members, but they were far from Communist agents. . . . They were just strong liberal people who took their lumps. . . . The producers carried it to ridiculous extremes and we did not stand up fairly to call a fair line. A line should have been called.[42]

A line was so difficult to draw because the crusaders were also transforming a popular culture that many had identified with the promise of a new American culture. Yet in the postwar era, Eric Johnston minced no words in explaining that films were now an agent of foreign policy. To ensure that movies shed gangster and populist ideals that might be interpreted as Communistic, Johnston, Brewer, and Reagan helped distribute a new film code. Written by Ayn Rand, a *Screen Guide for Americans* preached "Don't smear the free-enterprise system," "Don't deify the common man," "Don't show that poverty is a virtue . . . and failure is noble." Indeed, now the "nobility" of the "little people" was the "drooling of weaklings," and the screen had to show American heroes moving up the social ladder, solving problems through individual will. In such an atmosphere, Frank Capra, an enormously popular artist noted for dramatizing the "little peoples' " antagonism to monopoly, found his security clearance taken away. Likewise, a writer whose work for years had featured American heroes whose "fortune and happiness were threatened by a banker holding a mortgage over their heads," suddenly found these themes unmarketable.[43]

Similar pressures altered the image of the stars as well. No

longer did the Guild advocate vast parades supporting labor organizing, publish a magazine with ads calling for boycotts of
nonunion firms, praise radio shows in defense of labor, or mobi-
lize the members in vast public gatherings. Rather, a reporter
found that "many stars are worried that the public might have
received a very wrong impression about them, because of having
seen them portray, say, a legendary hero who stole from the rich
to give to the poor, or an honest, crusading district attorney, or a
lonely, poetic, antisocial gangster." "We've got to resolve any
conflicts," an actor remarked in 1948, "between what we are and
what the public has been led to believe we are. We can't afford to
have people think we're a band of strong men or crusaders."

The Guild nourished this trend by trying much of the stars'
élan to private rather than public life. A striking example of the
new thinking was a series of standardized speeches produced by
the Guild promoting the Hollywood celebrity as a symbol of a
family life unfolding in the suburbs. As such, the stars' charisma,
their glamour or ethnic roots or lower-class manners still represented a break from the stuffy styles of Victorianism. But their
vernacular and common touch was no longer vital for questioning
established institutions. Rather, their democratic personalities
reinvigorated a benevolent corporate consensus, focused on a
consumer-oriented home and children as a bulwark against communism. Listening to Ronald Reagan describe the transformation of Hollywood, a reporter from his hometown newspaper
recorded:

> Dutch gave a stirring defense of his new home town, Holly-
> wood. He compared it with other cities in America and
> pointed out that it leads the nation in church attendance on a
> per capita basis; that its schools are among the best in the
> nation; that the divorce rate in Hollywood is far below the
> national average. . . . He explained that it was only a few
> years ago that some churches wouldn't even bury an actor.
> That attitude he explained has changed today, because the
> film actors, unlike the thespians of old, now settle in one
> place, build homes, raise their children, attend school and
> churches and become part of the community. "You certainly
> couldn't expect an actor to live out of a trunk to do that."[44]

Yet the very success of these efforts to identify Hollywood
with status quo might well have killed the goose that laid the
golden egg. In striking contrast to the thirties and war years, pro-

ducers in 1947 found that box-office receipts fell dramatically, and membership in the Guild dropped from 7,898 in 1946 to 6,533 in 1949. Part of this erosion was due to the rise of television. But it was not until 1950 that even 10 percent of American families had receivers.[45] A more plausible explanation is that long before 1950 the anti-Communists destroyed the essence of mass culture's appeal, its linkage to a free social space, outside power and authority. The Hollywood reformers blacklisted writers and actors, pressured filmmakers to alter plots, and prevented the distribution of "undesirable" films, such as *Salt of the Earth*.[46] They also attacked major box-office attractions like John Garfield and Charles Chaplin, who gained success in films critical of established power. Both supported CSU rallies, refused to cross CSU picket lines, and backed Henry Wallace. Yet in the Cold War era these activities led to FBI investigations and to American Legion and IA boycotts of Chaplin's films. Shortly before the great clown left the country to avoid appearing before HUAC, Roy Brewer justified these actions:

> Mr. Chaplin has shown nothing but contempt for America and her institutions. His most recent statements that Hollywood has succumbed to thought control so far as I am concerned confirm the fact that his thinking is still in the Communist orbit of influence. This is strictly party line. . . . Nothing he has said or done would justify our assuming that he is on our side in this fight. Until we get such assurances, we are justified in resisting any further efforts to add to his fortune or influence.[47]

Today of course America's lovable tramp lies buried in Europe, and the Guild president became President of the United States, even appointing the IA leader Roy Brewer to a high post in the Labor Department. Given that Hollywood gave Reagan and Brewer their political baptism, what conclusions can we draw from these events? By now it should be clear that far from being an industry representing traditional America, Hollywood was at the center of a contest to determine the future of politics and national identity in the postwar era. The industry attracted such attention because ever since the teens it used the mass media to dramatize a revitalized middle-class life rooted in consumerism. Yet when that promise collapsed in the Depression, the stars aligned with workers in a radical labor movement dedicated to redistributing wealth and power. Drawing on the innovations unfolding in mass culture, and reconstructing an older republican tradition hostile to capitalism, the Guild leaders created a New Deal politics intent on realizing a new nationalism rooted in a welfare state, ethnicity, and consumption. The apolitical process of defense mobilization in World War II brought the cultural side of that promise to fulfillment, while wildcat strikes within the Guild brought the leadership into a closer relationship with big business.

Given the rise of the United States to world power, elitists like Eric Johnston sought to identify the corporate order with the realization of the new American culture pioneered in Hollywood. In the process, he worked to transform a New Deal tradition hostile to monopoly and to generate the support for economic and military expansion abroad. As the Cold War unfolded, as domestic anti-Communism served to discredit militant labor unions, the stars celebrated a cultural consensus where democracy was found less in the workplace than in a privatized consumer realm, open to ethnics and centered in the new middle classes. Small wonder that when the economic growth that promised to end wars and depressions appeared to be breaking down in the late sixties and seventies, Ronald Reagan should leave Hollywood to revitalize the "democratic capitalism" he had helped to create. A reporter interviewing the former Guild leader during his successful run for the presidency in 1980 found that these earlier events were still very much on his mind:

> Reagan, with no prompting from me, in what seems in fact to be a compulsive non sequitur, had resurrected events that took place some thirty years earlier, his wounds still raw and his hatred of the enemy unyielding. Most curious of all is that his view of the Soviet menace today is so deeply colored by events that took place in Hollywood more than a generation ago, as if today's Soviet government were simply the Hollywood communists projected on a larger screen.

Frank testimony, indeed, that the contest unfolding in postwar Hollywood continues to influence our lives.[48]

Notes

1.
Ronald Reagan and Richard C. Hubler, Where's the Rest of Me (New York: Dell Publishing, 1981), pp. 162–164, 189. Abraham Polansky, "How the Blacklist Worked in Hollywood," Film Culture 50–51 (Fall 1970), p. 44; Eric Johnston, We're All In It (New York: E. P. Dutton and Company, 1948), p. 69.

2.
Eric Johnston, "Utopia is Production," Screen Actor 14 (April 1946), p. 7, and (August 1946), pp. 14–15. For a full exposition of these ideas, see Eric Johnston, America Unlimited (Garden City, NJ, 1942). For Johnston's background see "Eric Johnston, 66, President's Aide Dies," New York Times, August 23, 1963; Karl Schriftgiesser, Business Comes of Age: The Story of the Committee for Economic Development and Its Impact upon the Economic Policies of the United States, 1942–1960 (New York: Harper and Brothers, 1960), pp. 13, 23, 73–75. For an insightful contemporary observation on the ideology of the "New American Century" advocated by Johnston and Henry Luce, see Dwight Macdonald, "The (American) People's Century," Partisan Review 9 (July–August 1942), pp. 295–310.

3.
The most valuable analysis of the national strikes can be found in George Lipsitz, Class and Culture in Cold War America: A Rainbow at Midnight (New York: Praeger, 1983), and Nelson Lichtenstein, Labor's War at Home: The CIO in World War II (New York: Cambridge University Press, 1983), pp. 210–245. On the Hollywood variant, see Anthony Dawson, "Hollywood's Labor Troubles," Industrial Labor Relations Review 1 (July 1948); pp. 638–647; Jeffrey Goodman, "Hollywood Local," The Sky's No Limit (Summer 1982); Life (October 14, 1946), pp. 29–33; Garry Wills, Reagan's America: Innocents At Home (Garden City, NY: Doubleday and Company, 1987), pp. 231–241.

4.
See, for example, William E. Leuchtenburg, Franklin Roosevelt and the New Deal: 1932–1940 (New York: Harper and Row, 1955); David Montgomery, Workers' control in America: Studies in the history of work, technology and labor struggles (New York: Cambridge University Press, 1979), pp. 153–181; Godfrey Hodgson, America in Our Time: From World War II to Nixon: What Happened and Why (New York: Random House, 1976), pp. 3–134; and Alonzo Hamby, Beyond the New Deal (New York: Columbia University Press, 1973).

5.
The most influential statement is in Warren Susman, Culture as History: The Transformation of American Society in the 20th Century (New York: Pantheon, 1984), pp. 150–211.

6.
For example, see Larry Ceplair and Steven Englund, The Inquisition in Hollywood: Politics in the Film Community, 1930–1960 (Berkeley: University of California Press, 1985); Victor S. Navasky, Naming Names (New York: Viking Press, 1980); Nancy Lynn Schwartz, The Hollywood Writers's Wars (New York: Knopf, 1982). For an overview of the literature and an analysis that stresses the importance of the film content to the red scare in Hollywood, see Thom

Andersen, "Red Hollywood," in Suzanne Ferguson and Barbara Groseclose, eds., Literature and the Visual Arts in Contemporary Society (Columbus: Ohio State University Press, 1986), pp. 141–196.

7.
Dore Schary, "Star System," speech to Hollywood Athletic Club, November 12, 1953, Screen Actor's Guild Files. Schary, a noted producer, referred specifically to the stars of the thirties. See also Lary May, Screening Out the Past: The Birth of Mass Culture and the Motion Picture Industry (Chicago: University of Chicago Press, 1983) and Roy Rosenzweig, Eight Hours for What We Will: Workers and Leisure in An Industrial City, 1870–1920 (New York: Cambridge University Press, 1983), pp. 191–230.

8.
Eric Johnston, American Unlimited (New York: Doubleday and Company, 1942), pp. 233–234. May, Screening, pp. 147–241. Budd Schulberg, Moving Pictures (New York: Stein and Day, 1981), p. 136.

9.
Lary May, with the assistance of Stephan

Lassonde, "Making the American Way: Moderne Theatres, Audiences and the Film Industry, 1929–1945," Prospects (May 1987). "Hollywood Turns to Personal Appearances," Motion Picture Herald (November 11, 1939), p. 13.

10.
For an example of Hollywood critics praising the new type films, see especially Dorothy Tree, "History of the Actor," a four-part series that ran in Screen Actor (July, August, September, and October 1943). This is the journal for the Screen Actor's Guild (hereafter cited as SA). For the general pattern, see Peter Roffman and Jim Purdy, The Hollywood Social Problem Film: Madness, Despair and Politics from the Depression to the Fifties (Bloomington: Indiana University Press, 1981).

11.
Movie directors were 8 to 1, executives 5 to 1, actors 7 to 1, and laborers 8 to 1 for Roosevelt in 1936. The poll was taken by the Hollywood Reporter, October 8, 1936. On the heavy proportion of the industry coming from immigrant and city backgrounds, see May, Screening, pp. 169–176, 188–190. On the total work force,

see Leo C. Rosten, Hollywood: The Movie Colony, The Movie Makers (New York: Harcourt and Brace, 1941), p. 373. On AFL ties, see "The Guild and the Labor Movement: A First Lesson on the Guild's Active Association with a Nation-wide Organization of Some Four Million American Trade Unionists," Screen Guild Magazine (July 1936), pp. 4–5.

12.
Rosten, Hollywood, pp. 381–394; "The Guild and the Labor Movement," pp. 4–5; "Actors Become Data," SA (December 1940), pp. 13–15.

13.
Two earlier works covered Hollywood unionization: see Murray Ross, Stars and Strikes: Unionization of Hollywood (New York: Columbia University Press, 1941) and Louis B. Perry and Richard S. Perry, A History of the Los Angeles Labor Movement, 1911–1941 (Berkeley: University of California Press, 1963). For a contemporary account that draws on these two books and incorrectly argues that the Guild was conservative and only a means for maintaining stars' high salaries, see Wills, Innocents At Home, pp. 215–223. Nunnally

Johnson, "American Epic," SA (August 1934), p. 4; Fred Keating, "Are We Laborers? Under Conditions of Modern Economic Society Motion Picture Actors Are Laborers Whether They Admit It or Not," The Screen Guild Magazine (August 1934), pp. 4, 18–21.

14.
Frank Scully, "Is the Middle Class in the Middle?" SA (December 1936), pp. 8–9. Anonymous, " 'I Am An Individual': Thinking Things Through, an Artist Reveals That Being an 'Individual' is Not All it's Cracked Up to Be," SA (January 1936), p. 5. Eddie Cantor, "What the Guild Stands for . . . ," The Screen Player (March 1934), p. 2; "The Wire to President Roosevelt and the Executive Order," The Screen Player (May 15, 1933), pp. 4, 16; "Text of Eddie Cantor's Speech at Annual Meeting," The Screen Player (May 15, 1934), pp. 1, 12; Editors, "The Menace of the Academy," The Screen Player (April 15, 1934); Minutes of the Board of Directors, August, 1933, March 1, 1937, and April 15, 1937, Screen Actor's Guild Records, Los Angeles, California (hereafter cited as Min-

utes). The literature on the republican tradition is vast. For summary of the arguments and appropriate scholarly literature, see Sara M. Evans and Harry C. Boyte, Free Spaces: The Sources of Democratic Change in America (New York: Harper & Row, 1986), pp. 1–25.

15.
For a general account of actors' outsider status, see Jean-Christophe Agnew, Worlds Apart: The Market and the Theatre in Anglo-American Thought (New York: Cambridge University Press, 1986), pp. 101–149. The Carnegie study only asked on its questionnaires who was foreign born; see Rosten, Hollywood, p. 335. For recollections of parental backgrounds by Guild leaders, see Jack Dales, SAG Oral History Interview, June 1979; Gail Sondergarrd, SAG Oral History Interviews, June 12, 1979; Robert Montgomery, SAG Oral History Interview, August 1979: For the Rich Brothers and actors' exclusion from graveyards, see Leon Ames, SAG Oral History Interview, August 1979. On racial tolerance, see "Combats Danger of Minority Baiting," SA (April 1946), pp. 7, 8. See also, Minutes,

November 9, 1939, p. 1307, where the leaders wrote that "all racial groups have access to the Guild." At Labor Day parades the Guild also proudly displayed "floats from each racial group"; see Minutes, August 23, 1937.

16.
See almost any issue of SA from 1935 to 1945 for the merging of labor news, endorsement of union firms, festivities, and ads for nightclubs and high level consumption. For boycotts and support of strikes, see Minutes, February 21, 1938, 714; for the displays at fairs, see Minutes, February 19, 1940, 1454; for radio programs, see Minutes, January 1938, 657, and May 15, 1939, 1162; and "Screen Guild Theatre Over CBS," SA (April 1941), p. 6. On FDR's hat, see SA (April 1941), p. 6. On the fairs and balls, see Minutes, August 23, 1937, and February 7, 1938, 665. For the Montgomery letter, see Minutes, March 2, 1936.

17.
"Labor Day Parade," Los Angeles Citizen, September 3 and 10, 1936. "Labor Day Parade," Los Angeles Citizen, September 3 and 11, 1937 "Guild Joins in Labor Day

Parade," The Screen Guild Magazine *(August 1936), p. 3.*

18.
For the ideology of the AFL toward capitalism, see Steven J. Ross, Workers on the Edge: Work, Leisure and Politics in Industrializing Cincinnati, 1788–1890 *(New York: Columbia University Press, 1985), pp. 318–319; Ross,* Stars and Strikes. *For the Board comments, see Minutes, January 15, 1937, March 1, 1937. Herbert Sorrell, "You Don't Choose Your Friends: The Memoirs of Herbert Knott Sorrell," UCLA Oral History Project 1963, Special Collections, UCLA, pp. 20–50, and Robert Montgomery, SAG Oral History Project, both explain how they worked to purge the IA of gangsters, through the use of national and local political influence. Sorrell's account of the CSU democratic style and its organizing white and blue collar workers is in Sorrell, "Memoirs," pp. 86, 77–78, 143–150, and "Testimony of Herbert Sorrell, Hearings Before a Special Committee on Education and Labor, House of Representatives,* Jurisdictional Disputes in the Motion Picture Industry, *80th Cong., 1st*

Sess., 1948, pp. 784–805 (hereafter cited as Jurisdictional Disputes).

19.
An example of their relation to popular culture is Hollywood Sun, *August 29, 1945, and "Cafe Man Lifts Light on Hollywood Night Life,"* Hollywood Sun, *July 25, 1945, clipping in Hollywood Studio Strike File (three boxes), folder 226, UCLA Special Collections (hereafter cited as* Hollywood Strike). *"Brother Eddie Cantor,"* Los Angeles Citizen, *10 September 1936. On Sorrell and members dressing like stars, see Sorrell, "Memoirs," p. 77. For Guild support of Sorrell's painters' unions and their rebellion from the IA̅, all the way from anti-Nazi leagues to common strikes, to unemployment conferences, see Minutes, April 15, 1937; February 21, 1938, 683, 714; June 13, 1938, 802; October 1938. For Sorrell's common alliance with SAG, see* Jurisdictional Disputes, *1847.*

20.
On the CSU and Communists, see Testimony of Herbert Sorrell, Jurisdictional Disputes, *1860–1903, and Sorrell, "Oral History," pp. 50–51, 86–87, 134, 169–*

170, 208. Testimony of Father George Dunne, Jurisdictional Disputes, *pp. 403–433, 443–456, and Father George H. Dunn, "Christian Advocacy and Labor Strife in Hollywood," UCLA Oral History Project, 1981, 52. For the leadership of SAG and their toleration of Communism in the thirties, see Montgomery, SAG Oral History Project. On IA anti-Communism and the CSU, see Testimony of Roy Brewer,* Jurisdictional Disputes, *pp. 1746–1805, and for his charge of "substantial" Communist influence of SAG before 1945, see p. 1786. For the Guild's earlier condemnation of the anti-Communist tactics of IA and the quote, see Minutes, March 1, 1937, 483.*

21.
On the war bringing to fulfillment a new American Way based on consumption and ethnicity, see John Morton Blum, V Was for Victory: Politics and Culture During World War II *(New York: Harcourt Brace Jovanovich), pp. 31–54, 90–17; and for ethnicity, see Philip Gleason, "Americans All: World War II and the Shaping of American Identity,"* Review of Politics *(October 1981), pp. 483–518. For antimonopoly spirit transferred against Fascists and*

dramatized by film-
makers, see John
Dower, War Without
Mercy: Race and
Power in the Pacific
War *(New York: Pan-
theon, 1986), pp. 15–
32.* This is the Army
file, *Museum of Modern
Art Film Library, New
York City, New York.*
See, *"Radio," SA (July
1942), p. 4,* where the
author proclaimed that
the purpose of Guild
radio shows was *"to
keep the audience at
such a pitch that it will
do anything the govern-
ment declares is neces-
sary for winning the
war." See also "Mo-
bilization," SA (June
1943), p. 4; "Home-
coming" SA (January
1944); "Marching
Men," SA (June 1942),
p. 13; "SAG Cited by
Army and Navy, SA
(April 1946), p. 4; and
James Cagney, "Spirit
of '42," SA (June
1942), p. 9.*

22.
The Johnston quote is
from Jurisdictional Dis-
putes, *p. 1342.* For the
larger context of John-
ston's ideology, see
Charles Maier, "The
Politics of Productiv-
ity," *International Or-
ganization 31:4 (1977),
pp. 607–632;* David
Eakins, "Policy Plan-
ning for the Establish-
ment," *in* A New
History of the Levia-
than: Essays on the
Rise of the American

Corporate State, *ed.
Ronald Radosh and
Murray N. Rothbard
(New York: E. P. Dut-
ton and Co.), pp. 189–
205;* Karl Schrift-
giesser, Business
Comes of Age: The
Story of the Committee
for Economic Develop-
ment and Its Impact
upon the Economic
Politics of the United
States, *1942–1960 (New
York: Harper, 1960);*
Johnston, American
Unlimited, *pp. 34–60;*
Eric Johnston, We're
All in It *(New York:
E. P. Dutton, 1948);
"Eric Allen Johnston,"*
The National Cyclopedia
of American Biography
*(New York: James T.
White and Company,
1952).* See also the cita-
tions in 2 above.

23.
On Wallace, see John
Morton Blum, "In-
troduction," *in* The
Price of Vision: The
Diary of Henry A. Wal-
lace, *ed. John Morton
Blum (Boston: Hough-
ton Mifflin, 1973), pp.
3–49;* Macdonald, "The
(American) People's
Century." In reference
to Johnston, the CSU
Bulletin observed, "The
boss and labor are lov-
ers in Eric Johnston's
code. But the boss gets
all the kisses while the
working stiff gets fired,"
in Hollywood Strike.
For the CSU mobiliza-
tion behind Wallace,
see Southern California

Progressive Citizen,
*July 1947–January
1947 in Hollywood
Strike, folder 226.* For
the participants' aware-
ness that this was a bat-
tle for national imagery
writ small, see Testi-
mony of Herbert Sor-
rell, *Jurisdictional Disputes, p. 2130.* On the
national strike wave,
see Lipsitz, Class and
Culture, *and* Lichtens-
tein, Labor's War at
Home. On the CSU de-
mands and Johnston's
comments on sick indus-
try, *see* Jurisdictional
Disputes, *pp. 769,
1343.*

24.
"More Trouble in
Paradise," *Fortune
(October 1946), pp.
154–157, 217–225.*

25.
On wartime strikes, see
Lipsitz, Class and Cul-
ture, *and* Lichtenstein,
Labor's War at Home.
On Sorrell being "fro-
zen out," of the wartime
prosperity, *see* Juris-
dictional Disputes, *p.
1233.* For the extras
controversy, see Min-
utes, *December 30,
1943, 2227; January 5,
1943, 2248; January 25,
1948, 2279; February
21, 1943; March 1,
1943; April 12, 1943;
May 24, 1943, 2353;
December 6, 1943, 2511.
July 31, 1941, 2638–
2664; December 18,
1944, 2704,* where the
Guild found that dissi-

dents' organization, The Screen Players Union (SPU) received a charter from Sorrell. In the Minutes, October 17, 1945, Sorrell told the board he would not settle his strike against the studios until the SPU problem was resolved in their favor.

26.
Jack Dales, the Guild's executive secretary, explained in reference to the extras "there was a quite understandable feeling that we had our heads in the sand, that we really did not understand their problems . . . and we viewed them as a bunch of malcontents who really didn't have a stake in the business"; see Dales, SAG Interview. On Sorrell organizing white-collar workers in war, see Testimony of Roy Brewer, House Committee on Un-American Activities, Hearings Regarding the Communist Infiltration of the Motion Picture Industry, 80th Congress, 1st sess. c. 1947, p. 353 (hereafter cited as HUAC, 1947), and Sorrell, "Memoirs," pp. 70–77. See also Kenneth Thomson, "Report on Extras," Minutes, March 14, 1943.

27.
For the key support of the CSU in 1945, see Minutes, October 16,

1945, 2884–2892, and for their support of CSU organizing of white-collar unions, see Minutes, October 16, 1945, 2915. Minutes, August 20, 1945, 2853–2854, show that the IA, Teamsters, and SAG members met with producers to successfully force them to recognize the Guild's union, the Screen Extras Guild, known as the SEG.

28.
The Minutes read that the board "found itself in a position of being unable to refuse . . . because of the unsolicited, militant support which the IA has given the SEG." The Minutes of February 18, 1946, state that the IA will give replacements for CSU jobs, but they must "have the support of the Guild." They had the support, but the Guild denied this cooperation; see Ronald Reagan to Honorable Ralph W. Gwinn, March 2, 1948, SAG Files. There Reagan claimed that the "charge of conspiracy and collusion between the producers and the IA," an absolutely accurate assessment, was "groundless" and "ridiculous."

29.
CSU News, June–August 1946, Hollywood Strike, folder 226, documents the boycotts of

the stars, and that for the pickets, the "actors seem to be a special object of their wrath." Sorrell also gave a speech in which he attacked the stars "who don't hide their contempt for us when they go through the lines."

30.
On earlier anti-Communist traditions, see John Higham, Strangers In The Land: Patterns of American Nativism, 1860–1925 (New York: Athenaeum, 1971), pp. 194–234, and Stanley Coben, "A Study in Nativism: The American Red Scare of 1919–1920," Political Science Quarterly 79 (1964), pp. 52–75. On the pro-Russian films and antagonism to early HUAC, see Mission to Moscow, ed. David Culbert (Madison: University of Wisconsin Press).

31.
For suggestions on how the stereotypes of total war were transferred to Communists, see Dower, War Without Mercy, pp. 308–310. Testimony of Roy Brewer, Jurisdictional Disputes, pp. 1746–1805. Testimony of Matthew Levy, Attorney for IATSE, Jurisdictional Disputes, pp. 2367–2371, 2429. On Levy's background, see "Matthew M. Levy, Justice, 72, Dead," New

York Times, *September 5, 1971, and "300 Attend Rites for Justice Levy,"* New York Times, *September 8, 1971.*

32.
For example, see Johnston, "Utopia is Production," Eric Johnston Testimony, House Committee on Un-American Activities, HUAC 1947, pp. 305–310, and We're All in It, pp. 1–60. What he shared with earlier anti-Communists, of course, was the fear of class conflict and a wish to contain the disruptive effects of an urban popular culture.

33.
Testimony of Roy Brewer, Committee on Un-American Activities, House of Representatives, 82nd Congress, 1st sess., 1951, p. 517 (hereafter known as HUAC 1951). For Reagan's family and politics, as well as his early years in the Guild, see Reagan and Hubler, Where's the Rest of Me?, *pp. 1–65, 147–230; Wills,* Reagan's America. *For Warner's, see Nick Roddick,* A New Deal in Entertainment: Warner Brothers in the 1930's *(London: British Film Institute, 1983). For Reagan as an FBI undercover agent, see*

Wills, Innocents at Home, *pp. 247–250. Quote is from "Ronald Reagan Testifies He Didn't Know Jeffers,"* Los Angeles Times, *unpaginated, undated clipping, probably January 1951, in Ronald Reagan File, Los Angeles Times.*

34.
Reagan and Hubler, Where's the Rest of Me?, *pp. 160–161. For Reagan and the extras, see Dales, SAG Oral History Project, 38; Dales, UCLA Oral History Project, 34, 51. On his "meteoric" rise and ability to "sell" people anything, see Dales, UCLA Oral History Project, pp. 20–40. For an account of the meeting where Reagan convinced the members to back the IA, see Minutes, Annual Meeting, October 2, 1946, 3092; "Special Membership Meeting," SA (January 1947), pp. 4–12.*

35.
For the board attack, see Minutes, September 27, 1947. The public assault on fellow Guild members' "devious aims" and "abuse of the democratic process" was the most vitriolic to date; see Screen Actor's Guild Intelligence Report, *May 15 and June 16, 1947. The result was that petitions*

no longer could come from the floor at annual meetings; more class "A" members had to sign petitions for a meeting; no alternative recommendations to the board were allowed on the ballots; and secret ballots, rather than public debate, determined voting. As a whole, this solidified power in the hands of the leaders and cut off democratic initiative from below. Lastly, the board also cut off the efforts of civil rights groups to pressure the producers to alter the "Sambo" type roles given to Negro actors; *see Minutes, May 24, 1943, and October 20, 1947.*

36.
Wills, Innocents at Home, *pp. 251–261. For SAG's financial and political support of MPIC, see Minutes, February 2, 1948, 3456, and January 20, 1949, 3750. For the MPIC as a model for business and labor harmony, see Eric Johnston, "Motion Picture Industry Council,* New York Daily News, *undated, unpaginated, article, 1948, in MPIC File, Academy of Motion Picture Arts and Sciences Library, Los Angeles, California (hereafter known as MPIC).*

37.
Eric Johnston, "Mr. Wallace Proposes Appeasement" undated, unpaginated clipping, MPIC, and Los Angeles Times, *January 16, 1948, unpaginated clipping, MPIC. Los Angeles Times, October 5, 1948, reported Ronald Reagan as chairman of AFL Film Council, and its first statement was to "denounce Wallace." "Hollywood AFL Shuns Aid to Candidate Trio," Los Angeles Times, October 29, 1948, unpaginated clipping, Roy Brewer File, Los Angeles Times, described the anti-Communist attack by the council on local Progressive Party candidates.

38.
On CSU campaign for Wallace, see CSU News, May 24, 1947, an account of a rally where Katharine Hepburn and Charles Chaplin were at CSU rallies for Wallace, and California Progressive Citizen, January 1948, in Hollywood Strike, 226. SAG Intelligence Report, February 7, 1948, denounced this alliance. The defeat of the CSU in the studios came because the new Labor Relations Board would not let the strikers vote on who would be their union. Since the CSU was locked out, and could not vote, the IA won; see Variety, September 9, 1949. Polansky, "How the Blacklist Worked in Hollywood," pp. 50–51.

39.
Navasky, Naming Names; Schwartz, Hollywood Writers's Wars, Ceplair and Englund, The Inquisition in Hollywood. For anti-Communist films, see Michael Rogin, Ronald Reagan, the Movie: and Other Episodes in Political Demonology (Berkeley: University of California Press, 1987), pp. 236–272. Johnston quoting from America Unlimited, pp. 152–160. Testimony of Herbert Sorrell, Jurisdictional Disputes, 1892.

40.
Richard English, "What Makes a Hollywood Communist?" Saturday Evening Post (May 19, 1951), pp. 30–31, 147–148. A recent comment by the son of a blacklisted actor caught the essence of this ideological intimidation: "The meaning of the blacklist . . . is the best experience in American history to date of how to silence the middle class. To silence people or to punish them for political associations . . . you attack the very things they have striven all their lives to achieve—a successful career. It is the nightmare of middle-class people." See, Conrad Bromberg, "A Son Writes About His Blacklisted Father," The New York Times, November 30, 1986. Bromberg's father was a member of the Guild.

41.
On the MPIC and blacklisting and clearing, see Wills, Reagan's America, pp. 251–261. For loyalty and SAG, see SAG Press Release, April 10, 1951; Board of Directors to Miss Gale Sondergaard, 20 March 1951; Ronald Reagan, "Inside Labor," Post-Hall Syndicate, 1951.

42.
B. B. Kahane to Mrs. Ronald Reagan, January 7, 1953, all in SAG Files. Jack Dales, SAG Oral History Project, 1979, pp. 12–13.

43.
See, for example, Testimony of Eric Johnston, HUAC 1947, pp. 305–310. Eric Johnston, The Hollywood Hearings (Washington, D.C.: Motion Picture Producers' Association, 1948), pp. 1–10. Screen Guide for Americans (Beverly Hills: Motion Picture Alliance for the Preservation of American Ideals, 1948), pp. 1–12. Lillian Ross,

"Onward and Upward With the Arts," The New Yorker *(February 21, 1948), pp. 32–48. Frank Capra, The Name Above the Title: An Autobiography (New York: Random House, 1971), pp. 425–430. How effective this was in altering the film content across the board is discussed by Andersen, "Red Hollywood." See also the citations in note 41.*

44.
The absence of boycotts, parades, and political mobilization is based on a survey of the Intelligence Report, *the journal which replaced* Screen Actor *after 1946. For Johnston and women, gender and the home, see* We're All In It, *pp. 59–61. Standardized speeches for the Guild during the 1950s are in "Speakers Kit," probably designed in 1950, SAG Files. See also Ronald Reagan, "Special Editorial to the* Hartford Times," *October 8, 1951, SAG Files. The quote is from* Dixon Evening Telegraph, *August 22, 1950, as in Wills,* Innocents at Home, *p. 144. For an example of how the transformation from a public life to privatized home did become the core of working-class comedies in television, see George Lipsitz, "The Meaning of Memory:*

Family, Class and Ethnicity in Early Network Television Programs," Cultural Anthropology 4 *(November 1986), pp. 355–387.*

45.
The most reliable figures for weekly admissions show that in 1935 42.9 million attended the movies. Admission then steadily grew to a high of 79.4 million in 1946. The next year, however, the decline began, as attendance went from 66.8 in 1947 to 62.4 in 1948 and 59.3 in 1950, falling to 37.7 in 1957. See Michael Conant, Anti-Trust in the Motion Picture Industry *(Berkeley: University of California Press, 1960), Table 1, p. 4. Tabulations of television ownership vary, but all agree that in 1949–50 only about ten percent of American families owned a set. See* Conant, Anti-Trust, *Table 6, and* Historical Statistics of the United States, *Part 2, 796. On the unprecedented decline in Guild membership, see* Intelligence Report *(July 22, 1949), SAG Files.*

46.
One side of the battle is told by the blacklisted director; see Herbert Biberman, Salt of the Earth *(Boston: Beacon*

Press, 1965). For the other side, see Salt of the Earth File, SAG Files. For other examples see MPIC and "Film Council Asks Ban on Import of Red Movies," Los Angeles Times, August 26, 1952.

47.
For analysis of how this crusade affected the directors of film noir as well as Garfield, see Andersen, "Red Hollywood," pp. 177–179. *For stories and pictures of Chaplin supporting the CSU, see* CSU News, May 24, 1947, *and* California Progressive, June 1948, in Hollywood Strike File, 226. "Roy Brewer Blasts Lessing for Branding IA 'Selfish,' Takes New Jab at Chaplin," Variety, 1952, *unpaginated, undated clipping in MPIC.*

48.
Robert Scheer, With Enough Shovels: Reagan, Bush and Nuclear War *(New York: Random House, 1982), pp. 42–43. Nor has Scheer been the only major journalist to observe the power of the Hollywood experience for Reagan's ideology; see* Bernard Weinraub, "Reagan's Early Encounters With the Left Seem to Key His Drive to Aid the Contras," New York Times, March 17, 1986.

Cultural Cartography: American Designs at the 1964 Venice Biennale[1]

Laurie J. Monahan

This society which eliminates geographical distance reproduces distance internally as spectacular separation.

Guy Debord, *Society of the Spectacle*

When Robert Rauschenberg won the Venice Biennale in 1964, the European press issued its verdict with headlines screaming. Italy's *ABC* lamented "Everything is Lost, Even a Sense of Shame."[2] The French periodical *Arts* raged "In Venice, America Proclaims the End of the School of Paris and Launches Pop Art to Colonize Europe."[3] The *France Observateur* provided its own graphic depiction of the situation: a storm cloud over Venice failed to dissuade America's pop-culture superhero from stealing away with the prize.[4] American critics explained Rauschenberg's victory in terms of aesthetic superiority;[5] Rauschenberg was the best artist there, and thus deserved to win. They argued that the French particularly were enraged because they had dominated the Biennale for years[6] and had been forced in 1964 finally to recognize they had been surpassed by a superior culture. Alan Solomon, the curator of the U.S. exhibition, summed up such sentiments in a public statement made just prior to the U.S. victory: "The whole world recognizes that the world art center has moved from Paris to New York."[7] Yet Solomon admitted pri-

Editorial Cartoon,
France Observateur,
June 25, 1964

vately that "we might have won it anyway (apart from the question of merit), but we really engineered it."[8]

Indeed, the Americans' exhibition in Venice was a marvel of cultural engineering. For the first time, the U.S. government was directly involved in the show, through the U.S. Information Agency (USIA), which was responsible for propaganda programs abroad. Hired by the USIA, Solomon planned a show far more ambitious than any before—indeed, a show so large that the Americans were allowed to extend their exhibition beyond the confines of the official exhibition grounds, the Giardini. They were the only participants ever to have the advantage of an annex while also maintaining a pavilion in the Giardini. This enlarged presentation of American art not only increased the number of works exhibited, but must be understood as symbolizing equally the fact of American cultural and political expansionism.

If Solomon missed these implications at the time of his decision to include the annex, European critics wasted no time making the connections for him once the Biennale had officially opened.

Solomon also successfully lobbied the president of the Biennale to appoint an American to the jury for the first time. Despite the difficulties of finding a willing American for the job,[9] eventually Sam Hunter was chosen. He was notified of his appointment through a telegram to Rauschenberg's dealer, Leo Castelli.[10] This is suggestive of where Hunter's interests lay, and it was no secret he was a promoter of Pop art. Indeed, he seemed unconcerned with maintaining an objective image, for he stated quite candidly on Italian television prior to the award that American art was far superior to anything Europe had to offer.[11]

Fueled by these events, rumors circulated that the U.S. was threatening to withhold funding from the ailing Biennale budget should they lose.[12] There were stories that the Americans' Mediterranean fleet was moving up to Venice to assure victory, and that the U.S. government was sending paintings on jet bombers. Given the tensions pervading the Giardini, Leo Castelli's promotional advertisement, which appeared in *Art International*[13] at the time, articulated in visual terms the "crisis" in Venice: Solomon directed the Americans' colonization of Europe with the aid of his cartographer, Castelli, who mapped out the targets and deployed the troops.

The volatile atmosphere ignited when Rauschenberg received the Grand Prize under even more unusual circumstances. His works had been exhibited in the U.S. annex, and the presi-

Advertisement for Leo
Castelli Gallery, Art
International, *July 1964*

dent of the jury, A. Hammacher, refused to give the prize to an artist who was not exhibiting on the official Biennale grounds, as this would be a violation of Biennale rules. Although Solomon had hoped to circumvent this problem by placing two small Rauschenberg works in the U.S. pavilion, Hammacher insisted these works were not enough to merit the Grand Prize. As a compromise, the Americans agreed to move several of Rauschenberg's works from the annex to their pavilion in the Giardini. The day the winner was announced, a photographer captured the transfer of Rauschenberg's works in the early morning, and the press widely reproduced the photographs as evidence of a secret deal worked out between Biennale officials and the Americans.[14]

I do not intend to argue for conspiracy, nor do I plan to justify the American prize on the basis of aesthetic superiority. It is my contention that Rauschenberg's work was particularly suited to the Americans' purposes in Venice, and that they set out to win the Grand Prize for reasons that extended beyond artistic considerations. The European and especially the French responses to Rauschenberg's victory in Venice spoke of colonization, tactical maneuvering, and complete defeat, while the Americans claimed absolute victory. These terms were indicative of the stakes, which were political as well as cultural. In this regard the French position is particularly interesting. France was the seat of Western culture and still laid claim to cultural superiority despite postwar economic and political hardships. The Biennale was one of the last strongholds where their cultural tradition was continually honored and recognized. The Americans chose to challenge this tradition at a moment when France was contesting American political hegemony in Europe, and this was to have profound implications in Venice.

Although the Biennale took place shortly after the assassination of John F. Kennedy, the plans for the show began in 1962 under the auspices of his administration. In that year the Museum of Modern Art announced it could not afford to sponsor the American exhibition for the 1964 Biennale.[15] While private sponsorship of the U.S. show had traditionally been interpreted as a mark of a free culture unfettered by official interference,[16] MoMA's financial circumstances placed the government in the happy position of "saving" modern art. Kennedy's liberal image was well-suited to the task, for the rhetoric he employed spoke of engagement, innovation, and challenge and gave his New Frontier administration its name:

*Transport of Rauschen-
berg's work from the
U.S. annex to U.S.
pavilion, 32 Venice
Biennale, Venice, 1964
(Photograph: Ugo
Mulas)*

We stand today on the edge of a new frontier—the frontier
of the 1960s, a frontier of unknown opportunities and paths.
. . . The new frontier of which I speak is not a set of promises—it is a set of challenges. . . . It would be easier to
shrink back from that frontier, to look to the safe mediocrity
of the past. . . . But I believe the times demand invention,
innovation, imagination and decision. For the harsh facts of
the matter are that we stand on this frontier at a turning
point in history.[17]

The staid cultural conservatism of the Eisenhower years gave
way to the progressive tone set by Kennedy, and this shift was
registered in the ideological strategies the U.S. employed in
Europe. Eisenhower's "programs of persuasion" and "campaigns
of truth" were designed to enhance European dependence on
American military and economic might in the face of the Communist threat. A 1951 *Collier's Magazine* cover exemplified the
Eisenhower strategy: under the guise of the United Nations, a
U.S. infantryman shielded the West from the encroaching Eastern bloc. Although the *Collier's* image inspired protests from
European allies objecting to its implications of American domination, dependence on American support made the issue moot.[18] By
the 1960s, however, the U.S. was mapping out a new strategy,
choosing a positive emphasis on the strengths of American society rather than stressing the "evils of communism" in its propaganda programs abroad.[19] While cultural programs played a
major role in all countries where the USIA operated, they had a
specific significance in Europe, as economic aid was increasingly
directed to underdeveloped Third World nations.[20] These programs became all the more important as officials noted European
hostility toward American culture. A 1961 article appearing in
Foreign Affairs reported that "the image of the U.S. as an intellectual wasteland and of American writers, artists and thinkers
as exiles in their own country . . . is almost uncontested in European intellectual circles today."[21] American society was increasingly regarded as a site inimical to culture, and the problem was
exacerbated by Soviet policies in Western Europe:

With the possible exception of Great Britain, anti-Ameri-
canism in the form of critical hostility toward American
thought and culture has actually been increasing. In recent
years it has been steadily promoted by Soviet cultural diplo-

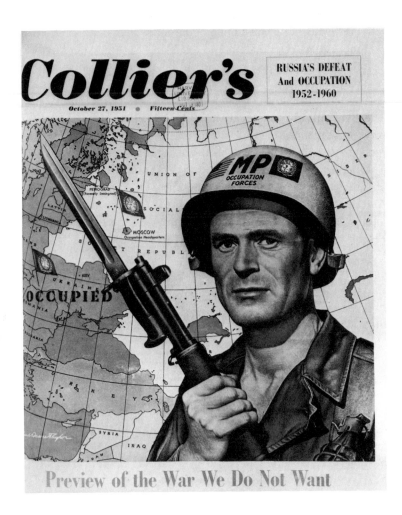

Cover of Collier's *magazine, October 27, 1951*

In light of the Soviet Union's cultural programs in Europe, an American counterbalance seemed increasingly necessary in European countries. Yet the United States somehow had to differentiate itself from other countries' cultural programs—that is, the government sought to foster a policy particularly *American* in its approach and content. Kennedy himself proposed a possible strategy:

> Above all, we are coming to understand that the arts incarnate the creativity of a free society. We know that a totalitarian society can promote the arts in its own way—that it can arrange splendid productions of opera and ballet. . . . But art means more than the resuscitation of the past; it means that free and unconfined search for new ways of expressing the experience of the present and the vision of the future. . . . A free government is the reflection of a people's will and desire—and ultimately their taste. It is also, at its best, a leading force, an example, and a teacher.[23]

The administration had found yet another "new frontier"—the avant-garde. By invoking cultural innovations, Kennedy differentiated U.S. policy from that of "totalitarian" society while simultaneously implying that his administration was a progressive example—even a teacher—to its citizenry. While the avant-garde had previously been enlisted in the Cold War cause,[24] Kennedy proposed to lead the battle himself. The New Frontier differentiated itself from previous cultural policies through its outspoken admission of an alliance between government and the avant-garde; the liberal tone of Kennedy's administration promised that progressive cultural programs would not be discussed in hushed tones, but presented as a part of the Chief Executive's overall policy.[25]

In keeping with the rhetoric of the New Frontier, cultural excellence was posed as a "problem" to which hard-hitting, pragmatic solutions offered by the administration could be systematically applied. In a 1962 speech outlining Kennedy's policy on culture, Arthur Schlesinger, Jr., explained that Americans faced a "critical moment" in culture; the nation could succumb to the leveling of culture, as predicted by the "pessimists," or rise to the "optimists' " vision of a new Renaissance.[26] Thus, the problem was posed in terms that allowed the Kennedy government to be seen as errant should it refuse to sponsor the arts:

> If our civilization is poised, so to speak, between vulgarization and fulfillment, then we would be remiss in not doing what we can for our country, as in the realm of defense of employment or civic freedom.[27]

Schlesinger's strategy not only laid the foundation for arguments in favor of government sponsorship, but also added a dimension of urgency to cultural programs by placing them on a par with defense and civic freedom. The fact that the argument issued from the presidency gave it further credence and legitimacy as a policy to be adopted by the government as a whole.[28] Government became the liberal sponsor of what Schlesinger termed the "new Renaissance,"[29] but the links between culture and more pragmatic issues of foreign policy were not to be overlooked. As Schlesinger continued:

> Our times require greatness as well as bigness—and greatness is a matter, not of the arsenal or of the pocketbook, but of the spirit. We will win world understanding of our policy and purposes not through the force of our arms or the array of our wealth but through the splendor of our ideals.[30]

Thus the Kennedy Administration developed a double-edged argument in favor of culture. On the one hand, there was a "community responsibility" to sustain culture as an essential component of a healthy society; on the other, the arts and humanities could serve as practical solutions to foreign policy problems where economic aid and military clout were not "enough." Domestic spending on culture might be justified by invoking national pride,[31] but investment in cultural "exports" such as state-sponsored exhibitions abroad required a more persuasive strategy, in which Schlesinger's "greatness of spirit" was only one component. Senator Jacob Javits, one of the most outspoken proponents of the arts, explained in more candid terms: "It is high time that we, as a people, realize that the visual and performing arts are not a luxury but a necessity in the defense of our free society against the backdrop of the cold war."[32]

This active cultural intervention must be considered in the

light of increasing European strength.[33] In response to the success of the European Economic Community (EEC), the *New York Times Magazine* reported in May 1962 that the renewed economic strength of Europe could be potentially threatening:

> The United States sees a danger in the [European economic] development that must be avoided at all costs. The danger is that a resurgent Europe would be tempted to discount the need for a close partnership with the United States, and would plunge into "go-it-alone" policies in economic, political and military matters—to the inevitable harm of Europe itself, America and free nations elsewhere.[34]

While American postwar policy had encouraged the development of an economically integrated Europe, the EEC threatened to impose prohibitive tariffs on American products. This was particularly problematic insofar as the EEC was proving to be a formidable trade competitor, edging out American products in Europe as well as within the United States. The problem was exacerbated by the fact that European countries were exchanging their large dollar reserves for gold, an exchange which the U.S. Treasury could not sustain indefinitely.[35] It was thus necessary to restore confidence in the dollar, while simultaneously bolstering the American economy through the expansion of trade abroad. To provide an alternative to prohibitive trade policies set by the EEC, as well as to offset the balance of payments problem by convincing the European allies to shoulder the financial burdens of NATO, Kennedy proposed his "Atlantic Partnership," a two-part plan tellingly dubbed the "Grand Design" by sympathetic journalists. On the Fourth of July, 1962, Kennedy introduced this program, calling for the Western Europeans to renew their ties in a "Declaration of Interdependence." First, the EEC's autonomy was to be linked to American tariff agreements to offset trade advantages within the community. This plan was enhanced by Kennedy's hope that Great Britain would be admitted to the Common Market for reasons explained by his advisor, Arthur Schlesinger, Jr.: "London could offset the eccentricities of policy in Paris and Bonn; moreover, Britain, with its world obligations, could keep the EEC from becoming a high-tariff, inward-looking, white man's club."[36]

Ostensibly Britain's "world obligations" to the United States would render it a more responsive ally of American interests in the EEC. If Britain were admitted to the EEC, British Prime

Minister Harold Macmillan could promote Kennedy's trade expansion act among Common Market countries and work to reestablish a close alliance between the United States and France.[37] The economic aspects of Kennedy's "Grand Design" were linked to a proposed military package known as the multilateral force (MLF), which would allow for an international seaborne force manned by NATO countries. It was designed to provide a sense of participation among European allies in NATO who had been excluded from the decision-making process during the Cuban Missile Crisis; Kennedy hoped it would offset suspicions regularly voiced by French President Charles de Gaulle that the U.S. would sacrifice Europe in the event of a nuclear war in the interest of its own preservation.[38] Yet the proposal did not substantially alter the existing power balance: the Americans would retain exclusive command and control of the nuclear forces, while simultaneously creating a trade agreement that would primarily benefit American investment.[39] Kennedy's "Atlantic Partnership" was thus a grand design, but one that chiefly enhanced the United States' economic and military control over Europe.

The Kennedy proposal was abruptly thwarted by an increasingly recalcitrant ally—France. Convinced that the U.S. had no intention of relinquishing its monopoly on nuclear weaponry, de Gaulle announced his intention to develop an independent nuclear defense force. De Gaulle's plan was sharply rebuked by Kennedy, who reminded him:

> [The American commitment] is to a common defense, in which every member of the Western Community plays a full and responsible role, to the limit of his capability and in reliance on the strength of others. . . . As long as the United States is staking its own national security on the defense of Europe . . . we will continue to participate in the great decisions affecting war and peace in that area. A coherent policy cannot call for both our military presence and our diplomatic absence.[40]

De Gaulle's decision challenged American power, and while it posed no immediate threat militarily, it had the effect of ideologically undermining U.S. hegemony in world affairs. France was bluntly reminded that the Americans had no intention of relinquishing their role in the "great decisions" regarding Europe. Yet de Gaulle persisted in his attempts to establish an independent

French policy; in January 1963 he announced his plans to veto Britain's bid for membership in the EEC and unequivocally rejected the American MLF proposal.[41] The announcement had the effect of publicly embarrassing those lobbying for Britain's admission to the EEC, since de Gaulle had circumvented diplomatic channels, opting instead to make a public announcement while negotiations were still in progress. By November of that year, he launched his slogan of "l'Europe europèenne," advocating an independent Europe pursuing its own interests rather than those of the United States.[42] De Gaulle felt he had successfully accomplished the goals he had set for France, goals that ran contrary to the kind of accords Kennedy had sought with Europe. The French president recalled the moment in his memoirs:

> In the eyes of the world, our country had suddenly become one of the principal actors in a play which hitherto she had been regarded as a supernumerary. And foreign governments . . . realized that we had entered a phase of politics in which France was once more in control of her own destiny and they had no alternative but to make the best of it.[43]

A newly-assertive France had thus initiated a policy that deliberately resisted American attempts to dominate the affairs of Western Europe at a time when the Kennedy administration was demonstrating with new insistence American authority.

Amid these events, the Americans began preparations for their exhibition at the Venice Biennale. The Museum of Modern Art was reluctant to organize and finance the show, prompting August Heckscher (Kennedy's special advisor on the arts, 1960–62) to contact both Edward R. Murrow (then director of the USIA) and Lucius Battle (Assistant Secretary of State for Cultural Affairs). He stated:

> We all feel the importance of having the United States represented at the biennials, particularly those of Venice and São Paulo which are generally regarded as the most famous international art festivals in the Old and New World, respectively. To have this country absent at a time when it is placing fresh emphasis upon the achievements of its cultural life would seem an unfortunate contradiction.[44]

The government was placed in a position to "save" modern art, thus reinforcing the advanced image the New Frontier administration wished to project. Further, it was an opportunity to implement Kennedy's cultural policies in an international forum: the Biennale provided the United States with an occasion to demonstrate that it was a society capable of producing not only material goods, but high culture as well—issuing not from isolated artists alienated from their country, but rather embraced and supported by direct government sponsorship.[45] The USIA was the logical choice for this task because it was the government agency officially charged with promoting American culture. Alan Solomon, then director of the Jewish Museum, was hired by Lois Bingham (chief of the Fine Arts Section, USIA Exhibition Division) because she was "looking for a scholar who would stand behind his convictions" and curate "a cohesive show which said something for America."[46] Solomon's work at the Jewish Museum made him a likely candidate for such a task; he had curated major shows of younger artists such as Rauschenberg, Jasper Johns, Kenneth Noland, and Helen Frankenthaler and had written catalogues which firmly supported an attempt to establish new trends in American art.[47] His involvement with the "neo-Dada" artists Rauschenberg and Johns was especially important because, according to Bingham, the Venice Biennale officials had specifically requested that these artists be included in the U.S. exhibition.[48] This poses some interesting questions: why would the Biennale officials request these specific artists and why is there no record of such a request in the USIA files? It is also curious that the USIA should take advice from Venice, thereby abdicating responsibility for the agency's own selection. Were the Italian officials actually determining the content of a show that was designed to "say something for America"? Whether the USIA chose to concede to the Italians or to determine their own artistic choices, certain trends became apparent in the early stages of the exhibition's organization: younger, relatively unestablished artists were the principal focus of the show, and they were to be presented as a cohesive group rather than as the eclectic assortment of artists typical of previous shows sponsored by MoMA, in which artists such as Ben Shahn, John Marin, and Edward Hopper had been included along with Abstract Expressionists. Additionally, the inclusion of Morris Louis and Kenneth Noland contributed another dimension to the show—that of abstract painting. The implications of presenting these works in the Biennale will be discussed below. At present, let us turn our attention to the circumstances surrounding the organization of the show.

Bingham and Solomon traveled to Venice in November 1963

to inspect the U.S. pavilion owned by MoMA. The space was deemed too small for the artists Solomon planned to feature; the U.S. organizers felt that Noland, Louis, Rauschenberg, and Johns (the "four germinal painters," as Solomon called them) could not be shown on an appropriate scale in the limited space afforded by the U.S. pavilion. The funding for the show—initially $34,000—precluded any major renovations to MoMA's pavilion, despite the fact that the USIA budget for the Biennale would more than triple to $102,977 by the June opening.[49] Rather than pare down the show by either eliminating artists or reducing the number of works included, the USIA sought an agreement with the Biennale officials whereby an annex located off the Giardini grounds could be used to exhibit works. As noted previously, the annex was an important element of the response to the U.S. exhibition; because of the problems the additional space created for the organizers (in both the logistics of the exhibition and the critical response to it), it is worth examining the negotiations for the annex and the structure of the exhibition itself.

According to Bingham, several possible exhibition spaces were offered by the Biennale officials, who were reportedly "enthused" about the possibility of a U.S. annex and who provided assurances that any artists featured in the annex would be considered eligible for the Biennale prizes.[50] The Americans readily agreed to expand the show beyond the perimeters of the Giardini, but rejected suggestions from Biennale officials and chose the former U.S. Consulate office that had been vacated six months prior.

Choosing the old consulate building proved a shrewd maneuver on the part of the USIA. Aside from the fact that the building had a history of official diplomatic service, thus providing an authoritative aura for its new cultural mission, it was ideally located for maximum exposure; though relatively removed from the Giardini grounds, it was situated on the Grand Canal. Its more central location promised greater accessibility to a public beyond the Biennale audience and was also likely to attract those avant-garde enthusiasts emerging from the nearby Guggenheim "Art of This Century" gallery.[51] The annex not only provided the U.S. with the opportunity to stage a fairly complete and comprehensive show, but also allowed for greater exposure, simply because the annex could stay open after dark, unlike the Giardini pavilions, which relied on natural light. Indeed, the USIA took advantage of the additional hours by hosting several openings prior to the official opening of the Biennale.

While the annex enjoyed certain advantages because of its location, it proved to be something of a mixed blessing for the U.S. organizers. Use of the consulate building required lengthy deliberations with the State Department, which was reluctant to rent it to the USIA. Despite several outright refusals from the State Department, which wanted to sell the structure, the USIA insisted that it was the only suitable exhibition space. Once the arrangements had finally been made, Solomon presented to USIA officials a concrete proposal that would expand the consulate exhibition to include younger artists who followed up on the developments made by the "four germinal painters." Yet the artists selected had stylistic affinities with only two members of the "germinal" group, Rauschenberg and Johns. Solomon explained:

> The situation in abstract painting is so fluid now by contrast with the clearly established group on the other side, that I do not think we could maintain the balance represented by the four germinal figures if we wish to illustrate developments among the younger artists. For this reason I would propose to extend the exhibition with a representation of the major figures of the so-called pop group, including one artist, Frank Stella, who actually stands between the abstract painters and the object painters.[52]

Such a statement is revealing, for it assumed the firm establishment of Pop art, which admittedly was gaining popularity; however, advocates of newer abstract painters would no doubt have argued that the "fluidity" of the abstract painting situation was insufficient grounds for dismissal.

Nevertheless, Solomon's proposal was accepted and the annex became the site for a large exhibition primarily composed of Pop art. Johns and Rauschenberg, benefiting from the additional space in the consulate, exhibited almost twice the number of works as Noland and Louis.[53] It is worth noting that the Pop artists were excluded from the Biennale grounds; in keeping with the USIA's original plan, the canvases of Noland and Louis were slated for the official pavilion in the Giardini, whereas the works of Rauschenberg and Johns, along with the "younger artists" Stella, John Chamberlain, Claes Oldenburg, and Jim Dine, were to be exhibited in the annex. The reasons for this split remain unclear. According to Bingham, the pavilion space was simply better suited to the works by Noland and Louis;[54] Alice Denney,

Solomon's assistant, claimed that Kenneth Noland insisted on being shown in the pavilion.[55] Whatever the reasoning, it was clear that by grouping all of the Pop artists in one large space, the annex show took on a more cohesive appearance, in keeping with Solomon's desire to present Pop art as a movement.

With the exhibition preparations underway, the annex again became a problematic issue for the USIA organizers. The Venice Biennale president, Mario Marcazzan, notified the USIA office that Biennale regulations prohibited considering any artists for prizes if their works were not located in the Giardini.[56] The statement generated a flurry of telegrams between the USIA and Marcazzan. The agency relied on verbal agreements between Bingham, Solomon, and the Biennale Committee during their first visit in November 1963, while Marcazzan insisted on following the regulations; once the show opened, he denied that the previous verbal agreements were ever made. Washington maintained that an annex was essential to the U.S. exhibition and contended that the artists in the former consulate office should be included in the competition. U.S. embassy officials in Rome hoped to use Rauschenberg, whom they considered "eminently eligible for [the] grand prize,"[57] in their argument to convince the committee to recognize the annex as an official part of the Biennale competition: if his works were included in the former consulate, they reasoned, Biennale officials could be persuaded to accept the annex. This strategy was predicated on the assumption that the committee would share the Americans' confidence in and enthusiasm for Rauschenberg, something the U.S. apparently miscalculated, since the committee sided with Marcazzan. From Washington, the USIA insisted by telegram that "any changes [in the] installation plan would mean new selection which [is] unfeasible at this late date."[58] The agency maintained that Rauschenberg, Johns, Noland, and Louis could not be exhibited in the pavilion as the space was simply inadequate.[59] Attempts were made to negotiate around the regulation; U.S. diplomats from the American Embassy in Rome (including the U.S. Ambassador) appealed to various officials to review the case. Efforts to negotiate with the Director of Cultural Relations, Italian Foreign Office, proved fruitless. The U.S. Embassy in Rome reported:

> Again our arguments to no avail. Italians adamant: only artists represented on Biennale grounds eligible for prize. This

of course is reversal of initial agreement as understood by us, Solomon and Bingham; but Post [U.S. Embassy] now convinced Italians will not change present position.[60]

Solomon and Bingham were faced with the choice of limiting the exhibition to a size suitable for the pavilion space or carrying out the plan to annex the show, at the risk of eliminating two of the "four germinal painters"—Rauschenberg and Johns—from the competition. In the end, the agency elected to take the risk, but Solomon included one work from both Johns and Rauschenberg in the U.S. pavilion, hoping that this gesture of compliance with regulations would satisfy Marcazzan and the committee.

The USIA purported to present the most exciting artistic innovations the United States could offer: Pop art and post-painterly abstraction. Noland and Rauschenberg, representatives from each movement, were initially considered likely candidates for the prize. The choice was not haphazard; Noland was the only living representative of post-painterly abstraction in the U.S. show, and Rauschenberg had had international exposure through two highly successful exhibitions in London the previous year. The two artists presented a balanced image of American culture as well: Noland's abstractions complemented Rauschenberg's figurative montages. As Solomon pointed out in the introduction to the substantial catalogue accompanying the American exhibit:

[Neo-Dada] has had a rapid and widespread impact in the last few years, because of the provocative and assertive nature of its ideas and practices. The new abstract movement, depending as it does on a more passive and contemplative condition, makes demands to which the response has been slower.[61]

It appeared that the U.S. artists offered something for everyone, from a more introspective aesthetic of abstraction to a daring, lively Dada. The distinction between the more culturally engaged neo-Dada movement and the withdrawn, cerebral abstraction was crucial to Solomon's discussion of the artists, for it allowed him to present two different readings of modernism in order to champion only one, that represented by Rauschenberg.

Solomon's introductory remarks indicated a hint of preference for the more "extroverted art" exemplified by Rauschenberg, if only through an estimation of its public impact. However, Noland's importance as a representative of American abstraction

could not be overlooked; indeed, the influential critic Clement
Greenberg had described Noland two years earlier as one of the
most important painters to develop from the Abstract Expressionist movement.[62] Like Greenberg, Solomon praised Noland's
works on the basis of formal "advances" made relative to the
previous generation of artists through his explorations of pictorial
surface and color. Noland's images evoked a kind of unresolved
spatial tension, a tension which created effects that were, in Solomon's words, "suggestive, imprecise in meaning, evocative and
equivocal."[63] This evocative formalism was integral to Noland's
success as an abstract painter, according to Solomon. But, paradoxically, these formal characteristics kept Noland in a more traditional realm, as Solomon explained:

> None of the abstract painters altered traditional attitudes to-
> ward materials or procedures in any substantial way, but
> Rauschenberg led a revolution which has rejected wholly the
> idea that one kind of materials [sic] or another are more or
> less appropriate to art.[64]

Noland's passive and contemplative aesthetic was hardly a challenge to the revolution led by Rauschenberg; rather, it served as
a foil for Rauschenberg's work, which, Solomon claimed, was
more advanced. Thus Solomon tipped the scales of the balanced
culture in favor of Rauschenberg—but Noland provided the
weight of the modernist tradition against which Rauschenberg's
works could be measured.

Still, it would seem that Rauschenberg's works labored in
the face of a tradition of over forty years of collage. How then, we
might ask, was Rauschenberg's development particularly innova-
tive? Solomon proffered a somewhat heavy-handed explanation:
unlike the Dadaists preceding him, Rauschenberg "has a positive
and constructive view of the world." Solomon added:

> He has no interest in social comment or satire, or in politics;
> he uses his previously inappropriate materials not out of a
> desire to shock, but out of sheer delight, out of an optimistic
> belief that richness and heightened meaning can be found
> anywhere in the world, even in the refuse found in the
> street.[65]

According to Solomon, the thrust of this "revolution" was crucially apolitical and affirmative; it was this that made Rauschen-

berg's work distinctive. His primarily figurative imagery, drawn from mass culture, was promoted for its multiplicity of meanings, which in turn produced an optimistic, new sensibility in the viewer. This view, however, dismissed too easily the potentially critical nature of Rauschenberg's work. In his combine-painting *Canyon* (1959), not all of the elements can be construed as strictly positive. An eagle, symbol of American strength, is stuffed and rests precariously on a cardboard box. Instability is suggested further by the imbalance created by the weight of the suspended pillow and the burden of images and objects resting on the eagle's outstretched wings. Yet any suggestively critical interpretation of the works was erroneous, according to Solomon; Rauschenberg's collages were a thoroughly positive exercise in "sheer delight," a delight produced by the artist's ingenious management of ambiguity.

Consider Solomon's statement about Rauschenberg's work:

> Since his paintings are never anecdotal or narrative in any sense, the agglomeration of images and objects has the sole function of generating a kind of irresolute tension with respect to the meaning of the relationship between the images. . . . Rauschenberg keeps the attention of the beholder by offering constantly vacillating alternative meanings, so that we can never arrive at a precise and resolved meaning for the painting.[66]

While Solomon claims no precise meaning is possible, he does not tell us there is no meaning. The meaning of the work resides, imprecise and irresolute, in the very multiplicity and ambiguity of which Solomon speaks. An important aspect of his analysis hinges on the viewer's willingness to suspend the possibility of a thematic connection between the elements in the works, so that the relationships between objects and images are vague and, at most, simply suggestive. Associations called up by each specific image diminish in relation to the ambiguity evoked through the interaction between images. Thus, the eagle, an astronaut, the Statue of Liberty in the photo-silkscreen *Tree Frog* (1964) have particular meanings in and of themselves; but their relationship to other images, less "loaded" symbolically, such as a sailboat, a car, a figure in a crowd, obscures their own constitutive value as meanings. To use the words of Roland Barthes, their "presence is tamed, put at a distance, made almost transparent."[67] The in-

Robert Rauschenberg,
Tree Frog, *1964.*
Private collection.
(Permission of Castelli
Gallery, New York)

dividual meanings comprising each image within the overall composition become secondary to the ambiguous meaning generated
by the picture as a whole.

The way in which ambiguity impedes a critical reading can
perhaps be seen more clearly by comparing Rauschenberg's
works to the pessimistic Dadaist vision he is credited with transcending. On this point, we can perhaps agree with Solomon's
analysis and take it beyond associative content to the very way in
which the images are constructed. Compare, for example, Hannah Höch's work entitled *Collage* (1920) with Rauschenberg's
Tracer (1964). Höch's disparate fragments, clipped from magazines and photographs, push against each other, form abrasive
seams, disrupting the ease with which we take in the images.
Thus the conjunctions created by the photograph of a woman's
head superimposed on the gesticulating, posed body or by the
beetle traversing the man's head disrupt the coherence of each
individual image. The overall effect, irreducible to a single meaning or a single set of meanings, is inflected by the disturbing tension created by the abrupt, often antagonistic transitions between
images. On the one hand, Rauschenberg's *Tracer* mitigates
against such disturbances. Ruben's *Toilet of Venus* coexists with
army helicopters and hard-hat workers; the seams between them
are not acknowledged as sites of abrasive disruption, and thus
serve as a kind of indifferent, connective tissue. In contradistinc-
tion to Höch's collage, Rauschenberg's work turns on an ambiguity which is produced through a multitude of representations
made equivalent, a process achieved through the ease of transition between disparate elements.

Rauschenberg's equivocality operates not only on a level of
signification and formal juxtaposition, but also in terms of distinctions regarding the interplay between high art and mass culture.
The distinctively ambiguous nature of the relationship between
Rubens's *Venus* and mass imagery in *Tracer* can perhaps be
made clearer by comparing it again to a Dadaist predecessor,
Kurt Schwitters. For example, in his *Die heilige Nacht von Antonio Allegri gen. Correggio, worked through by Kurt Schwitters*
(1947) a reproduction of Correggio's *Holy Night* is obscured by
signs of mass culture—ticket stubs, scraps of advertisements,
fragments of photographs and paper. Yet Correggio's image and
the scraps of refuse are polarized, maneuvering for position; take
for example the way in which the bent knee of the shepherd
punches out against the flattening scraps of paper surrounding it,

or the contrast between the confusion of written matter and the visual coherence of the Virgin and Child. At the same time, the reproduction of *The Holy Night* is as much a part of mass culture as the commercial refuse against which it plays off. In this sense, Schwitters's image refracts the ambiguous relation between high art and mass culture; they are at odds with one another and yet share an uneasy compatibility through their commercial equivalence.

Rauschenberg's *Tracer* also points to this relationship of equivalence, but the tension of high art in relation to mass culture diminishes in part through the very process of representation Rauschenberg employs. Rubens's image and the various photographs clipped from magazines are mediated through paint and the process of photo-silkscreen; the actual material differences, so pronounced in Schwitters's work, are themselves altered through the process of reproduction. The paradox produced by Schwitters's polarization of high and low is transformed by Rauschenberg's equivalency—the images are not of one world of culture or the other; they exist on ambiguous, common ground. This ambiguous territory might be judged the site for a cool, ironic statement about the ways in which high art and mass culture interact; yet Solomon claimed that these works were "positive and constructive,"[68] How was this equivocality in Rauschenberg's work made unequivocally affirmative? Such a transformation depended not only on the formal dynamics of the works, but also on the way in which ambiguity became a cipher for a broader cultural discourse.

In the Biennale catalogue, Solomon tells us that Rauschenberg "calls into question the standards by which, up to now, we have been able to make clear distinctions between the beautiful and the ugly, the obvious and the enigmatic, and so on." He adds:

> Rauschenberg too, then, shares that prevalent sense of the equivocal, of a new attitude to be brought to bear on the nature of experience and the meaning of existence. In a statement which has now become familiar he expresses the whole point of view of the movement for which he is the point of departure: "Painting relates to both art and life. I try to act in that gap between the two." In other words, the conditions he brings to his art are identical with the conditions he finds in the real world; meaning and value are inherent in both, we need only search them out.[69]

Hannah Höch, Collage, *1920. Morton G. Neumann Family Collection.*

Robert Rauschenberg, Tracer, *1964. Nelson-Atkins Museum of Art, Kansas City, Missouri (Nelson Gallery Foundation).*

Kurt Schwitters, Die
heilige Nacht von An-
tonio Allegri gen. Cor-
reggio, worked through
by Kurt Schwitters,
1947. Private collection.

At the crux of this new attitude, termed the "new sensibility" by Solomon, is a redefinition of the practices of modernism; instead of existing in opposition to the status quo, art should operate as an extension of the world—a juxtaposition of elements which would enrich the viewer's perception of life. This view had gained currency among leftist intellectuals such as Susan Sontag, who applauded this shift in her 1965 essay "One Culture and the New Sensibility":

> The Matthew Arnold notion of culture defines art as the criticism of life—this being understood as the propounding of moral, social and political ideas. The new sensibility understands art as an extension of life—this being understood as the representation of (new) modes of vivacity. . . . A great work of art is never simply (or even mainly) a vehicle of ideas or moral sentiments. It is, first of all, an object modifying our consciousness and sensibility.[70]

Sontag distinguished this "new sensibility" from a critical realm in order to argue for an art that would become an integral, affirming component of society. There was no room in this vision for "elitist" aesthetic theories that kept the world at bay; by expanding art's function to develop sensibilities hitherto untouched, art would connect to and enhance experience. It was this modification of consciousness that Solomon had extolled in Rauschenberg's "constantly vacillating alternative meanings"; aspects of the environment were represented in a way that served to refashion the viewer's perception of the world. Within this new sensibility qualitative judgments were based not on ideas and moral sentiments, but rather on the consciousness-expanding effect produced by the work. The implications of this shift were elaborated by Sontag:

> One important consequence of the new sensibility (with its abandonment of the Matthew Arnold notion of culture) . . . [is] that the distinction between 'high' and 'low' culture seems less and less meaningful. For such a distinction—inseparable from the Matthew Arnold apparatus—simply does not make sense for a creative community of artists and scientists engaged in programming sensations.[71]

The long-standing rift between high and low culture could be bridged, resulting in one culture for all. An ambiguous middle ground would break down the old polarities. In this sense, the new sensibility differed from the "bridges" built between modernism and popular culture; while modernism, from its earliest moments, had alternatively thrived on and exploited the differences between high and low forms, borrowing from the latter to rejuvenate its practices, the distinctions between the two remained. Sontag, on the other hand, proposed a fusion of these spheres in order to produce a more expansive culture.[72]

While Sontag's vision of an egalitarian age of culture had an admirable, anti-elitist, democratic appeal, her optimistic conception of the future did not convince everyone. Those who were critical of the new sensibility were not persuaded that the new Renaissance was at hand; indeed, they argued that the integration of high and low culture would not elevate but would level all culture. The debate had as its starting point varying views on the effects of mass culture. The leftist critic Dwight Macdonald expressed his concerns in his 1961 essay "Masscult and Midcult":

> Masscult is a dynamic, revolutionary force, breaking down the old barriers of class, tradition, and taste, dissolving all cultural distinctions. It mixes, scrambles everything together, producing what might be homogenized culture . . . [but] whereas the cream is still in the homogenized milk, somehow it disappears from homogenized culture. For the process destroys all values, since value-judgements require discrimination, an ugly word in liberal-democratic America. Masscult is very, very democratic; it refuses to discriminate against or between anything or anybody. All is grist for its mill and all comes out finely ground indeed.[73]

Macdonald identified the egalitarian aspects of mass culture, with its nondiscriminating character and its ability to eliminate class distinctions, but the point of contention between him and Sontag lay in their respective views of the effects of a "democratized" culture. Macdonald pointed to the fact that the resultant shift was merely quantitative (more cultural options are available if discriminating standards are eliminated) rather than qualitative. The situation did not promise to raise overall standards, as Sontag hoped, but precluded the possibility of such an occurrence, as Herbert Marcuse explained in his 1964 work, *One Dimensional Man*:

The range of choice open to the individual is not the decisive factor in determining the degree of human freedom, but *what* can be chosen and what *is* chosen by the individual. . . . Free choice among a wide variety of goods and services does not signify freedom if these goods and services sustain social controls over a life of toil and fear—that is, if they sustain alienation. And the spontaneous reproduction of superimposed needs by the individual does not establish autonomy; it only testifies to the efficacy of these controls.[74]

His words articulated a crucial oversight in Sontag's sanguine argument for the new sensibility; industrialization creates a demand for culture—a demand that increases as leisure time becomes more available—but satiates this demand with a culture, mass culture, that entertains and distracts from the real conditions of society, those which initially induced the desire for release from it.

Marcuse and Macdonald, along with other critics of mass culture and the "new sensibility," necessarily—and quite rightly, I think—based their critique on the belief that a genuine culture of the people could not be attained under the existing structure of capitalism, which by its very nature was alienating. This alienation had been assimilated by the art of the previous decade, and even flaunted as an emblem of freedom and individuality;[75] but as Solomon had pointed out in the introduction to the Biennale catalogue, a new generation of artists had matured beyond the angst of the previous decades, signaling the beginning of the "post-Freudian age."[76] Alienation was on its way out, and a new age was taking its place, as conservative sociologist Edward Shils explained:

This new order of society ["mass society"], despite all its eternal conflicts, discloses in the individual a greater sense of attachment to the society as a whole, and of affinity with his fellows. . . . The new society is a mass society precisely in the sense that the mass population has become incorporated into society. The center of society—the central institutions, and the central value systems which guide and legitimate these institutions—has extended its boundaries. Most of the population (the "mass") now stands in a closer relationship to the center than has been the case in either premodern societies or in the earlier phases of modern society.[77]

There was no need to talk of alienation produced by society when in fact the individuals within it were increasingly integrated through their "greater sense of attachment." These individuals converged to form a mass society which had as its focus a vital center of shared values and institutions. Whereas critics of mass culture claimed that mass society destroyed the individual,[78] the optimistic sociologist argued that mass society actually enriched the individual's potential:

> Mass society has aroused an enhanced individuality. Individuality is characterized by an openness to experience, an efflorescence of sensation and sensibility. . . . [It] has liberated the cognitive, appreciative and moral capacities of individuals. . . . People make choices more freely in many spheres of life, and these choices are not necessarily made for them by tradition, authority, or scarcity.[79]

The individual could develop his/her sensibility, unfettered by restrictive standards and constraints from without, because the "central institutions and values" had been internalized. While Marcuse argued that the choices were illusory since they only sustained alienation, Shils claimed that alienation no longer was an issue. Mass society paradoxically produced greater individuality. Sociologist Clyde Kluckhohn echoed Shils' view:

> Today's kind of "conformity" may actually be a step toward more genuine individuality in the United States. "Conformity" is less of a personal and psychological problem—less tinged with anxiety and guilt. . . . If one accepts outwardly the conventions of one's group, one may have greater psychic energy to develop and fulfill one's private potentialities as a unique person.[80]

If fulfillment could come only through individual potential, and this in turn depended on the individual's abilities to assimilate into society, certainly the greater range of opportunities in mass culture would only serve to enhance the possibilities for individuality. Was this not what Sontag had advocated in her plea for "expanding sensibilities"? There was no need for an oppositional culture when fulfillment was just around the corner.

This interpretation was bolstered by the contention of many intellectuals that society was in fact better than ever before. The cultural optimism expressed by leftists such as Sontag and conservatives like Shils found its political counterpart in the "end of ideology"—a concept introduced by Daniel Bell's 1961 book of the same name[81]—which formed a major focus for intellectual debate in the early 1960s.[82] Bell cited the fact that intellectuals were in agreement, for the most part, on political issues—notably that political pluralism and the welfare state proved to be the most viable means with which to improve society, after the hard-learned lessons of Stalinism had shown that political extremism of any kind resulted in totalitarianism. The situation, as Bell saw it, was:

> The old politico-economic radicalism (preoccupied with such matters as the socialization of industry) has lost its meaning, while the stultifying aspects of contemporary culture (e.g., television) cannot be redressed in political terms. At the same time, American culture has almost completely accepted the avant-garde, particularly in art, and the older academic styles have been driven out completely. The irony, further, for those who seek "causes" is that the workers, whose grievances were once the driving energy for social change, are more satisfied with society than the intellectuals. The workers have not achieved utopia, but their expectations were less than those of the intellectuals, and the gains correspondingly larger.[83]

Thanks to improvements within the system, Bell claimed, critical intellectuals such as Marcuse and Macdonald were the only disgruntled members of society; indeed, he implied that their critique was redundant in a society which had become so progressive that it could accept the avant-garde. For Macdonald, this latter feature was hardly reassuring; in accepting the avant-garde, society developed a new twist in mass culture of consumerism: he called it "midcult."

> In Masscult the trick is plain—to please the crowd by any means. But Macdonald has it both ways: it pretends to respect the standards of High Culture while in fact it vulgarizes them. . . . It is its ambiguity that makes Midcult alarming. For it presents itself as a part of High Culture. Not that coterie stuff, not those snobbish inbred so-called intellectuals who are only talking to themselves. Rather the great and vital mainstream, wide and clear though perhaps not so deep.[84]

But the ambiguous middle ground Macdonald found so alarming was, of course, the place where cultural gains could be made, according to the proponents of the new sensibility. Perhaps the expanding sensibilities of the new art would not produce a cultural utopia, but by modifying expectations, the gains could be correspondingly larger. What was good for the worker was good for the intellectual.

For those intellectuals who abandoned their critical stance for Bell's accommodating position, Kennedy's progressive image confirmed that the welfare state could, with a bit of fine tuning, redress the problems of society. The views of Cold War liberals and "leftists" advocating liberalism in the name of populist values converged with Kennedy's promise of a new and better society. Under the aegis of the New Frontier, culture could provide society with a wider range of sensibilities and sensations by abdicating its oppositional position; like the intellectuals, it could operate most effectively in concert with a system that had proven itself to be the best. The end of ideology signaled the institutionalization of liberalism, and as culture came under its wing, it too was liberalized in the name of democracy and anti-elitism.

Clearly the optimistic trappings of the new sensibility lost some of their luster when introduced into the charged atmosphere of the Biennale. The circumstances of the show—the annex, the transfer of paintings, and so on—all served to color the response to Rauschenberg's work. The French press, almost without exception, made mention of the unprecedented annex, while the other countries had to contend with the limited space of their pavilions:

> The Americans, in 1964, have invaded with a completely missionary zeal. Not content to exhibit in their pavilion in the Biennale gardens, they have organized a gigantic retrospective of their two stars, Johns and Rauschenberg—plus their accomplices—in the palace of the old U.S. consulate.[85]

The *France Observateur* complained that the Americans had infringed on "the elementary rules of 'fair play' " by extending their exhibit beyond the Giardini grounds.[86] Other reports described the situation in much stronger terms, such as those used by Pierre Cabanne in *Arts*:

> [Solomon and his associates] have treated us as poor backward Negroes, good only for colonization. The first com-

mando is in place: it's called "Pop Art." The invasion does not take place in the official pavilion. It occurs at a distance, choosing expansionism instead. The old American consulate . . . is transformed into a temple for the new religion. The pope officiates there: Rauschenberg, surrounded by his great priests, Johns, Oldenburg, Dine, and Stella.[87]

Even the French critic most supportive of the Americans, Pierre Restany, opposed the expansiveness of the U.S. exhibit; speaking of the additional space and the artists featured there, he commented:

> [I] have the greatest esteem for these artists . . . but I vigorously contest the validity of the proceedings which created an unfortunate precedent and contributed to the production of an aura of cultural imperialism around the Americans.[88]

For those less inclined to give the United States the benefit of the doubt, the Americans profited from unfair advantages over every other country participating in the event. Their large exhibition was already an affront, but the fact that an artist exhibiting off the grounds was awarded the major prize, following the surreptitious transfer of his works back to the American pavilion, was an outrage.

These were the circumstances that surrounded the events in Venice; but what of the actual jury deliberations? The international jury, ostensibly objective, pooled from the various nominations submitted by each participating country, had selected Rauschenberg from all the artists at the Biennale. Was this not evidence of the superiority of Rauschenberg's work? Like everything else at the Biennale that year, the situation was not as clear-cut as it appeared. As previously noted, Solomon was able to secure the appointment of Sam Hunter to represent the Americans on the jury, but it was not immediately clear whether Hunter was an asset or a liability for the Americans' cause. Solomon later noted, "When Hunter arrived he was impossible about proving his purity, to the point where the Italian jurors wondered if he wanted the prize to go elsewhere,"[89] that is, to someone other than Rauschenberg.[90] The Italian jurors' comments apparently referred to their concern that Hunter's obvious bias would rule out the possibility of a Rauschenberg prize, since the jury might feel compelled to vote for another artist as evidence of their objectivity. The reasons for the Italians' unequivocal support of Rauschenberg remain unclear. The Swiss member of the jury that year, Franz Meyer, suggested that, according to the Italians, the Americans were threatening to withdraw from the Biennale:

> The jury had naturally in no way been confronted with the financial status of the Biennale as such and the importance of an eventual financial support by the U.S. I am quite certain about that. But I remember that the Italian jurors [Giuseppe Marchiori and Marco Valsecchi] told us that the American officials had been more and more disillusioned by the fact that all efforts to show important American art in the previous Biennales had not been rewarded by a prize. I cannot remember the exact phrasing of Marchiori's and Valsecchi's information. But they may have spoken of the danger that the U.S. would not come to Venice anymore if a prize was not given this time.[91]

It is uncertain whether the Americans had actually offered the Italians financial support for the Biennale. The French magazine *La Cote des Peintres* reported that the Biennale was criticized for its cost (over 200 million lire) and that the Americans had promised to absorb the deficit;[92] *Le Figaro* also mentioned that the Biennale was endangered financially,[93] but this cannot be confirmed until State Department documents become available.[94] Alan Solomon suggested that the Americans' chances for a prize "began with the simple pure fact that certain Italians wanted an American prize for general altruistic reasons, and proceeded to work for it,"[95] but their reasons for being so inclined remain ambiguous.

Not all the members of the jury agreed with the choice of Rauschenberg, however. Rauschenberg had received the majority of the votes (four to three); those in favor included Hunter, Marchiori, Valsecchi, and Julius Starzinski, the Polish judge.[96] Meyer, the Brazilian judge Murillo Mendes, and the president of the jury, Hammacher, apparently opposed Rauschenberg initially, and their final votes remain unclear. Recall that it was Hammacher who had threatened to resign if the prize was given to Rauschenberg on the basis of one work exhibited in the Giardini. Apparently, an offer had been made to give the award to Kenneth Noland, but Solomon announced that if Rauschenberg was disqualified, all the American artists would be withdrawn

from the competition.[97] Meyer eventually supported Rauschenberg, as he later explained:

> When Bob Rauschenberg's name came up (maybe proposed
> by one of the Italians, too), I remember that I tried for a
> moment to extend the discussions to other names of Ameri-
> cans (Mike Sonnabend reminded me years later, that I had
> told him I would rather have voted for Jasper Johns), but—I
> think that especially Sam Hunter made it clear to me—the
> only American of this generation, who . . . could eventually
> qualify for the chief-prize was Bob Rauschenberg.[98]

Yet while Meyer eventually supported Rauschenberg, it still remained to convince Hammacher to accept the jury's decision.
Prior to the compromise reached with the transport of Rauschenberg's work to the official pavilion, Rauschenberg's close friend
Merce Cunningham and his dance troupe performed at the Venice theater La Fenice. Rauschenberg was responsible for all the
set designs, which consisted of Italian stagehands "moving about
in the background, pushing brooms or carrying props."[99] The
event was well attended, and Hammacher was reportedly won
over by the performance and Rauschenberg's sets.[100] The following day he agreed to the compromise, and Rauschenberg
emerged as the winner of the Grand Prize for painting.

As noted earlier, the French response to the American victory was based largely on their perceptions of Solomon's handling
of the show and the circumstances prior to the award. It was also
difficult for them to accept the major change at the Biennale—a
young artist who was relatively unestablished had taken the major painting prize traditionally given to an "old master" of modern
art. In 1964 the French featured a major retrospective of the abstract painter Roger Bissière (see his *Gray Composition*, 1964);
on the basis of awards made at the Biennale in previous years,
Bissière seemed a likely contender for the prize. His reputation
was long-standing as a major painter (he received the Grand Prix
National des Arts in 1952, the first to be given to a painter), and
his work was championed for its affinities with a particularly
French aesthetic of fine technique and refinement:

> His painting has remained non-figurative but today we can
> see that its qualities are traditional and French: it is humble
> and intelligent, never dogmatic, harmoniously tuned to the

Roger Bissière, Gray
Composition, *1964.*

simple emotions inspired by silent meditation before the spectacle of reality which is thereby freely and discreetly transcended.[101]

These particular qualities were considered essential to represent adequately the culture of France, in which tradition formed the solid foundation for aesthetic enterprise. This was of course a culture made in the image of Gaullist France, one which relied on the past for prestige and power—a culture with a "mission civilisatrice," transcending the everyday world.[102] These were the terms Raymond Cogniat, art critic for the conservative *Le Figaro*, emphasized in his summary of the French pavilion at the Biennale:

> [Bissière] is certainly the painter most qualified to illustrate the peaceful permanence and continuing invention which one feels the need to experience even more vividly today. His exhibition is one of such unquestionable dignity and refinement that the international jury, although tempted by more vehement and hazardous statements, nevertheless expressed its desire to pay homage to him.[103]

The French had hoped to win as they always had, on standards that had been tested throughout the history of the Biennale and had proven most durable—and more necessary, Cogniat would argue, given the "more hazardous" aesthetic statements issuing from the Americans' exhibition. Bissière's work was the French answer to the new sensibility, providing a quiet, aesthetic retreat, as critic Pierre Schneider explained:

> Bissière practically never departs from the post-Cubist gridiron. He tends it with the loving care of a suburban gardener, extracting the maximum produce from each little plot. The general effect is that of a gentle, tightly woven Impressionistic patchwork: soft, quilted blankets for eyes prone to chills.[104]

For those who had taken to bundling up in these protective, comforting aesthetics, Rauschenberg's work, with its engagement with mass culture, was anathema.

Yet it was not only images from popular culture that the French had to contend with; in Rauschenberg's silk-screens, political and military images appear repeatedly. Despite Solomon's assertions to the contrary, it is difficult to imagine that such images could be perceived as ambiguous, particularly given the charged atmosphere at the Biennale. Under the cloud of cultural imperialism, how were images that included Kennedy, the author of the Grand Design for Europe, the army helicopter, the city, and of course the omnipresent eagle, emptied of their associative values, as Solomon argued? Given the political tensions between the United States and France, it would seem that these images would be especially loaded. Yet oddly, the French critics made no reference to the military and political connotations of the work. Their silence was covered by a more overt concern with the "positive sensibility" perceived in the reproduction of mass-media images. Leonard, a critic for the leftist *France Observateur*, explained,

> For these everyday objects, deformed, splattered, meticulously reconstructed in enormous dimensions, these "comics" scrupulously reproduced on a scale of panoramic cinema screens, these collages of magazine photographs, all the bric-a-brac that constitutes 'Pop Art'—it is this which constitutes a grotesque plagiarism of Dada. . . . Dada was an essentially revolutionary movement . . . an attack on bourgeois society . . . but the Neo-dadaists, by contrast, are locked in a passionate embrace with bourgeois symbols.[105]

While Solomon had made a point of promoting the positive in Rauschenberg's work, it was precisely this quality which the French critic found so objectionable. The work was problematic *because* it remained detached, simply presenting objects without comment, reflecting consumer society and, worse, aestheticizing the process that "engenders publicity campaigns."[106]

This observation presents an interesting contradiction with respect to the possible readings evoked by Rauschenberg's works. Given the political relations between France and the U.S., the images of eagles, marines, military helicopters, and Kennedy appearing in the combines and photo-silkscreens were potentially political, aggrandizing U.S. power; these would seem to be an obvious point of focus for critics objecting to the American victory. Yet Leonard—and others—ignored these issues and chose to focus on the mass imagery employed in Rauschenberg's works, with its detached and almost apolitical tone. The associative meanings and content in the images were in fact neutralized for French critics, leaving only form as the focus for critique. It was this which Leonard seized upon, by identifying Rauschenberg's connections with Dada; he concluded that the political nature of the works was debased, a "grotesque plagiarism." Political statement of any kind was neutralized by the artist's embrace of mass culture—he made no comment on Kennedy, he merely reproduced an image sapped of its meaning as it funneled through mass media.

Unlike Solomon and American enthusiasts of Rauschenberg's work, French critics saw neither ambiguity nor expanded meanings in his imagery. For conservative critics, Rauschenberg's works threatened to destroy the aesthetic refuge they found in Bissière's works by dragging high art through the sludge of the commonplace; Pierre Schneider described the process as a shift from "hyper-idealism" to "hyper-materialism."[107] Alternatively, critics such as Leonard worried that by abandoning a critical posture, art would become one with consumer culture, a kind of "positive sensibility" which was particularly American:

> Pop Art is a brutal representation (characterized by giganticism) of elements from the American way of life, picked from the urban context. Consumer products have been worshiped in this civilization of comfort; it is therefore comprehensible, although sad, that food, cars, the American symbols of health and well-being, that is, all the germ-free and assembly line odds and ends have become the major preoccupation of the North American artists.[108]

According to Solomon, the meanings of objects or images were transposed when they were placed in the completely different context of a Rauschenberg combine; it was this which evoked a "new sensibility." But the signs of mass culture refused to recede for the French critics; the works functioned as a metaphor for the materialism and consumerism "worshiped" in American society. And while the purveyors of the new sensibility saw in Rauschenberg's work a positive way to come to terms with the American environment, it was precisely this process of assimilation that the French had hoped to stave off.

Although the French were unwilling to accept the new sensibility represented by the Rauschenberg victory, they were unable to compete with the New Frontier. And competition was what the Biennale had always been about, as juror Franz Meyer later pointed out:

Pressures and playing off of influences by dealers and government officials have always been the daily bread which fed the whole [Biennale] machine. If the Americans had for one moment threatened not to come anymore without the prize this time, they only would have used the natural language of the place. The government officials of all the countries and all the dealers went to Venice interested in certain artists, trying to bring the prize home and they always engaged all the expedients they could think of. If in 1964 the Americans finally succeeded, you may say against them that their aim had been no less nationalistic than the one defended by the French or English in other Biennale years.[109]

Certainly the Americans had unprecedented advantages in 1964, and they used these to press their claim to the prize, but the French had long been exerting pressures to maintain their hold on the Biennale, one of the last places they hoped to retain some semblance of cultural hegemony amid the onslaught of Abstract Expressionism and, by 1964, Pop art. What made the American triumph particularly difficult was the fact that it pointed to a victory in a larger, extra-aesthetic realm: while the United States managed to wrest the prize from the French with its new avantgarde, it was its economic power that had already won the battle. The force of the new issuing from American shores had already succeeded in dominating the world with its movies, its magazines, its culture. Rauschenberg's triumph signaled that the game was up, with the terms and materials of the victory made over into art. And in this sense, the Americans' design in Venice only mapped out in spectacular terms the symbolic separations that had come to replace geographical distances.

Notes

1.

This paper grew out of
research done while at
the University of British
Columbia; I am espe-
cially grateful to Dian
Kriz and David How-
ard, University of Brit-
ish Columbia, and Amy
Kurlander, Harvard
University, for their in-
sights and criticism at
various stages of this
project.

2.
ABC, June 28, 1964.

3.
Pierre Cabanne, "A
Venise, L'Amérique
proclame la fin de
l'Ecole de Paris et
lance le Pop'Art pour
coloniser l'Europe,"
Arts, June 24, 1964.

4.
Editorial cartoon,
France Observateur,
June 25, 1964.

5.
Calvin Tomkins, "The
Big Show in Venice,"
Harper's Magazine
230 (April 1965), pp.
98–104.

6.
The Grand Prizes
awarded in the postwar
period prior to 1964
were as follows: 1948,
Georges Braque; 1950,
Henri Matisse; 1952,
Raoul Dufy; 1954, Max
Ernst; 1956, Jacques
Villon; 1958, Osvaldo
Licini; 1960, Jean

Fautrier; and 1962, Al-
fred Manessier.

7.
John Ashbery, "Venice
Biennale the Center of
Controversy," New
York Herald Tribune,
June 23, 1964.

8.
Undated correspon-
dence from Alan Sol-
omon to Lois Bingham,
Venice Biennale Files,
USIA (64–045) (Wash-
ington, D.C.: National
Museum of American
Art, Smithsonian Insti-
tute). Hereafter referred
to as VB files. Lois
Bingham was chief of
the Fine Arts Section,
USIA Exhibition
Division.

9.
Solomon expressed his
frustration over "the
willingness of people to
serve on the jury, for
personal reasons, which
were apparently quite
petty. One of them (and
this I know to be true of
Martin Friedman) was
that they didn't want to
help me win a prize. I
think that [William]
Seitz had feelings like
this, but more with re-
spect to the museum [of
Modern Art], which af-
ter all had never won
it." Ibid. Walter Hopps
and James Johnson
Sweeney had also de-
clined the invitation,
according to Emile de
Antonio, telephone in-
terview with the author,

September 28, 1985. De
Antonio knew Solomon,
Castelli, Rauschenberg,
and Hunter and at-
tended the Biennale in
1964.

10.
De Antonio interview.

11.
The incident was re-
ported by Gerald Gas-
siot-Talabot, "La
Biennale d'Art mod-
erne, ou les Américains
à Venise," unidentified
newspaper clipping,
Leo Castelli Gallery
Papers (Washington,
D.C.: Archives of
American Art), micro-
film, frame 257, and it
was alluded to by
Pierre Restany, "La
XXXII Biennale de
Venezia, Biennale della
Irregolarità," Domus
417 (August 1964),
p. 37.

12.
[D.C.], "Pop'Art &
Dollars, ou la semaine
de Venise," La Cote des
Peintres 2 (July–Au-
gust 1964), p. 25, and
Pierre Mazars, "Venise:
les grandes manoeuvres
du 'Pop'Art'," Le Fig-
aro, June 25, 1964.

13.
Art International, June
1964. It also appeared
in L'Oeil, July 1964.

14.
Tomkins, "The Big
Show in Venice," pp.
100–103.

15.
Correspondence from August Heckscher (Special Advisor on the Arts to the President), to Edward R. Murrow (Director, USIA) and Lucius Battle (Assistant Secretary of State for Cultural Affairs), May 10, 1962, VB files.

16.
See Eva Cockcroft, "Abstract Expressionism, Weapon of the Cold War," Artforum 12 (June 1974), pp. 39–41.

17.
John F. Kennedy, quoted in Arthur Schlesinger, Jr., A Thousand Days (New York: Fawcett Premier, 1965), p. 772.

18.
Critics charged that Collier's was serving as a front for the State Department, and objections culminated in a formal protest issued by United Nations officials over the use of the UN insignia. See "Editorial," Collier's Magazine, April 1952.

19.
Phillip H. Coombs, "The Past and Future in Perspective," in The American Assembly, Cultural Affairs and Foreign Relations (Englewod Cliffs, NJ: Prentice-Hall, 1963), p. 144. Coombs was appointed Assistant Secretary of State for Educational and Cultural Affairs by Kennedy, a position he held until April 1962, when he resigned to rejoin the Ford Foundation.

20.
W. McNeil Lowry and Gertrude S. Hooker, "The Role of the Arts and the Humanities," ibid., pp. 72–73. Lowry was director of the Ford Foundation Program in the Humanities and the Arts; Hooker was with the Cultural Affairs Division of the U.S. Information Service in Rome (1951–59) and in Paris (1959–61).

21.
Julian Marias, "The Unreal America," Foreign Affairs 39 (July 1961), p. 589.

22.
Lowry and Hooker, "The Role of the Arts," p. 73.

23.
[John F. Kennedy], "The Late President's Last Reflections on the Arts," Saturday Review 47 (March 28, 1964), p. 17.

24.
See Serge Guilbaut, How New York Stole the Idea of Modern Art (Chicago: University of Chicago Press, 1983) and Cockcroft, "Abstract Expressionism," passim.

25.
In this respect, the government's overt role in cultural sponsorship had advanced considerably from the initial postwar period, when Truman pronounced judgment on Yasuo Kuniyoshi's Circus Girl Resting, featured in the State Department exhibition Advancing American Art (1946–48). Truman's comment ("If that's art, I'm a Hottentot") did not keep his administration from using the avant-garde to advance its ideological aims, but officially the hand of government did not touch such hot issues, having been burned so badly by the public reaction to the State Department's show.

26.
Arthur Schlesinger, Jr., "Government and the Arts" (speech to the American Federation of Arts, April 12, 1962). Reprinted in U.S. Congress, Senate, 88th Cong., 1st sess., August 15, 1963, Congressional Record 109 (part II), p. 15136.

27.
Ibid.

28.
Culture and its role in government policy were increasingly considered in Congress; see for example U.S. Congress,

House, Representative Kearns speaking for the Establishment of a Federal Advisory Council on the Arts (H.R. 4172), 87th Cong., 1st sess., September 20, 1961, Congressional Record 107 (part 15), pp. 20487–20489 and U.S. Congress, Senate, "Freedom versus Coercion," Senator Pell speaking for USIA cultural programs, 88th Cong., 1st sess., November 5, 1963, Congressional Record 109 (part 16), pp. 20957–20958.

29.
Schlesinger, Congressional Record, p. 15136.

30.
Ibid.

31.
See Gary O. Larson, The Reluctant Patron: The United States Government and the Arts, 1943–1965 (Philadelphia: University of Pennsylvania Press, 1983), pp. 159–60 for a brief discussion on the success of this strategy.

32.
Correspondence from Javits to Arthur Goldberg (Secretary of Labor), November 1962, ibid., p. 160, note 15.

33.
For a discussion of the impact of the EEC on the American economy, see Ernst Van der Beugel, From Marshall Plan to Atlantic Partnership: European Integration as a Concern of American Foreign Policy (New York: Elsevier Publishing, 1966), pp. 395–400.

34.
Sidney Hyman, "In Search of 'The Atlantic Community,'" The New York Times Magazine, May 6, 1962, reprinted in Robert A. Divine, ed., American Foreign Policy Since 1945 (Chicago: Quadrangle Books, 1969), p. 150.

35.
Richard J. Barnet, The Alliance (New York: Simon and Schuster, 1983), p. 200.

36.
Schlesinger, A Thousand Days, p. 772.

37.
Barnet, The Alliance, p. 214.

38.
For de Gaulle's fears in this regard, see Lois Pattison de Ménil, Who Speaks for Europe? The Vision of Charles de Gaulle (New York: St. Martin's Press, 1977), pp. 107–108.

39.
Seyom Brown, The Faces of Power (New York: Columbia University Press, 1968), p. 297.

40.
Kennedy, speech delivered at Conference on Trade Policy, Washington, D.C., May 17, 1962, reprinted in Allan Nevins, ed., The Burden and the Glory: President John F. Kennedy (New York: Harper & Row, 1964), p. 105.

41.
Brown, The Faces of Power, pp. 303–304.

42.
Philip M. Williams and Martin Harrison, Politics and Society in de Gaulle's Republic (London: Longman Group, Ltd., 1971), p. 48. Of course, de Gaulle's ambitions to forge a European alliance included his vision of France as the leader, with Germany as a junior partner.

43.
Charles de Gaulle, Memoirs of Hope: Renewal and Endeavor, trans. Terence Kilmartin (New York: Simon & Schuster, 1971), p. 206.

44.
Correspondence from August Heckscher to Edward R. Murrow and Lucius Battle, May 10, 1962, USIA file 64–045, "Miscellaneous."

45.
Indeed, it appears that the government was intent on making public

its role in the exhibition, since alternatives to official sponsorship were rejected. For example, on behalf of the American Federation of Art, Roy Neuberger, wealthy collector and then a trustee of the AFA, wrote to the USIA: "The AFA is willing, indeed anxious, to replace MoMA but would need help from the U.S. government." USIA correspondence memo, May 15, 1962, VB files.

46.
Interview with Lois Bingham, June 30, 1984.

47.
See for example Second Generation (Jewish Museum, 1957), The Popular Image Exhibition (Washington Gallery of Modern Art, 1963), Robert Rauschenberg (Jewish Museum, 1963), and Jasper Johns (Jewish Museum, 1964).

48.
Bingham interview. I attempted to confirm Bingham's story with the Venice Biennale archivist Dr. Umbro Apollonio (a member of the Biennale Committee in 1964) but received no response. The matter is complicated further by Alice Denney (Assistant Director of the American Pavilion, 1964

Venice Biennale), who claims that neither the Biennale nor USIA officials had anything to do with the selection of artists; according to Denney, the entire show was devised by Solomon with her help. Interview with Alice B. Denney, January 11, 1985.

49.
USIA Budget, VB files.

50.
Here again ambiguities emerge as stories diverge. The USIA maintained that agreements had been made with Biennale officials whereby the annex would be considered an official part of the U.S. exhibition. Unfortunately, the USIA never had these agreements put in writing, an oversight that was to become problematic later when Biennale officials denied that agreements had ever been made.

51.
The proximity to Guggenheim's gallery provided an interesting contrast in terms of the trends of modern art. Guggenheim herself detested Pop art and championed Abstract Expressionist works. In 1964 this created a situation where the avant-garde gallery was showing work from the previous decade, while the USIA was ex-

hibiting the latest, more controversial work in its annex.

52.
Correspondence from Alan Solomon to Lois Bingham, February 12. 1964, VB files.

53.
The show featured twenty-two works by Rauschenberg and twenty-one by Johns, whereas Noland and Louis had thirteen canvases each.

54.
Bingham interview.

55.
Denney interview.

56.
Telegram from U.S. Embassy, Rome, to USIA, Washington, D.C., April 21, 1964, VB files.

57.
Telegram from U.S. Embassy, Rome, to USIA, Washington, D.C., April 28, 1964, VB files: "Would be useful to know whether planned to locate Rauschenberg works in consulate building. This might be clincher argument as he is considered eminently eligible for grand prize."

58.
Telegram from USIA, Washington, D.C., to U.S. Embassy, Rome, April 28, 1964, VB files.

59.
Bingham interview.
Lawrence Alloway
claimed that Noland re-
fused to give up any of
his space in the pavil-
ion, citing as his source
Tomkins's piece in Har-
per's Magazine; how-
ever, this is not stated
in Tomkins's piece, nor
did Denney or Bingham
offer this as an expla-
nation; see Alloway,
The Venice Biennale
1895–1968, from salon
to goldfish bowl (Green-
wich, CT: New York
Graphic Society),
p. 150.

60.
Telegram from U.S.
Embassy, Rome, to
USIA, Washington,
D.C., May 7, 1964, VB
files.

61.
XXXII International
Biennial Exhibition of
Art, Venice, 1964,
United States of
America, unpaginated.
Hereafter referred to as
"VB catalogue."

62.
See Clement Greenberg,
"Louis and Noland,"
Art International (May
1960), p. 29. For Green-
berg's more theoretical
account of the reasons
for championing No-
land and the post-
painterly abstraction-
ists, see his "Modernist
Painting," Arts Year-
book 4 (1961), pp.
102–108, and "After

Abstract Expres-
sionism," Art Interna-
tional 6 (October 25,
1962), pp. 24–32.

63.
VB catalogue, n.p.

64.
Ibid.

65.
Ibid.

66.
Ibid.

67.
Roland Barthes, My-
thologies, trans. An-
nette Lavers (New York:
Hill & Wang, 1981),
p. 118.

68.
It should be noted that
other critics shared this
view; see for example
Max Kozloff, "Art,"
The Nation 197 (Decem-
ber 7, 1963), pp. 402–
403. Even some hostile
critics commented on
the affirmative, uncrit-
ical nature of the work;
see Irving Hershel
Sandler, "Ash Can Re-
visited, A New York
Letter," Art Interna-
tional 4 (October 1960),
pp. 28–30.

69.
VB catalogue, n.p.

70.
Susan Sontag, Against
Interpretation (New
York: Farrar, Straus,
Giroux, 1966), pp.
299–300.

71.
Ibid., p. 302.

72.
There are distinctions
to be made, of course,
between the terms that
have been used here—
"popular," "mass,"
"low" culture—that are
more than mere matters
of nomenclature. For
instance, in terms of
production, popular
culture might be asso-
ciated with localized,
small-scale, artisanal
forms of labor, while
mass culture might be
associated with large-
scale commercial enter-
prises, with the latter
often seeking to appro-
priate the "look" of the
former. Further, low
culture can be said to
include both mass and
popular forms, in con-
tradistinction to high or
elite culture. The mean-
ings of the various
terms shift both with the
particular objects and
historical periods under
consideration. For fur-
ther discussion of these
and related issues, see
Meyer Schapiro, "Cour-
bet and Popular Im-
agery. An Essay on
Realism and Naïveté,"
Journal of the Warburg
and Courtauld Insti-
tutes 4 (April–June
1941), pp. 164–91;
Clement Greenberg,
"Avant-Garde and
Kitsch," Partisan Re-
view 6 (Fall 1939), pp.
34–49; Thomas Crow,
"Modernism and Mass
Culture in the Visual
Arts," in Modernism

and Modernity: The
Vancouver Conference
Papers, eds. Benjamin
H. D. Buchloh, Serge
Guilbaut, and David
Solkin (Halifax: Press
of the Nova Scotia Col-
lege of Art and Design,
1983), pp. 215–64.

73.
Dwight Macdonald,
Masscult and Midcult
(New York: Partisan
Review Series, No. 4,
Random House, 1961),
reprinted in his Against
the American Grain
(New York: Vintage,
1965), p. 12.

74.
Herbert Marcuse, One
Dimensional Man (Bos-
ton: Beacon Press,
1964), pp. 7–8.

75.
Guilbaut, How New
York Stole the Idea of
Modern Art, pp. 158–
159.

76.
VB catalogue.

77.
Edward Shils, "Mass
Society and its Cul-
ture," Daedalus 89
(Spring 1960), p. 288.

78.
See for example Mac-
donald, "Masscult and
Midcult," p. 11.

79.
Shils, "Mass Society
and its Culture,"
p. 290.

80.
Clyde Kluckhohn,
quoted by Seymour
Martin Lipset, "A
Changing American
Character?" in Culture
and Social Character:
The Work of David
Riesman Reviewed,
eds. Seymour Martin
Lipset and Leo Lowen-
thal (Glencoe, IL: Free
Press, 1961), p. 171. It
is interesting to note
that the collection of
essays reviewed the
implications of David
Riesman's The Lonely
Crowd, which studied
the tendencies to con-
form in society as a
result of alienation
produced by it. Many
of the essays disagreed
with his proposal, and
Riesman himself sug-
gested that his critique
was probably "too
harsh."

81.
Daniel Bell, The End
of Ideology (New York:
Colliers, 1961).

82.
For an overview of the
central arguments of
and participants in this
debate, see the essays
collected in Chaim
Waxman, ed., The End
of Ideology Debate
(New York: Funk and
Wagnalls, 1968).

83.
Ibid., p. 404.

84.
Macdonald, "Masscult
and Midcult," p. 37.

85.
Jean-François Revel,
"XXXIIe Biennale de
Venise: Triomphe du
Réalisme National-
iste," L'Oeil 115–16
(July–August 1964), p.
5: "Les Américains, en
1964, ont envahi Venise
avec une énergie toute
missionaire. Non con-
tents d'exposer dans
leur pavillon, à l'in-
térieur des jardins de la
Biennale, ils ont organ-
isé une gigantesque rét-
rospective de leurs deux
vedettes, Jasper Johns
et Rauschenberg—
plus les comparses—
dans le palais de l'an-
cien consulat des
Etats-Unis."

86.
Leonard, "Des dollars
chez les Doges," France
Observateur, June 25,
1964 ("enfreindre les
règles du 'fair play' ").

87.
Cabanne, "A Venise,
L'Amérique proclame
. . .": "nous ne sommes
plus que de pauvres
nègres arriérés, tout
juste bons à être colon-
isés. Le premier com-
mando est sur place: il
s'appelle le Pop'Art.
L'invasion ne met même
pas les formes, négli-
geant le pavillon offi-
ciel des Giardini, elle
prend ses distances et
choisit l'exterritorial-
ité: l'ancien consulat
américain . . . trans-
formé en temple de
la nouvelle religion.

La pape y officie: Rauschenberg, entouré de ses grands prêtres, Johns, Oldenburg, Dine, Stella."

88.
Restany, "La XXXII Biennale di Venezia . . .," p. 37 (although text appeared in both French and Italian I will quote only the French text here): "[Je] ayant pour ces artistes . . . la plus grande estime. Mais je conteste avec la plus grande énergie le bien-fondé du procédé qui crée un précédent fâcheux et contribue à susciter autour des américains un halo d'impérialisme culturel." Restany's favorable review of the Pop artists is understandable when one considers that he was promoting the "new realists" in France (Niki de St. Phalle, Yves Klein, Arman, César), and thus had much to gain if Pop art was accepted and recognized internationally.

89.
Solomon, undated correspondence to Bingham, VB files.

90.
Despite my repeated attempts to elicit comments from Hunter, he would not discuss the implications of Solomon's statement. Perhaps the "purity" of

which Solomon spoke may have been a reference to Hunter's indiscretion with the Italian press, but this is a question that is still unresolved; Bingham also had no comment when asked to what Solomon was referring (Bingham interview).

91.
Franz Meyer, correspondence with the author, February 21, 1986.

92.
"Pop'Art & Dollars . . .," p. 25.

93.
Mazars, "Venise: les grandes manoeuvres . . .," n.p.

94.
Umbro Apollonio, the Biennale Archivist (and also a member of the Biennale Committee in 1964) did not respond to my inquiries about the jury deliberations and the financial agreements the committee made with the Americans, leaving many questions regarding the Italians' role unanswered. In a draft of a report submitted to Senator Jacob Javits by Alan Solomon, the U.S. Commissioner obviously felt betrayed by the Italians' refusal to abide by the agreements which would have made the artists in the annex

eligible for the prize. After they rescinded on these arguments, Solomon charged: "Subsequently, the Biennale officials were most devious in their attempts to compromise their own political (and financial) problems with their evident desire for significant American participation. We were forced to accept their rather arbitrary behavior without making a major issue of the matter." Whether this implies that certain financial agreements had been made between the U.S. and Biennale officials (in which the Italians subsequently renegged on their "part of the bargain") is unclear. In any case, this portion of the report was deleted by USIA official Robert Sivard. See U.S. Government Memorandum (Robert Sivard to Lois Bingham), VB files.

95.
Solomon, undated correspondence with Bingham. These "certain Italians" apparently extended beyond the jurors themselves. In the same letter, Solomon mentioned, "It was Falzoni who brought off the whole prize thing." Giordano Falzoni was a USIS interpreter who worked for Solomon and Denney who had been

discharged by the government but kept on at Solomon's insistence (Solomon had credited Falzoni in the Javits report, but USIA officials edited out this portion in the final version.) According to Alice Denney, Falzoni was very enthusiastic about the American exhibit but did not do that much regarding the final prize (Denney interview). Lois Bingham was unsure who Falzoni was, thinking he might have been a juror when I asked her to comment on Solomon's statement (Bingham interview). Emile de Antonio noted that Italian artists who had seen Rauschenberg's work in Italy before pressured Marchiori and Valsecchi to support Rauschenberg (de Antonio interview).

96.
Sam Hunter claimed that Starzinski had voted with the Italians from the beginning and that Meyer supported Rauschenberg on the second vote, after having opposed him initially, with Kenneth Noland as his first choice (de Antonio interview).

97.
Tomkins, "The Big Show in Venice," p. 102.

98.
Meyer, correspondence with Emile de Antonio, September 19, 1985. Mike Sonnabend and his wife Ileana Sonnabend were the major dealers of American Pop artists (including Rauschenberg and Johns) in Paris at the time. Ileana Sonnabend was formerly married to Castelli, and their business connections remained when Sonnabend relocated in France. Here there is some ambiguity if, as Hunter claimed, Meyer had intially favored Noland. Perhaps he preferred Johns over Rauschenberg once it became clear that Noland had little chance of winning the prize.

99.
Tomkins, Off the Wall, p. 10. The performance also included music by John Cage.

100.
De Antonio interview.

101.
Jean Yves Mock, "Notes from Paris and London: Bissière at the musée d'art moderne," Apollo 69 (June 1959), p. 195.

102.
Barnet, The Alliance, p. 207.

103.
Raymond Cogniat, "Curieuse attitude agressive des Etats-Unis," Le Figaro, June 23,

1964: "[Bissière] est certainement le peintre le plus qualifié pour illustrer la permanence calme et l'incessante invention dont on ressent si vivement le besoin aujourd'hui. Son ensemble est d'une dignité et d'un raffinement si indiscutables que le jury international bien que tenté par des affirmations plus vehémentes et plus hasardeuses, a cependant exprimé le désir de lui rendre hommage."

104.
Pierre Schneider, "Art News from Paris," Art News 61 (October 1962), p. 48.

105.
Leonard, "Des dollars chez les Doges": ". . . ces objets usuels, déformés, bafoués, minutieusement reconstruits à d'énormes dimensions, ces fragments de bandes dessinées (de 'Comics') scrupuleusement reproduits a l'échelle des écrans de cinéma panoramiques, ces collages de photographies de magazine, tout ce bric-à-brac qui constitue le 'Pop'Art,' qu'estce d'autre qu'un plagiat grotesque de Dada . . . Mais Dada fut un mouvement essentiellement révolutionnaire. . . . C'était une attaque de cette société bourgeoise. . . . Mais les néo-dadaistes

*embrassent au contraire
le symbole bourgeois
et sont fermés a la
passion."*

106.
*Ibid.: [Pop'Art] nais-
sent du même processus
qui engendre les idées
publicitaires."*

107.
*Pierre Schneider, "La
Biennale de Venise,"*
Paris L'Express, *July
22, 1964.*

108.
*Gassiot-Talabot, Cas-
telli Papers, Archives
of American Art, frame
257: "Le Pop Art est,
on le sait, une représen-
tation brutale, général-
ement empreinte de gi-
gantisme, d'éléments
choisis parmi le con-
texte urbain de la vie
des Etats-Unis. Cette
civilisation du confort a
en quelque sorte divin-
isé le produit de con-
sommation, et il était
naturel, par une sorte de
logique assez triste,
mais inéluctable, que les
denrées alimentaires,
l'automobile, les sym-
boles de l'hygiène et du
bien-être américains, en
somme tout le bric-á-
brac de l'objet aseptisé
et produit en série, de-
viennent la préoccupa-
tion majeure des
artistes
d'outre-Atlantique."*

109.
*Meyer, correspondence
with de Antonio, Sep-
tember 19, 1985.*

Contributors

Jean Baudrillard

is a well-known writer who teaches sociology at the University of Paris. His publications include *The Mirror of Production* (1975) and *For a Critique of the Political Economy of the Sign* (1981). His reflections about contemporary Western culture have been a major force behind the reappraisal of modernity.

Benjamin H. D. Buchloh

is a critic and Assistant Professor of the history of art in the School of Architecture at the Massachusetts Institute of Technology. His extensive work on post-1945 art and theories has been published in France, Germany, and North America.

Timothy J. Clark

teaches art history at the University of California, Berkeley. He has published two books on French art and the 1848 revolution, *The Absolute Bourgeois: Artists and Politics in France* and *Image of the People: Gustave Courbet and the 1848 Revolution* (1973), and is the author of *The Painting of Modern Life: Paris in the Art of Manet and His Followers* (1985).

Thomas Crow

teaches history of art at the University of Michigan. He is the author of *Painters and Public Life in Eighteenth-Century Paris* (1985) and "Modernism and Mass Culture in the Visual Arts," in *Modernism and Modernity* (1982).

Thierry de Duve

teaches at the University of Ottawa and is the author of *Nomalisme Pictural: Marcel Duchamp, la peinture et la modernité* (1984), *Essais Datés* (1986), *Au Nom de l'Art* (1989), and *Resonances du Readymade* (1989).

François-Marc Gagnon

is Professor of Art History at the University of Montreal. He has published extensively on the French-Canadian painter Paul-Emile Borduas and on early Canadian art. He is currently preparing a major retrospective of the painter Jean-Paul Riopelle, to be held in Montreal in 1992.

Serge Guilbaut

is Associate Professor of Art History at the University of British Columbia. He edited the volume *Modernism and Modernity* (1982) and is the author of *How New York Stole the Idea of Modern Art* (1983). He is currently at work on *The Expressionist Triangle*, a book about cultural relations in Paris, New York, and Montreal between 1945 and 1956.

John-Franklin Koenig

is an artist currently working in Seattle and France. Since he began exhibiting in 1952, he has had over 125 one-man shows. He helped found the Galerie Arnaud in 1951 and the contemporary art magazine *Cimaise* in 1952.

Lary May

is Associate Professor of American Studies and Art History at the University of Minnesota. He is the author of *Screening Out the Past: The Birth of Mass Culture and the Motion Picture Industry* as well as the editor of *Recasting America: Culture and Politics in the Age of Cold War*.

Laurie J. Monahan

is a doctoral candidate at Harvard University. She is currently working on Surrealism in the 1930s.

Constance Naubert-Riser

is Associate Professor of Art History at the University of Montreal. She has recently been the guest curator and author of the catalogue of the first major retrospective of Jean McEwen's work, *Color in Depth*, at the Montreal Museum of Fine Arts.

John O'Brian

Assistant Professor in the Department of Fine Arts at the University of British Columbia in Vancouver, is the editor of *Clement Greenberg: The Collected Essays and Criticism*. He is the author of two books, *David Milne and the Modern Tradition of Painting* (1983) and *Degas to Matisse: The Maurice Wertheim Collection* (1988), and is currently at work on a study of the reception of Matisse in America.

Fourth printing, 1995

First MIT Press paperback edition, 1992

© 1990 Massachusetts Institute of Technology

This book was set in Univers and Bodoni by Achorn
Graphics and printed and bound in the United States
of America.

Library of Congress Cataloging-in-Publication Data

Reconstructing modernism : art in New York, Paris, and Montreal,
1954–1964 / edited by Serge Guilbaut.
    p.   cm.
Papers from the hot ɾaint for cold war symposium, held at the University
of British Columbia, Vancouver, Canada, Sept. 1986.
ISBN 0-262-07120-7 (HB), 0-262-57092-0 (PB)
    1. Modernism (Art)—New York (N.Y.)—Congresses. 2. Art,
Modern—20th century—New York (N.Y.)—Congresses. 3. Modernism
(Art)—France—Paris—Congresses. 4. Art, Modern—20th century—
France—Paris—Congresses. 5. Modernism (Art)—Québec (Province)—
Montréal—Congresses. 6. Art, Modern—20th century—Quebec
(Province)—Montreal—Congresses. I. Guilbaut, Serge.
N6535.N5R4   1990
759.06′09′045—dc20   89-13760
                                              CIP